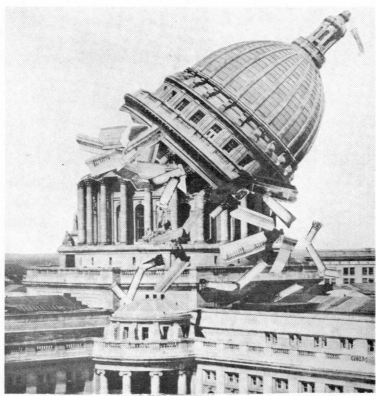

WISCONSIN'S CAPITOL COLLAPSES

This faked picture, showing the dome of the Wisconsin State Capitol at Madison collapsing, appeared on page 1 of the Madison *Capital-Times* April 1, 1933. Although "April Fool" appeared in small type in the caption and at the end of the accompanying article, readers were shocked. Typical of many letters to the editor was the following: "I was filled with indignation over your April Fool joke on the front page of the *Capital-Times* of April 1. There is such a thing as carrying a joke too far and this one was not only tactless and void of humor as well, but also a hideous jest."

HOAXES

by
CURTIS D. MacDOUGALL

DOVER PUBLICATIONS, INC.
New York • New York

This Dover edition, first published in 1958, is a revised and enlarged version of the work originally published by The Macmillan Company in 1940.

Standard Book Number: 486-20465-0
Library of Congress Catalog Card Number: 58-12615

.

Manufactured in the United States of America
Dover Publications, Inc.
180 Varick Street
New York, N.Y. 10014

PREFACE TO SECOND EDITION

SINCE this book first appeared in 1940 the Cardiff Giant has come to rest in Cooperstown, N. Y.; a French court has finally decided, after more than a century and a half, that there was no Lost Dauphin; the Bardstown paintings have been stolen and recovered and their spurious nature proved in a federal court; the Smithsonian Institution has sponsored another report on the Minnesota Kensington Stone; the sealed Lincoln papers have been opened and examined by scholars, and leaders of the pacifistic Veterans of Future Wars have fought in World War II.

All these and many other recent developments have been recorded in this edition which has been updated throughout. Mention of more than twenty-five entirely new incidents also has been added: discovery of the spuriousness of the Piltdown Man; the fictitious Flying Figments of Plainfield Teachers College; the masterful forgery of the Dutch artist Jan Vermeer by Hans van Meegeren; *The Man Who Wouldn't Talk;* several ingenious war hero and Hollywood impersonations and others.

Except for the inclusion of this new material and the correction of a few typographical errors, the present edition is the same as the earlier one. Nothing has been deleted so the book remains a compendium of accounts of how forgers, swindlers, impostors and other hoaxers have thrived on human gullibility through many centuries. It is the author's hope that it will serve as a warning to potential victims so that they will be fewer in number in the future than in the past.

1958   CURTIS D. MACDOUGALL

What Is a Hoax?

HUNDREDS or thousands of miles from a scene of action, a newspaper editor may gain and deserve a reputation for outspokenness, courage, or fearlessness. On home-town matters, however, the same editor may be controlled by the belief that discretion is the better part of valor.

This is especially true of routine non-political news about the comings and goings of the socially important. The society page is edited with the aim of making friends for the paper, and the lowly average reporter becomes used to a eulogistic or self-expurgated type of writing and almost convinces himself it is consistent with the highly moral tenet that news is news and editorial opinion is editorial opinion.

Almost but not quite. Lurking in the back of the mind of many a veteran writer is the ambition once in his career to tell the truth, the whole truth, and nothing but the truth as he sees it.

Imagine, therefore, the professional hullabaloo in January, 1930, when one newspaperman seemed to have realized that ambition. It was the Fountain Inn (South Carolina) *Tribune,* edited and published by the eccentric columnist Robert E. Quillen, that printed the apparently bona fide account of a local wedding on its society page. The story began ordinarily enough with the names of the principals, the time and place, and continued as follows:

The groom is a popular young bum who hasn't done a lick of work since he got shipped in the middle of his junior year at college. He manages to dress well and keep a supply of spending money because his dad is a soft-hearted old fool who takes up his bad checks instead of letting him go to jail where he belongs.

The bride is a skinny, fast little idiot, who has been kissed and handled by every boy in town since she was 12 years old. She paints like a Sioux Indian, sucks cigarets in secret and drinks corn liquor when she is out joy riding in her dad's car at night. She doesn't know how to cook or keep house.

The house was newly plastered for the wedding and the exterior painted, thus appropriately carrying out the decorative scheme, for the groom was newly plastered and the bride newly painted.

The groom wore a rented dinner suit over athletic underwear of imitation silk. His pants were held up by pale green suspenders. His No. 8 patent leather shoes matched his state in tightness and harmonized nicely with the axlegrease of his hair. In addition to his jag he carried a pocket knife, a bunch of keys, a dun for the ring and his usual look of imbecility.

The young people will make their home with the bride's parents—which means they will sponge on the old man until he dies and then she will take in washing.

The happy couple anticipates a blessed event in about three months.

POSTSCRIPT BY EDITOR: This may be the last issue of THE TRIBUNE, but my life ambition has been to write one wedding and tell the truth. Now that is done death can have no sting.

This journalistic classic quickly made the rounds. Near-by editors, of course, picked it up promptly. Some suggested that it was just another of Quillen's jokes; several upbraided him for berating people so cruelly. The *American Press,* newspaperman's magazine, reprinted it in full, but the late Marlen S. Pew omitted the line above the postscript in reprinting the story in his "Shop Talk at Thirty" column in *Editor and Publisher. Publishers' Auxiliary* used the abridged version but offered to send subscribers an unexpurgated copy upon request; the response ran into the hundreds.

Mr. Quillen readily admits that a few neighboring editors who knew him best and reproduced the story as an example of a joke guessed correctly. "The story was written as humor," he explains, "and was understood as such in this region. It was so preposterous that I thought no one would take it seriously."

The wedding story, in other words, was a hoax. It had no basis in fact. Whether its author intended it to be accepted as a fact is immaterial for my purpose: to illustrate my definition of "hoax" as a deliberately concocted untruth made to masquerade as truth. Hoaxes, then, are distinguishable from honest errors in observation or judgment to which everyone is subject.

Of relative insignificance for harm, the credulous reprinting and retelling of the wedding story suggests the influence which hoaxers may exert —and the value of a study of the hoax as a means of swaying public opinion. Too often, scholars, taking a current belief or custom, laboriously strive to trace it, step by step, back to its origin. The result, as crossroad after crossroad is reached and researchers differ on which route to take, is failure or, at best, controversial confusion. The origin of much contemporary thought remains as mysterious as ever. On the other hand, by working "forward" instead of "backward," would it not be easier to discover how a belief, opinion, or custom originates, is disseminated, leads to overt behavior, and ultimately, perhaps, becomes a permanent influence on thought and action?

This book originated in the belief that the answer to this question is affirmative. Intentional hoaxes are natural case material for such a study. Discovering and telling the stories of several hundred important fakes, furthermore, has been fun for the writer and, it is hoped, will be for the reader as well.

We are concerned first with why such whoppers as the Quillen wedding story are accepted as factual. Human events and thought seem to have been determined as much by what is untrue as by what is true, and it is important to dip deep into the well of human credulity and find what is at the bottom. Part I of this volume is devoted to that task, using a cross-section of all types of hoaxes about which facts were gathered as case material.

Part II is devoted to an examination of how important hoaxing has been in many fields of human thought and activity—government, science, religion, literature, and so forth—and with an analysis of how a hoax spreads and acquires influence.

It would be interesting and certainly significant, of course, to examine also the make-up of those who have undertaken, regularly or occasionally, to concoct hoaxes. Although the present study casts a sidelight upon the nature of the inventor of humbug—who is not essentially different from his inveterate victim—the careful investigation of the psychology of the swindler, forger or impostor is to be undertaken only by a psychoanalyst. And psychoanalysis of the hundreds of dead mentioned in this book would be extremely difficult.

In addition to throwing light on the culture of hoaxes, and thus upon the entire problem of how public opinion operates, this study is intended to form a fairly complete record of fakery throughout history. Footnotes and elaborate references have been avoided, but the writer can cite authority for any statement. Valuable assistance was received from several libraries (notably those of the University of Wisconsin, the Wisconsin Historical Society, Northwestern University, the University of Chicago and the Chicago Public Library) and from a number of persons to whom the writer is deeply grateful. Among these are: Kimball Young, eminent social psychologist, who inspired it; the late Joseph F. Kwapil, librarian of the Philadelphia *Public Ledger;* Elmo Scott Watson, editor of *Publishers' Auxiliary;* Charles E. Brown, director of the Wisconsin State Historical Museum; Henry L. Mencken, of the Baltimore *Evening Sun;* Arthur Davison Ficke and Witter Bynner, poets; Edward Richardson and M. D. Hinshaw, Ladysmith, Wis., journalists; the late Halbert L. Hoard, publisher of the Fort Atkinson (Wis.) *Jefferson County Union;* Hugo Ballin, painter; George S. Chapell and Paul Jordan Smith, authors; Robert C. Vose of the Robert C. Vose Galleries, Boston; William W. Ferguson of the Los Angeles *Times.* Others made contributions that will be noted in the chapters to follow. R. E. Wolseley, author and professor of journalism at Syracuse University, read the original manuscript and gave valuable criticisms.

More than anything else *Hoaxes* should serve as a warning to all of us on our beliefs, attitudes, opinions, prejudices, and biases. What about the "facts" we cite when called upon to defend them? Throughout history, mobs have formed and become hysterical; governments have fallen; reputations have been made and destroyed; international relations have been strained, and wars have been fought, all as a result of hoaxes which were exposed too late. Scholars have met in serious conclave, or have traveled to all parts of the earth; navigators have sailed the seas; audiences have filled halls; the stock market has risen and fallen; newspaper offices have been raided and closed and court trials have dragged on for months, merely because some person or persons had to have his or their joke.

Many a hoax, intended to have a fleeting effect or no effect at all, has attained gigantic proportions of influence. Though exposed time and again, it has refused to die; though interred at one time, it has been exhumed at a later date with confusing results or worse. Whether the public likes to be fooled, as the great Barnum declared, or is fooled for other reasons, it always has been. And it probably always will be. Nevertheless, knowledge of the nature and importance of many of the outstanding humbugs of the past may be insurance for the future. At least, let us hope so.

CONTENTS

ILLUSTRATIONS

PART I

WHY THEY SUCCEED

CHAPTER I

Why We Don't Disbelieve: Indifference

A YOUTHFUL REPORTER on a small New England newspaper needed one hundred fifty dollars. In August, 1895, even more than today, that was a lot of money for one in his position. It was not soon saved out of his regular wages or raised through payments from metropolitan dailies for items submitted—not at least for the type of news which Louis T. Stone was sending to New York from Winsted, Connecticut.

Still, the one-fifty had to be raised, and, to the cub, there was only one way out: if routine news from Winsted was not worth that much to big-city papers, the news would have to be changed to increase its value. Stone changed it, and with it the reputation of his birthplace for almost forty years.

The first fake of the "Winsted Liar" was an account of a wild man at large in the Connecticut woods; but the young man did not allow for the New York editor's sending his own man to investigate such a story from an inexperienced correspondent. It is not recorded whether Stone ever collected the money from the big-city star to whom he revealed the truth after a week of frenzied search and frantic journalism. What is known is that Stone learned a lesson in the type of news which intrigues metropolitan editors, so that ultimately the reputation he acquired as the century's outstanding teller of tall tales meant many times the one hundred fifty dollars both to him and to Winsted.

Stone's contribution to Winsted's reputation was acknowledged by inscriptions on roadside signboards to greet the visitor approaching this town of eight thousand:

Winsted, founded in 1779, has been put on the map by the ingenious and queer stories that emanate from this town and which are printed all over the country, thanks to L. T. Stone.

It is indicated also by a plaque on the building of the *Evening Citizen*, of which Stone was managing editor at his death, March 13, 1933, and by a bridge over Sucker Brook, erected in 1938 and named for him.

Here are the high lights of only a few of the tales by which Stone earned his reputation:

A tree on which baked apples grew.
A farmer who picked his hens for market with a vacuum cleaner.
A rooster that stopped a train.
A deaf and dumb pig.
A three-legged bullfrog.
A hen that laid a red, white, and blue egg on July 4.
A Plymouth Rock hen that hopped off a railroad engine's cowcatcher when "Plymouth" was called, and left an egg "to pay for her ride."
A cow that grazed in a horse-radish patch and gave burning milk.
A cat with a harelip that whistled "Yankee Doodle."
A modest cow owned by two old maids that refused to allow a man to milk her.
A maternal bulldog that set on hen's eggs.
Three tunneling trout that burrowed their way underground from Highland Lake to Mr. Stone's brook and received their New Year's Day meal annually from Mr. Stone's hand.
A man who painted a spider on his bald head to keep the flies away.
A squirrel that brushed its master's shoes with its tail.
A watch in the stomach of a cow that lost only two hours over a period of years because the breath of the animal acted as an automatic winder.

These tales and many, many others in the same vein are virtually all examples of unnatural history which will receive more extensive treatment in the next chapter.

Who believed these extremely odd oddities? Virtually everyone who read them, except wise editors who came to be skeptical of anything submitted by Stone but printed the stories anyway because of their reader interest.

Why are such whoppers believed? Because man is ignorant, suggestible, influenced by the prestige of a newspaper printing them, glad to believe the thrilling and spectacular since it entertains as fact but would not as fiction? Certainly, all these factors and others enter in. However, with the concoctions of the Winsted Liar and several others who have shown facility in this sort of production, probably a stronger element is the indifference of the average person toward a large part of what he reads in his daily newspaper. He will scan news items which cannot possibly affect him or someone whom he knows; and where his prejudice or sympathy is not stirred he may chuckle over an item or relate it to a near-by relative or acquaintance and then forget it.

After all, what difference does it make to the average newspaper reader whether any or all of the nature freaks invented by Louis T. Stone ever existed? What concern has he, furthermore, with a large proportion of the news of routine comings and goings of his coevals? What does he care about the creation of a new school of poetry or art, or the appearance of a new book of memoirs, an adventure story, scientific discovery, or historical theory? There is no incentive to trouble about judging most such news, no reason to be incredulous about it.

In fact, there is no reason to be amazed because the ordinary person believes anything. Belief is natural and pleasant. The child begins life by believing everything. He has to be taught skepticism before he will doubt that there is a Santa Claus, or that the moon is made of green cheese.

There was nothing unpleasant about any of the freakish accounts which emanated from Winsted. Neither was there in the inventions of a number of other contributors of unusual but innocuous news items which editors have published, sometimes aware and sometimes ignorant of their veracity.

One noted predecessor of the Winsted Liar was Joseph M. Mulholland, a traveling salesman of Washington, Pennsylvania, who wrote under the pseudonym of Orange Blossom in the eighties and nineties and read his semiplausible yarns in many a serious publication, principally the Philadelphia *Public Ledger*.

Among the most fantastic of Orange Blossom's stories was of a blazing meteor which fell in western Pennsylvania, spreading havoc and setting fire to a large portion of the country. Ultimately, according to the *Ledger,* his signature "came to be known as a sign-manual of a modern Munchausen and his stories were read as the entertaining product of a brilliant imagination and nothing more."

Another raconteur of the unusual who was not a newspaperman himself was Captain I. D. Howard of North Geneva, Ohio, of whose friendship with its correspondent in that city the Cleveland *Plain Dealer* boasted in its Sunday magazine section of January 24, 1937. Among the retired sailor's achievements, which the *Plain Dealer*'s man dutifully chronicled for publication in his paper, were increasing of the daily output of Bessie, his cow, to fifty quarts of milk through feeding her Vitamin D breakfast food; discovery of a pet rattlesnake using a stick to rob the nests of Howard's hens, and subduing of his pet goat, Oscar, by planting the animal's horns in the ground.

Relating mostly to old age, life, and death, and never revealed as anything but authentic were the frequent front-page "fillers" in the Chicago *Daily Tribune* under a Whitesburg, Kentucky, date line. Typical items:

an elderly Negro preacher who turned white and said incessant praying did it; the holding of a funeral sixteen years after death; an eighty-five-year-old woman who refused to take a ride after seeing an automobile for the first time; a ninety-six-year-old who was thrilled by her first ride; a piece of property claimed by twenty-five churches; a minister who preached his own wife's funeral, and innumerable accounts of shootings as the result of feuds among mountaineers.

Attracting suspicion by their frequency, these Whitesburg stories separately are easy to believe. It would be the casual reader who doubted one that would excite a psychiatrist's interest, not the reader who accepted it along with similar shorts from other parts of the world.

How much less strange journalistic fiction often is than journalistic fact may be learned from regular reading of Robert Ripley's authenticated "Believe It or Not" items. In 1935, furthermore, Bruce Catton made a collection of "Dizzy Doings in the News" including a woman who traced her ancestry back to Adam and Eve, a repentant burglar arrested while confessing in a Salvation Army meeting, a beaver that severed a wooden leg from its owner while he slept, a relief client who asked for two dollars for fishing tackle and to be taken off the rolls, and many other "liftings" from the day's press. Mr. Catton did not trace down these stories to determine their accuracy; instead, he accepted them as authentic, and so, unquestionably, did other readers who knew that, in a scientific age, to doubt is heretical. Annually the Burlington (Wis.) Liars Club awards prizes for the best of such whoppers. Incidentally, the club itself began as a creature of the imagination of Manel Hahn, Milwaukee *Journal* correspondent. When Hahn found himself "on the spot" as the result of his hoax, the natives made an honest man of him by actually organizing a club which has won national fame.

As a result of the human propensity to accept as true whatever is learned through the normal channels of communication, many amusing hoaxes have helped stimulate subscriber interest in newspapers and magazines. Notable among them have been the following cases:

A young man whose story appeared in an early edition of the San Francisco *Mail,* according to Evelyn Wells' *Fremont Older,* desired to end it all because of a disappointment in love. To make certain that he would not fail he not only tied a rope around his neck but also took poison and held a pistol. As he jumped from a cliff, however, the shot missed and severed the rope, whereupon he fell into salt water which acted as an emetic and prevented the poison from working.

Almost everyone who ever enjoyed the friendship of Eugene Field had to pay for it by becoming the object of some joke in the eminent humorist's column in the Chicago *Daily News*. One of Field's favorite victims was Edward W. Bok, editor of the *Ladies' Home Journal*, whom Field once had engaged to Miss Lavinia Pinkham, granddaughter of Mrs. Lydia Pinkham, and again to Mrs. Frank Leslie, both announcements being made shortly before Bok actually married Miss Curtis. Field also printed a fake interview with Bok "at quarantine" upon the latter's return from a European trip. Even Bok's Philadelphia office was fooled and prepared for his arrival. The interview pertained to changes in women's fashions in Paris and was copied by fashion papers.

Slason Thompson called himself running copy for Field for seven years, among the printed rumors being that Thompson was a British subject, even a British spy. A frequent Field trick was to introduce a controversial subject through a mythical contributor. In that way he often raised the question as to whether Colonel John A. Joyce was the author of a poem accredited to Ella Wheeler Wilcox, only to refute the arguments vigorously.

Following the adjournment of the 1933 London economic conference the London *Morning Post* printed what ostensibly was a diary hurriedly left behind by a stenographer for a member of the American delegation. It consisted of mingled gentle and biting satire for many of the principals who labored for weeks without accomplishing anything of international importance. Typical entry, that of June 10, was: "Left Maxine to type out the secretary's speech again. I've done it seven times now and her only three, and anyhow I'd some private work for the boss. They must have seen we were there, because when the movie was over the band played 'My Country 'Tis of Thee' and all the folk stood up to look at us. Was I embarrassed!"

The story of a Long Beach, California, reporter who attempted to inject a little brightness into the otherwise tragic story of how fifty-three persons lost their lives during the California earthquake in the spring of 1933, was told by Marlen Pew as follows:

It's the little disappointments that create the tragedy of life. I have been smacking my lips for weeks over a story from Long Beach, Calif., published at the time of the earthquake, about the barber who stopped shaving his customer as the first temblor shook the earth and took the first train to Nashville, Tenn., arriving just in time for the tornado, which disaster caused him to write to his old boss: "California's safer than this and I'll be back on first train." That story must have made millions laugh at fate. My well developed sense of appreciation of newspaper talent caused me to ring up a good score for the alert reporter who picked that jewel out of the rack and ruin. But, alack and alas! I hear that the story was faked by a Long Beach reporter who, in writing a second-day story, labored under the righteous conceit that it was up to him to throw a little humor into an otherwise desolate situation. The same journalistic missionary coined the nature fakes about the hen that was so scared by the recurrent temblors that she laid seven eggs running, and the King snake in the Zoo that vomited up a live mouse. I suppose this was good comedy relief. But I wanted the barber story to be true. Sort of hurts my feelings that it was only imaginative.

In the July 5, 1933, issue of the *Christian Century* a woman reader suggested that Protestants emulate the Catholic practice of maintaining nunneries. "The Pilgrim" in a September, 1933, issue of *America,* Jesuit publication, announced discovery of just such an institution in Rhode Island: the Harmonian Sisterhood. After the story was reprinted widely it was admitted to be a fake.

Newspapers of course are not always to blame for spurious items, and most of them show commendable alacrity in following up unintentional hoaxes with adequate corrections.

One of the most recent such stories was that of freckled-faced Della DeHaven, eleven-year-old Ogden, Utah, schoolgirl who came home November 12, 1936, screaming that she had met a man who frightened her with the sight of the headless body of a woman. After posses had searched and the entire country paid attention for a whole day, she confessed that she concocted the story to escape a spanking for tardiness in arriving home.

The same day the nation's press also carried the account of a big black dog which came out of the scrub pine forest near Pearl River, Louisiana, to present Mrs. Louis E. Crawford with a day-old male child whom she and her neighbors immediately called a "second Moses" because of the circumstances of his arrival. The following day, when public authorities threatened to remove the baby, Mrs. Crawford confessed that she had attempted to hoax her husband regarding a child born to her of which he was not the father.

Assigned in 1911 to write the account of an imaginary murder, a junior journalism student at the University of Kansas, at his home in Olathe, Kansas, for a short vacation, made his task easier by killing a chicken and obtaining some black hair combings from his sister. With a friend he went to an abandoned mill, smeared one of the upper floors

TWO NEWSPAPER APRIL FOOLS

(Above.) This picture of a man flying by his own lung power appeared in the 1934 April Fool edition of the *Berliner Illustrirte Zeitung* and was distributed in the United States by International News Photo.

(Below.) The Philadelphia *Record* tried to fool readers with this composite picture, "Deep Sea Monster Visits Philadelphia," April 1, 1936.

APRIL FOOL IN HONOLULU

(*Above.*) Discovery of the remains of an ancient Viking ship in Hawaii was announced April 1, 1936, by the Honolulu *Star-Bulletin*.

(*Below.*) April 1, 1939, the same newspaper ran this picture of "the largest fish ever caught" about which, according to Managing Editor Vern Hinkley, it told "the longest fish story ever told."

with the blood, scattered some of the hair, scarred the floor, and left a club near by.

The "murder" evidence was discovered by a night watchman. The Kansas City *Star,* St. Louis *Post-Dispatch,* and several other papers accepted accounts of the search for the murderer written by William W. Ferguson, later of the Los Angeles *Times,* the hoax's originator.

An impostor who took in a number of newspapers from coast to coast in 1936 gave the name of Wilbur Pledge Brown, said he was from the Ketchikan *Alaska Chronicle,* sold articles generally derogatory to the government's Matanuska Valley resettlement project, cashed checks which later proved valueless and moved on until he was caught stealing a typewriter in a New York hotel. Exposés appeared in both newspapers and news magazines.

After kidnapings became important front-page news early in the 1930's, several persons, seeking publicity, feigned abductions. Two such cases were those of Caleb Milne IV and R. H. Askew, disciple of Aimee Semple McPherson, both of whom disappeared and then sent ransom notes to friends and relatives. The newspapers printed stories of the searches for these and others who made similar bids for attention and also gave prominence to the solutions of the cases.

It is not known whether a newspaperman or someone else was responsible, in April, 1938, for the faked story of the birth of sextuplets to a San Salvador mother. The story was run seriously one day, declared a hoax the next. It is known, however, that when a London illustrated newspaper in 1936 reprinted from a French publication the pictures of six babies supposedly born to a southern Frenchwoman, it was duped by an April Fool's Day feature. And in 1952 newspapers on both American continents were the original victims of multiple birth notices. Early that year the Chicago Herald-American streamer headlined, "Mother Here Expects 5 or 6 Babies." It did so on the authority of one of its own reporters, Hugh S. Stewart, who refused to reveal his news source even to his editors whom he asked to trust him. Stewart explained one delay in the announced delivery date as caused by medication. Finally, after almost six months of it, the suspicious editors wrung a confession out of their employee and published an abject apology for the benefit of readers.

The reported birth of septuplets, all girls, in Santiago, Chile was not branded a "vulgar hoax" by police until after all but one local newspaper had issued extra editions with banner headlines and American and other foreign newspapers had given prominent space to press association accounts on Nov. 28, 1952. The hoax was a prank by students who sought to advertise a spring festival.

Until they caught on to the Continental journalistic habit of running faked stories and pictures each April 1, many American newspapers and picture services innocently broadcast sensational photographs. None attracted more attention than that which appeared in numerous American papers in 1934 showing a German pilot flying through the air with the greatest of ease by his own lung power, utilizing the rotor principle by blowing into a box on his chest to create a suction into which the flying man, with skis on his feet for landing gear and a finlike tail, was drawn.

A story of the efforts of Archibald MacLeish, librarian, to obtain loan of a draft of the Declaration of Independence written by Thomas Jefferson for display in the Library of Congress appeared in the New York *Daily News* in April, 1943. The priceless document presumably was owned by the Adams family in Massachusetts and finally was received in the mail by MacLeish, done up in ordinary brown paper and insured for only $25. Actually the manuscript, in the hand of John Adams rather than Jefferson, belongs to the Adams Manuscript Trust and was loaned through the Massachusetts Historical Society. It was insured for $5,000 and was delivered to Washington by the Princeton University librarian accompanied by a Library of Congress guard.

To clinch the contention of this chapter—that what normally enters the mind is accepted as true unless there is reason for disbelieving—the following from the anonymous author of *Sketches of Imposture, Deception, and Credulity,* published in 1837 in London, is as apropos today as it was more than a century ago:

A certain extent of credulity, or, more properly, belief, may, indeed, be considered as absolutely necessary to the well-being of social communities; for universal scepticism would be universal distrust. Nor could knowledge ever have arrived at its present amazing height, had every intermediate step in the ladder of science, from profound ignorance and slavery of intellect, been disputed with bigoted incredulity.

CHAPTER II

Why We Don't Disbelieve: Ignorance and Superstition

"ADMITTING the point of your entire first chapter," the reader may declare, "knowing that the average person scans his newspaper indifferently and doesn't ponder over the plausibility of an unusual item which has no personal effect upon him, it still seems that some people must be awfully stupid to believe the tall tales of the Winsted Liar and others."

To this point of view the answer is, "That's right."

Whereas indifference accounts for our not disbelieving a great many of the trivia with which our favorite newspaper or magazine is made more interesting, ignorance and superstition cause us to accept a great many more of them and much in addition which is of greater significance.

Consider, for instance, the fertile field in which the Winsted Liar and other fakers of animal stories work. Their yarns may be directed not only to the unschooled but also to well educated and intelligent people who nevertheless await February 2, ground-hog day, or July 15, St. Swithin's Day, to learn what the weather will be for the next six weeks, and whose ideas about animals and their ways include the following erroneous ones: that the weather also can be forecast by the activity of squirrels in gathering their winter's store of nuts, or by the length of an animal's coat; that owls are especially wise, cannot see in the daytime and relish the taste of human ears; that opossums steal shoelaces to use in their nests; that ostriches hide their heads in the sand; that giraffes, although possessed of no vocal cords, utter a death cry; that bats are blind and like to roost in growing human hair; that elephants are afraid of mice lest they crawl up their trunks; that camels' wounds won't heal; that the age of rattlesnakes can be told by the number of rattles, and that these reptiles will not crawl over horsehair ropes; that most snakes hypnotize birds, swallow their young when danger is near and, if captured, commit suicide with their own venom; that ants are overly wise, and that some squirrels use their tails for sails in crossing water on chips of bark.

Few of the feats of the animal friends of Louis T. Stone were much more remarkable than these fictitious accomplishments of familiar animals. Equally credible, in the light of contemporary ignorance in zoology, were the inventions of Elmer Lee Summers, reporter for the Houston (Texas) *Chronicle,* who delighted his editor with stories of a bantam rooster which killed a huge hawk in defense of one of its barnyard companions; of twenty ducks trained to draw a farmer's boat through marshlands and to serve as decoys for wild ducks, and of two clams that killed a giant alligator by fastening themselves to the saurian's jaws, thus preventing him from opening his mouth and starving him to death.

Almost certain to be believed, because of widespread ignorance regarding the animal's real nature, are newspaper accounts from all parts of the world, generally during the seasons when other news is scarce, of wolves in packs conducting wholesale massacres of humans. The classic wolf story, which Vilhjalmur Stefansson says made one of its earliest appearances in Willa Cather's *My Antonia,* is that of the wedding party. One by one the wedding guests are sacrificed to the baying, slavering beasts. As journalism the story ends with the eating or the escape of the bride and bridegroom and is one which may have an American or foreign date line; always it gets good front-page play. Stefansson has traced numerous wolf stories and is adamant in his belief that wolves neither travel in packs nor attack humans; he also upbraids the authors of modern geography books for perpetuating many untruths.

A story reminiscent of Sindbad the Sailor and suspiciously resembling many of the publicity stunts to be described in a later chapter appeared early in the thirties in the *Vineyard Gazette* describing the bomb-dropping sea gulls of Marthas Vineyard. These remarkable birds, it seems, dropped quahaugs on hard-surfaced roads to break them preparatory to eating. When field mice attempted to make off with the gulls' meal, the latter accurately dropped other quahaugs on the mice, killing them and providing themselves with an augmented menu.

Exaggeration may be suspected or even expected in the accounts of record growths of tomatoes, corn, sunflowers, and the like, and of the accomplishments of laying hens, breeding cattle, and other domesticated fowl and animals. No denizen of the barnyard ever was credited with a better record, however, than the White Rock hen exhibited at the Wisconsin state fair in 1919 by a West Salem, Wisconsin, farmer. It supposedly was capable of producing upwards of a half-dozen eggs at one laying.

Professor John Barry Hayes, of the University of Wisconsin College of Agriculture, attracted by the publicity given the bird, made a day's investigation. He saw a young farm hand, a reform-school parolist, slip additional eggs under the hen. Hayes kept the secret, but fair-goers became skeptical when eggs of all shapes and colors, even petit bantam eggs, began to appear together in the nest; other poultrymen from whom they had been collected gave the show away.

When Robert Ripley included the West Salem hen in his "Believe It or Not" column a few years ago, Professor Hayes lost all respect for that type of sensational journalism.

Regardless of the degree of belief he gives to their existence in the more or less remote past, the modern traveler to far-away places no longer fears meeting a centaur, unicorn, sphinx, phoenix, roc, dodo, dragon, gargoyle, mermaid, behemoth, pegasus, seven-headed hydra, lamia, mantichore, satyr, or other fabulous creature—many of them partly human— which stud the accounts of earlier seagoing and land tourists. Nevertheless, belief in the existence of strange monsters, as yet unrepresented in contemporary zoological gardens, continues today almost as strong as in the days of Marco Polo, Benjamin of Tudela, Pliny, Sir John Mandeville and other trail blazers into the vast unknown when so-called civilization was restricted to Europe and near-by parts of Asia Minor and northern Africa.

"Ocean travelers are again on the lookout for sea monsters," wrote Marshall Sprague in the New York *Times* for June 6, 1937. "Recent reports have it that a giant sting-ray measuring fifty feet across battled the freighter *Lewis Luckenbach* for two days in Mexican waters; that a thirty-foot sea serpent with a flowing red mane and dinner-plate eyes appeared briefly off the Scottish coast; that Mediterranean fishermen near Tripoli barely escaped death at the hands—or horns—of a monster with moose-like antlers and elephant ears."

In its issue of May 31, 1938, the *Christian Science Monitor* reported that within an eighteen-months period at least eight sea monsters had been reported at various points in British lakes or off the coast of Great Britain. Most famous internationally is the alleged horrific denizen of Loch Ness, near Inverness in the Scottish highlands, whose appearance has been announced each spring since 1933 when it first became a boon to Scotch tourist bureaus and business men. Variously reported as from thirty to three hundred feet long, from three to five feet thick, with a long tapering neck and tail, button head, a rough skin with a dark ridge down the back, with two appendages, possibly gills, and two or four propelling paddles or fins, "Nessie," "Bobby," or "Loopy" had an early able defender in Lieutenant Commander R. T. Gould, R.N., retired, author of *The Case for the Sea-Serpent,* who collected fifty-one eyewitness accounts on the basis of which he sought an act of Parliament to protect the what-is-it.

Footprints on Loch Ness' banks were discovered by a fellow of the Royal Geographical Society but were discredited by the Natural History Museum in London; pictures taken by Malcolm Irvine, of Scottish Films, Ltd., were too indistinct to be impressive. Nevertheless, the Loch Ness monster continued to have observers and believers among scientists and laymen of probity, and in 1938 there was organized Loch Ness Monster Company by Captain Donald John Munro, R.N., C.M.G., to make a careful investigation. Said Sir Arthur Keith, famed British anthropologist, drawn into the controversy along with almost every other important scientist of the British Isles: "Strange to say, it is just the great number of witnesses and the discrepancy in their testimony that have convinced professional zoologists that the 'monster' is not a thing of flesh and blood. I have come to the conclusion that the existence or non-existence of the 'monster' is not a problem for zoologists but for psychologists."

In this country the Lake Champlain sea serpent has appeared at intervals since 1817 and has been investigated with negative results by the Linnaean Society. It was not until April, 1934, that its cousin, the Lake George serpent known as a "hippogriff," which terrorized vacationists thirty years earlier, was revealed by its inventor, the late Harry W. Watrous, widely known painter, to have been a ten-foot log anchored and regulated from the shore by means of a rope and pulley.

Other marine monsters are reported with regularity from almost every part of the world, often by reputable citizens and even by persons of scientific training or interest. Unfortunately, however, none of the following which excited more than usual interest ever was captured or even photographed: the "ogopogo" of Okanagan Lake, British Columbia, observed in October, 1933, by F. W. Kemp, member of the provincial archives staff, and by Major W. H. Langley, clerk of the British Columbia legislature; the Hiaschuackaluck sea serpent "seen" by Captain W. N. Prengel of the Grace Liner *Santa Lucia* and investigated futilely in the Straits of Juan de Fuca by a Victoria newspaper; the abnormal monsters which almost annually frighten seamen or bathers off the New Jersey and Pacific coasts; the Wading River, Long Island, "thing" for which posses searched in July, 1936; the Sterling, Illinois, "it" of October, 1937, or the unknown visitor to Wasaga Beach, Ontario, in June, 1938. All, however, received a very good press and quantities of sandwiches and soft drinks were sold to thousands of quidnuncs.

Just as terrifying as sea monsters in the habits attributed to them are the fearsome creatures that form a part of the folklore of the American timberlands. Their tales, in the Paul Bunyan tradition, still are told to tenderfeet on hunting or camping expeditions, and not infrequently news stories of startling discoveries by horror-stricken persons of repute appear. Not many years ago, for instance, from the vicinity of Beaver Falls, Nebraska, came the report of terrible devastation of cattle and horses from the stings of the hoopsnake, familiar to students of such folklore as the reptile taught by its mother to use the force of gravity by rolling into a ball and swooping down hillsides to surprise victims.

Never captured for either zoo or museum or photographed but believed in by the excusably gullible are the whirling whimpus, which spins like a top so rapidly that its physical characteristics cannot be determined; the rubberado, which bounces when shot and, if eaten, causes the consumer to bounce; the rackabore, which is either left- or right-handed and incapable of turning in the other direction; the tripodero, which has extensible legs like a photographer's tripod and kills its prey by hitting it with pellets of mud; side-hill gougers, badgers and sheep with legs shorter on one side than on the other to make easier horizontal progress on slopes; the wampus cat, treesqueak, cross-feathered snee, snow snake, snoligostus, and many others.

Recent additions to unnatural history, all of which received space on press association wires, include: a breed of sheep that cannot jump and is addicted to fainting spells, reported by R. J. Goode, insurance man of Birmingham, Alabama, and member of the Alabama state legislature; the Australian bunyip, resembling a bullock in size with a head and back of an emu, a thick mane of hair from the top of the head to the shoulders, three webbed toes and a tail of a horse; an eighty-four-year-old talking mongoose named Gef on the Isle of Man about which Harry Price, president of the London Society for Psychical Research, and R. S. Lambert, investigator of the supernatural, wrote *The Haunting of Cashen's Gap;* a "specter moose" reported to have appeared again in the woods of Maine after having previously been seen in 1901, 1917, and 1932.

In 1875 the New York *Herald* printed an amazing story by R. B. Davenport, its correspondent accompanying the Newton-Jenney expedition to the Black Hills of South Dakota. It was based on the explanation of the skeleton of a bull elk discovered by Davenport as supplied by California Joe, famous scout. Joe identified the bones as those of a "camelce," the result of the mating between native elks and Asiatic camels which he said the government once used as pack animals in the deserts of Arizona.

Among the most sensational yarns was that which appeared in the *Arkansas Gazette* of Little Rock in 1897, of the killing of a "gowrow" by one William Miller, friend of the author, Elbert Smithee, who had Elmer Burrus make a drawing of the dead creature. The kill was said to have been made by a posse in Searcy County, Arkansas, after the gowrow, so named because of its cry, had terrorized the countryside and slaughtered cattle and other animals. The description was of an animal twenty feet long, with a ponderous head, two enormous tusks, short legs, web feet with claws, green scales, a back with short bristling short horns, and a long, thin tail. Before it was killed it shook the ground like an earthquake and caused huge waves on the lake.

The annals of American journalism include mention of none who made greater capital of the frontiersman's delight in the marvelous than E. J. ("Stroller") White, for thirty-five years editor and publisher of the Juneau *Stroller's Weekly*.

Stroller's story begins with his arrival in Dawson during the gold rush of 1898 and his immediate crashing of the door to local fame with the printing of a few hundred sheets of stationery for the Sour Dough Hotel. "They sold like hot cakes—at two dollars a dozen sheets," said Stroller. "In fact the things are still selling in all Alaskan towns. Newcomers think it is a good joke to write home to their folks on it."

The letterhead locates the Sour Dough Hotel at 1323 Icicle Avenue. Among the house rules are: towels changed weekly; spiked shoes must be removed at night; anyone troubled with nightmare will find a halter on the bedpost; don't worry about paying your bill—the house is supported by its foundation, etc. This foolery landed White a job on the *Klondike Nugget,* where news was scarce during the storms which cut off communication with the outside world.

To keep the presses going during one particularly cold spell, Stroller announced a heavy fall of Mark Twain's blue snow and the appearance in adjacent glaciers of the ice worms which came to the surface "to bask in the unusual frigidity in such numbers that their chirping was seriously interfering with the slumbers of Dawson's inhabitants."

Incredible as it may seem, virtually the whole town believed this story, according to its inventor. Immediately every saloon in town advertised "Ice-Worm Cocktails." White decided to try one and observed its preparation by the bartender who dropped a six-inch squirming worm extracted from a cake of ice. When he bravely gulped it down the bartender in a whisper confessed: "Say, Stroller, we couldn't get any of the real thing, so we faked 'em by poking spaghetti through gimlet holes and letting it swell. But don't tell any of the boys the difference."

Alaskan postcards still show bearded miners pulling ice worms from a glacier.

Stroller White also tells the story of Casey Antonio Moran, Irish reporter with an imagination. During another news famine Casey returned with an affidavit signed by an Indian chief that a "house big as a white man's town built in a big canoe" which he had discovered on Mt. Koyukuk resembled the picture of Noah's ark in a Bible shown him by Moran.

"The other two dailies, having been scooped, tried to discredit Casey's story by calling it a hoax," said Stroller, "but in vain. It was printed wherever the Associated Press flashed its service, and even today, after more than thirty years, it is still going the rounds."

Aside from synthetic monsters inspired by publicity men, to be treated in a later chapter, one outstanding exception to the rule that a monster of either sea or land never is captured and examined must be mentioned. This is the "bovine spirituallis" or "hodag," trapped alive at Rhinelander, Wisconsin. Its ferocity can be conjectured from picture postcards still on sale in northern Wisconsin showing a beast with the head of a bull, the grinning face of a giant man, thick short legs set off by heavy strong claws, the back of a dinosaur, and a long tail with a spear at the end.

Advertised seriously as the transmigrated soul of an ox used by Paul Bunyan and other early-day loggers, its capture, as told by Eugene S. Shepard and two companions, coincided with what would be expected of Bunyan's ox. Tradition tells that that animal, although burned for seven years to rid it of all the profanity of its many masters, arose from the ash pile and exhaled an obnoxious odor, making the earth tremble with the lash of its tail. It was the odor which drew Shepard's attention near the headwaters of Rice Creek, Oneida County.

Visitors crowded to observe the beast after its incarceration. Because of a dim light it was not known for some time that the animal actually was a large dog over which a decorated horse's hide was stretched. The name "hodag" was a combination of "horse" and "dog."

In sending the story of the monster's capture to metropolitan newspapers, according to Jack Cory, editor of the Rhinelander *Daily News,* the theory was advanced that the hodag was "the long-sought missing link between the ichthyosaurus and the mylodoan" of the Ice Age. This interested eastern scientists and circus owners, and the hodag created a sensation for weeks and months.

After the original hodag's death a stuffed successor was exhibited at fairs for two years. Whenever a convention meets at Rhinelander the fame of the monster lives anew, stuffed hodags being manufactured for floats or other displays. Luke Sylvester Kearney in 1928 published a book, *The Hodag*. W. J. Lemke, head of the news bureau of the University of Arkansas, states that during his boyhood at Wausau, Wisconsin, "large photographs of the hodag on a fallen log, surrounded by a group of his captors armed with axes, pitchforks, etc. were fairly common. Many of them were used as decorations in the saloons."

Early in 1937, the Associated Press reported that Sir Alexander Seton had sent back to Egypt a bit of bone supposedly from a Pharaoh's skeleton —concrete evidence that it is not only regarding mundane animal life that the twentieth century man is superstitious and ignorant. Confusing coincidence with cause, as men have done since the beginning of history, Sir Alexander got rid of the bone because visitors to his home had complained of shadowy things, two fires had broken out in his house, the maid of a surgeon to whom he had loaned the relic had broken her leg, several members of the family had become ill, and a number of other calamities had occurred.

Despite the advance which science has made, moderns still avoid opening an umbrella in the house, lighting a third cigarette with the same match, spilling salt, breaking mirrors, walking under ladders, crossing the path of a black cat, and the number thirteen in any social gathering or as a house or telephone number. To them a howling dog portends death; but there are lucky days, numbers, and signs. Four-leaf clovers, horseshoes, rabbits' feet, and rapping on wood help in the defense against unseen forces which, in rational moments, many would deny but regarding which it is still best to play safe and take no chance.

In 1935 Dr. Reese James of the University of Pennsylvania found that his students avoided passing anyone on a stairway, throwing a hat on the bed, giving a knife to a friend, and writing an examination paper with a new pen or pencil. Although they shamefacedly admitted their credulity they said there probably was "nothing to it." Nevertheless, they counted nine before reentering a room they had just left, crossed their fingers and muttered spells.

A study in the same year conducted by Professor George J. Dudycha of Ripon College among seniors in seven middle western colleges revealed widespread belief in fortune telling by palm readings, the danger of Friday the 13th, the injudiciousness of beginning an important task on a Friday, birthmarks as a result of a pregnant woman's social experiences, astrology, ghosts, and many other unscientific anachronisms.

If such is the situation as regards the minority in the population given the advantage of higher education, what must be the case of those not so fortunate? In one field, that of medical magic, Dr. Joseph L. Miller of Thomas, West Virginia, reported to the Medical Library Association, there persists among his patients faith in the efficacy of the following folk remedies:

asafetida suspended in a little sack from the neck to prevent acute infectious diseases like measles, diphtheria, whooping cough;
necklaces of amber to prevent and cure goiter;
coral or kernels of red corn to stop nosebleed or other hemorrhages;
a coin held under the upper lip and a cold key dropped down the back to stop a nosebleed—if these fail, let the blood drip on an ax or knife and bury it in the ground;
peony roots to prevent epilepsy and convulsions;
and many more of the same sort.

In *Don't Believe It!* Dr. August A. Thomen debunks, among others, the following popular beliefs: that eating green apples will cause stomach ache; that the heart is situated in the left side of the chest; that a "compound fracture" is one in which a bone is broken in a number of places; that beef tea is very nourishing; that singeing the hair is beneficial, aiding it to grow more abundantly; that reading light should come over the left shoulder; that it is more dangerous to prick oneself with a pin than with a needle; that baldness is due to the too frequent wearing of hats, or to tight hatbands; that individuals with high color or florid complexions are especially healthy; that thunder sometimes causes milk to sour; that a person's hair grows after death; that any method of using one's handkerchief is quite satisfactory, and that we have only five senses.

As illustrated by these studies, there is a difference between superstition and mere ignorance, although the dividing line sometimes is difficult to draw. Superstition, however, is responsible for the anxiety with which recipients of certain chain letters, threatening misfortune if instructions are not complied with, take pen in hand to keep the chain unbroken. One such letter, which has been going the rounds longer than most, is the alleged epistle of Jesus Christ, said to have been found under a stone near Iconium where it was deposited by the Angel Gabriel to be broadcast throughout the world. Professor Edgar J. Goodspeed of the University of Chicago writes of its contents:

It consists principally of some artless precepts about attending church and observing the Sabbath, but its text has been so often debased by inaccurate reprinting that it is sometimes difficult to make out just what the original meant to say. I have not been able to learn anything about its age or author, but it seems to have originated in England, forty or more years ago. . . .

Religious superstition and fear always have provided fertile soil for the sower of supernatural lore. A complete list of religious fakers and fanatics would be interminable. A typical case was that of Joanna Southcott (1750–1814), a farmer's daughter of Gittisham, Devonshire, who set October 19, 1814, as the date for the fulfillment of the following prophecy from Revelation 12:1–2: "And there appeared a great wonder in heaven; a woman clothed with the sun, and the moon under her feet, and upon her head a crown of twelve stars: And she being with child cried, travailing in birth, and pained to be delivered."

Not only that: she also cleared up the question of the identity of the woman. It was not "Mother Ann" Lee (Mrs. Standerin or Stanley, founder or the Shakers), but Joanna, a part of the Deity itself, spiritually ordained to "seal" 140,000 of the faithful to be saved for eternity after the Second Coming.

William Sharp press-agented the prophetess in London, and she found the years after 1792, when she made her prophecy, until the date of her death, October 29, 1814 (ten days after her miscalculation), very lucrative. Her box of "treasures" was guarded for one hundred and four years. In 1928 it was found to contain only miscellaneous objects, but in 1939 the Panacea Society, which perpetuates the memory and teachings of Joanna Southcott, claimed to have the true box which their prophet ordered to be opened in a time of great crisis in the presence of twenty-four bishops. The Church of England ignored a petition to assign the bishops to preside at an opening ceremony.

Financed by the bequest of a rich widow named Essam, a man named Roberts devoted years to the preparation of *Observations of the Divine Mission of Joanna Southcott,* which contained sixty illiterate works by the prophetess.

Superstition has received no greater boost from the press of the world than through its handling of the deaths of members of the party which in 1922 entered the inner part of the tomb of Tutankhamen, Egyptian mummy. The story, which resulted in exceptionally good news-stand sales, had it that the tomb carried the inscription: "Death shall come on swift wings to him that touches the tomb of Pharaoh."

Actually there was no such inscription, and eleven years after opening of the tomb all ten men who were present when the mummy was unwrapped were alive, including Howard Carter who actually pierced the door of the tomb. The average age at death of the first six of the expedition who died was fifty-nine years, and none died from unknown causes. Carter died early in 1939 at the age of sixty-six years.

Despite the public statements of eminent archaeologists and historians, especially following the death in 1935 of Dr. James H. Breasted, noted University of Chicago archaeologist who was a member of the King Tut party, and despite the iconoclasm of many editorial writers, who have tried valiantly to offset the evil done in the news columns of the newspapers with which they are connected, the average reader probably will react to the next recorded death of a member of the expedition in orthodox shuddering manner.

How can readers do otherwise when the papers persist in printing such nonsense as the following account sent out April 10, 1939, by the Associated Press:

The "curse of the Pharaohs" has taken one more of the party of Lord Carnarvon, which explored the 32-centuries-old tomb of the boy King, Tutankhamen.

Dr. Jean Ahmid Brochet, Los Angeles endocrinologist who was killed a week ago in a traffic accident, was an archaeologist with the Carnarvon expedition his widow, Joan Brochet, said today.

For his superstition and his scientific ignorance—especially the latter —modern man should not be censured too unkindly. In an age of radios, sputniks, H-bombs, Rhines, quanta, and fifth dimensions, is it any wonder that the bewildered newspaper reader or radio listener also gives an ear to the phrenologist, numerologist, spiritualist, fortune teller, alchemist, or possessor of a divining rod?

In a scientific age to doubt is sacrilegious. "Fundamentalist" is a term of opprobrium which even conservatives wish to avoid. With the exception of a laughable minority men today accept without question or proof the statement of scientists that the earth is round and rotates about the sun. The main tenets of evolution are coming to be accepted similarly. From the standpoint of the average person, however, both the rotundity of the earth and modern biology are matters of undemonstrated faith; and the same is true of almost every other belief he cherishes.

This being so, is it any wonder that people have believed newspaper stories originating in Whitesburg, Kentucky, and Tulsa, Oklahoma, of a Negro who has discovered the secret of turning his black skin white? According to Stefansson there is no place in the Arctic where the sun doesn't shine for at least a few seconds every day of the year. Eskimo mothers do not carry their babies in their hoods, Eskimos do not drink oil, and any statements regarding them are likely to be incorrect inasmuch as there are many types, widely separated in space and customs. Nevertheless, schools and lecturers perpetuate these untruths, and interviews with careless observers who have made quick trips to the polar regions—or, in fact, to any other part of the world—get good newspaper space: the more startling the statements, the greater the space.

How prophetic a scientific hoaxer may be was illustrated by the famous diaphote hoax of Dr. H. E. Licks, who related it in his *Recreations in Mathematics*. Although commercial television is commonplace everywhere today, this marvelous instrument, with its name derived from the Greek *dia* signifying "through" and *photos* signifying "light," was a sensation when the first account of it appeared February 10, 1880, in a Pennsylvania newspaper.

The instrument contained four essential parts: a receiving mirror, transmitting wires, a common galvanic battery, and a reproducing speculum. Light, Licks said, caused momentary chemical changes in the mirror which modified the electric current, and caused similar changes in the remote speculum, thus causing an image which might be seen readily or thrown upon a screen by a second camera.

Licks predicted the use of the discovery in connection with interlocking railroad switch systems to enable the central office to see many miles of track at one time, thus lessening the probability of accident. In connection with photolithography, he said, it could be employed so that the great English newspapers could be printed in New York a few hours after their appearance in London.

Plausible as these predictions may seem today, based on the principles expounded by Licks, they were ridiculous. Nevertheless, within a week the original article was copied in part or in whole by numerous other papers through the United States, many of which commented editorially on the great possibilities of the marvelous diaphote. Some said sunlight would be transmitted by it from the sunny side of the earth to light the side which was in darkness. The New York *Times* said, "The imagination almost fails before the possibilities of what the diaphote may yet accomplish." The only paper, according to Licks, which recognized the fake was the New York *World*.

Within a month items appeared in papers announcing the invention in Pittsburgh of an instrument called the "telephole" by which two persons at a distance could see each other as they talked over the telephone, and by which any written or printed document could be transmitted instantaneously to any distance. The inventors of this instrument, it was stated, had labored many years in making experiments. While Dr. Licks used seventy-two wires, the Pittsburgh inventors used but one, and their applications for patents were soon to be granted.

News soon spread to Europe, and in due time, according to Licks, stories came of wonderful inventions made there. For instance, the news came in 1889 that a young German named Korzel had exhibited an instrument by which a person in one city could read a newspaper held before a receiving plate in another city.

Of "petrified" men there have been many. One of the earliest was that exhibited at the World's Columbian Exposition in 1893 in Chicago—the Forest City Man from somewhere in the Dakotas. It was manufactured out of a human skeleton, was buried near the Little Cheyenne River by James Sutton of Redfield, South Dakota, and was dug up by a friend of his, after which it was taken on tour.

This hoax probably was inspired by the most famous of all such—the Cardiff Giant, to be described later. Another imitation of that phenomenon was the solid image (later found to be made of water-lime, sand, and gravel by William Ruddock of Thornton, St. Clair County, Michigan) discovered in 1876. G. A. Stockwell wrote in the June, 1878, *Popular Science*:

This hoax obtained some local celebrity, and even found its way into the general press. Several rural clergymen made it an especial topic in their Sunday discourses; and certain agricultural papers, backed by letters from these same teachers, assured the world that the "Pine River man" was no Cardiff giant, but a *bona-fide* "creation of God!"

The great Barnum advanced two thousand dollars to facilitate the making of the Colorado Man at far-away Elkland, mountain town in northern Pennsylvania, where its instigators presumably operated a summer resort and mountain sanitarium.

This Colorado Man was an ambitious effort. It was given real bones and other human ingredients made from ground stone, clay, plaster and dried eggs, well baked for two weeks. Its four-inch tail and its arms proportionally longer than its legs made it a monstrosity.

When a traveling "geologist" discovered the body in its Rocky Mountain burial place, Barnum "happened" to be in the neighborhood on a temperance lecture tour. The great showman offered $20,000 for the find, scientists were permitted to bore into certain prepared parts. It was Yale's Professor Marsh, who also had exposed the Cardiff Giant, who proved Barnum's nemesis. He took one look at the figure and said its rotundity was incompatible with the theory of one who had died and become fossilized; in such case the abdomen naturally would have collapsed. Despite this exposé the Colorado Man entertained western newspaper readers for some time; but it is doubtful if its promoters earned much on their investment.

It was a mistaken interpretation of a cablegram regarding the distress of a ship near Bermuda that inspired a series of newspaper yarns over a period of years which contained such absurdities that it is difficult to believe they were as widely accepted as is known to have been the case. Author of them was the late Frank Ward O'Malley, New York *Sun* columnist, who thought it very funny when the cable desk took the last word of the message, "Wobble," to be the name of the vessel rather than the code word for "cable instructions."

According to O'Malley's running account, the *Wobble* was equipped with only one paddle-wheel which handicapped navigation. Its commander was Captain Heinie Hassenpfeffer; its cargo included subways and artesian wells. Its chief officer was a second-story man who went insane when he tried to operate in Africa and discovered that the houses were only one story high. Often the ship became lost in Michigan or the Hippodrome.

The predilection of otherwise intelligent persons to accept as true whatever reaches them through a source considered trustworthy, and the inability of many to apply the ordinary tests of probability to fictitious accounts, are strikingly illustrated by the experience of a Connecticut tall-story teller—C. Louis Mortison of the Waterbury *Republican* and *American,* who made Prospect, Connecticut almost as famous as Winsted.

THE RUBBERADO bounces when shot. Anyone who eats it bounces, too

THE RACKABORE, an offspring of the javelina, is legged for sidehills. There are two types, right and left-handed

THE TRIPODERO

When it spies another beast, the tripodero stuns it with a clay pellet from its blowgun proboscis

THE WHIRLING WHIMPUS

"Outdoor Life"

IMPROBABLE QUADRUPEDS

Tenderfeet on camping trips are thrilled by the stories old-timers tell them of fabulous beasts. If they existed, some of these creatures would look like this.

W
Ph

Courtesy, E. C. Kropp Company, Milwaukee

THE CAMERA CAN LIE

(Above.) An obviously faked picture purporting to be the famous Loch Ness serpent which the Wide World Photo Service jocosely sent out as an "unretouched photo rushed here from London by radiograph."

(Below.) This postcard view of the Rhinelander, Wis., hodag shows the interesting results of a taxidermist's art.

Unlike Stone, Mortison writes all his stories about the same character and his family. As Prospect correspondent for the *Republican* and *American* years ago, he began substituting the name "Lester Green" for those of real persons in stories with which he knew they wouldn't want their names connected, but which nevertheless made good copy.

Gradually Lester's exploits increased and, after a short period during which metropolitan editors blue-penciled all mention of him and his family, came to be eagerly sought by out-of-town papers.

Among the doings of Lester Green and his family which have made news are the following:

One fall Lester flooded a meadow to insure a good ice crop for the summer. While cutting ice during February he found a setting of hen's eggs in a block of ice. These he placed in a pan on top of his furnace to thaw out. A few days later he found eight Leghorn chicks in the pan, each covered with what resembled fur instead of feathers.

When Lester's chimney caught fire he went to the roof and threw sand down it. His wife, excited, mistook washing soda for salt and filled the stove with it. The fire fused the two materials and filled the stovepipe and chimney solidly with glass.

Hearing of Thomas A. Edison's experiments to extract rubber from goldenrod, Lester invented a system for producing dairy products from milkweed stems. He attached Mrs. Green's vibrating machine and churned the juice of the plants so that the leaves exuded butter.

Finding a snapping turtle that had been scared out of its shell, Lester made another for it out of concrete into which the turtle crawled and rewarded its benefactor by keeping his feed house free of rats and mice.

To assure a winter crop of fresh apples Lester sprayed his trees with glue which prevented the fruit's dropping off in the fall. During the winter a fresh apple always was available merely by washing off the glue.

While butchering a hog Lester discovered the fluid responsible for the curl in a pig's tail. By rubbing it on their hair Mrs. Green and her daughter produced beautiful permanent waves.

Ridiculous as some of these stories may appear, the following results are on record:

A Canadian farmer tried to buy a pair of the fur-coated chickens. Mortison answered that they had sweltered to death in the warm weather.

Two prominent chemical engineers tried to find the Green home to investigate the chimney filled with glass.

American and Canadian glue manufacturing concerns sent letters addressed to Lester Green asking what kind of glue he used for his apples, and a representative of a Boston concern came to Prospect to investigate.

Mrs. Green was inundated with requests for the exact method of extracting the pigtail fluid. One man offered to buy the secret to use it in making bedsprings.

In the February 9, 1935, issue of *News-Week*, page 23, one of Mortison's whoppers was printed soberly as fact as follows:

LOGIC: Lester Green of Prospect, Conn., puts two setting hens on his automobile motor cold nights. "A setting hen's temperature is 102," Green explained, "and consequently two hens is 204. With that heat the engine is sure to start the first time it kicks over."

On its editorial page April 20, 1939, the Kansas City *Times* reprinted the following from the sober "It Takes All Kinds" column of the *American Magazine:*

Lester Green, a farmer of Prospect, Conn., has trained his hound dog to run away from foxes, not after them, thus developing what he claims is a successful new system of fox hunting. It works like this: Hound finds fox, legs it for home; fox chases dog; then as both round the corner of the barn, Farmer Green blazes away.

At the other end of the country another Winsted-inspired character acquired nation-wide fame. That was Pelican Bill, creation of the conductor of the Coconut Club Press whose dispatches originated with the *Florida Keys Sun* of Key West.

This awkward bird, according to a series of news stories which were given wide circulation, was dissuaded from killing the famed albatross of the Ancient Mariner when they met in combat in 1931 near the Florida shore only by fear that he might be doomed to roam the South Seas forever. Saved from such a fate by his own prudence, the bird attached himself to the good ship *General Debility* which sails the Gulf Stream. Always eluding capture, he was reported from Havana, Yucatan, and other places. At first he wore a scarlet tie, and later a green one. When last heard from, Pelican Bill was on his way to Ireland in search of a shillelagh, relic of the rebellion of 1798.

The Pelican Bill stories were not the only ones from the Coconut Club Press. In mid-July, 1930, when the nation was sweltering from the heat, it issued a dispatch telling of the freezing over of the docks of the Peninsular and Occidental Steamship Company at Key West. An order of one hundred pairs of skates received from Baltimore sold out in an hour, and another shipment was ordered. The ice was of cerulean blue, and news-reel photographers were reported to be taking colored pictures of it.

Hens intoxicated from drinking rum runners' whisky, a guide named Lucius Llewellyn Lucifer who lighted campfires by deflecting the sun's rays from his red hair, rule fish, athletic mosquitoes, skate fish, a Japanese lantern tree, and many other phenomena were reported in Coconut Club dispatches.

Ora L. Jones, managing editor of the *Florida Keys Sun,* writes in part:

For many months we ran a column of similar foolishness, made up for the most part of seemingly plausible stories of freaks of nature and imaginary monstrosities. While most of our readers recognized such articles as pure fiction, a certain number—and not always the feeble-minded readers either—were continually being fooled by them. So much so, in fact, that we finally abandoned the feature.

Among the outstanding articles that deceived many people and caused them to go looking for something that did not exist were the following:

Twenty-four chickens hatched from a dozen double-yolked eggs.

The capture of an 850-pound Chelenoid, described as a testudinate reptile, which many wanted to see.

And there is still one man here who insists that he saw a number of stray icebergs moving southward in the Gulf Stream near here—as described by the SunOgram writer. The fact that the Gulf Stream flows northeast by here failed to convince this man that the bergs didn't come this way.

CHAPTER III

Why We Don't Disbelieve: Suggestion

REREAD the last paragraph of the quotation with which the preceding chapter ended—the one about the man who was certain he saw the icebergs off the coast of Florida. He illustrates what is meant by "suggestion," a word which Kimball Young, professor at Northwestern University, in *Social Psychology* says is "used to describe a certain form of social stimulation wherein the vocal or other stimuli of a person or persons set off images, ideas, attitudes or acts on the part of another person or other persons because other images, ideas, and attitudes do not inhibit them."

The suggestible person either is disposed, because of his attitudes, opinions, prejudices, etc., to act as the person offering the suggestion wants him to act, or at least has no reason for not acting in that way. Note that suggestion calls for response by its recipient, if only the expression of an opinion, whereas the indifferent or ignorant or superstitious reader or hearer of a tall tale may remain perfectly passive. Little thought or deliberation precedes action as a result of a suggestion; if it did the response frequently would not be the same, as the "victim" would "know better" than to do as he had been told.

To accept suggestions that things be accepted as they appear to be is to travel the normal path of least resistance. The success of a suggestion depends in large part upon two factors: (1) interest; (2) familiarity. That is, if a person does not believe his well-being is affected, doubt does not arise when a new idea is presented to him; if, on the contrary, the matter is one of personal concern, he rejects the suggestion, or at least considers before he acts. Often, the tendency to disbelieve what does not square with preconceived notions is a factor in the rejection of what may be true.

In their laboratories experimental psychologists have proved the suggestibility of all types of persons. In Gardner and Lois Murphy's *Experimental Social Psychology* are to be found the results of many of these tests. For instance, one professor sprayed pure water about a schoolroom, telling the students to raise their hands when they detected an odor; 73 per cent did so. Of 381 children shown a toy camel and told it would be seen to move when a windlass turned, 76 per cent said they saw the motion. A coin about the size of a fifty-cent piece was passed around a class of forty-eight boys from fourteen to seventeen years of age with instructions to examine it carefully. At the end of the class period the instructor asked each boy to draw a picture of the coin, indicating the position of the hole in it. Although there was no hole, all but four of the forty-eight indicated one, some even drawing two holes. Of the four only one, the bad boy of the class, unaccustomed to obeying orders, was positive that there was no hole.

The importance of familiarity in its effect upon suggestibility was demonstrated by A. T. Poffenberger, who investigated the conditions of belief in advertising. Subjects were asked whether they believed certain advertisements. Although one of these, a picture of an elephant standing on a trunk to test its strength, was not a fake, 38 per cent doubted the statement that the trunk would withstand such a test, 24 per cent believed the photograph was not genuine, and 21 per cent simply said it was impossible to build a trunk that strong.

On the truism that belief rarely is the result of reasoning based on observations in everyday life, "Ginger," a veteran newspaperman, wrote in the *American Magazine* for December, 1912, after confessing the authorship of a long series of fake stories: "Sometimes I used to wonder whether we had not accidentally hit upon truth. I have had men of undoubted probity declare the stories true, although insisting that some of the details were wrong."

He had published a fictitious account of a sock-darning contest arranged among the eligible young women in a small Kentucky town, the winner of which was to become the bachelor minister's bride. "More than a year later," commented Ginger, "I met a staid and respected citizen of that place who gravely informed me that every word of the story was true, and he went further, and added details concerning the happiness of the married life of the couple."

To the credit of the same pseudonymous Ginger, on his own authority, were the following tall tales:

A Plymouth Rock hen was said by its owner, a Mrs. Jones of California, to be the reincarnation of a great-great-great-grandaunt, Ann Purkiser. The story in various forms appeared in more than a score of newspapers all over the country. A psychical research society in London wrote for additional information on the case, which Ginger sent. Out of gratitude the society voted him an honorary membership.

A schoolboy vowed to lick his teacher when he grew up. Year after year the older man, however, won. The former student married his opponent's daughter, but the annual combat continued. The editor of another department of the paper put the date of the next meeting in his record book and, when the month rolled around again, wired a correspondent to watch out for the fisticuffs. The correspondent rose to the occasion, sending in a half-column on the latest victory of the schoolmaster. The next year this new writer in the case queried his paper on how much was wanted.

A hoodooed chair was advertised as part of the furnishings of a real hotel. Anyone who sat in it was supposed to come to grief. The hotel proprietor seized upon the idea, enclosed the chair, and put up a chain to protect guests. Five years later the chair was a superstitious legend.

In his *Candid Chronicles,* Hector W. Charlesworth tells of a practical joke played by Charles Langdon Clarke, widely known Canadian newspaperman, upon a proud member of the Scotch clan of Maclean. It was a story in the Toronto *Mail and Empire* that the cowardice of the Macleans caused the defeat of Bonnie Prince Charlie in 1756 at Culloden. Another journalist, with a grudge against a member of the Canadian parliament named Maclean, saw the story and declared himself familiar with *History of the Scottish Clans* by an author named Stranways on which it presumably was based. He said Stranways' work was "based on material not accessible to other historians." There was, of course, no book and no Stranways.

Following publication in 1909 of *The Old Librarian's Almanack, 1773* as No. 1 of an alleged Librarians' Series under the editorship of John Cotton Dana and Henry W. Kent, its real author, Edmund Lester Pearson, had much to say about the erudition of certain book reviewers.

The presumed original editor of the almanac had signed himself "Philobiblos" in Greek letters, but internal evidence, according to the preface, was said to indicate he must have been Jared Bean, born in New Haven about 1705 or 1706 and curator about 1754 of the Connecticut Society of Antiquarians.

The curiosity was received seriously. Of the reviews quoted in the *Book Review Digest* for 1910, only one, in the weekly *Independent,* called it "one of the cleverest hoaxes of recent years." Pearson, then literary critic for the Boston *Transcript,* insisted that it never was intended as anything else. He explained later, in *Books in Black or Red:*

The point of the thing was this: it was designed to delude any intelligent reader for no longer than five minutes. It was purposely sown thick with anachronisms; its language was made unduly archaic; it contained innumerable clews of modern origin; and it ended with an outrageously farcical parody of an ancient cure for rattlesnake bite "made Publick by Abel Puffer of Stoughton."

As soon as the New York *Sun* reviewed the book seriously for a column and a half, Pearson disillusioned the critic. Nevertheless, serious acceptance continued for two months, when the "exposures" began and continued for two years.

The "discoverers" of the modern origin of the Almanack balked at the name of the veritable Abel Puffer, but swallowed the fictitious Jared Bean without a struggle. They became owlish about typography, paper, and the biographies of Eighteenth Century almanac-makers and printers. Light broke in upon them when they discovered obscure and recondite "clews" of their own invention—after they had passed by a dozen obvious indications of modernity. They found jokes and allusions which were quite unknown to the author, just as the commentators on every writer from Shakespeare to Lord Dunsany have invented meanings of their own for various passages. They found "really modern" expressions which, as a matter of fact, were not modern at all; they walked past signs which were wide as a church-door, to pick up microscopic imaginings of their own. . . .

Every sea-serpent or monster scare affords the opportunity to observe the operation of suggestion on a wide scale. In 1922 Ware, Massachusetts, since then known as Alligator Town, with a baseball team called the Alligators and with places of business popularly designated by the same name, had such a mass fright.

It all began when Stephen Fabirkiewicz of Gilbertville breathlessly reported that upon passing Dismal Swamp on the Ware-Gilbertville road he suddenly was confronted by a horrific beast six or eight feet long. Posses, newspapermen, and photographers searched in vain although the names of twenty-four persons who swore they had seen the menace appeared in the *Ware River News.*

According to George E. Clapp, then a member of the staff of the Springfield (Mass.) *Union,* capture of a two-foot baby alligator a month later solved the mystery. This reptile, Clapp said, had been received from a Florida friend by a resident who, not caring to keep it as a pet, set it loose. Says Mr. Clapp: "The alligator took up residence in the swamp and was getting along swimmingly until the simple folk took fright."

In the opinion of William H. Dearden, editor of the *Ware River News,* however, the baby alligator was only a "plant" of a motion picture house manager; the identity of the creature which terrorized the countryside, Dearden contends, never was determined. "It was not a fake," he writes, "and is still an unexplained mystery, with a great many men convinced they saw an alligator and others believing it may have been a large stray otter which are sometimes seen hereabouts."

A better example, involving a terror about the specious nature of which there can be no question, is that of the Jersey Devil, incarnated in 1906 as a publicity stunt and today still firmly believed in by many rural citizens of New Jersey and eastern Pennsylvania.

Inspiration of the 1906 devil was an old book, the authorship of which seems to have been forgotten, which tells the story of a mother who placed a curse on her seventh child about to be born. Her blasphemy was the wish that it might be a devil. It was, and, immediately after birth, flew up the chimney and away.

It was a copy of this book which Norman Jefferies, publicity manager for C. A. Brandenburgh's Arch Street Museum in Philadelphia and much in disrepute in newspaper offices in that city because of previous stunts, found in Leary's bookstore. It gave him the idea needed to revive flagging interest in the show.

In a few days there appeared in a small-town paper in south Jersey the following news story:

The "Jersey Devil," which has not been seen in these parts for nearly a hundred years, has again put in its appearance. Mrs. J. H. Hopkins, wife of a worthy farmer of our county, distinctly saw the creature near the barn on Saturday last and afterwards examined its tracks in the snow.

Other versions of this item vary somewhat in structure and give the name of Mrs. D. C. Rees, or of Mrs. J. K. Mooney. Perhaps there were several items, one of which at least reached the office of the Philadelphia *Press* in December, 1906. From there it was relayed by the Associated Press.

From then on accounts agree. Reporters gathered, plaster casts were made of footprints in the snow, reports poured in of prominent citizens who staggered home in dilapidated condition as the result of meetings with the creature, women were found in hysterics on lonely roads.

Said one writer:

And the devil was seen. Reputable citizens described in detail his horrific form, the great wings, the frenzied countenance, half human and half animal, the long tail, the eleven feet, the deadly vapors which were exhaled in a mixture of fire and smoke. The fiend was ubiquitous. He was seen all over the southern part of the state. He was seen in the rural parts of Pennsylvania, Delaware and Maryland, all on the same night.

It was impossible for the learned to avoid being drawn into the controversy. An expert of the Smithsonian Institution said that the appearance "bore out his long cherished theory that there still existed in hidden caverns and caves, deep in the interior of the earth, survivors of those prehistoric animals and fossilized remains. . . ." The devil, he concluded, must be a pterodactyl.

As the terror spread, several mills in Gloucester closed because their female operatives were afraid to go home after dark. Phil Nash, noted theatrical manager, who had leased the Broadway Theater in Camden, was compelled to close for several nights. When the devil was reported seen in California on the same night that it also had appeared in New Jersey, Professor Samuel P. Langley, of aviation fame, was consulted. He examined descriptions of the wing spread and opined that the beast easily could fly the distance in a night, considering the difference in time.

Only one editor is said to have even suspected Jefferies, and he was not certain when he challenged the press agent to have the beast captured. Photographers were conveniently present at Hunting Park when a group of "farmers" was found surrounding a bizarre monster chained to a tree.

The devil actually had appeared and had been trapped. Its body was that of a kangaroo, but there were green stripes running its full length. It had huge wings and green whiskers. News of its capture and subsequent exhibition in the Arch Street Museum was reported seriously by the papers, and the crowds gathered for a look. It was only a fleeting one that they got, but it was all that they wanted. When the curtain of the devil's cage was drawn, the beast with a roar leaped forward, and the crowd cleared the way for a new influx of customers.

Jefferies' creation was an imported kangaroo obtained from an animal dealer in Buffalo. The wings were of bronze fastened by a rabbit-skin harness. The leap was inspired by a small boy with a stick.

The importance of this hoax lies principally in the fact that the 1906 episode was only the first. It apparently served merely to establish in the minds of the populace the belief that such a monster existed and might reappear at any time.

Which it did. The next report of which there is a record was an Associated Press story June 28, 1926, under a West Orange, New Jersey, date line. An armed posse was reported hunting a "flying lion" which had frightened two ten-year-old boys. One of the cubs was said to have been recovered from a swamp.

July 24, 1930, at Mays Landing, New Jersey, the devil appeared again, according to a Philadelphia *Evening Ledger* report. Mrs. William Sutton, a farmer's wife, positively saw it in her cornfield. A man stopped a car driven by Charles Mathis and begged to be taken from the scene of his meeting with "a horrible monster." A thirteen-year-old boy saw it peering at him through his bedroom window.

The January 21, 1932, "return" of the devil was more important than any other since 1906. It was the occasion for much burlesque journalism, but to John McCandless of Swarthmore, Pennsylvania, the experience was a terrifying one. Five miles north of Downingtown he was attracted by mysterious moans and observed in the brush a hideous form, half-man, half-beast, on all fours and covered with dirt or hair. McCandless and a score of friends hunted with pistols and guns for a week, as other persons of the vicinity, mostly small children and farmers' wives, said that they, too, had seen the monster.

Before this book is published the Jersey devil may have appeared again.

Sometimes a satirist, with no intention to deceive, simulates reality so closely that he is taken more seriously than he intended. Such was the experience of both Daniel Defoe and Benjamin Franklin. The former's *The Shortest Way with the Dissenters* was intended as a satire on existent religious persecution: it was taken seriously by high churchmen, who had the author pilloried and imprisoned for several months.

Franklin wrote *An Edict of the King of Prussia* to burlesque the demands of the British on the American colonies. Because Great Britain was settled by Saxon colonists, Franklin had the German monarch declare himself ready to exact his just dues. The British failed to see the joke, and there was considerable excitement over the threatened German diplomatic difficulty.

To the power of suggestion must be credited the success of most practical jokes. Often, to act as the joker intends one should is the only intelligent thing to do, as in the case of guests of the late Colonel Edward

H. R. Green, son of the fabulous Hetty Green, who slowed down their automobiles as they observed the signs on his estate warning them of rough roads—which, however, did not materialize. Green, known as a practical joker, also liked to offer to exchange a $20 bill for $5. "Examine it closely before you decide," he would say cannily, thus suggesting that there was something wrong with it; almost always the offer was refused.

Typical of the jokes which succeed because unusual situations are simulated cleverly was that which Thomas Parnell perpetrated upon Alexander Pope. Overhearing Pope read the description of the toilet from his unpublished *The Rape of the Lock* to Dean Swift, Parnell's remarkable memory enabled him later to write it down, versify it and translate it into Latin. The next day, when Pope read his work to other friends, Parnell produced what appeared to be an old monkish manuscript on which he had transcribed the translation. It was some time before Pope recovered, and longer before he learned what had happened. In a footnote to his *Life of Thomas Parnell* Oliver Goldsmith tells of a similar hoax played on John Dryden, one of whose friends pasted on the bottom of an old hatbox the celebrated passage, "To die is landing on some silent shore, etc." Dryden also was alarmed and amazed at having been a plagiarist unwittingly.

Some of the journalistic jokes of the great humorist, Eugene Field, were told in the first chapter. Melville E. Stone, publisher of the Chicago *Daily News,* related that Field requested a suit of clothes one Thanksgiving instead of the customary turkey. Stone responded by presenting his columnist with a convict suit of stripes, which Field accepted calmly. He got his revenge when country editors visited the *News* office by coming out in his stripes to poke the furnace, sweep the floor, and do other menial work. Said Stone:

> The editor would join with the sympathetic reporter (showing him around) in denouncing the outrage while Field, the wretched convict (supposedly sent up from the state prison to be janitor), was chuckling over the prank. In one case a week later, down in central Illinois, a weekly paper appeared with an editorial pouring out its virus of wrath upon Major McClaughry (the warden) and myself for this shameless performance.

Leading the list of more ambitious practical jokes is the famous Berners Street hoax of the noted prankster, Theodore Hook, which in 1810 won for him a bet that he could make an obscure thoroughfare the most talked-about street in London.

From a near-by house Hook and the friend with whom he had made the wager observed the events by which the former won. First there was delivered at a quiet house a load of coal. Then came a vanload of furniture, followed by a hearse with a coffin and a train of mourning coaches. Two fashionable physicians, a dentist, and an accoucheur arrived. After these "preliminaries" the neighbors of the widow who lived in the house were amazed to see the Archbishop of Canterbury drive up. Also a cabinet member, the governor of the Bank of England, the Lord Chief Justice, and finally the Lord Mayor himself. The last mentioned had been summoned to receive the deposition of a dying person who wished to make an important confession. Others were appealed to in similar ways.

Police protection did not prevent the overturning of some of the vans and goods, nor the congestion of traffic almost all day.

A similar hoax was perpetrated against Henry Labouchère, who made himself repulsive to opponents by keeping alive the memory of the chicanery by which the Irish hero, Charles Parnell, was almost convicted of complicity in a murder (see Chapter XIII). In retaliation they sent representatives of crematory companies to call on him, had a wedding cake delivered to his home, placed orders in his name for beds, coal, clothing, a billiard table, prints, carpets, beer, spirits and wine, an umbilical belt for hernia and many other things. Physicians replied with prescriptions to letters sent in his name; cabins were engaged for him to India, the United States and other parts of the world. Gladstone received a gift of salmon as from him; Asquith got a traveling bag; Sir George Trevelyan, a haunch of venison, and other friends, other gifts. Invitations were issued in the name of a mythical niece for a party and dinner at his home.

Because undertaking establishments called to inquire the number of men needed to carry the coffin, the "funeral" plans did not carry through. Labouchère commented: "Had the hearses arrived it would have been curious, as the mutes would probably have disputed in which I was to be moved off, and would have had to appeal to me eating my marriage cake and arrayed in my umbilical belt to decide to which I would give my preference."

In 1936 a Springfield, Illinois, prankster revived the old joke by ordering a quantity of merchandise, from roses to coal, to be delivered to the residence of E. B. Grunendike.

To issue invitations to a fictitious celebration, demonstration, parade, or other special event is a popular kind of trick.

Liverpool, one day in 1807, was placarded with bills announcing the arrival at one o'clock on a certain afternoon of a model of a ninety-eight-gun man-of-war, constructed on the Lord Stanhope plan, which would reach Chisenhale Street bridge by the canal from Wigan. A barge to precede the battleship, it was stated, would carry the show sight of the day, Polito's hippopotamus. It is estimated that ten thousand persons were disappointed.

About twenty thousand are said to have gathered June 19, 1812, for a grand military review on Wimbledon Common. These merrymakers refused to be convinced by the announcement of a government official that the affair would not take place, that the announcement was a forgery. As the crowd's anger grew the heath was set on fire, and the police were unable to handle the disturbance which threatened. A detachment of guards was rushed from London to parade to fulfill the expectations of the twenty thousand.

Both sides of the river between Pittsburgh and Allegheny City were crowded one day in 1845 following newspaper advertisements that a man was to demonstrate the possibility of human flying with a take-off from the center of the Hand Street bridge. Promptly at the hour announced a wag slipped through an opening from the wagon road to the footpath of the bridge, made his way to the railing and flung a live goose into the air, and then disappeared.

Invitations to the "annual ceremony of washing the white lions in London Tower" were received in 1860 by many prominent Londoners. Guards at White Gate thought the persons presenting cards were lunatics, until the number began to grow.

Responding to notices in florid German official style a few years after World War I, many prominent citizens of Leipzig rushed to the City Hall to pay the "bobbed-hair tax" which, the notices said, the feminine members of their families had neglected to honor. A roomful of anxious persons was kept waiting several hours before the hoax was exposed as the work of an anonymous humorist.

Richard Reid in *The Morality of the Newspaper* relates that his newspaper, the Augusta (Ga.) *Chronicle,* once announced that a battleship would come up the Savannah River in order to demonstrate that the river could float such a ship and to prove the river's value in national defense. At six A.M., the hour set for the warship's arrival, the banks of the river were crowded, among the spectators being Senator Patrick Walsh. "It was a long time before the people of Augusta could bring themselves to believe any unusual news in the *Chronicle,*" writes Reid.

Foreign ambassadors to the Court of St. James's were spared being the victims of an annually attempted hoax in 1925 when the Home Office warned them to disregard invitations to a memorial service to the "brave of all nations," issued for Southwark Cathedral, July 25. The year before, American Ambassador Frank B. Kellogg and others had appeared at St. Paul's for a similarly announced program.

In all of the preceding cases the victims acted normally, just as the magician's audience does when it responds to his suggestions, directing its attention away from the trick. The prestidigitators testify that children and mentally inferior persons who do not follow suggestions discover more magicians' secrets than do the normal.

College undergraduates are especially adept at practical joking. A familiar trick which has been tried successfully many times, mostly by Princeton students, is to invent a mythical classmate, and enroll for extra courses in his name. An early instance of this was Joe Gish, invented by a group of the Princeton class of 1905; Joe's identity was revealed when five of his originators accidentally signed chapel cards for him the same day. In 1908 Princeton had another ghost student named Henry Thompson, invented by a member of the mathematics department who playfully filled out papers in his name while supervising entrance examinations in Chicago; Thompson was admitted but never appeared to register.

The most ambitious Princeton ghost-student attempt was Ephraim di Kahble in 1935. For him a group of freshmen rented and furnished a room; then they advertised that di Kahble was willing to pay ten dollars for a ticket to the Dartmouth-Princeton football game, that he wanted to take students in his expensive car to the Yale game "for the company," and finally that the phenomenal freshman desired an orange and black guinea pig because he believed the tiger too ferocious to be the symbol of an "ivy league" university. Unfortunately, visitors always found that di Kahble had "just stepped out."

In 1937 the Princeton idea spread to Iowa State College, where a band of seniors actually persuaded their psychology, botany, and chemistry instructors to give A rating to a mythical Cuthbert Gleep.

Although they should be accustomed to hoaxes by now, Harvard students seldom fail to "fall" for a new journalistic hoax perpetrated by the *Lampoon,* humorous publication, on the *Crimson,* regular undergraduate newspaper. Familiar stunt is for the *Lampoon* to issue a burlesqued issue of the *Crimson* in orthodox dress. In one of the earliest of such attempts news items concerned the upsetting by a janitor of a jar of microbes, a crew man who rowed himself out of his shell, a proposed honorary degree for President William McKinley, and an announcement that half of the yearly subscription to the *Crimson* would be refunded. It is reported that a Boston newspaper, taking these articles seriously, copied some of them, but that they were caught in proof and deleted by the suspicious managing editor. In February, 1933, before Dr. James Bryant Conant had been named as successor to former President A. Lawrence Lowell, the *Lampoon,* in another faked edition, announced the election of a nonexistent Dr. Henry Eliot Clarke of Evanston, Illinois, as the new president and included a message of congratulation to Clarke from President-elect Franklin D. Roosevelt, "a former classmate." Clarke, in his letter of acceptance, pledged himself to continue the policies of Dr. Lowell and Charles W. Eliot.

May Day, 1939, Edward C. K. Read, *Lampoon* editor, disguised as a girl, won the annual Wellesley College hoop race and was rewarded by being thrown into a near-by lake by the irate girls.

In *Books in Black or Red,* Edmund Lester Pearson relates that several Oxford undergraduates once impersonated the crown prince of Abysinnia and his suite and were received on H.M.S. *Dreadnaught* with salutes and a ceremony. Namur University, Belgium, hoaxers with similar success were honored as supposed Indian princes. It is related of the late William Horace DeVere Cole, brother-in-law of former British Prime Minister Neville Chamberlain, that when a student at Cambridge he impersonated the Sultan of Zanzibar and was given a champagne dinner by university and city authorities and that, on another occasion, he was shown through H.M.S. *Dreadnaught* by naval officers in full regalia while he posed as a widely known Indian potentate.

In later life Cole, who became known as Great Britain's leading practical joker, once took charge of a section of workers whom he found loafing in Piccadilly Circus without a foreman. He marched them a few blocks and then directed them in digging a ditch across a leading thoroughfare, unsuspecting bobbies assisting in redirecting traffic. He also impersonated Ramsay MacDonald, Labor leader and twice prime minister, whom he resembled greatly in appearance, and delivered an impassioned Tory speech to an audience of trade unionists.

A lecture on spiritualism by the late Sir Arthur Conan Doyle, Pearson relates, once was advertised by Cambridge students. After an hour's wait the audience was treated to a large billboard, reading, "Sir Arthur Conan Doyle Has Failed to Materialize."

The American counterpart of William Horace DeVere Cole is Hugh Troy, widely known muralist. As a Cornell undergraduate he once painted a professor's rubbers white to resemble feet, then covered them with lampblack which washed off in the rain, giving the appearance of their owner's being barefoot. Troy also emulated Cole's Piccadilly stunt by leading a group of conspirators in workers' overalls to New York's Fifty-fourth Street and Fifth Avenue where they erected red flags and "Men at Work" signs and ripped up the pavement. At another time he managed to get arrested several times during the same day by carrying a bench in Central Park. One policeman after another thought it was public property and took him to headquarters until the desk sergeant, familiar with the sight of Troy's bill of sale, ordered him taken home under police escort.

The success of these pranks is seen to lie in the careful simulation of familiar situations. It is easy to laugh at your friend for telephoning the zoo on April 1 to ask for Mr. Wolf or Mr. Fox, but actually he would be a much more ludicrous person if he were not punctilious about attending to such messages. The victims of most practical jokes act rationally upon suggestions to which theirs are normal reactions.

CHAPTER IV

Why We Don't Disbelieve: Prestige

PITIRIM A. SOROKIN, Harvard University sociologist, obtained the cooperation of 1,484 human guinea pigs, 32 of whom he tested individually and the rest in twenty-one groups ranging in size from 4 to 299. To them all he played two phonograph recordings of Brahms' Opus 68, Symphony No. 1 in C minor, Part VI. Preceding each rendition, the statement was made that musical experts had selected one (sometimes the first, sometimes the second) as the better. Purpose of the test, it was announced, was to determine if laymen agreed with critical opinion.

Although actually the same record was repeated, 95.6 per cent accepted the dogmatic suggestion that the two playings were different. The judgment of the supposed critics was accepted by 58.9 per cent. In part summary of his findings in the March, 1932, *American Journal of Sociology,* Sorokin wrote:

> Thus a mere dogmatic statement, bluntly put, that the records were different dimmed their sense of discrimination and led them to an entirely wrong conclusion, in spite of the contrary evidence to the reality—the real sound stimuli. . . . On a large scale, and in thousands of forms, facts of this kind happen daily in social life, especially on various political platforms, in discussions, clubs, various lectures, and so on.

At Dartmouth College, Professor Henry T. Moore repeated a set of tests involving the expression of opinions, first announcing what the opinion of a respected authority in the particular field involved happened to be. Scored on the basis of acceptance of the opportunity to reverse their original judgments favorable to that of the supposed authority, the subjects showed the following shifts of opinion: in the language tests, 48 per cent; in the ethical judgment tests, 47.8 per cent; in musical appreciation tests, 46.2 per cent.

Professors Sorokin and Moore established experimental evidence of what? Of the thesis of the preceding chapter that a powerful determinant of opinion is suggestion and, more pertinent to the subject of this chapter, that an influential factor in suggestion is prestige. In other types of experiment success often is dependent upon the prestige of the experimenter. Classmates seldom get the results that instructors and professors do; subjects just do not feel shocks, see lights and experience other sensations upon the authority of a person whom they do not regard with respect or awe. When, however, it comes "out of the horse's mouth," to borrow a phrase from Aldous Huxley's *Brave New World,* it is as from on high and is accepted without mental reservation.

The prestige of the printed word was a contributing factor in causing belief in many of the newspaper tall tales related in earlier chapters. Despite their frequent fulminations regarding the daily newspaper, ordinary readers derive from it most of their knowledge of what is going on in the world; they can and do rely upon most of what reaches them through that medium.

Likewise, they have come to respect the radio as a trustworthy medium of information. Certainly, when they tune into a description of a sports event or other special occasion they do not think it is faked. So, the millions of listeners to a British Broadcasting Company program the evening of January 16, 1926, reacted normally by becoming extremely alarmed when a speech being broadcast from Edinburgh was interrupted to permit an eyewitness account of epoch-making occurrences in London. The following is part of the excitable announcement at which they were understandably horrified:

The Houses of Parliament are being demolished by an angry mob equipped with trench mortars. The clock tower 320 feet in height has just fallen to the ground, together with the famous clock, Big Ben, which used to strike the hours on a ball weighing nine tons. One moment, please. Fresh reports announce that the crowd has secured the person of Mr. Wurtherspoon, the minister of traffic, who was attempting to make his escape in disguise. He has now been hanged from a lamp post in Vauxhall. London calling. That noise you heard just now was the Savoy Hotel being blown up by the crowd.

Englishmen rushed to their telephones and telegraph offices to ascertain the safety of loved ones and to make inquiries of newspaper offices and of official sources. The Admiralty was asked when the fleet would proceed up the Thames. Denials from all sources were unavailing. "We heard it over the radio," was the customary reply. So intense did feeling become that the radio company had to issue an official explanation and the full text of the program, which had been announced by the Reverend Ronald A. Knox, son of the former Bishop of Manchester. Apparently few auditors who had listened to the first part of the broadcast remembered the statement that all to follow was a burlesque. The majority took seriously the news flashes about the unemployed riot in Trafalgar Square, led by Mr. Popplebury, secretary of the National Movement for Abolishing Theater Queues.

Americans laughed at Britons in 1926, but the situation was reversed October 30, 1938, when thousands of Americans from coast to coast became panicky over the radio dramatization by Orson Welles and other Mercury Theater players of H. G. Wells' fantastic *The War of the Worlds.* By shifting the locale from England to New Jersey and by adopting radio news broadcasting technique, Welles convinced unthinking listeners that the accounts of the heat-ray-spurting Martians were as authentic as those regarding the Czechoslovakian crisis to which they had become accustomed a month earlier.

To the state of anxiety engendered by the turbulent European affairs of 1938, many psychologists credited the belief given to the broadcast despite announcements at the beginning and end and in the middle of the regular program that it was a dramatization of an old novel.

As a result of what Dorothy Thompson called "the story of the century," thousands of New York and New Jersey citizens left their homes to seek refuge; hospitals treated hundreds of patients for shock; citizens got out firearms and hastened to the vicinity of Princeton, where the rockets containing the octopus-appearing invaders supposedly had landed. Radio, newspaper, and police headquarters in many cities were swamped with telephoned inquiries; the staff of the Memphis *Press-Scimitar* was called back to put out an extra edition; church services were interrupted in several cities by frightened persons spreading the alarm; the devout met to pray in numerous places.

Proving, according to Miss Thompson, that "Mr. Orson Welles and his theater have made a greater contribution to an understanding of Hitlerism, Mussoliniism, Stalinism, anti-Semitism and all other terrorisms of our times than all the words about them that have been written by reasonable men."

Other commentators, including many eminent scientists, deplored modern education, which does not teach the modicum of rational thinking that would have been necessary to detect that the broadcast was not authentic; that science, instead of making people more logical, has caused them to be more gullible because of its demonstration that feats once deemed impossible can be achieved, and that emotional suggestibility is a stronger determinant of human activity than calculated thought.

When the hoaxer is a famous scientist whose years of careful work and many contributions to human knowledge have made him universally respected, he can get away with almost anything. At least that was the experience of David Starr Jordan when, through the medium of *Popular Science Monthly* for September, 1896, he set a trap for writers who contended that mind can control matter without intervening agencies.

Jordan's announcement, made over his name, concerned the astounding success of an experiment in photographing the composite mental picture which seven persons had of a cat. With scientific minuteness the author described a lens with curved facets arranged on the plan of the eye of the fly. To each of the seven facets led an insulated tube through which electric or odic impulses could be transferred from the brain or retina through the eye of each of the different observers to the many-faced lens. From the lens the impulses would be converged on a sensitive plate as the rays of light are gathered together in ordinary photography. What, therefore, would be shown was the "innate idea of the mind or ego itself . . . the impression of ultimate feline reality," provided all seven experimenters followed directions and concentrated properly.

Accompanying the article was a reproduction of the photograph obtained. In Jordan's words, "The photograph assumed to have resulted from this process was very striking—a comfortable cat at rest, with various shadowy feline faces in the background." A black spot on the cheek of the largest image, it was suggested, might be the blind spot, or the yellow spot, *macula lutea,* the point of acute vision where the odic forces were absent.

This nonsense, it must be recalled, was for the consumption not of hillbillies or undergraduates but of reputable leaders in the scientific world. Only the magazine's editor, William Jay Youmans, knew Dr. Jordan's intention. Instead, however, of being recognized as satire, the article was taken seriously both by those whom it was intended to satirize and by others. In his autobiography Dr. Jordan commented on the incident in part as follows:

The satirical nature of my story I had supposed sufficiently clear, especially my proposition similarly to photograph "the cat's idea of man." But the scientific minuteness of detail proved to be fatally complete, and a surprising number of people took the thing seriously. One clergyman even went so far as to announce a series of six discourses on "the Lesson of the Sympsychograph," while many others welcomed the alleged discovery as verifying what they had long believed, and an eminent professor soberly opined that my reputation as a psychologist would not be enhanced by such discoveries!

That it is not only the half-witted who are the victims of deceptions also was proved in March, 1926, by the late Halbert Louis Hoard, eccentric editor-publisher of the *Jefferson County Union,* Fort Atkinson, Wisconsin, who obtained the signatures of twenty-seven of the city's leading citizens to a petition to be sent to Congress protesting against the wearing of brassières by women.

As printed in his paper, together with the names of the endorsers, Hoard's petition read in part as follows:

The undersigned note with alarm the increase in divorce since the Nineteenth Amendment—the woman suffrage law. We note many more women wearing breeches than before. We can stand that, but this new fad—slab-sided dresses flat in front—showing women in the fashion pictures as flat-chested as man, we regard with jealous eyes as an infringement. . . .
We ask that the Congress of the United States do its utmost to break down these brassières as an evil that menaces the future well being of society.

Although his campaign was endorsed by the Juneau, Wisconsin, Welfare League and by other organizations, the editor was getting the worst of it until Dr. J. J. Seelman of the State Board of Health, issued a statement that brassières cause rickets in babies. Thus, what began as a protest against "a usurpation of masculine rights and destruction of feminine beauty" developed into a discussion of this new point.

In a subsequent editorial Mr. Hoard wrote:

There are cow-milk-fed babies right in this city that are gasping for breath, the doctor at his wit's end to nourish them properly. They could live on monkey's milk, because monkeys are related, but there are no monkeys around except the mothers who dawdled fatally with the deadly brassières and few of them are giving milk.

Mr. Hoard was not the only storm center. Each of the twenty-seven signers received calls from indignant subscribers, mostly women; home life became unpleasant for a few of them who were told they "ought to be ashamed," and should "mind their own business."

The explanation of one signer was reported by the Milwaukee *Journal*: "Well, it happened like this. We all know Bert here and he and his paper advocate some very good things. We are good friends and he came to see me when I was busy and said something about a new movement, and I saw some writing and a list of names, so I just signed it. I didn't think any more about it—until I got home the night after and the paper was out." Others in the "movement" were quoted similarly.

Ranking with the foremost literary hoaxes of history, perpetrated by one of the most serious-minded and hence most respected literary groups in America, was the Larrovitch "revival" staged by the Authors Club of New York in 1918.

A framed portrait of a scholarly-appearing Russian, a pressed flower, and a page of manuscript on the wall of the club today testify to the abortive effort to do honor posthumously to "the father of Russian literature," to whom all subsequent Russian writers were said to be indebted. Still available for sale are some copies of *Feodor Vladimir Larrovitch: An Appreciation of His Life and Works,* edited by William George Jordan and Richardson Wright.

Larrovitch originated during a chess game between William George Jordan and Gustave Simonson—"a bibliophile with a photographic mind who never forgot a typed page once his eyes fell on it," according to Richardson Wright: Jordan made a move, kicked Wright's shin under the table, and asked Simonson, "Did you ever see a copy of *Vyvodne* by Larrovitch published in Paris in 1868?" After several minutes of contemplation over the chessboard, the encyclopedic Simonson said: "I never even heard of Larrovitch."

For several weeks Simonson was the sole victim of Jordan and Wright's fun. Then the joke began to spread all over the club. Wright challenged Jordan to deliver a lecture on the much-abused Russian. Jordan did. The club, impressed, decided to do justice to Larrovitch, and on April 26, 1917, more than three hundred members attended one of the largest dinners in the organization's history to listen to the reading of selections from the great Russian's poems, to hear him eulogized, and to observe the unveiling of the portrait, the pressed flower from the grave at Yalta, and a page of the manuscript of *Crasny Baba.* Other souvenirs of Larrovitch included a picture of him as a young man; his embroidered shirt; pictures of his mother and father, of the room in which he died, and of his grave; and miscellaneous items, such as his icon, pen, inkpot, and padlock for his house.

Before the book honoring Larrovitch appeared—almost two years after the beginning of the hoax—the officers of the club and the majority of the members were "in" on the secret. The list of contributors to the volume is impressive. Professor Franklin H. Giddings wrote "A Prolegomenon to Larrovitch"; Jordan discussed "The Personal Side of Larrovitch"; Richardson Wright translated fragments of his works, and George S. Hellman did the same for three incidental poems. There were five letters edited by Thomas Walsh, and "Talks with Larrovitch," by Titus Munson Coan, M.D.

Of Coan, Wright writes, "The only man who was not quite sure was Titus M. Coan. He was quite old at the time and his memory of Larrovitch visiting the American Legation in Paris was halting and very touching." A bibliography was prepared by Dr. Arthur Colton.

Few newspaper or magazine reviewers were deceived when the volume appeared. The Boston *Transcript* reviewed it seriously, as did several New York newspapers. The spelling of the name with two *r*'s instead of one proved a clue, which hardly was necessary in view of many others. Not until 1932, however, did anyone discover the most obvious key to the hoax, which was a letter deliberately signed, "Alexis Larrovitch." The critic who found it, furthermore, was a sports writer for the Swedish newspaper *Stockholms-Tidningen*. For the most part, magazines printed burlesqued reviews of the book, although some critics seemed to admire their own cleverness in being able to detect the fraud.

Richardson Wright explains the hesitancy of some critics to question the existence of Feodor Larrovitch in these words:

One of the reasons why the book was taken seriously is that the Authors Club is an organization of tremendous age and dignity. The membership at the time consisted largely of college professors and literary gentlemen. . . . Consequently when this society put out the Larrovitch book no one in literary circles in New York dared question its sincerity and truth at the first glance. It was too much like imagining your great-grandmother getting drunk.

Creation of a mythical author is the device by which a number of pathetic figures in the history of literature, doubtful of their ability to succeed in their own right, have attempted to gain fame. Most tragic of these was Thomas Chatterton, eighteenth century youth, who took his life at seventeen because of his failure to convince literary London that his compositions were the work of a fifteenth century monk named Thomas Rowley.

Because of his precocity and early death Chatterton often has been compared to Keats, who admired him so much that he dedicated *Endymion* to his memory. Why a person of his ability threw his life away in an attempt to perpetrate a fraud rather than seek fame in his own name, has been the subject of a sizable literature.

Chatterton's career of forgery began before he was twelve years old, when he submitted *Elinoure and Juga* for the approval of a friend. Next he palmed off on Henry Burgum, a pewterer, a de Bergham pedigree and other evidences of Burgum's descent from an ancestry as old as the Norman conquest. In 1768, at the time of the construction of a new bridge at Bristol, England, his home, he submitted to the newspaper *Felix Farley's Bristol Journal,* in the name of Dunelmus Bristoliensis, an ancient manuscript, *A Description of the Fryars Passing Over the Old Bridge,* allegedly written by Rowley, parish priest of St. John's Church, during the reign of Henry II. Upon demand he produced the manuscript, which, as the result of patient doctoring, had all the appearance of antiquity, and which he maintained he had found in a collection formerly in the treasure room of the old Church of St. Mary Redcliffe, of which his uncle was sexton.

The poems all dealt with the early history of Bristol. William Barrett, a surgeon, included specimens in his *History of the Antiquities of the City of Bristol* and used others as source material. It was when the boy attempted to increase his sphere of activities that he met disaster. Learning that Horace Walpole was gathering material for *Anecdotes of Painting in England,* he sent some manuscripts. Suspicion was aroused when his contributions became too plentiful. Mason and Gray, poets, denounced certain specimens as spurious. After a short stay in London, where he attempted unsuccessfully to dispose of his Rowley creations, Chatterton retired to his lonely attic and took his life.

Among those who acclaimed Thomas Chatterton as a genius were Byron, Shelley, Coleridge, Southey, and Wordsworth. Among those who accepted the Rowley poems as genuine were Dr. Milles, dean of Exeter and president of the Antiquarian Society, and Dr. Fry, president of St. John's College at Oxford. Many editions of the poems have appeared with increasingly long introductory eulogies. In Redcliffe churchyard at Bristol there is a monument to Chatterton with the inscription taken from his will:

To the memory of Thomas Chatterton. Reader! judge not! If thou art a Christian, believe that he shall be judged by a Superior Power. To that Power only is he now answerable.

Two others of whom somewhat the same might have been written were Charles Vanderbourg and the eminent nineteenth century French writer, Prosper Mérimée. Of the former, J. A. Farrer wrote in *Literary Forgeries:*

One is left to wonder that a poet capable of producing poems so good as Clotilde's were admitted to be should have spent some years of his life building up a reputation for an imaginary ancestress when he might with no more labour have permanently established his own.

Clotilde was a poetess of the time of Charles VII and a friend of the Duke of Orleans, according to her creator. Her full name was Marguérite Eléonore Clotilde, depuis Mme. de Surville. Her poems, whose themes included the relief of Orleans by Joan of Arc in 1429 and the victory of Fornovo by Charles VIII in 1495, were "discovered" in 1782 by a descendant, Joseph Etienne, Marquis de Surville, in the family archives. Many of them were said to have been lost during the Revolution; but some copies were preserved and given by Joseph's widow to Vanderbourg.

Critics soon began to find allusions to events which Clotilde could not have known, and a quotation from Lucretius, who was not known in France until a half-century after her death. Also there was mention of the seven satellites of Saturn, the first of which was not discovered until 1655 and the last not until 1789.

Clara Guzla was the most important of the fictitious literary figures created by Mérimée. Her *Dramatic Works* appeared in 1825 with the explanation in the preface of how the supposed translator, Joseph L'Estrange, had met her at Gibraltar. Two years later a purported translation from the Illyrian of Hyacinthe Maglanovich fooled Sir John Bowring, a competent Slav scholar, and the Russian poet, Pushkin. Hyacinthe had no more reality than Clara. Mérimée also wrote a letter in Robespierre's handwriting and sold it as genuine to Cuvier, noted autograph collector. The watermark proved the forgery.

Washington Irving at first disguised himself as Diedrich Knickerbocker, and Nathaniel Hawthorne attributed "Rappaccini's Daughter" to a French writer named Aubépine, which is French for his own name. Many another successful author, of course, has used a nom de plume, but not for the purpose of creating belief in the existence of another writer; friends, publishers, and ultimately the literate public have learned an author's private as distinguished from his public name.

Most outstanding case of author-invention in the second quarter of the twentieth century has been the best-selling *Diary of a Young Lady of Fashion, 1764-1765,* which appeared in 1926 and apparently gave the "inside dope" on eighteenth century society as observed by Cleone Knox, who was kissed on both cheeks by the King of France at Versailles, introduced to Voltaire in Switzerland and acquainted with the elite in England and on the Continent. The book was published as a find of Alexander Blacker Kerr, descendant of Cleone.

Not until after the narrative had reached nine editions in two months in America was it revealed that the real author was a nineteen-year-old Irish girl, the daughter of Admiral Sir George King-Hall of the British Navy. The girl, Magdalen King-Hall, said that she had written the story in a few weeks with no intention to deceive. She dashed it off without a definite plan at Portaferry, county Down, Ireland, where she received inspiration from Quinton Castle, called Castle Kearney in the diary. Her knowledge of eighteenth century life was gleaned from books in the Brighton town reference library.

Lord Darling, famous former judge of the English High Court, was among those who praised the book highly. He felt it should rank with Pepys' famous diary as a record of its time, and that it should be accepted as of equal authenticity with the accounts of Smollett and the Abbé Prévost.

In the field of music, similarly, to win better audience acceptance concert artists have invented names of composers for selections of their own. Most outstanding case was that of the eminent violinist, Fritz Kreisler, who confessed in February, 1935, that for thirty years in playing his own works he had credited them to such minor early masters as Vivaldi, Couperin, Porpora, Pugnani, and Padre Martini, saying he had discovered them during his world tours.

Kreisler explained that, as a young man without a reputation, it would have been impossible for him to offer a program consisting entirely of his own compositions; hence the invention of fictitious names.

The Philadelphia *Record* commented upon the confession:

In the first place, no one would have wanted to hear the pieces if they had been ascribed to the then unknown Kreisler. In the second place, no one would have bought them. In the third place, rival players would

not have put them on their own programs if they had known ¹
composer really was. . . . We like to think of the composer as
high above sordid earthly cares and of a virtuoso as one who
thought for anything but his music. The glimpse here given ⸻
maneuvering and strategy sometimes demanded by the divine art will
comfort realtors, morticians and bond salesmen. Business is, as the saying goes, business.

And the Portland *Oregonian* asked editorially:

What if Fritz Kreisler had died without making confession that over
a period of thirty years he had been composing music and signing to it
the names of half-forgotten composers of former times? What if he had
left no list of his works? The mess in the musical field would be
comparable to the mess which Mr. Shakespeare left in the literary field.

Other twentieth century musicians who have hesitated to rely upon
the prestige of their own names' appearing too often on their programs are
Josef Hofmann, the distinguished pianist, and Henry Wood, eminent
British orchestra conductor, and Hans Kindler, cellist.

For years Hofmann sponsored compositions by one Dvorsky, supposed
to be a Polish invalid languishing in southern France. Then some one
realized that Dvorsky is the Polish translation of Hofmann, whereupon
the latter confessed.

Wood capitalized upon the glamour which Anglo-Saxons attach to a
Slavic name. From October, 1929, until September, 1934, when he confessed, Wood used the name of Paul Klenovsky on his programs as the
transcriber of Bach's organ toccata and fugue in D minor as played by
Wood's orchestra in Queen's Hall, London.

Wood explained that Klenovsky was "a young man believed to have
lived in Moscow" whose recent death had robbed the musical world of a
genius. About to publish a score of the toccata and fugue five years later,
Sir Henry confessed the hoax and added that in the future he intended to
use the pseudonym for all his scoring as he found the "sky" an attention
getter.

Because of the greater thrill-producing potentialities of the true story,
upon which a sizable number of pulp magazines are capitalizing lucra-
tively today, it was the practice of novelists two and three centuries ago to
encourage the belief that the characters and episodes in their books had
counterparts in real life. Readers of Hawthorne's *The Scarlet Letter,* for
instance, are familiar with the lengthy introduction in which the author

tells of the discovery in an old warehouse of documents relative to Hester Prynne and to the scarlet letter itself. Defoe's *Robinson Crusoe,* Scott's exciting tales of Scotch heroism, Cooper's Leatherstocking Tales, and, in fact, a majority of the romantic literary masterpieces were accepted as grounded substantially on facts.

Typical example of a nineteenth century best seller whose author profited by the readers' predilection for believing whatever they are not warned is make-believe, is *Lady Willoughby, or Passages from the Diary of a Wife and Mother in the Seventeenth Century.* The publisher's preface to the second edition, in which the name of the author, Mrs. Hannah Mary Reynolds Rathbone, still was omitted, read in part: "The author, who in this work impersonates a lady of the seventeenth century . . . This is an unmasking of the character assumed at the first publication when the reader was left to solve his own doubts as to the authenticity of the work as an ancient Diary." Such a confession was the exception rather than the rule.

A type of autobiography which never fails to become the subject of critical debate is the diary of a child prodigy. Two which have drawn especial attention during the twentieth century are *The Young Visiters,* by Daisy Ashford, nine-year-old English girl, and the diary of Opal Whiteley, a six-year-old girl in Oregon lumber camps.

The Ashford book was edited by the eminent James M. Barrie, who insisted upon its genuineness. Irvin S. Cobb, who wrote the introduction to the American edition of *Daisy Ashford: Her Book,* which appeared the next year, vouched for its youthful authorship. Hugh Walpole says he has met Daisy Ashford, now Mrs. James Devlin. Nevertheless, skeptics persist in believing Daisy to have been another of Barrie's familiar fantasies.

Opal Whiteley's diary appeared in 1920, when the author was twenty-three years old. Under the eye of Ellery Sedgwick, editor of the *Atlantic Monthly,* she worked for nine months piecing together the torn parts of the diary kept seventeen years earlier.

Although, or perhaps because, the book turned out to be a remarkable account of life in a number of Oregon lumber camps, "exposés" of Opal began almost immediately. Her giving of classical and historical names such as "Oliver Goldsmith" and "Lars Porsena of Clusium" to barnyard pets seemed too precocious despite her explanation that she took them from two old copy books. Her statement that she was an adopted child was denied by her parents and other relatives, and physical resemblances were noted between her and other members of the family.

Leaders in the attacks upon Opal Whiteley were Professor E. S. Conklin of the University of Oregon, and Elbert Bede, editor of the Cottage Grove (Ore.) *Sentinel*. In 1933 Bede published a series of articles denouncing Opal's claim to be of noble French parentage and presenting strong arguments against the authenticity of her entire life's story.

Most familiar way of attempting to achieve financial success in literature, through the illegitimate capitalization upon prestige, is to forge. Hardly an important writer of the three centuries preceding the present has escaped being a victim of forgery, as will be related in a later chapter devoted to literary hoaxes. In this country the rise to fame of the beloved Hoosier poet James Whitcomb Riley generally is credited to his successful forgery of a poem advertised as by Edgar Allan Poe.

With the cooperation of Oscar Henderson, editor of the Kokomo (Ind.) *Dispatch*, Riley published "Leonanie" and displayed a fly leaf from an old dictionary on which it was written, apparently in Poe's handwriting. A butcher friend stuck steadfastly to the story that he found the faded volume while out collecting bills, and the butcher's customer joined the plot by "remembering" a dissipated young man who had left the dictionary in a room of his grandfather's hotel in Richmond, Virginia, many years before.

Critics the world over acclaimed "Leonanie" as a Poe masterpiece. To capitalize upon its fame Riley, of course, had to reveal his own authorship, which naturally caused a critics' storm. Although many refused to accept Riley's confession, the young writer's name became widely known so that his signed writings commanded attention. Nevertheless, the poems in the collection *The Old Swimmin'-Hole and 'Leven More Poems* originally appeared in the Indianapolis *Daily Journal* as by Benjamin F. Johnson, a Boone farmer, which was Riley's *nom de plume*.

An attempted forgery which couldn't possibly have had a long life, even if publication plans had progressed further, was that of a Los Angeles mail carrier, George R. Gage, who almost duped Gordon Dorrance, Philadelphia publisher, into accepting a manuscript, *We Fly,* as an authentic sequel to Charles A. Lindbergh's *We*. Because he was able to intercept mail, Gage for months corresponded with Dorrance in the name of Daniel Keyhoe, Lindbergh's agent. Dorrance became suspicious, however, when he learned of a visit by the real Keyhoe to Washington after the Keyhoe of the correspondence had written that he would not be East.

Investigation revealed that Gage, in the name of Keyhoe, had written to Mrs. Theodore Roosevelt, Sr., for incidents of the boyhood friendship between Lindbergh and her son Quentin, and that he had accumulated dozens of photographs of the famous aviator. Lindbergh himself was on a Caribbean good-will trip at the time. His signature to the publisher's contract, however, was declared genuine by handwriting experts; and other authorities said, "Only an experienced airman could have written the book."

One of the oldest, most frequent and most successful devices of the hoaxer is imposture, the acquiring of undeserved prestige by which to make easier the attainment of his ends. Wear the proper clothes, assume the correct "airs," and your awestricken victims will not detect the joke, swindle, or fraud.

As a master of bluff none ever excelled William Voigt, a cobbler remembered by the sobriquet of Captain von Köpenick (after the small suburb of Berlin where, October 16, 1906, he executed his famous coup).

Masquerading in the uniform of a Prussian army captain, Voigt, an ex-convict, placed himself at the head of a detachment of grenadiers, marched to the town hall, arrested the burgomaster, examined the municipal accounts, seized ready cash to the sum of two hundred pounds, commandeered telephone and telegraph services "for state business," and sent the burgomaster in custody to Berlin military headquarters.

When, nine days later, Voigt was arrested and, within six weeks, sentenced to four years' imprisonment, the attention of the entire world was directed to alleged abuses in the German prison system. Either because of the tremendous public opinion which was aroused or, as some say, because of being amused, Kaiser Wilhelm pardoned Voigt by imperial edict despite the impostor's record of twenty-seven years in prison for petty offenses.

Six years later, according to an Associated Press dispatch which appeared in the Atlanta *Constitution,* German newspapers received notices of Voigt's death. In orthodox fashion they reviewed his life and unwittingly gave valuable publicity to a vaudeville company to which the Captain von Köpenick belonged. In 1932 a motion picture, *Der Hauptmann von Köpenick,* starring Max Adalbert, was based on Voigt's escapade.

Another superimpersonator, with a keener eye for his personal advantage, brought to their knees the shrewd Jay Gould, Horace Greeley, Colonel Thomas A. Scott, vice president of the Pennsylvania Railroad, and a number of other leading financiers of the last quarter of the nineteenth century.

The bogus Lord Gordon-Gordon had arrived in the United States in 1871 and gone to Minnesota, where he deposited $40,000 in banks and announced his intention of investing one million dollars in railroad lands. The $125,000 which he possessed at the time, it was learned later, came from a diamond theft in Edinburgh.

Accompanied by state officials and officers of the Northern Pacific Railway, which paid all expenses, Gordon-Gordon made an inspection tour of the state, locating sites for cities and naming them. After being dined and wined elaborately he left for the East, ostensibly to raise the money. Colonel John S. Loomis, land commissioner of the Northern Pacific, gave him a warm letter to Greeley.

When the bogus lord announced his ownership of 60,000 shares of Erie Railroad stock, which meant control of the next election of the board of directors, he brought Greeley, Scott, and Gould to his feet. Magnanimously he agreed to permit Gould to continue as manager but insisted on selecting the directors himself. Gould purchased 20,000 additional shares for Gordon-Gordon, who haughtily refused to give a receipt, saying his word was sufficient. Later Greeley deposited 40,000 more shares with the new financial force. In all, it is said, Gould placed a half-million dollars' worth of securities and greenbacks at Gordon-Gordon's disposal and also handed him his resignation as director and president of the Erie line.

Some of these securities Gordon-Gordon succeeded in selling on Wall Street and in Philadelphia before Gould discovered what he was doing. When the financier brought suit to recover, however, Gordon-Gordon already was in Canada. When he was reported at Fort Garry, Manitoba, a half-dozen Minneapolis citizens crossed the border and captured him. Canadian authorities, however, stopped the abductors just below the international boundary line. Extradition papers were obtained in Washington and the Canadian government released the prisoner under bond.

The Minnesota kidnapers again closed in on Gordon-Gordon, whom they found asleep in a cottage near Toronto. While they were waiting for him to dress, he committed suicide. Three of the kidnapers later were elected to Congress, and two became governors of Minnesota.

With three thousand claimants to foreign titles in New York alone, in 1936, the Baron Giorgio Suriani di Castelnuovo, who suspected that not more than eight hundred were genuine, organized the Noblemen's Club to function as a central clearing house to authenticate or deny titles as held by persons residing in this country. Nevertheless, the avidity of kingless and titleless Americans for the company of the presumed superior clay of other lands probably will continue to provide pretenders as well as genuine members of the nobility with sycophants.

No more glamorous personality ever stimulated the heartbeats of American mammas with marriageable daughters, even despite innumerable arrests and exposés, than that of His Imperial Highness Prince Michael Alexandrovitch Dmitry Obelensky Romanoff, frequently proved to be merely Harry F. Gerguson (or Gaygusson), whose birthplace may have been Russia, as immigration authorities declare, or New York, as he himself has confessed more than once, or Hillsboro, Illinois, or some other place.

An orphan at an early age, Harry in 1902 was a problem of New York social welfare associations. At one time he lived in the home of F. L. McDavid, vice president of the Montgomery Loan and Trust Company, and also was the charge of former Congressman Gordon Russell of Tyler, Texas. He has been deported but has returned to the United States under assumed names; apprehended, he has claimed American citizenship. He has fooled former President A. Lawrence Lowell of Harvard with stories of records destroyed during the Russian Revolution; he has impersonated Rockwell Kent, artist and author, who once filled an agreement made by Gerguson in his name to illustrate a book because the publishers had hastened to advertise the fact; he has sold paintings from the Cleveland Museum of Art to purchasers who were told they were from the Russian Romanoff collection and the property of the bogus prince, and he has been as ubiquitous as "One Eye" Connolly at Kentucky Derbys, world series baseball games, and other important events.

In March, 1935, Gerguson figured in a $500,000 conspiracy suit in New York which resulted in a $25,000 award to Mrs. Wilma E. Gould who charged her brother-in-law, former Congressman Norman J. Gould, and other relatives with having hired the "prince" as a co-respondent to inveigle her into a compromising situation so that her husband, Edward Gould, might obtain a divorce. Shortly afterwards he turned up at Fredericksburg, Virginia, as John William Adams, professor of history. Although soon exposed, he continued to operate the estate of a New York broker, making occasional trips to New York and Washington without getting into any trouble over the checks that he cashed. In 1939 he landed in Hollywood, where he operates a succesful restaurant.

Closest rival of Prince Mike for the honor of being known as the leading impostor of modern times in America is George Robert Gabor, Hungarian youth, who disregarded the debutantes and used about thirty aliases to go after big game. As G. E. von Krupp, Jr., on this side of the Atlantic and as Taft Thew, Jr., "son of the former ambassador of the Court of St. James's," on the other, he numbered among his scores of victims Henry Ford, Harvey Firestone, Thomas A. Edison, Myron T. Herrick, and Alanson B. Houghton.

His story in America was that he was here studying industrial conditions preparatory to assuming control of the great Krupp works. Social Registerites vied with one another to engage him for teas, banquets, receptions. He was entertained at West Point with a dress parade. Edison had him as his guest at West Orange. Henry Ford received him at Detroit, but did not present him with an automobile as Gabor declared. He visited the steel works at Pittsburgh, the powder works of the Du Ponts at Wilmington, and the rubber plants at Akron, where Harvey Firestone entertained him.

Arrested in Albuquerque for bad checks, he was deported in 1926, but returned two years later on a forged birth certificate and with a genuine letter from Ambassador Myron T. Herrick. It was said he imposed on Herbert Hoover at Palo Alto during the 1928 campaign, but Mr. Hoover has no recollection of the incident and believes it impossible because he had met the real Baron Krupp. For impersonating a third solicitor general of the United States, he served eighteen months at McNeill Island, and at the expiration of his sentence was taken to New York to be deported again.

In London he phoned Ambassador Houghton, posed as W. C. Widener of Philadelphia, and asked Houghton to "keep an eye on my nephew, Taft Thew, Jr." The ambassador called on "Thew," entertained him at the embassy and at a polo game. In Paris Gabor represented John W. Davis in a telephone conversation with Ambassador Herrick and again asked favors for Thew. Herrick bought him a first-class ticket to Halifax on the *Lapland* and wrote a letter: "The bearer is an American citizen in whom I am interested."

In 1935 Kansas City newspapers described Gabor's trial in federal court on a charge of posing as an attaché of the United States embassy at Tokyo as the most dramatic in that city's legal history, and Judge Merrill E. Otis expressed regret at having to sentence him to Leavenworth penitentiary, from which place he was released June 23, 1936, on parole for deportation. He was deported July 22, 1936, to Hungary. At the time of his arrest in Newark, New Jersey, he had completed two and a half years as general manager of a doll factory and could prove that he virtually dictated the NRA code for the doll manufacturers' industry.

Of pretenders to the throne of almost every European nation there have been many; and of confusion among historians regarding the fates of royal heirs who have disappeared, or about whose time and place of death there was uncertainty, there has been more than a little. Later chapters will contain the details. Of the scholarly controversy to which such a case gives rise there is no better illustration than the young woman whose passage was paid to this country in 1928 by Mrs. W. B. Leeds of Philadelphia, formerly Princess Xenia of Russia, in the belief that she was Anastasia Romanoff, daughter of the assassinated Czar Nicholas II.

The alleged youngest daughter of the last czar has been disowned by almost every other member of the Romanoff family; but her claims were defended by Sascha, former nurse in the royal household, and by Gleb Botkin, son of the czar's physician and childhood playmate of Anastasia.

The young woman first attracted attention in 1920 when she was rescued by Berlin police after an attempted suicide by drowning. For a time she remained in Dahldorf Insane Asylum at her own request, although adjudged sane by physicians. A fellow inmate, a Mrs. Teupert, upon her release spread the story.

While ill from tuberculosis the girl was visited by members of the Romanoff family. She is said to have recognized each as he entered and to have identified photographs and other family heirlooms. She also bore certain physical traits, especially a protruding bone in the left foot which led a physician who had attended the czar's daughter to believe she was Anastasia. She also had bruises and bullet and bayonet wounds as the result, she said, of her treatment by the Bolshevik soldiers at Ekaterinburg in 1918 when they thought her dead along with other members of the family.

The girl's story includes her rescue by a young Red soldier who noticed life in her body and escaped with her into Rumania upon the approach of the Russian White army. She married her deliverer and became Mme. von Tschaikovsky, bore a son, but shortly was widowed when her husband was killed in a Bucharest traffic accident. Leaving the baby in an asylum, she made her way to Berlin in quest of relatives.

Disbelievers in the girl's story point to the lack of evidence regarding either the husband's death or the child and to her refusal to talk either Russian or English. They say she is Franziska Schanzkowski, a Polish peasant, who lived with a Berlin family from 1915 to 1920 and returned for a three days' visit in August, 1922. The latter dates are said to synchronize with ones on which Anastasia was strangely missing after her release from the asylum.

Knowing the weakness of Hollywood motion picture producers for foreign talent, many an American-born girl has gotten her start as a film star by playing a successful impersonating role to obtain a job. Among the first was Theda Bara (really Theodora Goodman, the daughter of Theodore Goodman, a Cincinnati storekeeper), who gave her racial origin as Arabian. After the DeMille studios had ballyhooed the engagement of a dazzling new Russian star, Sonia Karlov, it was revealed that she was Jean Williams, Broadway chorus girl.

Arriving in Hollywood as an unknown, Katharine Hepburn did not discourage reports that she was the niece of Baron Hepburn and heir to $16,000,000. Joan Woodbury obtained a Spanish girl part in *The Eagle's Blood* by posing as Nina Martinez. Prominent in the "all-British" cast in *Cavalcade* was Margaret Lindsay, who waited until she had obtained fame before confessing she was Margaret Kies of Dubuque, Iowa, and had spent a half-year in England acquiring an accent after having been refused employment in Hollywood as an American-born actress. Robert Cummings of Joplin, Missouri, did the same thing, changing his name to Blade Stanhope Conway, bribing a London theater janitor to put his name in lights and returning to Broadway to go places with his new way of speaking. Before he really "landed" in Hollywood he once obtained a part in "So Red the Rose" posing as a Texan, Bryce Hutchens.

Called by Samuel Goldwyn "the greatest hoax in box-office history" was the case of Sigrid Gurie, presumably Norwegian theater star whom Goldwyn secluded and taught English for more than a year before starring her in *The Adventures of Marco Polo*. When she brought suit for divorce from Thomas Stewart shortly after release of the picture, it was learned that Miss Gurie, really Sigrid Haukelid, was a native of Brooklyn.

Because she had olive skin and the Good Neighbor policy had made South Americans popular, in 1942 an Arapahoe Indian from Ozone, Wyo., posed as Burnu Acquanetta and was called "the Venezuelan Volcano" by the press agent who took her to Hollywood from New York where her ruse had gotten her employment as a Powers model. Her motion picture career began with a small part in *The Arabian Nights* after which she was cast opposite Charles Boyer in *Flesh and Fantasy*. She was exposed when she applied for membership in Screen Actors Guild which requires proof of birth.

Ten years later the Indian angle was worked in exactly the opposite fashion by Anthony Quinn, an American of Irish and Spanish descent. With a knowledge of Spanish and a swarthy appearance, he got a part in *The Plainsman* for which Cecil B. DeMille wanted a genuine Indian.

When she was asked to remove her shirt during a lawn mowing scene in her second picture, Tanis Chandler balked and revealed she was not Robert Archer, under which name she previously appeared in *The Desert Song*. Miss Chandler pretended to be a man at a time, 1944, when there was a wartime shortage of male actors.

After Marlon Brando married in October, 1957, a Cardiff, Wales factory worker announced that newspaper pictures revealed the bride was not an Indian but his daughter, Johanna O'Callaghan. He said the actress who called herself Anna Kashfi was born in Calcutta where he had been a railroad worker but that both he and the girl's mother were London-born. The actress Anna Kashfi's first Hollywood role was in *The Mountain* starring Spencer Tracy in 1955.

Impersonation often seems to fill an overpowering psychological need, the outstanding contemporary example being Ferdinand Waldo Demara, Jr. Although he never finished high school, he impersonated known scholars and taught college classes in psychology and zoology. He also was a Trappist monk and then a brilliantly successful surgeon in the Canadian navy. Glowing newspaper accounts of his work during the Korean war led to his exposé by the Canadian surgeon whose name he used. In 1955 Demara was exposed as lieutenant of the guard at Texas' Huntville Penitentiary where he posed as a doctor of education. In 1957 he was caught teaching high school at North Haven, Me.

Similarly, Marvin Harold Hewitt taught relativity, theoretical physics, electrical engineering and similar intricate subjects in seven schools and universities although he never finished high school. He got the positions by using the names of real scholars and faking reference letters.

In 1953 Harold K. Rain was sentenced to three years imprisonment for having duped doctors and hospitals in eight states by posing as an experienced physician, Dr. Samuel P. Hall.

Most headlined case of many World War II fake heroes was that of Douglas Stringfellow who resigned as a Utah Republican congressman when his cloak-and-dagger account of wartime exploits for the Office of Strategic Services was exposed as fictitious by the *Army Times*.

Most notorious Canadian counterpart, George Dupre, was a Calgary, Alberta Boy Scout leader and Sunday School teacher who fascinated audiences with a tale of how he spied by posing as a mental defective in a Normandy village. Quentin Reynolds wrote Dupre's story, *The Man Who Wouldn't Talk* which Random House published in 1953 and *Reader's Digest* condensed. A former R.C.A.F. officer exposed Dupre by means of photographs which showed him in Canada when he said he was being tortured in France.

CHAPTER V

Incentives to Believe: Financial Gain

NO MATTER how intelligent or careful you are, at least once in your life you will be swindled, according to the National Better Business Bureau, which, since 1911, has attempted to reduce the annual average of $2,500,000,000 (fifteen dollars for every man, woman and child) collected by racketeers and confidence men in the United States.

If you are in the automobile insurance or restaurant business, you will pay your part of the $15,000,000 collected annually by fraudulent accident claimants.

If you handle money—and we all do—you are likely to pass on unwittingly some of the half-million dollars' worth of counterfeit bills or some of the $25,000 worth of altered money, or some of the $50,000 worth of counterfeit coins which are discovered yearly, and for manufacturing which more than 2,000 persons are convicted.

As a housewife you may send money in response to a telegram, presumably to an absent husband at an address where he will not receive it; as a widow you may pay bills which your recently deceased husband did not contract, or you may subscribe to a nonexistent or worthless memorial scroll or buy a cemetery lot of equal "value."

As a business man you may grant too much credit to a company which recently has had a change in ownership; or you may subscribe to a puff sheet or magazine or clipping bureau to see your name in print in a manner of no credit to you; or you may succumb to the eloquence of written requests for philanthropy (each Christmas more than 100,000 such letters pass through the New York City post office alone), or to fake charities which cost about $150,000,000 annually.

As a householder you may purchase furniture in the false belief that you are obtaining bargains; or you may buy some of the $300,000,000 worthless insurance sold yearly; or you may invest in some of the $100,000,000 worth of valueless real estate. .

Whoever you are, you may entrust money to some unscrupulous person; or you may invest in worthless stocks, bonds, or business enterprises; or you may take correspondence courses or attend classes without improving your chances of success; or you may contribute part of the $100,000,000 of which the public is mulcted annually by fraudulent "homework" promoters.

In a multitude of cases in every category, the victims can be exonerated of blame for contributory negligence. In as many others, their "lapses" are explainable by their ignorance of legal procedure, by the cleverness with which the cheaters have simulated reality, or by the false fronts and words by which they have been beguiled.

However, besides these reasons for not disbelieving—the same indifference, ignorance, suggestibility, and prestige which were illustrated in other fields in the first four chapters—the psychological factor popularly known as "wishful thinking" is strongly operative in that phase of human activity involving investment and purchasing.

Wishful thinking is believing what one wants to believe instead of what factual evidence shows to be true. It is the cause of almost incredible gullibility in otherwise intelligent people, especially—to repeat—when the rainbow seems to lead to a pot of gold.

And so we take a chance: We take part in office pools on athletic events. We play punchboards with all the winning numbers already removed. We play policy or numbers games. We keep chain letters going. We act upon rumors in the hope that "something may come of it," as thousands of us did recently when it was whispered about that the Ford Motor Company would make a present of its latest model to anyone sending in a coin minted in 1922, and that the Seeing Eye Foundation would deliver a dog free for every 25,000 empty book-match covers. Although two out of three tickets for the Irish sweepstakes lotteries sold in this country are counterfeit, and although each American holder's chance is estimated at from one in a million to one in three million, three times annually ten or fifteen million of us take part, and then go to the motion picture theater—on bank night, of course—to see the joyful faces of the janitor from Hoboken and the schoolgirl from Tisch Mills who won fortunes, after having forgotten the $2.50 they sent across the Atlantic. If we are economically in the "big time," we are easy prey to the Ivar Kreugers, Serge Staviskys, Richard Whitneys, and Musica-Costers.

With such a gambling public the hoaxer has little difficulty achieving success. To prove exactly this point, but laudably not to profit personally, a French journalist inserted the following advertisement:

I promise nothing; I engage to perform nothing. But send one franc fifty centimes in postage stamps. Somewhere there is a little surprise in store for you. Who knows? Address "F.D." Post Office.

The surprise was the embarrassment, in which many prominent persons shared, of seeing the sizable list of answerers in the same newspaper with the announcement that their contributions would be donated to a creditable charity.

Also to expose human cupidity but, one suspects, with some maliciousness, as early as 1815 an advertiser in a Chester, England, newspaper offered "sixteen shillings for every athletic full-grown cat, ten shillings for every adult female puss, and a half crown for every thriving kitten that can swill milk, pursue a ball and thread or fasten its young fangs in a dying mouse"—ostensibly in an effort to relieve a rodent plague on faraway St. Helena where Napoleon Bonaparte was languishing. The following day five thousand cats were recovered from the Dee River when the three thousand persons who responded to the address given in the advertisement found an empty house. During World War I the same joke was played on New Yorkers, the felines being advertised as needed in German military camps by American soldiers.

No small part of the $1,000,000,000 which the Post Office Department estimates is collected annually in mail frauds changes ownership in what is known as the Spanish prisoner game—since the outbreak of the Spanish Civil War, the Mexican prisoner game. Ostensibly written by a person unjustly incarcerated in a foreign country, the Spanish prisoner letter enjoins absolute secrecy and asks for a sum of money to be sent to a friend to assist in obtaining the release of a sizable fortune in the United States. Despite innumerable official warnings, this old one still is being worked profitably. In March, 1939, the Department of State announced the old hoax's most recent appearance as a form letter from Mexico offering a one-third interest for assistance in recovering $285,000 in a trunk in an unspecified custom house somewhere in the United States. In 1947 and 1953 a new wave was reported by the Post Office Department.

No more trusting or wishful souls exist than those who entrust their savings—sometimes all of them—to promoters who convince them they are the rightful heirs to some nonexistent estate the assets of which can be released for division only after costly court proceedings.

Over a period of years almost every common name has been used by the heir chasers who astound those on their lists with the "revelation" that some distant relative whom they remember indistinctly, if at all, died fabulously wealthy. Most dramatic of all such rackets is the Drake Estate swindle, whose victims are told that the notorious Elizabethan buccaneer Sir Francis Drake left a fortune still tied up in English courts. Despite repeated warnings by both British and American governments that no such estate exists, the racket was promoted successfully as late as 1935. Oscar Hartzell of Iowa alone made over $1,000,000 before being sent to Leavenworth for life. He took up the racket himself after being duped by Sudie Whitaker of Chicago.

Another is the Edwards Heirs fraud started in the 1880's by Dr. Herbert H. Edwards of Cleveland, Ohio, who said he was descended from Robert Edwards, alleged owner in 1770 of sixty-five acres of Manhattan Island, including the site of the Woolworth Building. Dr. Edwards founded the International Edwards Heirs Association, which his son continued, to recover the property—lost, he said, through legal chicanery.

Twenty-six dollars was the enrollment fee, and a carpenter, Milo Pressel, was engaged to make genealogical investigations of applicants. Hundreds joined, one Tennessee man paying the initiation money for himself and forty-seven others. When the Post Office Department exposed the fraud, there was $10,000 in the "treasury."

An example of Pressel's work was his discovery of evidence of the marriage of Blount J. Hassell to Frances Kirk, November 1, 1885—eleven years before the birth of the bridegroom and thirteen years before the birth of the bride. Not the least factor in keeping up the spirits of the victims was an annual picnic at which was sung enthusiastically an "alma mater" of which the first two verses and chorus were as follows:

> We have rallied here in blissful state
> Our jubilee to celebrate.
> When Fortune kindly on us smiled,
> The Edwards Heirs now reconciled.
>
> Our president deserves our praise,
> For strenuous work through dreary days,
> In consummating our affairs
> And rounding up the Edwards heirs.
>
> Chorus:
> We're Robert Edwards' legal heirs,
> And cheerfully we take our shares.
> Then let us shout with joy and glee
> And celebrate the jubilee.

Also especially long-lived is the Baker Estate case, for promoting which convictions were still being handed down in 1938. In 1936 government officials declared that more than $3,000,000 had been collected from 3,000 persons who hoped to share in the imaginary $300,000,000 fortune supposed to have been left in 1839 by Jacob Baker of Philadelphia, largely in the form of valuable real estate in that city given him by a grateful government for his service in the Revolutionary War.

In 1938 and 1939 the Office of Indian Affairs of the Department of the Interior warned Indians against swindlers who were collecting a dollar apiece from them and for their dead relatives in the expectation that they would receive $3,000 each during the next session of Congress. Representative Usher L. Burdick of North Dakota actually was induced to introduce such a bill—which, however, he withdrew when it was proved to him he was being "used."

Impressed by the glibness and flattery of high-pressure salesmen who use telephone and telegraph to convey their "inside tips," thousands who should know better have borrowed, mortgaged, and otherwise raised funds to invest in cemetery lots in the hope that an increased population would make them valuable; to raise silver foxes, rabbits, muskrats, or bullfrogs; to obtain liquidating interests in oil wells; to enter into partnerships with strangers, and to obtain worthless stocks and bonds of virtually every type of business existent.

Although Grant's Tomb and the Woolworth Building seldom are sold nowadays to greenhorns on their first visit to New York, not long ago an Italian immigrant purchased the information booth in the Grand Central Station for a fruit stand. Up the river at Yonkers four big city slickers took $135,000 from prospects to whom they showed steam shovels and grading equipment left by a road construction gang and then offered gold mine stock certificates so that the work of "extracting gold" might be resumed. Across the ocean in England two women reaped a half-million-dollar profit in what is known as the Gift Family swindle; the victims handed over their savings, which the promoters said they could quadruple by a "divine source." Similarly in Boston, in the early 1920's, Charles Ponzi grew rich by offering investors a 50 per cent return in ninety days by a secret unexplained method of manipulating foreign exchange.

By no means, furthermore, is it only the ignorant poor, eager to obtain the opportunity of a lifetime, that fall. In *The Run for Your Money,* E. Jerome Ellison and Frank W. Brock nominate the American business man as the "national open champion dupe" and say of him:

Certain factors in the businessman's make-up make him abnormally susceptible to the sharper's wiles. He is unconscionably vain; he is eager to increase the volume of his business; he has reams of "accounts receivable," many of them "bad debts" he is anxious to liquidate; and he is habitually courteous to customers or clients. For his vanity, the racketeer obligingly provides "puff sheets," "mug books," medal-awarding societies and "press associations" which purport to spread his fame to the admiring world through the magic of the printed word. For his desire to expand his business, there are "group buying syndicates," promising to place his product in the hands of millions of customers, and "trade stimulators" to zoom his local sales. His eagerness to convert his bad debts into cash is met by a rabble of gyp "collection agencies"; his courtesy to customers is exploited by ingenious racketeers in the guise of clients.

One of the most successful swindles, whose victims included a number of America's shrewdest investors, was the Ralston's Diamond hoax of 1871. Impressed by the bagful of diamonds, sapphires, rubies, and emeralds which two bearded prospectors wished to place in a deposit box in the Bank of California of San Francisco, William C. Ralston, the bank's president, raised $700,000 from among such notables as General George B. McClellan, Charles Lewis Tiffany, Horace Greeley, and Baron Rothschild to buy the miners' interest. After a $10,000,000 corporation had been formed, two suspicious government geologists discovered that the gems had been "planted" and that the value of those which had dazzled Ralston was $20,000, not $1,250,000 as the banker's local expert had estimated. Ralston took his loss in cavalier fashion, paying back the investments of the others.

Outstanding British swindler of all time is believed to have been Whitaker Wright, who founded forty-two companies with a total capitalization of $110,775,000; all but $10,000,000 was revealed to be water when the Boer War caused a stock-market slump and Wright tried to escape to the United States. Wright owed his fabulous success to his skillful cultivation of British royalty—even the Prince of Wales, later Edward VII, being a guest in 1895 on his yacht.

When Wright's fictitious empire collapsed, two prominent Englishmen lost social position as well as riches with him. They were the Marquess of Dufferin and Ava, formerly governor general of both Canada and India and ambassador to both Russia and France, and Lord Loch. They were officers and directors in many of his companies, most of which purported to be engaged in gold mining in Australia. The Duke of

Connaught, brother of the Prince of Wales, was a heavy purchaser of stock, as was Prime Minister Balfour.

While it lasted Wright had a grand time, purchasing a palatial home from William Ewart Gladstone, building another $2,500,000 home in Surrey, going in heavily for racing yachts, and entertaining lavishly. He awed guests with a billiard room beneath a lake; it had a glass ceiling through which the players could watch the fish.

While being sentenced after his conviction for fraud and forgery, Wright swallowed poisoned pills. Dufferin and Loch already were dead from shame.

To the "credit" of Mrs. Cassie Chadwick, called the most romantic schemer of the century and "Cleveland's headache," are the failure of the Citizens' National Bank of Oberlin, Ohio, runs on several other banks, and the loss to financial houses and individuals of about $1,500,000. An ex-convict and ex-clairvoyant with many aliases, Mrs. Chadwick posed as the natural daughter of Andrew Carnegie and obtained her fabulous loans by displaying forged signatures of Carnegie on promissory notes totaling more than $5,000,000. As she offered 25 per cent interest and repaid her early borrowings, she was considered a wonderful opportunity by the bankers and other creditors. One, however, became suspicious, and in 1905 she was convicted and sentenced to ten years in prison where she died two years later.

In France, scene of several first-class swindles, one of the most astounding also was instigated by a woman, Marthe Hanau, in whose pyramid of holding companies investors in 1928 lost more than $4,000,000. Her system was to take options on good real estate and to issue stock against them. She gained prestige by inducing many prominent leaders of the government, including Premiers Poincaré and Briand, to contribute to her newspaper, *La Gazette du Franc et des Nations*. With her were associated her divorced husband, Lazare Bloch, and a Mademoiselle Joseph, who finally broke with her and tipped off the authorities. As generally happens in France when a financial scandal is revealed, a political crisis followed her conviction; at the Ministry of Agriculture royalists beat up employees, and mobs shouted that the Republic could not offer adequate protection to small investors.

Failure to make the proper investigation cost French bankers, merchants, and others an estimated $11,000,000 over a twenty-five-year period ending in 1902, when it was revealed that the Humbert Millions were nonexistent. Ten creditors committed suicide when the safety deposit box supposed to contain securities worth $20,000,000 was opened and found to contain $1,000 in negotiable paper, an empty jewel box, a few copper coins and a brass button.

Perpetrator of the swindle, beginning in the late seventies, was a peasant girl, Thérèse Daurignac, who announced herself as the sole heir to the estate of Robert Henry Crawford, an American millionaire whom she had nursed during an illness. Delay in liquidating the estate supposedly was caused by the legal activities of two nephews whom Thérèse and her husband, Frédéric Humbert, son of a cabinet member, always beat in the courts only to have them take appeals. In the meantime the Humberts became patrons of art, bought estates, and lived handsomely on credit for the incredible period of a quarter-century. Convicted after a suspicious creditor investigated and found no trace of the Crawford family, the Humberts obtained short sentences.

Two cabinets fell and at least forty deaths resulted from murder or suicide following exposure of the greatest French swindle of all—the Stavisky case, which came to a head in 1934. Serge Alexandre Stavisky, the Russian-born principal, who killed himself to escape arrest, received protection through connections with governmental and police officials which never were explained satisfactorily.

Before he got into the pawnshop business, his last and best racket, Stavisky had been apprehended for operating a fake casting bureau, a diagnostic clinic where he claimed to be able to detect pregnancy by means of an invention he called a matroscope, and a narcotics ring and had been accused more than once of forgery. He remained at liberty, however, and consorted with members of one cabinet after another. On the advice of Premier Chautemps, the minister of colonies, Albert Dalimier, advised insurance companies it was legal to invest in pawnshop securities.

The names of many leading politicians were found on the stubs for more than $3,000,000 worth of checks which Stavisky issued during his heyday. Parisian Police Prefect Jean Chiappe was forced to resign and the mangled body of Magistrate Albert Prince, judge of the Paris Appeals Court, was found on a railroad track just before he was to testify regarding Stavisky's early career. Royalists stormed the Chamber of Deputies, crying, "The rottenness of Republicanism." Thousands of investors never recovered millions of dollars with which they had purchased worthless stock, and it was long before France again had a cabinet which could command respect and confidence.

So internationally shocking was the suicide in 1932 of Ivar Kreuger, Swedish and world match king and the subsequent revelation that the stock in his four hundred companies was not worth a fraction of the $724,000,000 which millions of investors had paid for it, that for years rumors persisted that Kreuger still was alive and his supposed fortune intact.

Everyone had confidence in Kreuger, one of the world's leading financiers. Typical example of this confidence was the purchase by the Boston investment house of Lee, Higginson of $150,000,000 worth of Krueger & Toll, Inc., securities without knowing the nature of the X.Y.Z. contracts on which many of them were based. Lee, Higginson took Kreuger's word that their nature must be kept confidential.

Kreuger collapsed after the first accounting audit of his empire was made in the early days of the world-wide depression which began in 1929. He fled to Paris, purchased a gross of pistols and a box of cartridges and shot himself in a hotel room. After his death examination revealed that at least $100,000,000 worth of Italian government bonds in his vault in Stockholm were forgeries.

In the United States during the depression years the revelation of fraud in connection with one gigantic failure after another almost immunized the newspaper reading public against shock. In 1938, however, two outstanding cases jolted the most lethargic back to attention.

The first was that of Richard Whitney, for years head of the New York Stock Exchange. He guessed wrong when he invested heavily in stock of Distilled Liquors, manufacturers of applejack, and used $105,000 worth of clients' funds, in addition to his own, to keep the stock from falling and to forestall the banks, with which he had deposited it as security, from calling his loans. Taking his medicine with his chin up, Whitney went to Sing Sing for from five to ten years and became a utility outfielder on the penitentiary's famed baseball team.

More intriguing to the lover of detective fiction was the Musica-Coster case, in which the principal was Philip Musica, the Brooklyn-reared son of an Italian immigrant. He had got into trouble several times and served a three-year sentence, after which he changed his name to F. Donald Coster and became president of McKesson & Robbins, one of the country's leading drug distributors. Although "Coster" had been paying blackmail to the remnant of the Mafia gang for almost two decades, it was not until after the firm's treasurer, Julian F. Thompson, discovered an $18,000,000 shortage that his identity generally became known. He saw federal agents approaching his Fairfield, Connecticut, home, went to the bathroom, and shot himself to death.

Musica first got into trouble in 1909, when he bribed customs officials to mark down the weights on invoices for cheese his father imported from Italy. On the assumption that the federal employees were more to blame than he, President William Howard Taft pardoned him. Four years later Musica, his father, brothers, and sisters were in New Orleans about to embark for Honduras, which had no extradition treaty with the United States, when they were arrested for their part in the United States Hair Company $2,000,000 swindle. A raid of their headquarters in New York had revealed virtually no human hair, in which the company was supposed to deal, and no assets. Philip sacrificially assumed the entire blame and served three years in New York's Tombs.

He emerged in 1916 to become a stool pigeon for Merton E. Lewis, New York deputy attorney general, using the name of William Johnson. In 1919 he was indicted for perjury in connection with the trial of Joseph Cohen, for the murder of Barnet Baff, and also was revealed to have forged affidavits linking prominent Americans with Bolo Pasha, notorious French intriguer.

Four years later, leaving his past behind him, he landed in Mount Vernon, New York, with $2,000, under the name Frank D. Coster, and started Girard & Company, dealers in hair tonic. Prohibition agents never were able to prove that Girard & Company were bootleggers, and in 1924 Coster was able to obtain a $1,000,000 loan from Connecticut bankers to buy McKesson & Robbins. Five years later the expanded company floated a $10,000,000 stock issue and expanded further. The president, now F. Donald Coster, later got into *Who's Who in America* with a fabricated autobiography making him a student for the M.D. and Ph.D. degrees at Heidelberg University, Germany, during the years he was languishing in the Tombs.

Although, in his suicide note, Musica-Coster assumed full blame for his last and most colossal hoax, his three brothers, who were associated with him under the names of George Vernard, George Dietrich, and Robert Dietrich, were indicted several times, pleaded guilty and served short prison sentences.

In view of the record of the supposedly shrewd business leaders who were victimized by Stavisky, Kreuger, Whitney, and Musica-Coster, and of the National Association of Credit Men's estimate that credit system racketeers collect about $20,000,000 annually, the investment gambles of some of the more impecunious and supposedly less erudite do not seem so stupid. Who would say, for instance, that the gasoline filling station employee who presumably filled the tank of a motorist with water and then saw the latter drop in two capsules to convert the fluid into motor fuel acted foolishly when he paid out as much as he had in his pocket for some of the magic pills?

Many an equally worthless invention has seemed just as enticing to more experienced investors. Prominent among them was the Keely engine, designed and exhibited during the last quarter of the nineteenth century by John E. W. Keely, who never managed to make good his promise to run a train of thirty cars from Philadelphia to New York at the rate of a mile a minute with one small machine consuming a quart of water for fuel.

From November 10, 1874, when he first demonstrated his vibratory generator with a hydro-pneumatic-pulsating vacue machine, to his death, however, he worked incessantly on the commercial possibilities of his invention and deluded a host of investors and others who came to believe in him as some would in a religious prophet.

Mrs. Clara Jessup Bloomfield-Moore, Keely's most ardent champion, in an article which she wrote in his defense, explained what Keely claimed to be doing. It was the release of

the force which Kepler predicted would in this century be revealed to man. The divine element is shown by the laws of etheric force to be like the sun behind the clouds, the source of all light though itself unseen. It is the latent basis of all human knowledge, as latent aş caloric and electricity are the base of all material forms.

Keely himself explained:

With these three agents alone [air, water, and machine], unaided by any and every compound, heat electricity and galvanic action, I have produced in an unappreciable time by a simple manipulation of the machine, a vaporic substance at one expulsion of a volume of ten gallons having an elastic energy of 10,000 pounds to the square inch. . . . It has a vapor of so fine an order it will penetrate metal. . . . It is lighter than hydrogen and more powerful than steam or any explosives known. . . . I once drove an engine 800 revolutions a minute of forty horse power with less than a thimbleful of water and kept it running fifteen days with the same water.

Keely's scientific language was too profound for the stockholders, who in 1872 had organized in New York the Keely Motor Company. As business men, however, they knew that the return on their investment was not very great. Whenever resentment grew intense, Keely would announce himself on the verge of his greatest discovery; and the suckers who had sunk thousands in the project put in more to save what they already had thrown away.

In the meantime Keely continued to give marvelous demonstrations in his Philadelphia workshop. He poured a pint of water into a cylinder, the gauge showed a pressure of over 50,000 pounds per square inch, great ropes were torn apart, iron bars were broken or twisted out of shape, bullets were discharged through twelve-inch planks by a force which could not be determined.

Immediately after Keely's death two University of Pennsylvania professors, a prominent electrical engineer, and Clarence B. Moore, son of Mrs. Moore, investigated Keely's home and found in the cellar the secret of Keely's success—a compressed-air apparatus which connected through the floor with the wonder-producing demonstration machine. It is significant that Keely left no fortune; he had put back into his experiments all he gulled from credulous investors.

The unexploited commercial value of water also was the talking point of Prescott Ford Jernegan, Baptist minister of Middletown, Connecticut, in 1897. With an accomplice, Charles E. Fisher, he, however, went Keely one better in that he was able to display an apparatus which apparently worked. It was a gold accumulator which, covered with mercury and lowered into the ocean, after a suitable period came up coated with gold.

It was not until after a $300,000 stock issue had been sold out that it was discovered that the secret lay in Fisher's ability as a deep-sea diver. Jernegan and Fisher left town, the former escaping to France with $110,000. Remorseful, he refunded about $75,000 to investors and later returned to the United States to end his life creditably.

When virtually every one in Middletown with any spare money was rushing to invest it in Jernegan's Electrolytic Marine Salts Company, the gold extraction swindle assumed the proportions of a local craze. War excepted, throughout history there has been no more potent stimulant to what the social psychologists call a mass movement than the yearning for financial profit. The three outstanding cases are the South Sea Bubble, the Mississippi Bubble, and the Tulipomania. The first was promoted by John Blount, who persuaded the English Parliament in 1711 to authorize his South Sea Company to purchase the nation's entire $150,000,000 debt on subscription, exchanging its own stock, which thereupon soared as much as 1,000 per cent as everyone wanted to speculate. When it dawned on the helpless that the South Sea Company had no plans for its exclusive trade with the South Seas, the promoter had disappeared.

Despite the example across the Channel, nine years later the French went equally enthusiastic over John Law's Company of the West, to which Louis XV gave the exclusive right to exploit and settle the American Louisiana territory.

For more than two years, 1634 to 1636, life in Holland was at an abnormal pitch as the Dutch saved every florin to invest in the tulip trade, until it became so topheavy that no one could profit.

That all victims of confidence men have larceny in their own hearts is the inclusive generalization of Herbert N. Graham, veteran post-office inspector. Newman F. Baker, Northwestern University professor of law, began an article in *Police "13-13"* for May, 1936, with virtually the same statement:

It is remarkable how much the swindler and trickster rely upon the victim's cupidity or inherent dishonesty in the framing of get-rich-quick schemes.

If these two authorities are correct, the huge annual traffic in "smuggled" goods—furs, laces, rugs, etc.—and of "extras" which "truck drivers" either can return or can dispose of for personal profit is not surprising. Neither is the amount of betting on supposedly "fixed" sports events or the cases in which the victim is "double-crossed" while believing he is assisting in the fleecing of some one else.

The perfectly honest seeker after bargains, however, is in as great danger when he patronizes auction sales, bankruptcy and closing-out sales, cut-rate furniture stores, and, especially, wholesale establishments of certain types. In his eagerness to obtain goods below retail cost, he is likely to pay more than reputable places of business charge for merchandise of the same quality. The National Better Business Bureau warns that house-to-house peddlers without adequate credentials seldom have genuine oriental rugs or Irish linens; that the household belongings offered in an auction at a residence often are newly stocked (the "stuffed flat" racket); that furniture stores which are "just out" of advertised goods, or whose salesmen attempt to sell something "a little bit better," often are what is known as "borax" establishments (which take about $50,000,000 annually from customers for bargains that fall apart in a few weeks or months); that courtesy cards offered by retailers enabling buyers to obtain wholesale prices usually are fraudulent to the extent that the $10,000,000 annually collected from customers using them is largely on merchandise sold above rather than below prevailing prices; that the sample displayed by an auctioneer or "pitch man" may have no resemblance to the articles wrapped up for successful bidders; and that, in general, bargains are less to be trusted than standard-priced goods.

In all cases (the warning is *not* superfluous) anything to be signed should be read first. Otherwise, the householder may discover that the receipt which he initialed to indicate he had received a free roof, in exchange for the obligation to permit potential customers to inspect it, actually was a purchase agreement or a wage attachment. Or, after his death, his widow may learn that the microscopic type on his protection certificate (not insurance policy) relieved the society (not company) of any obligation. Carelessness in an eager moment to get something below cost has upset many a thrifty home.

In a society which overwhelms its entertainers with fame and fortune, it is natural that the sharpers should find a lucrative field of operation among the thousands of clerks, shopgirls, day laborers, schoolteachers, and others who dream of seeing their names in bright lights. Leading the sucker encouragingly, step by step, up the supposed ladder of success, the unscrupulous dramatic schools charge for rehearsals, auditions, and other training which the client is convinced is necessary preparation for his debut as a stage, motion picture, or radio starlet.

The reputable Radio Institute of the Audible Arts estimated in 1935 that there were more than one hundred radio schools whose graduates would be no nearer a bona fide broadcasting contract than before they laid out their hard-earned money. Under the leadership of Dr. Marion Sayle Taylor (radio's "Voice of Experience") the Lambs, a club of actors, formed a committee in 1934 to combat such swindles. In 1936 in Japan, 150,000 mothers entered their daughters in a fake contest to discover a Japanese counterpart of Shirley Temple. Three years later two employees of M.G.M. studio were convicted of having forged the signature of Louis B. Mayer while signing up several of Hollywood's foremost players to fictitious special contracts.

No matter how trashy it may be, any scenario synopsis submitted to a large number of writers' agencies will receive praise, and its author will be induced to pay for its revision into form suitable for submission to some producer. The music sheet, radio script, and authorship rackets are worked similarly, much to the detriment of the reputable agencies serving only clients who display ability.

Writing in the *Bookman* for August, 1932, an experienced subeditor for a manuscript agency described its clientele partly as follows:

They included religious cranks, broken-down school teachers, office workers, over-emotional ladies with no outlet, letter carriers who have gone over the same route too long, elderly retired lecturers, and so on. Some of them were just plain people who want to write and who believe in the integrity of American ballyhoo. These need to be burned only once in order to understand the nature of fire.

Fortunately for the racketeers, once is enough to make the talent-school swindle profitable. As early as 1887 at least £2,400 was the take of the promoters of the International Society of Literature, Science and Art, which offered a free diploma, the privilege of wearing a cap and gown and the right to use the initials M.S.L. or F.S.L. Purpose of the society was to "edit, purchase and sell manuscripts of members, to bestow prizes for meritorious works and inventions and productions leading to employment of the masses."

In comment upon the swindlers, chief of whom was W. J. Morgan, the *Spectator* said:

They had evidently sounded the depths of human folly very carefully, and had come to the conclusion that it was impossible to make a prospectus too absurd, if only it were addressed to aspiring authors and artists. They saw with wonderful cleverness that the weakness of plain people of the present generation is the desire for literary and artistic distinction and they set themselves to exploit this weakness to the best of their ability.

Not only in the talent field but also in virtually every other in which it is possible to earn a living, the frauds are difficult to distinguish from the genuine agencies of assistance.

After studying 294 men who had tried to improve their occupational status by correspondence study, Professors Charles Bird and Donald G. Paterson, of the University of Minnesota, found that only 6 per cent who paid an average of $120 for their courses completed them, and that 78 per cent of the students would be misfits if they should obtain employment in the field studied. The four hundred Boston waiters who, in 1937, paid $11 each in the belief they would obtain positions, paying $120 a month, on a millionaire's yacht during an eight months' cruise, are typical of the thousands in lower economic levels who allow their desire to get work to shadow their reasoning powers. The increased success of all types of financial swindles—gambling, investment, purchasing, and job security— during a depression proves this chapter's thesis that, when the victim's wish is strong, the hoaxer's task is easier.

CHAPTER VI

Incentives to Believe: Vanity, Conspicuous Waste

EVEN after he learned that several paintings which he had purchased as by outstanding artists were forgeries, the late John G. Johnson, "most catholic of picture collectors," kept them on his walls, maintaining that he had bought them "not for their name or even for their honesty" but because he liked them, and that he still liked them.

Mr. Johnson was exceptional. To most collectors the masterpieces which they have been displaying to friends with boastful explanations become mere daubs upon proof of their spuriousness. Hilaire Belloc, proud of having passed off some lines of his own in "Favorite Extracts from Shakespeare" prepared for an English editor, says of the attitude of a majority of connoisseurs:

I have never understood why a good fake should not be as valuable as an original. If a man can reproduce an article so that not one man in 10,000 can tell the difference between the model and the copy, what element is it in the model which gives it its value? . . . I think we owe a great gratitude to the hosts of men who have learned how to make counterfeits.

Anyone who, like Mr. Belloc, fails to understand the non-artistic purchaser's mind, should read Thorstein Veblen's *The Theory of the Leisure Class,* especially the parts about the conspicuous waste to which the well-to-do resort in order to fortify themselves in their self-satisfied feeling of social superiority.

In the preceding chapter were considered the many pitfalls into which the person desirous of improving his financial status may stumble. This chapter is concerned with the purchase of luxuries rather than necessities; the type of wishful mind under consideration, consequently, is that of the comparatively wealthy patron of the arts.

Today, government and insurance company sleuths and art critics agree, effete Americans are the most gullible customers for forged paintings, sculpture, and other pieces of art, for faked first editions, association copies, and autographs, for specious genealogies, and for all kinds of antiques and objects of a hobbyist's fancy. That personal vanity was a motive even during the Renaissance, furthermore, is attested by many biographers of the great Michelangelo. The story is that, either from disgust at critics' incessant praise of things classical or, as most authorities believe, upon the suggestion of Lorenzo de' Medici, the youthful, unknown Michelangelo passed off a Cupid on an amateur collector, Raffaello Riario, Cardinal di San Giorgio, as a genuine antique. He had carved his initials under one of the wings to protect himself against a possible charge of willful deceit; but when the buyer learned he had been imposed upon he returned the article indignantly, in true twentieth century style, and demanded return of his money.

The history of art is replete with similar cases. Early in the second quarter of the present century the Dutch art critic De La Faille discovered, just before publishing a complete catalogue of the works of the nineteenth century Dutch master Vincent van Gogh, that at least thirty of the works credited to that painter in various European galleries were forgeries. Immediately De La Faille had a supplement to his catalogue printed, mentioning the suspicions, and then set out to trace the deceptions. All thirty which had been questioned were traced to a Berlin art dealer named Walker who was tried and convicted.

Meier-Graefe, the German critic, remarked at the trial:

Critics aren't much use anyway, but if a purchaser insists on trusting expert opinion, rather than his own sense of appreciation, he deserves to be cheated.

It must be a great pleasure to Herr Meier-Graefe to know that although Anthony Van Dyck painted only about seventy canvases, at least two thousand have been sold as by him; also, that in 1935 five American millionaires paid an average of $300,000 each for copies of da Vinci's famous "Mona Lisa," now in the Louvre at Paris, in the belief they were obtaining the original; also, that in the same year Professor André Mailfert of Paris admitted that for five years he had employed two hundred workmen to turn out the entire product of the eighteenth century "Loire School" of provincial furniture of inlaid lemon wood whose leader, he had declared in his lectures, was a certain Jean François Hardy; also, that, on the authority of Dr. George de Cornell, director of the Fine Arts Guild of America, "out of 3,000 Corots 8,000 are in the United States and England—only Corot never painted 3,000 pictures."

Especially amusing to the German authority during the amazing year of 1935 must have been the conviction in France of Jean Charles Millet, grandson of Jean François Millet of the Barbizon School, and a confederate, Paul Cazot, for forging the name of the great painter to many paintings. "You can sell anything to Americans and Englishmen," pleaded the wayward grandson. "They know nothing about art; even their experts know nothing. All you have to do is to ask a fabulous price."

Greatest art sensation of the present century was the revelation in 1928 concerning the work of Alceo Dossena, Italian sculptor. This modern artist was the innocent tool of unscrupulous art dealers who for about ten years placed his work in some of the leading private and public collections of Renaissance sculpture throughout the world. In 1938 controversy still raged regarding the genuineness of a tomb for which the Boston Museum of Art had paid $100,000 in the belief that it was by Mino da Fiesole, Renaissance sculptor.

Dossena's amazing career as an imitator began when he concluded that Simone Martini, fourteenth century painter, also should have been a sculptor. Dossena projected himself into the personality of Martini and, for a decade, produced a fair-sized gallery of sculpture for Petrarch's friend. The antique dealer Alfredo Fasoli purchased these and imitations of other Renaissance masters, including Nicola Pisano, for an average price of $200 each. Exposure of Fasoli's reselling them as genuine articles came in 1928 when Dossena sued for $66,000 allegedly due him in back wages.

During the suit it was revealed that Dossena's work had been bought at fabulous prices by the Metropolitan Museum of Art in New York, the Cleveland Museum of Art, many European museums, and several leading private collectors, such as William Randolph Hearst and Helen Clay Frick.

After Dossena had been absolved of the title "world's greatest forger" in March, 1933, a public auction of his work was held in Manhattan's National Art Galleries. Each purchaser received an official document of the Italian government attesting that the work was a genuine fake.

Another recent emulator of the Michelangelo technique was Francesco Cremonse, obscure Italian sculptor, who buried a Venus sans nose, one arm, and lower legs in the turnip patch of a French peasant near St. Etienne, in south-central France. Plowed up in 1938, it was accepted by art critics as a priceless relic of the Roman invasion of Gaul, a perfect example of the neo-Attican period from seventeen hundred to twenty-five hundred years ago. After the French government had issued a decree classifying the Venus de Brizet, as it was called, as one of France's art treasures which were not to be sold abroad without official permission, Cremonse came forward with the missing parts and produced the nightclub singer who had been his model. As soon as the spurious nature of the sculpture became known, its value dropped in the estimation of those who previously had been lavish in their praise.

With the increased use of the X-ray and other means of scientific detection, the chances of a serious art collector's being fooled by a forgery have been lessened. Nevertheless, whenever there is a demand there will be a supply, and so, long after the art galleries and museums have been purged of their spurious contents, faked Rembrandts and Whistlers still will be found in private collections. They will be admired, furthermore, by their proud owners' friends seated on imitation antique furniture with their backs to shelves, mantels, and whatnots containing modern manufactured artifacts which will become family heirlooms. In a corner of the room may be a handsome violin with "Antonius Stradivarius Cremonensis Faciebat Anno 17—" on the inside; but it will not be a genuine instrument by the great eighteenth century violin maker. And on the wall may be a human figure with the head of Abraham Lincoln grafted onto the body of John C. Calhoun, Henry Clay, or someone else more given to being photographed than the Great Emancipator—the mutilation, of course, being unknown to the picture's owner.

According to the United States Treasury Department, in the first twenty-eight years after the passage in 1906 of an act exempting from duty antiques predating 1700, at least 75 per cent of all antiques imported into this country have been spurious articles. In 1906 the "works of art"—not all of them fakes, of course—admitted under the act were valued at $478,000; in 1910 the figure was $2,500,000, and in 1919 it was $21,619,543. Since about 80 per cent of these imports were from Great Britain, federal authorities have no doubt that a majority are fraudulent; otherwise, there would be no relics left for the British to display to gullible American tourists.

American collectors of antiques about the turn of the century did not have to go to Europe, Asia, or Africa to be swindled. In almost every state of the Union they could purchase prehistoric stone implements made by Lewis Erickson, Medina Township, Dane County, Wisconsin.

Acme

ART FAKES FOOL EXPERTS

(Above.) The Boston Museum of Fine Arts bought this sculptured tomb monument in the belief it was the fifteenth century work of Mino da Fiesole. Evidence now points to the belief it was made, or at least restored, by Alceo Dossena in the twentieth century.

(Below.) An obscure Italian sculptor, Cremonse, constructed this Venus which later was dug up and believed to be a genuine antique. After President Lebrun of France signed a decree requisitioning it, Cremonse produced the missing arms and nose and the model.

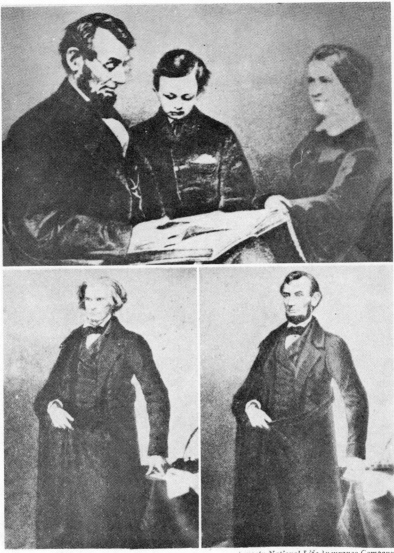

PHOTOGRAPHING "OLD ABE"

Because there were few "heroic" photographs of Abraham Lincoln, many fakes have been produced to supply the lack. In the picture above of Lincoln and his family, the likeness of Mrs. Lincoln has been superimposed. On the left below is an authentic "heroic" portrait of John Calhoun which was mutilated to place the head of Lincoln on Calhoun's shoulders. The reconstructed fake is to be seen in many public-school classrooms.

Erickson, according to his own story, learned the art of making antiques by an apparently new method when he accidentally bit a piece off a flint arrowhead to amuse himself while ill at his home. With steel pincers he was able to form a fairly sharp apex and gradually to produce implements still to be found in the collections of experienced archaeologists who paid extravagant prices for them.

Professor Albert Ernest Jenks, of the University of Minnesota, told the story of Erickson's detection by some would-be customers who were admitted to his workshop during his absence. According to Charles E. Brown, director of the Wisconsin State Historical Museum, it was Erickson's father who thoughtlessly opened the workshop for the visitors.

Professor Jenks' exposé appeared in 1900. More than ten years later there walked into Mr. Brown's office a man with a face wreathed in smiles. Identifying himself as Erickson, he asked for a copy of *A Remarkable Counterfeiter* which, with Jenks' consent, he had reprinted in 1912 for proud distribution among friends.

"Old Noah Surely Wrote His Diary on Carbon Paper" was the headline given by the Detroit *Daily News* to one of a series of stories with which it helped to expose an extensive fake relic ring in 1907. This antique factory was as remarkable for the men involved as for the ingenious methods employed to obtain eyewitness testimonials to archaeological finds in all parts of Michigan.

According to the group's own advertising, "No discovery since the exhuming of the city of Pompeii has created such widespread interest, and no set of views is complete without these curiosities." This was to sell stereoscopic views of the various finds.

According to the *News*, "The scheme is so unique as to win absolute admiration for the perpetrators. If committed in a spirit of humor, it is the most colossal hoax of a century."

Head of the Detroit fakers was Daniel E. Soper, deposed secretary of state of Michigan. The procedure by which he and his accomplices duped many wealthy antique collectors was to plant bronze tablets, Indian copper implements, wonderful battle axes of leaf copper, spearheads, etc., some of them bearing hieroglyphics and symbols of the biblical deluge and the tower of Babel. A year or so later some member of the ring would appear in the community selected for the discovery to organize a committee of foremost citizens to act as witnesses of the excavations. In that way they filled a fat file with testimonials as to the genuineness of their offerings.

The attention of Mr. Brown was attracted to Soper and his companions by H. P. Hamilton of Two Rivers, Wisconsin, a collector who already had made some minor purchases from Soper, but who became suspicious when offered a copper tablet purporting to be the diary of Noah.

It was Mr. Brown who obtained the cooperation of the Detroit *News* in the campaign. Because the state statutes at the time provided no basis for prosecution, the appeal the paper made was to public opinion.

Suspected with Soper were James O. Scotford, a sign painter, and his relative, Alpheus D. Scoby, Adolphe B. Covert, curator of the University of Cincinnati Museum, and many others. Others who helped investigate and expose some of the discoveries as fakes included Professor G. B. Brown, of the University of Pennsylvania department of archaeology; J. E. Talmage, director of the Deseret Museum of Salt Lake City, and Warren K. Moorehead of Phillips Academy, Andover, Massachusetts.

The result of the activity of these men was that Soper and his gang disappeared for a time. Not for long, however. In addition to further discoveries there followed pamphlets, articles submitted to reputable publications, and lectures in several states. The deaths of most of the principals finally ended the frauds, but generations to come will admire the astounding relics which today form the nucleus of many a private collection.

To gratify the vanity of collectors of first and rare editions, association books and autographs, there is an army of fakers even larger than those of which the art and antique lovers must beware. Among literary dilettantes, again, it is the Americans who are the most easily fooled. Deprived of a long literary history, these patriotic aesthetes are ready to relieve peddlers of coffee-stained manuscripts written in ink made from iron filings to suggest antiquity.

In the better libraries, of course, scientific examination is made of paper and printing whenever a doubtful item is offered for sale. Nevertheless, in the famous Huntington Library at San Marino, California, are to be found fifty-four of the fifty-five spurious first editions of the Victorian school published in England about the turn of the century. Most notable of these is Elizabeth Barrett Browning's *Sonnets from the Portuguese*. Kipling, George Eliot, Stevenson, Tennyson, Dickens—in fact, almost every British writer of the latter half of the nineteenth century—is represented in the collection of literary hoaxes of all times, which the Huntington Library now values highly as such. In many cases the unknown fakers took long poems or essays out of already published volumes and published them in pamphlet form under earlier dates than the authentic first editions.

In the annals of literary hoaxing there is no more humorous story than that of the Fortsas Catalogue which, August 10, 1840, caused the leading bibliophiles of all western Europe to flock to the obscure town of Binche, Belgium, bidding for titles in the private library of the late Jean Nepomucene-Auguste Pichauld, Count de Fortsas. A sixteen-page pamphlet announcing the auction, printed at Mons, had drawn their attention with the statement that the eccentric count had refused to own a book of which any other copy was known to exist.

So rare an opportunity did the sale seem to provide that Baron de Reiffenberg, director of the Belgian Royal Library, obtained a special appropriation to buy several of the treasures. Techener, Van de Weyer, and Crozat all wanted No. 36 on the list; Princess de Ligne wrote to a friend to buy No. 48, no matter at what expense, because she feared it was a revelation of the foibles of her grandfather, the Grand Monarch. Charles Nodier, French bibliophile, was there, although it has been said that he suspected a hoax.

Police, regarding the foreigners with suspicion, were relieved when the Brussels newspapers of the evening before carried a notice that the sale had been called off following the purchase of the entire collection by the people of Binche out of regard for the collector. It was some time before the irate visitors could accept the denials by the authorities that they had purchased any books, or knew anything about Count Fortsas or M. Moulon, notary, at whose address the sale was advertised to take place.

Sixteen years after the incident the printer of *Documents et Particularités Historiques sur le Catalogue du Comte de Fortsas,* revealed that the hoaxer was Renier Chalon, antiquarian and author, who was remembered to have mingled with the bibliophiles the day of the abortive auction. At a sale in New York in the 1930's, Baron de Reiffenberg's copy of the Catalogue, containing quotations, brought forty dollars as a curiosity.

During the past one hundred years the autograph of almost every important historical personage has been trafficked by swindlers. Most notorious of these fanners of vanity was Robert Spring, native Englishman, who in 1858 opened a bookshop in Philadelphia and went in for forging the signatures of George Washington, Benjamin Franklin, and others on canceled bank checks, on the flyleaves of books and on letters.

Outstanding creation of this master of the spurious was Fanny Jackson, fictitious daughter of "Stonewall" Jackson, to whom Spring had the Confederate general write hundreds of letters. The signature of Jackson still is being forged to battered Bibles which a ragged gentleman of the South offers for sale while tearfully relating how long it has been in the family, and how it grieves him that poverty has driven him to such straits. Each Bible is sold as the one found on Jackson's body after his accidental death at Chancellorsville.

The Salem witch warrant racket also usually is a lachrymose act. To help out a "stranded antique dealer," a "war veteran," or some similar itinerant, many a soft-hearted layman, often a country newspaper editor sensing a good feature article, has purchased or advanced a loan upon a death warrant for a witch at Salem, Massachusetts, dated late in the seventeenth century. It carries the signatures of Cotton Mather, Samuel Sewall, John Winthrop, King Philip, and several other historical figures. It, furthermore, always is certified to by a little card beneath glass signed by the curator of some museum or historical society.

A genuine death warrant for a Salem witch would be a valuable collector's item. Death warrants have been reported from all parts of the country. Often they are made the subjects of newspaper feature articles. Among the fictitious names to be found on the certification cards are William F. Warren, curator of the Boston University Museum, and J. A. Skaggs, curator of the South Carolina Historical Society. Investigation by the Kansas City *Star* revealed that the latter, at least, is nonexistent along with his society. Others have pointed out that both Winthrop and King Philip died in 1676.

Other rarities included in the swindler's collection may be forgeries of the signatures of Abraham Lincoln and of signers of the Declaration of Independence. The swindler often identifies himself as a World War veteran with discharge papers signed by Pershing himself, as the man who taught Lindbergh to fly, or as a Texas antique dealer.

Among the most popular items in the inventories of twentieth century faked autograph peddlers have been signatures of Mozart, Handel, Wagner, Lafayette, Hardy, and Marie Louise. Even the Library of Congress was taken in by Tobia Nicotra, an Italian who posed as the deceased Richard Drigo, former conductor of the czar's orchestra. The many lapses in the voyages of discovery of Christopher Columbus have inspired numerous simulators of water-soaked parchment to attempt to supply the lack. This has been true particularly since the publication in 1875 of *Historia de las Indias,* by Bartolomé de las Casas, found in a Madrid museum.

A statement in the account to the effect that Columbus, fearing his fleet would go down and the King and Queen of Spain would never know its fate, had written on parchment a full account which he rolled in waxed cloth and threw overboard in a large wooden cask, suggested the forgery. The world had not to wait long for it. Less than a month after the American edition appeared, the original log was presented to Miss Helen U. Kiely, in charge of the American Writing Company's booth at the San Francisco fair, by two men who wished her to establish its age. After chemical analysis she told them it was not over thirty years old.

A few weeks later the log was purchased by Angel Delmete, a lawyer of Mexico City, Mexico; but it was not established whether it was the copy found to be spurious in California. There is no doubt of its having been soaked in salt water. The cover was damaged badly, and small shells and sand were embedded in it. The writing, all in German, however, was plainly visible, including an explanation that Columbus used German so that his crew might not read his entries.

Shown a photograph of several pages of the "find," Professor Adriaan J. Barnouw, Queen Wilhelmina professor of the history, language, and literature of the Netherlands at Columbia University, burst out laughing. According to him, a new "original Columbus log" appears every few years. The New York *World* of September 14, 1924, declared that a few years previously an edition of several thousand copies had been printed, the forger being a German who used excellent modern grammar rather than that known by Luther when he translated the Bible less than a half century later.

Hobby collectors are lucrative bait for the racketeers and near-racketeers. After recounting the disgust of many stamp dealers with foreign countries, mostly small, which bolster their national treasuries by frequent changes in stamp designs, Alvin F. Harlow declared:

But the great mass of collectors just love to be kidded; they love the pretty colored pictures of bridges and trolley cars and penitentiaries and kangaroos and poets and town pumps, and they cherish the belief that some of them may be quite valuable some day.*

* *Saturday Evening Post,* April 18, 1936.

From this it would seem that the hobby collector has the dual motivation of vanity, through the possession of a rare article, and potential profit. Although philatelic societies keep such sharp watch that few experienced collectors are fooled by false issues, thousands of inexperienced persons are the counterfeiters' meat.

Historically, vanity is discovered to have been one of the earliest traits upon which professional hoaxers depended for success. T. F. Tout in his *Medieval Forgers and Forgeries* wrote:

> Many medieval forgeries have their roots in no worse than vanity. A church or family was anxious to prove its origin was more ancient than it really was and to claim as its founder or ancestor one of the great names of old.

Universities had their origin in the twelfth century; by the thirteenth and fourteenth they were so strong that they wanted to appear old. Therefore, the University of Paris said that Charles the Great was its founder. Tout continued:

> Oxford found its origin in the schools of Alfred the Great, Cambridge went one better and traced itself back to King Arthur or to a Spanish prince named Cantaber.

As with institutions so with individuals. Unaware of or unimpressed by mathematical logic, belittling the importance of descent from a Revolutionary hero or Pilgrim father, thousands of American families proudly display genealogical tables allegedly proving that the roots of the family tree on this side of the Atlantic are grounded in colonial Massachusetts or Virginia. In Great Britain family pride goes even further, causing fallacious pride in supposed descent from Norman conquerors or earlier denizens of the island.

In *The Hero*, Lord Raglan scoffs at the idea that any Englishman can prove his pedigree to the Norman Conquest, and contends it would mean nothing if he could. Studying many genealogies, he discovered serious anachronisms, as the assigning to pre-Conquest Saxons of Christian names. Concluding his scholarly analysis of how these family trees have continued to spread, he wrote:

> We thus see arrayed in defense of false genealogy the powerful forces of religion and patriotism; of custom and tradition; of family pride and individual vanity, and of Eupemerism and rationalization, not to mention the popular love of the marvelous and the romantic. On the other

side are only the puny and disunited columns of critical investigation. It is not surprising that, although hundreds of them have been proved false and none have been proved true, the traditional pedigrees still hold the field.

Although small numerically by comparison with the persons who have a few cents or dollars to gamble or invest recklessly, those vain wishful thinkers to whom possession of a rare object gives assurance of elevation above the common clay of mankind are so well fixed financially that satisfying their aesthetic pride gives a good living to a small army of artistic hoaxers.

When one of these aesthetes or the "experts" on whose judgment they rely blunders badly, the unsophisticated chortle. In 1947 the artistically illiterate had a huge guffaw when a hitherto obscure Dutch painter proved that he had fooled many leading collectors, art dealers and museums. The hoaxer was Hans van Meegeren and his confession followed his arrest, at war's end, as a Nazi collaborator. He defended himself by declaring the canvas, *Christ and the Adulteress* which he had sold to Hermann Goering, No. 2 Nazi, for $256,000, was not the work of the master Jan Vermeer (1632-75) but his own creation. He further confessed that *Men of Emmaus* which the Boymans Museum, Rotterdam had purchased for 500,000 guilders after its supposed sensational discovery in a Paris linen closet, was his work as were also five other supposed Vermeers, two Pieter de Hoochs and one Terborch.

When the same critics who had called him a second-rater refused to believe his confession, van Meegeren painted *Jesus in the Temple,* in Vermeer's style while under guard in prison. Chemical and x-ray examination also proved his fakes. Van Meegeren explained his motive was not financial gain but revenge on the critics who rejected his early work. He went to Nice, France where he invented a collection of Vermeer's works supposedly done during a 12 year period in the great artist's life about which little was known.

Van Meegeren was acquitted of collaboration but convicted of fraud and sentenced to one year imprisonment. He died from a heart attack at 57, however, before he could start serving it.

CHAPTER VII

Incentives to Believe: Promoting a Cause

MORE than a year before the 1936 presidential campaign began, E. P. Cramer, Washington, D. C., advertising man, confessed to a Senate committee investigating lobbies that he was the instigator of a "whispering campaign" to spread the rumor that President Franklin D. Roosevelt, candidate for reelection, was either incompetent or insane.

Despite the official exposé of its origin, this canard persisted and was fortified by numerous others. Nevertheless, President Roosevelt was reelected by an overwhelming majority as has been virtually every other presidential candidate similarly maligned, including George Washington. Explaining the indulgence in personalities which characterizes American politics, James Truslow Adams, eminent historian, in an article, "Our Whispering Campaigns," in the September, 1932, issue of *Harper's,* pointed out that the United States is the only great nation which elects its most powerful official, and that in this country men always count for more than measures.

"So long," wrote Adams, "as our politics are primarily concerned with men rather than with measures, it will be the men who will be attacked; characters, not ideas. The attack will be planned not with reference to the real characters of the men themselves; for almost every charge ever made has been abominably false, but with reference to the dominant prejudices or standards of the voters to be influenced. If these prejudices or standards should change, the slanders of the politicals would change."

Throughout our existence as a nation the prejudices or standards have remained remarkably the same. Sexual irregularities, drunkenness and mixed blood have been the charges most frequently whispered against candidates for high office; and any candidate of which one of these was true was considered, under existent standards of public morality, to be unworthy of the respect of his fellow citizens. That ten of the sixteen men against whom the whisperers have directed their most virulent attacks have been elected, while two of the four defeated lost to candidates similarly attacked, indicates no lack of cleverness or viciousness on the part of the attackers. Rather, it suggests that, although the whispers may tend to fortify the prejudices of some voters, they have little or no effect on others who are disinclined to think ill of the subjects of them. That is, in politics as in everything else, *people believe what they want to believe and disbelieve what does not square with preconceived ideas.*

During his investigation of spurious literature the writer addressed a questionnaire to readers of unreliable books on lists supplied by libraries. One, who read John Hamill's *The Strange Career of Mr. Hoover Under Two Flags* in good faith, answered: "The book confirmed my opinion of the true character of Mr. Hoover if the truth was really told, in this work or others." Although this book's publishers guaranteed its genuineness and announced that the author had encountered great difficulty in obtaining material which mysteriously disappeared from foreign libraries and other places, Hamill admitted that it was a collection of misrepresentations when he was haled into court on the complaint of a New York policeman that he deserved to share in the book's royalties. While copying records, he testified, he interpolated passages to change their meaning. This was true, among others, of a quotation tending to show that Mr. Hoover might have saved the life of Edith Cavell, World War I nurse who was executed by the Germans, had he cared to do so.

The enemies of every other prominent person, already holding a low opinion of him, have been ready to believe the worst about him. President Washington complained that attacks on him were in terms so exaggerated and indecent "as could scarcely be applied to a Nero, a notorious defaulter or a common pickpocket." It is believed by some historians that his decision not to seek a third term resulted largely from his desire to avoid slurs on his character.

Thomas Jefferson was accused by the Reverend Timothy Dwight, president of Yale University, of planning to overthrow the churches and banish religion. It also was whispered that Jefferson was a rapist and had mulatto children.

The death of Mrs. Andrew Jackson followed by three weeks publication of a story that she and the General had lived in sin before their marriage thirty-seven years before. The fact was that the Jacksons were wed in the belief that the state of Virginia had granted her a divorce from her drunken first husband, whereas all that had been permitted was the privilege to sue; two years later, when they learned the truth, the Jacksons were remarried.

To counteract the scandal against Jackson the story was circulated that John Quincy Adams, while minister to Russia, had obtained an American girl to be mistress for a rich Russian nobleman. Martin Van Buren was said to be the illegitimate son of Aaron Burr, and his running mate was called a part Negro. William Henry Harrison was called a drunkard. The Negro-blood charge also was made against Hannibal Hamlin, vice president under Lincoln, and against Warren G. Harding. Ulysses S. Grant, Grover Cleveland, Theodore Roosevelt and Alfred E. Smith were accused of heavy drinking.

Most frequent has been the sexual delinquency whisper, on the popularity of which James Truslow Adams commented thus: "It has been said that in England the open possession of a mistress would very seriously damage the career of a public man, in France it would make no difference, in Italy it would help. . . . In America, at least, it would damn him bitterly." In the same way, it may be noted that politicians "consider the people to be deeply opposed to a candidate who might be so unfortunate as to have been an illegitimate child."

Of Henry Wilson, Grant's vice president, it was said that he was an illegitimate child; of James A. Garfield that his wife planned to sue for divorce after the election; of Chester A. Arthur that he was involved in a scandal with a society woman; of Horatio Seymour that he was hopelessly insane; of William McKinley that he was pro-Catholic; of William Howard Taft that he was godless because of his membership in a Unitarian church; of Woodrow Wilson that he was estranged from his wife, immoral with other women and, near the end of his term, hopelessly insane.

In some cases, of course, stories of past indiscretions were true. Both Alexander Hamilton and Grover Cleveland, confronted with having fathered illegitimate children, bravely confessed. For many other charges against Cleveland, however, apparently there was no basis in truth, and the incident of which so much was made occurred in his early youth. Mrs. Cleveland publicly denied that her husband was cruel to her, and Mr. Cleveland was in no way responsible for the Murchison letter which, more than anything else, caused his defeat by Benjamin Harrison in his second campaign. In that letter, which bore a fictitious signature and was addressed to Sir Lionel Sackville-West, British ambassador to the United States, the writer represented himself as a naturalized Englishman in doubt as to how to vote. Sackville-West's tactless reply, suggesting that a vote for Cleveland would be useful to England, was interpreted as proof that the Democratic policy to reduce the tariff was British-inspired.

Cleveland demanded and obtained the ambassador's withdrawal, but Harrison won the election.

In no campaigns has more mud been slung than during those in which Cleveland and James G. Blaine opposed each other. In 1884 Blaine credited his defeat to his unfortunate overlooking of an introduction of him by the Reverend Samuel D. Burchard to a delegation of Protestant clergymen in which the minister defined the issues of the campaign as being "rum, Romanism and rebellion." Because Blaine neglected immediately to correct the impression that he was prejudiced on these three points, he lost the sympathies of large sectors of the electorate. Another clergyman, the Reverend C. H. Pendleton, persisted in circulating the charge that Cleveland was a drunkard and cruel to his wife; Mrs. Cleveland publicly denied the canard but, as Robert Littell and John J. McCarthy declared in an article, "Whispers for Sale," in the February, 1936, *Harper's*, "Rumor has wings; the dirtier the rumor the bigger the wings."

In 1888, contributing to the defeat of Blaine for the Republican nomination was a story that he and his wife had been immoral before their marriage. Appearing, supposedly, first in the Indianapolis *Sentinel* for August 8, 1888, the charge was illustrated by the picture of a tombstone in an Augusta, Maine, cemetery, indicating that the first child of Mr. and Mrs. Blaine had been born only three months after their marriage. The explanation was that, because of differences in state laws, the Blaines went through a second ceremony more than a half-year after the first.

The celebrated Mulligan letters were investigated by a congressional committee and called fictitious. If genuine they would have proved that Blaine had been connected with questionable actions in connection with legislation favorable to certain railroad interests. The letters, supposedly passing between Blaine and a business associate, Warren Fisher, were used in the campaigns of 1876 and 1884.

James A. Garfield successfully overcame the adverse effects of a last-minute attempt to defeat him in 1880 by means of a forged letter supposedly addressed by Garfield to H. T. Morey of the Employes Union of Lynn, Massachusetts. In it, contrary to the party platform, the candidate opposed immigration restrictions on Chinese labor. The letter was released to the press and given nation-wide publicity. Beginning with its issue of October 23, 1880, the New York *Herald* printed results of a diligent search for the forger. He was found to be Kenward Philip, a Brooklyn journalist, who was tried and convicted.

Finding easy credence among northern Republicans during the early decades after the Civil War, when fear persisted that southern Democrats

were conniving to bring back slavery, was a propaganda piece in the form
of a bill of sale for a Kentucky auction in 1840. Included with a list of
horses, cows, liquor and farm equipment were six slaves, making an eloquent appeal in the *Uncle Tom's Cabin* tradition. This curiosity apparently was printed in great numbers, for even today it is not uncommon
for a copy to be discovered in an attic trunk containing family heirlooms.
Numerous newspaper editors have received copies from subscribers, and
many feature articles about it have been written. With skepticism, a few
years ago, *Publishers' Auxiliary* reprinted the Kentucky bill of sale. One
of several letters received was from Sam W. Davis, of the *North End
News,* Wichita, Kansas, and contained the following:

The bill may have been actually printed and circulated for sale, but of
this I have always had my doubts. Back in Parke County, Indiana, this
bill was used as political ammunition in the campaign of 1870 or 1872 to
show the awfulness of slavery and the danger of electing Democrats to
office for fear that the Fifteenth Amendment would be abolished and the
black man would again be enslaved. At that time I was the "devil" in the
old *Parke County Republican* office . . . and I have a faint recollection
that the job department printed one lot of these bills for home circulation
during the campaign in an effort to defeat the late Hon. Daniel W.
Vorhees, "the tall sycamore of the Wabash," for congressman from the
district. At various times during the past fifty years the old "chestnut"
has bobbed up in some section of the country.

Shortly after James Bryce, the author of *The American Commonwealth,* returned to England in 1897 from a visit to this country, and a
few days before the New York mayoralty campaign, there appeared in the
New York *World* an alleged shipboard interview with Bryce on the
qualifications which a mayor should have. That the description fitted
Seth Low, the *World's* candidate, was obvious.

When a copy of the interview reached Bryce in Aberdeen, Scotland, he
promptly wrote to the editor of the New York *Evening Post* vigorously
denying having seen a reporter of the *World* or of any other newspaper
while in New York. "All that I am reported to have said is an invention
from beginning to end," he wrote under date of October 26, 1897. "I saw
no reporter of the *World* or of any other newspaper when I was in New
York, now nearly a month ago."

The New York *Sun* reprinted the letter November 4, 1897, and commented upon it editorially under the title "Pulitzer's Fake Mill Busy." I
could find no subsequent reply in any issue of the *World,* but the files to

which I had access are confined to early mail editions, so that Pulitzer may have done what one would have expected him to do—explained the situation in some way.

"Marse Henry" Watterson, eminent editor-publisher of the Louisville *Courier-Journal,* invented a light-hearted hoax in January, 1908, to fortify the prejudices of those eager to believe the worst about Theodore Roosevelt. It was to the effect that an old southern woman thought "the South is coming into its own" because the son of Martha Bulloch, a southern woman, was in the White House to stay. Her plan was a third term for Roosevelt and then life tenure, à la Louis Napoleon. Watterson ended his sketch: "If out of the mouths of babes and sucklings, why not out of the brain of this crazed old woman of the South?" Because of other important news the day the story came out, it received a "bad press," which resulted in a "kidding" letter from the president, Watterson wrote in his autobiography, *Marse Henry.*

Until 1936 the most vicious presidential campaign of recent years was that of 1928, when religious, social and moral prejudices were exploited to discredit Governor Alfred E. Smith of New York, Democratic candidate. It was rumored that, after his election, the pope would be invited to move his headquarters to the United States. Both Mr. and Mrs. Smith were described as uncouth, illiterate and socially philistine.

In addition to the whispers regarding the physical and mental health of President Roosevelt, the 1936 campaign evoked the rumor that he actually was a Jew named Rosenfeldt and that a majority of his close advisers were Jewish. Both the president and Secretary of Labor Perkins publicly denied that they were Jewish or foreign-born but stated that they would have been proud to admit it if it had been true. Other fakes of the campaign included:

A story was printed prominently by the Chicago *Daily Tribune,* that American Communists had been instructed by Moscow to vote for Mr. Roosevelt. The Chicago *Times* discovered that the quotations used in the alleged order were taken from a speech by Earl Browder, Communist candidate for president, in which he predicted most of the members would vote for Mr. Roosevelt instead of for himself. The *Times* offered $5,000 for proof to the contrary, and the challenge was not taken.

Members of the Republican National Committee hired a farmer and six cows to promenade on a sidewalk built by Works Progress Administration workers in Arcadia, Missouri, to make it appear federal money had been spent to construct a footpath for cattle.

The false allegation was made that 500 pies and 800 loaves of bread, ordered for workers on the tide-harnessing project in Passamaquoddy Bay, Maine (which ended when Congress declined to extend its appropriation), were being sold to pig raisers for fodder.

The story was sent to numerous newspapers over different signatures, that a farmer who never made more than $400 a year raising hogs was receiving $1,000 from the Agricultural Adjustment Administration for not raising them.

The charge was made by Senator H. Styles Bridges (Republican, New Hampshire) that the Tennessee Valley Authority paid $2,500 for a jackass and $2,080 as traveling expenses for a group of experts to find a perfect "jackass." It was revealed that the senator had misunderstood the purchase of a mechanical jack used for lifting purposes at Norris Dam, and that the only animal purchased by the authority had been bought for $290 and sold for $350. Nevertheless, others continued to spread the story.

A telegram supporting the Democratic primary candidacy of Representative Thomas L. Blanton (Democrat, Texas) was faked as having come from James A. Farley, chairman of the Democratic National Committee. Mr. Blanton said it was an attempt to make it appear he had forged Mr. Farley's signature.

The attempt was made to show that the Resettlement Administration had faked pictures of drought conditions in North Dakota. Investigation revealed that a picture distributing syndicate had put misleading outlines on pictures showing a rotting steer's skull on a stretch of parched alkali ground and, ten feet away, upon a patch with scrubby underbrush. The Fargo *Forum,* which first cried "fake," retracted its charge as to a view of cattle grazing near the state capitol at Bismarck. Actually, the capitol is on the outskirts of the city, and the cows were being driven by on the way to a waterhole. It was charged that the New Deal agency had attempted to create the impression the animals were driven, through starvation, to seek the last remaining grass in the state in the capitol grounds.

Most of the political fakes just described are "roorbacks"—"fictitious reports circulated for political purposes." The word entered the language following one of the first important attempts to discredit a candidate through deliberate falsehood. August 21, 1844, there appeared in the Ithaca (N. Y.) *Journal* a letter from a reader containing what purported to be a quotation from a book, *Roorback's Tour Through the Western and Southern States in 1836.* It contained the startling and unpopular revelation that the English traveler had discovered forty-three abject

THE ALLEGED PERAMBULATING SKULL

When sent out by the Resettlement Administration in 1936, the top picture was captioned, "Dry and parched earth in the Bad Lands of South Dakota," and the lower one, "Over-grazed land, Pennington County, S. D." Republicans charged that the New Deal used the skull shown as a "moving prop" in the attempt to indicate South Dakotan cattle had died during the drought.

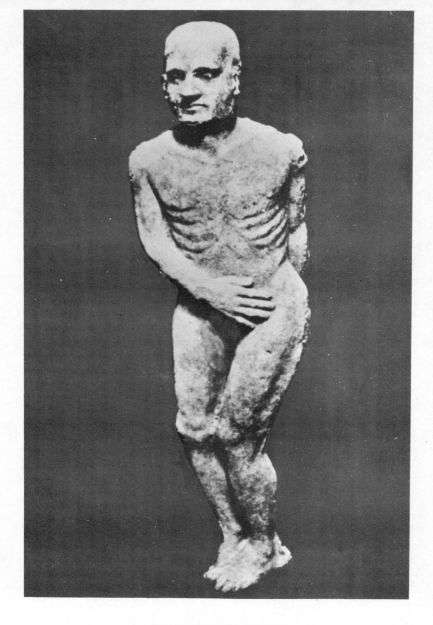

THE CARDIFF GIANT

This creation in gypsum was considered both as a petrified man and as a statue until proved to be a modern fake. Then it became a carnival attraction.

slaves branded with the initials of James K. Polk, candidate for the presidency against Henry Clay. After being reprinted widely by Whig newspapers, the quotation was proved by the New York *Evening Post* to be an interpolation of an extract from a real book of travel, *Excursion Through the Slave States,* by a British writer, George William Featherstonhaugh. There was no reference in that creditable work to Polk.

Exceeding even the predilection of political partisans to believe the best about their standard-bearers and the worst about their opponents is the zeal with which religious fanatics grasp at any supposedly factual straw to support their beliefs. When one identifies himself with an institution or cause, its gain or loss is his also. What tends to confirm his convictions is accepted as true; what tends to discredit his prejudices is rejected as untrue.

An amusing example was that related by Hector Charlesworth in his *Candid Chronicles* of the evangelist who attended the World's Fundamentalist Conference in Toronto and became a victim of one of Charles Langdon Clarke's jokes. To consume time Clarke was given to inventing news items based on biblical stories for the Jerusalem *Times,* the Babylon *Gazette* and similar fictitious organs of public information. After attending one lecture by the religious leader, in his capacity of reporter for the Toronto *Mail and Empire,* Clarke concocted the story of the discovery in the Holy Land by two scientists, Dr. Schmierkase and Dr. Butterbrod, of the remains of a whale with a sort of muscle arrangement working a trapdoor which gave access to its stomach. This dispatch, presumably offering support to the story of Jonah's having been swallowed by a big fish, was sent to the evangelist, who delightedly mentioned it in his next sermon. After a rival newspaper seriously reviewed the speech, the *Mail and Empire* exposed the hoax and translated the scientists' names as meaning Dr. Cheese and Dr. Bread and Butter.

Much desired by Christian scholars and laymen alike is proof, other than that contained in the New Testament itself, of the historical actuality of Jesus Christ. In addition to the valid evidence that has been discovered, there have been numerous attempts to supply the lack which scholars have believed it to their benefit to expose as false. Among the most important are the Archko Volume, also known as Pilate's Letter, and the Benan Letter.

The first, debunked by Dr. Edgar J. Goodspeed, of the University of Chicago, in his *Strange New Gospels,* was perhaps first published in 1879 at Boonville, Missouri, by the Reverend W. D. Mahan, a Cumberland

Presbyterian minister. Still going the rounds, it consists of an allegedly official report on the trial and death of Jesus made directly to the Emperor Tiberius by Pontius Pilate. Also included are accounts of Jesus' ministry as observed at first hand by Pilate and of a meeting of the two shortly before the arrest and trial.

The Reverend Mr. Mahan's story was that he had learned of the existence of the report in the Vatican through a visiting German scholar, Henry C. Whydaman, who in 1856, snowbound, spent several days at the Mahan home in De Witt, Missouri. Through a Father Peter Freelinhusen, chief guardian of the Vatican, Mahan obtained a copy of the Latin text for $62.42 and a certificate of its genuineness. In 1884 Mahan published *The Archaeological and the Historical Writings of the Sanhedrin and Talmuds of the Jews, translated from the Ancient Parchments and Scrolls at Constantinople and the Vatican at Rome,* in which he amplified the original story. In the introduction he claimed to have made a trip to Rome, where he saw the original of the Pilate report and also other documents giving hitherto unknown incidents in the life of Jesus.

The Pilate Letter has been republished many times, first in 1880 by the Reverend George Sluter of Shelbyville, Indiana, together with almost one hundred pages of introduction and notes under the title *The Acta Pilati.* Later in the same year William Overton Clough published it in Indianapolis as *Gesta Pilati.* When Mahan's second work appeared, it was reprinted in St. Louis in 1887; in Dalton, Georgia, in 1895; in Philadelphia in 1896; in Topeka, Kansas, as *The Archko Library,* in 1904; in Philadelphia again in 1905 as *The Archko Volume*; a third time in Philadelphia in 1913; in Chicago in 1923; several times in Grand Rapids, Michigan, the last time in 1929; in Oregon and in Washington. It also was translated and printed in Germany and other European countries. Recently it appeared as *Letter of Pontius Pilate to Caesar,* published by the Free Tract Society of Los Angeles. During the summer and autumn of 1926 it was read over the radio during Sunday evening programs from Davenport, Iowa, and the bulk of it was printed in *American Weekly Magazine,* December 4, 1927. Original printings have been sold for $50 as rarities.

Dr. Goodspeed revealed that there never was a Father Peter Freelinhusen connected in any way with the Vatican Library. Nor is there any record of a German scholar, Henry C. Whydaman. No such letter ever was found in the Vatican or anywhere else.

To supply additional facts concerning the boyhood of Jesus the spurious *Benan Letter* was published in 1910 in Berlin under the editorship of

Ernst, Edler von der Planitz. It supposedly had been discovered in 1860 in the Coptic original text, based on a lost Greek original, by Freiherr von Rabenau, a scholar and universal historian who died in 1879 at Munich. Planitz, a friend, said he obtained possession of the manuscript which Rabenau had recovered from the ruins of the village of Mit Rahinê, south of Cairo.

Benan, the author of the epistle, is identified as a writer of the first century supposedly converted by Jesus to the Hebrew God. The recipient of the letter was supposed to be Strato, a rhetorician and formerly private secretary of Emperor Tiberius. The letter is dated A.D. 83, after the eruption of Vesuvius brought Benan and Strato together as fellow victims.

The letter begins with the discovery of the Christ child by Putiphra, an astronomer at the observatory of Anu-Heliopolis, who had been sent by the high priest of the temple to observe the star Sinus in the land of the Hebrews. Putiphra obtained the permission of Mary and Joseph to take the babe back to Egypt where he was instructed in philosophy and religion by Ranebchru and Pinehas, high priests of the Jewish Onias Temple, until he was twelve years old when he returned for a visit to his parents and astounded the best Hebrew scholars in the temple at Jerusalem.

Before beginning his missionary work, the letter continued, Jesus practiced medicine and obtained a reputation for his cures. At the age of twenty-six he was visited by Philo of Alexandria, and later he had a romantic courtship with Asartis, daughter of a rich grain dealer. Shortly before his thirtieth birthday he returned to Palestine. At the end of three years Benan was sent to learn what had happened to him. Dramatically Benan reached Jerusalem on the day of the crucifixion and was present at the sepulcher Easter Sunday to observe the risen Christ.

Exposé of *The Benan Letter* is accredited to Dr. Carl Schmidt, professor of church history at the University of Berlin, and Dr. Herman Grapow, Egyptologist. They showed that no such historian as Rabenau ever lived, and that virtually all the names, dates and lore of the story were borrowed from works of J. F. Lauth, a Munich professor who died in 1895.

Scientific proof with which to refute skeptics regarding the virgin birth of Jesus also long has been a desideratum of religionists. In the seventeenth century it was contained in a letter humbly addressed to the British Royal Society. Titled "Lucina sine Concubitu," the report related the results of an experiment which proved "by most incontestable Evidence, drawn from Reason and Practice, that a woman may conceive, and be brought to Bed, without any Commerce with Man."

Written in plain but scientific language, the curiosity is to be found today in the first volume of *Fugitive Pieces on Various Subjects,* signed by Abraham Johnson but believed to have been the work of Sir John Hill, who described himself as "a physick and male midwife."

By means of "a wonderful, cylindrical, catoptrical, rotundo-concavo-convex machine," the author asserted, he captured from the air "floating animalcula" which under a microscope proved to be minute men and women. These embryos, it was contended, were intended to be breathed in by women and needed only a warm shelter to develop into babies.

The discovery, it was predicted, would clear the reputations of many ladies, abolish matrimony (long a nuisance), end venereal disease and possibly coitus. The author suggested a royal edict preventing copulation for one year to permit further experimentation.

Dwarfing all other examples of religious wishful thinking, so fantastic as to be almost unbelievable but attested to by numerous reputable scholars, is the case of Leo Taxil and a group of followers who pretended to expose the "Satanic rites" of the Freemasons. For five years (1880 to 1885), through the Society of Freethinkers which he founded, Taxil openly attempted to fight popery. In 1881 at Montpellier he published *The Secret Amours of Pius IX.* Found guilty of libel and fined 65,000 francs, he appeared in court and obtained a quashing of the indictment. Among his other early books was *The Scandalous History of the Maid of Orleans.*

In 1885 Taxil's sobs astounded his followers as he proclaimed repentance and announced his intention of repairing the harm he had done. This was after the April 20, 1884, encyclical of Pope Leo XIII which divided the human race into "two diverse and adverse classes, the kingdom of God on earth—namely the true church of Jesus Christ—and the realm of Satan." The headquarters of the latter group was alleged to be the Masonic lodge.

The first book by Taxil after his "conversion" was a four-volume history of Freemasonry. It contained eyewitness verification of the Satanic rites of the Masons. In 1892 under the pseudonym of Dr. Karl Hacks, a collaborator of Taxil, a Dr. Bataille published *The Devil in the Nineteenth Century,* purporting to be the observations of a ship's surgeon. Really a burlesque of the encyclical, it was received seriously by the Catholic press, as had been Taxil's book.

The chief character of Hacks' creation was a Sophia Walder. A second mythical character was introduced by Taxil as a descendant of the Rosicrucian alchemist and Oxford professor, Thomas Vaughan. She, Diana Vaughan, was said to possess a copy of a written pact between Satan and her ancestor signed March 25, 1645. Having questioned the impeccability of Judas Iscariot, Diana was said to have been tortured by her associates. The inquisition was a clever travesty of the Roman Catholic ceremonial for expulsion of an evil spirit.

Dr. Michael Germanus in *Secrets of Hell* seriously accepted an anecdote supposedly growing out of the jealousy between Diana and Sophia. The former, according to the story invented by Taxil and accepted by Germanus and other defenders of the church, played a joke on the latter by dropping in her lemonade a few drops of Lourdes water which caused great pain. Relief was obtained only by vomiting fire. This Dr. Germanus accepted as proof that Sophia was "possessed." Dr. Germanus also considered highly interesting the signature of Bitrus (Satan).

Diana's salvation resulted from her admiration of Joan of Arc. One day she was attended by Asmodeus, Astaroth, Beelzebub and Moloch and invoked Joan. The devils immediately were stripped of their disguises and stood before her in their true characters as imps of hell, with horns, and emitting a terrible stench. After this Diana went to a cloister, paid penance and joined the church. Her memoirs caused a sensation. The pope himself sent congratulations after the publication of *Eucharistic Novena,* a prayer book by Diana containing forms of supplication against unbelief, worldly indifference and lukewarmness, hardness of heart, blasphemy and unchastity, etc.

E. P. Evans quotes Taxil as follows:

> Sometimes I fabricated the most incredible stories, as, for example, that of the serpent inditing prophecies with its tail on the back of Sophia Walder, or that of the demon who, in order to marry a Freemason, transformed himself into a young lady and played the piano evenings in the form of a crocodile. My colleagues were aghast and exclaimed, "You'll spoil the whole joke with your nonsense." "Bah," I replied, "let me be and you will see."
> And they did see how eagerly such gross falsehoods were accepted as positive facts. Protestants without exception are denounced as apostates. Every Lutheran is a Lucifer in disguise.

The climax came with a conference called for April 19, 1897, at Paris at which Taxil promised to introduce the reformed Diana. Taxil took the

platform and confessed. After thanking the clergy for their aid in carrying out his scheme and attributing their cooperation chiefly to ignorance
and imbecility, he escaped amid much confusion.

A month later at Milan was published *Osservatore Cattolus* in which a
Catholic writer contended the Masons had held Taxil captive during the
conference and that the man who took the platform and made the startling announcement was an impostor. Another writer said that Diana
failed to appear because the Masons had bribed Taxil to place her in an
insane asylum.

One of many contenders for the title of "greatest hoax of all times"
was the Cardiff Giant whose story illustrates how, confronted with a mystery, exponents of particular theories are wont to explain it as a substantia-
tion of what they want to believe. The story of the "discovery of the
epoch" October 16, 1889, at Cardiff, New York, was as follows:

When neighbors employed by William C. Newell, a farmer, to dig a
well reached five feet below the surface of a hillside, they stopped thunder-
struck. There, unearthed, lay the figure of a giant, twelve feet long, four
feet broad and twenty-two inches thick. It was supine with the legs
slightly drawn upwards as if in agony.

Twenty-four hours later a tent had been erected and admission was
being charged to hundreds and thousands who reverently tiptoed to the
brink of the excavation, murmured, "Lot's wife," "The Scriptures are ful-
filled," or some similar expression of piety, and left. Four local doctors
examined the body and announced it to be a petrifaction, but Dr. John F.
Boynton of Syracuse, a physician with some antiquarian knowledge,
declared it was a statue three hundred years old, probably made by the
Jesuits known to have settled in the vicinity about that time.

The statue theory grew with proof that the figure was made of a sort
of gypsum. Because this rock was not indigenous to the region, Alexander
McWhorter, a resident graduate of Yale Divinity School, prepared an
article advancing the theory that the American Goliath was a Phoenician
idol of the "winged" or "cherubim" type. He described outlines of folded
wings of which "even the separate feathers are clearly distinguished."
Also he saw what none else did—a crescent-shaped wound on the left side,
and also an inscription.

A deputation of regents of the state university inspected the giant,
which was raised and exhibited in Syracuse. Dr. James Hall, the director
of the New York State Museum, "perhaps the most eminent American
paleontologist of that period," was baffled by it. Ralph Waldo Emerson

pronounced it beyond his depth, very wonderful and undoubtedly ancient. A whole evening was devoted by the Boston Thursday Evening Club to the giant, the president contending in a learned address that it must be modern because its features were Napoleonic.

Supporting the belief in the petrified man theory, an Onondaga squaw was said to have declared it was the body of a gigantic Indian prophet who, many centuries before, foretold the coming of the palefaces and prophesied just before his death that his descendants would see him again.

Some sense began to be introduced into the controversy with the arrival of Professor O. C. Marsh of Yale, eminent paleontologist, who also knew something of sculpture. He promptly said the giant was neither a human body nor a good piece of art—which Andrew D. White, of Cornell University, had been maintaining all along; but he was no hero in his own locality.

Professor Marsh was right. A Chicago stonecutter, Edward Salle, had made the giant from a block of gypsum sent to him from the vicinity of Fort Dodge, Iowa. The originator and chief profiteer was George Hull, formerly a Binghamton, New York, tobacconist and a relative of the farmer Newell. The hoax, which cost several thousand dollars, was partly a money-making scheme and partly, Hull admitted, an attempt to gull an evangelist, the Reverend Mr. Turk of Ackley, Iowa, to whom Hull had lost an argument on the existence of giants in biblical times.

After the giant was carved, a mallet with darning needles was used to create pores, and the figure was sponged with water and sand to make it appear water-worn. Erosion on the lower side for a time baffled investigators. A sulphuric acid bath further created the appearance of antiquity, but the absence of hair, recognized by Hull as a defect, was one of the first clues to its true nature.

From Chicago the giant was shipped to New York and buried, about a year before it was dug up, while Newell's family was away on a visit. Neighbors, however, remembered a wagon with a large box which arrived by express, and helped solve the mystery.

The fame of the giant attracted the attention of Phineas T. Barnum who tried in vain to purchase it. Then the great showman had an exact replica made which he exhibited as the original. When Hull reached New York on his tour he found that his potential customers already had been entertained at Wood's Museum by the giant's double.

Confusion exists to this day among some writers who do not distinguish between the original Cardiff Giant and Barnum's imitation. The writer has found several references to Barnum's giant, and in 1902 G.

Fabrico Sala, the sculptor who worked on the second figure, was interviewed and written up as though his creation had been the one and only phenomenon.

Cyrenus Cole wrote in *A History of the People of Iowa:*

From it all, Fort Dodge gypsum gained renown and in 1871 the first mill for its utilization on a commercial basis was built, the beginning of one of the state's important mineral industries.

Benjamin F. Gue, in his *History of Iowa,* agreed with this opinion. Since 1948 the giant has been on exhibit in the Farmers' Museum of the New York State Historical Association at Cooperstown, New York.

That the potential hoaxer's task is made easy by the predisposition of his intended victims to give credence to whatever fortifies them in their beliefs concerning a cherished cause has been the burden of this chapter's argument. As Hilaire Belloc asked in the *New Statesman* for October 8, 1921:

Have you noticed how men, eager to call "a forgery" any false document supporting an historical view they disapprove, will eagerly swallow whatever flatters their own errors?

CHAPTER VIII

Incentives to Believe: Chauvinism

NEWCASTLE and Portsmouth, New Hampshire, believe that the "shot heard round the world" was fired in their vicinity rather than at either Lexington or Concord.

Bardstown, Kentucky, insists that Stephen Foster received the inspiration for and probably composed "My Old Kentucky Home" there, and that the art treasures in its St. Joseph's Proto-Cathedral were the gifts of King Louis Philippe of France.

Sanford, Maine, is certain Louis Philippe, while king, stopped at a tavern there in 1797 on a trip from Portsmouth, New Hampshire, to Portland, Maine.

Few North Carolinians question that the great Marshal Michel Ney of France is buried near Cleveland, North Carolina.

Fredericksburg Virginians know the exact spot where the youthful George Washington chopped down a cherry tree.

Hogansburg, New York, is convinced a ramshackle cabin there once was the residence of Louis XVII, lost dauphin of France.

Madison County, New York, is proud of the "fact" that Charles X of France was an incognito exile there early in the nineteenth century.

Frederick, Maryland, has made a shrine of a house in West Patrick Street where ninety-five-year-old Barbara Fritchie, according to John Greenleaf Whittier, refused to take down the Stars and Stripes to please "Stonewall" Jackson's men.

Philadelphians and, in fact, thousands of other Americans pay homage to Betsy Ross in the Arch Street house where she presumably made the first American flag.

Because historical evidence to the contrary often is inconclusive, some, possibly all, of this local pride may be justified. Significant, in connection with the subject of interest in this book, however, is not the validity or falsity of any of these bids for distinction, but the indubitable fact that a majority of the champions in every case are home-grown. Foreign skepticism and incredulity may reach avalanche proportions and may be buttressed by seemingly incontrovertible authority; nevertheless, faith in the indigenous scholarship remains unswerving.

How this ubiquitous chauvinism may be utilized effectively by the historical hoaxer is obvious. Exalt "my own, my native land" and you exalt every individual who associates himself with it. Political demagogues know this, chambers of commerce know it, travel bureaus know it, and they who do the exalting come to be called blessed. The seriousness of the results when hoaxers also take advantage of it will be detailed in Chapter XII. It is this chapter's purpose to prove the power of wishful thinking in distorting judgment in historical research and thus to offer further explanation as to why we believe the untrue.

First, let us consider the cases already mentioned.

"The town of Newcastle will be pleased to have you visit and see the exact spot at Fort Constitution, formerly Fort William and Mary, where the first shot of the Revolution was fired on Dec. 14, 1774," the selectmen of Newcastle wrote Representative Sol Bloom, chairman of the Constitution Sesquicentennial Commission, in 1936.

It may well be, as many reputable historians have contended, that the embattled farmers who, four months later, resisted the redcoats on their march from Boston to Lexington and Concord, were not the first to take pot shots at the enemy. The offer regarding the "exact spot," however, is going a little too far after thousands of tourists have made their pilgrimage to the Minuteman monument at Concord. Until a Ralph Waldo Emerson or Henry Wadsworth Longfellow elects to compose a jingle commemorating the incident dear to the hearts of Newcastleonians, however, children's history books will continue to quote from the "Hymn" and "Paul Revere's Ride" to teach the "facts" regarding the origins of the colonists' fight for freedom.

Although Kentucky senators and other dignitaries have delivered eulogies at Federal Hill, one-time home of Judge John Rowan, relatives and biographers of Stephen Collins Foster deny that he could have written the state's song there because there are no records that he visited Rowan, a cousin, within several years of its composition in 1852. Furthermore, since the song's original title was "Poor Uncle Tom, Good Night," it is doubted even that the old house was its inspiration. Nevertheless, Kentuckians have contributed $65,000 to restore Federal Hill as a national shrine and museum.

To further set the Stephen Foster legend straight, his niece furnished proof to the operators of Greenfield Village, Henry Ford's historical museum at Dearborn, Michigan, that the "little white house with green shutters" exhibited there as that in which her uncle was born, was built in Pittsburgh years after his birth. The real birthplace, records show, was torn down. Nevertheless, when Alfred M. Landon, Republican presidential candidate, visited the museum in 1936, the dwelling was pointed out to him as the authentic home of the composer of the campaign song, "Oh! Susanna," as it has been to thousands of other visitors.

The only evidence to support the belief that the nine paintings, resembling old masterpieces in Bardstown's St. Joseph's Roman Catholic Proto-Cathedral were presented Father Benedict Joseph Flaget by the citizen king of France is a bill, introduced in Congress in 1824 and 1832, to exempt the bishop from paying duties on "certain paintings and church furniture presented by the then Duke of Orleans, now King of the French, to the Bishop of Bairdstown." Presumably, the gift was in gratitude either for the care extended to the duke by the bishop during the former's one-day illness from colic in the small Kentucky town, or for having helped raise money to assist his return to France in 1800.

Although for more than a century many art critics, historians and others had expressed doubt of the pictures' authenticity, it was not until 1953 that there was an airing in court of expert opinion and scientific evidence. Nov. 12, 1952 all nine paintings were cut from their frames and stolen. In April, 1953 Federal Bureau of Investigation agents had recovered four of them in New York and the other five in Chicago. In U. S. District Court in the latter city a former assistant U. S. attorney, Norton L. Kretske, was convicted of the theft and sentenced to six years in prison. During the trial it was established that the supposed Rubens actually was a lost work by the 17th century Italian painter, Marria Preto, worth over $5,000, but that the other paintings were *not* by prominent artists such as Van Dyck, Van Eyck and Murillo, and had slight value. If authentic the collection would have been worth $675,000, as authorities of the Chicago Art Institute testified.

In *Trending into Maine,* Kenneth Roberts pointed out the impossibility of the claim to fame of Sanford, Maine. He showed that, contrary to the bronze tablet which reads, "Site of Tavern at which in 1797 Louis Philippe, King of France, Accompanied by His Two Brothers, the Duke of Montpensier and Count de Beaujolais, and Tallerand, Afterwards the Noted French Diplomatist, Stopped on Their Way From Portsmouth, N. H., to Portland, Me.," Talleyrand did not spell his name Tallerand and was not in America in 1797, having sailed in November, 1795, and Louis Philippe did not become King of France until 1830.

Because he deserted with his army to Napoleon Bonaparte, whom he had been sent by Louis XVIII to bring back to Paris in an iron cage after the escape from Elba, Marshal Michel Ney, called by the Little Corporal "the bravest of the brave," was killed December 7, 1815, in Luxembourg Gardens, according to orthodox historians. Because they were his former comrades, the members of the firing squad allowed the marshal to escape to America where he became a schoolteacher under the name of Peter Stewart Ney, according to North Carolina patriots.

The American Ney, who confessed his identity on his deathbed, according to the stories about him, arrived at Charleston, South Carolina, in January, 1816. After being recognized by some French refugees at Georgetown, he moved to Brownsville and, in 1830, settled in Iredell County, North Carolina. In the library of near-by Davidson College he read recent French history books in which he corrected statements regarding Marshal Ney and Napoleon. Upon hearing of the emperor's death at St. Helena, he fainted.

In 1887 the grave in the Third Creek Presbyterian Church Cemetery near Cleveland, North Carolina, was opened but presumably without sufficient proof being obtained. Over the grave in Paris' Père-Lachaise Cemetery, where the executed Ney supposedly is buried, now stands a three-tiered monument to his memory.

With white-haired seventy-year-old George Steptoe Washington, a family descendant, present, February 22, 1935, a group of Virginians planted another cherry tree on "the exact spot" where the father of his country hacked down "the" cherry tree. No longer generally taught in the schools, the anecdote of George Washington's adolescent honesty has been debunked thoroughly in recent years. Nevertheless, for more than a century after it first appeared in 1806 in the fifth edition of the *Life of George Washington* by Parson Mason Locke Weems, it was a tremendous influence because of its effect upon little boys and girls whose fathers and mothers and teachers wanted them to grow up to be good.

Origin of the cherry-tree myth has been traced to a story by Dr. James

Beattie, *The Minstrel,* published in London in 1799, which Weems plagiarized. The same book also contained the anecdote of cabbage seeds which grew up to form a person's name, another credited by Weems to Washington.

The effect upon a biographer of the popular disposition to accept a fake or two about a national hero is emphasized by Albert Bushnell Hart, who wrote in the *American Historical Review* for January, 1910, as follows:

Weems lived in a period when it was thought a moral duty to look upon the patriots of the Revolution and the fathers of the Constitution as demigods; it did not expect its historians to search for elaborate details and infinitesimal finish of statement. They wanted a good round mouthful of biography just as they wanted a boiling hot sermon on perdition.

Lawrence C. Wroth, biographer of Weems, points out that the generation in which the parson wrote was a sterile period in the production of books for young people or for the less cultured of their elders. The *Encyclopædia Britannica* explains the success of Weems' book as due in large part to the scanty knowledge regarding the life of Washington.

The tree planted in 1935 on the Ferry Farm near Fredericksburg was the gift of Traverse City, Michigan. The following year two hundred Japanese cherry trees, a gift from the Japanese government, were planted along with two hundred fruit-bearing cherry trees which were a gift from the states of Ohio, Pennsylvania, New York, Michigan and Wisconsin, each state giving forty trees. At the same time Walter Johnson, one-time star baseball pitcher of the Washington American League baseball club, the Senators, threw a silver dollar across the Rappahannock River from a spot where George Washington was said to have thrown a Spanish dollar across the river.

At one time there were twenty-seven pretenders saying they were Louis XVII, son of Louis XVI and Marie Antoinette, who died of scrofula because of harsh treatment by his jailers according to an official record at the time. Not the least entrancing of the many lost-dauphin legends was that related by a part-Indian missionary, Eleazar Williams, in the February, 1853, issue of *Putnam's Monthly.* Eleven years earlier, Williams confessed, he was visited, near what is now Green Bay, Wisconsin, by the Prince de Joinville, son of Louis Philippe, then king, and told that he was the dauphin who had been rescued by friends who substituted the dead body of another child to deceive the French Revolutionary guards. The prince's visit was to persuade Williams, until then unaware of his identity, to sign a statement of abdication.

The story supplied material for a best-selling novel, *Lazarre,* by Mary Hartwell Catherwood, but historians never have given any credence to it. Williams' Indian father died without making any statement regarding his son's supposed paternity; his mother and other relatives refused to substantiate the story, and it was extremely unlikely that Louis Philippe would have invited more trouble than he already had. The Prince de Joinville denied the yarn. Nevertheless, the Hogansburg shack became a landmark, and the Daughters of the American Revolution of Green Bay, Wisconsin, also have marked with a plaque Williams' supposed house there.

Not far from Hogansburg, in Madison County, New York, the Mystery of Muller Hill is a perennial source of material for newspaper feature writers. It pertains to the arrival, about 1800, of a French stranger who, in the name of L. A. Muller, lived a secluded existence there until 1814, after the Battle of Waterloo, when he departed and did not return until ten years later. Historians who have taken the trouble to investigate think the exile might have been some minor figure such as the Comte d'Artois, the Duc d'Angoulême or General Charles Dumouriez, but local legend insists that it was Charles X himself. "Madison County holds fast to the pleasant belief that it once sheltered a king and defies historians to prove otherwise," F. Reed Alvord of Hamilton, New York, wrote in *Letters* for October 26, 1936.

John Greenleaf Whittier himself declared that he exercised considerable poetic license when he wrote his patriotic poem about "yon gray head" which appeared at a Frederick Town window to snatch Old Glory before it reached the ground. Because Dame Fritchie was in ill health at the time, dying three months later, because the main body of Jackson's troops did not pass within two blocks of her home and because the general left his troops to visit a friend in another part of the city, Whittier's story is doubted on its own merits. In addition, there is the version of Mrs. Mary A. Quantrill who was thirty-two years old at the time. The wife of a Washington compositor, she stood at her front gate with her daughter, who was waving a Union flag, the day the Confederates marched into Frederick. Once a lieutenant cut the flag from the child's hand; but she picked it up and began waving it again. Someone reminded the soldiers that General Jackson had ordered that the civilians should not be molested, and so the column marched on. One officer saluted Mrs. Quantrill, explaining, "To you, madam; not your flag." Until recently, keepers of Barbara Fritchie House and Museum admitted exact details "have been obscured in such a fog of controversy that they will probably never be certainly known." Although admitting Whittier did not verify the details, they said of his poem: "in the spirit we know it to be true."

Regarding the demand in January, 1939, by the New Jersey department of the Veterans of Foreign Wars that Congress investigate both whether Betsy Ross actually made the first Stars and Stripes and whether she lived at 328 Arch Street, Philadelphia, the Philadelphia *Record,* January 10, 1939, said: "The opinion of most of the persons who have interested themselves in the dispute (and probably of the majority of Philadelphians) is that the Betsy Ross story is, like the Santa Claus story, believed in for its spirit, just as many other intrenched—and demonstrably wrong —patriotic legends are believed in. In other words, if research shows some of the facts to be wrong—so what?" Nevertheless, the V.F.W., led by Theodore D. Gottlieb, Newark attorney, is very serious about the matter as have been scores of others, both iconoclasts and faithful, including numerous first-rate historians.

Local patriotic pride is seen strongly in the reception by natives of Minnesota and North Carolina respectively of the genuineness of the Kensington Stone and the Mecklenburg Declaration of Independence. The historical and legislative bodies of those states stand virtually alone in accepting as authentic what other, impartial experts apparently have proved to be spurious.

The history of the pre-Columbian exploration of the North American continent by the Norsemen would have to be entirely rewritten if the Kensington Stone, a slab of soft calcite found in 1898 near Kensington, Minnesota, were accepted as genuine. It would show that as early as 1362 white men penetrated that far inland and left a record in runic characters for posterity of their visit.

Unfortunately for those who intended the discovery to be taken seriously, only one investigator, Hjalmar R. Holand of Ephraim, Wisconsin, has made any effort to establish the Kensington rune-stone as an authentic fourteenth century invention. Mr. Holand's insistent writings on the subject for nearly twenty-five years, however, have forced other scholars to devote more attention to the matter than they feel it merits. Undaunted by the verdicts of authorities in runic characters, both in America and in Europe, Holand persisted for half a century in lecturing and writing about the stone. In 1932, after a quantity of magazine articles, he published his conclusions in book form, *The Kensington Stone: A Study in Pre-Columbian American History,* privately printed at Ephraim, Wisconsin. This converted several former skeptics, including Professor Sigurdus Nordal, University of Iceland scholar, but others, especially the philologists, remained adamant in disbelief. In 1940 Holand published *Westward from Vinland* in which he attempted to answer his critics.

Leaders in the attempt to refute Mr. Holand's claims have been professor George T. Flom, of the University of Illinois, and Professors Rasmus Anderson and Julius Olson, of the University of Wisconsin. The museum committee of the Minnesota Historical Society in 1911 reported in favor of the genuineness of the stone.

The controversy between these scholars began more than ten years after the digging up of the stone by Olof Ohman and his small son, Edward, on Ohman's farm. When Professor George O. Curme, of Northwestern University, to whom the stone was sent, declared it a forgery, the discoverer used it as a doorstep for his granary. There it was found by Holand, who purchased an interest in it and began advertising it.

The inscription, translated, reads:

Eight Goths and twenty-two Norwegians upon an exploring journey from Vinland very far west. We had camp by two skerries, one day's journey north from this stone. We were fishing one day, when we returned home we found ten men red with blood and dead. A.V.M. [Ave Virgon Marie] save us from the evil. [We] have ten men by the sea to look after our vessel forty-one [or fourteen] days journey from this island. Year 1362.

Holand took the stone to Europe where he also attempted to trace a similar find, alleged to have been made in 1738 by Chevalier de la Verendrye and given to Jesuit scholars at Quebec before being sent to France. Holand's trip was a great disappointment, for not only could he find no scholars to agree with him as to the stone's genuineness, but his search of museums and of documents for the alleged other stone was futile.

Nevertheless, Holand pieced together a story based on an incomplete 1348 record of an expedition which left Norway and did not return until 1364 and of another small vessel which entered the harbor of Straumfjord, Iceland, in 1347. He answered all objections regarding the probability of the Norse expedition, but historians consider him badly defeated when it comes to a scholarly consideration of the runic characters themselves.

Professor Flom in his report to the Illinois State Historical Society proved countless anachronisms in the dialect alleged to be fourteenth century. Both he and Professor Anderson mentioned Andrew Anderson, brother-in-law of Ohman, and a Reverend Svend Fogelblad, who were known to have produced rune stones for pleasure, as possible originators of the hoax. Professor Anderson reported a meeting with Andrew Anderson which, he said, left no doubt in his mind of that person's guilty knowledge. In 1954 the Smithsonian Institution published the adverse opinion of Johannes Brondsted of the Danish National Museum.

Thomas Jefferson was a plagiarist when he composed the Declaration of Independence if five resolutions written from memory in 1800 actually were adopted May 20, 1775, by citizens of Charlotte, Mecklenburg County, North Carolina.

The Mecklenburg Declaration was first published April 30, 1819, in the Raleigh *Register,* and in 1830 Jefferson issued a trenchant denial of its authenticity. John M. Alexander, recording clerk at the alleged convention, wrote the resolutions from memory in 1800, and many others came forward to say they had been in attendance when they were adopted. No original of the resolutions, however, ever was found. It was said to have been sent to England by Governor Josiah Martin. James K. Polk, when president, ordered Ambassador George Bancroft to make a search for it because he (Polk) believed an ancestor of his, Colonel Thomas Polk, military commandant, to have been among the signers. Both Bancroft and an earlier ambassador, Andrew Stevenson, were unable to find the document.

Leaving for the historians the dispute of whether there actually was a Mecklenburg Declaration of Independence, it is certain that one attempt to prove its existence was a fake. This was the facsimile of the first page of a newspaper, the *Cape-Fear Mercury,* for June 3, 1775, published, with an article by S. Millington Miller, in *Collier's* of July 1, 1905. On the first page of the newspaper is a complete set of the resolutions.

A. S. Salley, Jr., secretary of the Historical Commission of South Carolina, and Dr. Worthington Chauncey Ford, chief of the Division of Manuscripts of the Library of Congress, exposed the spuriousness of the *Cape-Fear Mercury* in the *American Historical Review* for April, 1906. Among other things they showed that June 3, 1775, was not a Friday, as indicated in the paper, that the numbering of the edition was wrong, that the type was not the same as that on known genuine copies of the *Mercury* and that the paper suspended publication before June, 1775.

The copy from which the facsimile was made was supposed to be the one which Governor Martin sent to London in 1775 but which was removed by Ambassador Stevenson August 15, 1837, from the British Foreign Office. An allusion to the *Resolves of the Committee of Mecklenburg* is made in a letter supposedly from Martin to the Earl of Dartmouth, British secretary of state for the American department. Martin refers the Earl to the newspaper for knowledge of the resolutions but does not explain their contents. Evidently Ambassador Stevenson never made a report to Washington, if it was really he who removed the copy.

Upon the great seal of the state of North Carolina today is emblazoned the date of the Mecklenburg Declaration. By legislative action May 20 is a holiday; the declaration is engrafted upon the statute books of the state.

Outstanding in English literary history, so good that they are still given to college students to read, are the poems of Ossian, the success of which is attributed by Henry Hewlett to their author's having turned to account the national enthusiasm of 1762, and by Dr. Samuel Johnson, no admirer of the Scotch, to the intense patriotism of the Highlanders. Of the Ossianic and other Highland ballads, the great lexicographer said:

A Scotchman must be a very sturdy moralist who does not love Scotland better than truth; he will always love it better than inquiry, and if falsehood flatters his vanity, he will not be very diligent to detect it.

In like vein, Joseph Ritson, authority on Scotch literature, declared: "The history of Scottish poetry exhibits a series of fraud, forgery and imposture, practiced with impunity and success."

The author òf the Ossianic poems was James Macpherson (1736–1796) with the possible assistance of Lachlan and Evan Macpherson. Upon repeated urgings of friends to settle the matter, Dr. Johnson, who is said to have carried an oak cudgel to protect himself against possible attack by Macpherson, finally made a trip to the Hebrides. Upon his return he reported that no such stories existed among the native legends; and a similar report was made in 1805 by a committee of inquiry appointed by the Highland Society.

Fragments of Ancient Poetry, Collected in the Highlands of Scotland, and Translated from the Galic or Erse Language appeared in 1760 and was received enthusiastically by Dr. Hugh Blair, leading critic, who published several books in defense of the genuineness of this and later publications in the Ossianic series. *Fingal* and *Temora* followed, but the only original ever exhibited was part of the last named.

No other scholar in search of Gaelic folklore ever came across anything resembling the Ossianic tradition. After the death in 1767 of Lachlan Macpherson, who accompanied James on his two trips to the Highlands, there was found in his repositories, a Gaelic copy of the seventh book of *Temora* in his own handwriting, with the notation, "First rude draft of the seventh book of *Temora.*" Scholars also have pointed out that the author was not well grounded in Gaelic speech, history and archaeology.

In his will Macpherson left five hundred pounds for a monument to himself which stands at Bellville, Kingussie, today. His request to be buried in Westminster Abbey also was granted. Coleridge wrote two poems said to be in imitation of Ossian, and Byron's "Hours of Idleness" also shows the Ossianic influence. Napoleon Bonaparte was an avid reader of the poems.

Wenceslaus Hanka, Bohemian philologist, fabricated another collection of manuscripts, of whose influence for more than a century Dr. Joseph Chador in *The Czech National Revival* said: "They were one of the great motivating forces of Czech nationalism . . . created much excitement at home and abroad, imbued the Czechs with a greater feeling of nationalism and for a time at least served as models in the evolution of a new type of literature."

These documents, allegedly found by Hanka in 1817 and 1818 in an old church tower, presumably were of the thirteenth and fourteenth centuries. They came opportunely at a time when Bohemian scholars were attempting to re-create the old Czech culture and rebuild the national language, as they seemed to prove the existence of a high degree of Bohemian civilization as early as the ninth century.

After Hanka's death rough drafts of some of the poems in his handwriting were found in his library, and chemicals he had used to give his "discoveries" the appearance of age; but controversy continued as to whether the truth should be acknowledged, or, for the sake of the glory of Bohemia, be denied and concealed. Thomas Masaryk, teacher at the University of Prague, who later became the founder and first president of Czechoslovakia, failed to obtain a full professorship because he insisted on the truth and published iconoclastic articles in the *Athenaeum,* literary periodical of which he was editor.

It was purely a patriotic impulse which prompted two public-spirited citizens of Florence to raise 10,000 francs to purchase a bust of Savonarola, believed to be of the fifteenth century, to prevent its loss to the city. According to Dupra, critic, the bust equaled Michelangelo in force and Robbia in exquisiteness of treatment and might have been the work of either.

Photographs were made of this new discovery. A noted painter, Sir Frederick Leighton, obtained one and placed it at the head of his bed "like a sacred image." It is said that for a while Grand Duchess Marie of Russia considered constructing a temple to house it alone.

When asked abruptly one day if he were the real author, Bastianini, a Florentine sculptor, without hesitation admitted that he was. The same frankness revealed that a bust of Benevieni, sixteenth century Florentine poet, sold to the Louvre by an art dealer for 13,000 francs, was not a genuine antique. Bastianini began his career as an imitator of antiques in the shop of an antiquarian named Freppa; faking became his life work.

The tendency of scholars to divide along nationalistic lines in defense or adverse criticism of a scientific find was demonstrated when a human jaw was discovered March 28, 1863, in a gravel pit near Abbeville, France, a famous Lower Paleolithic site. The finder was Boucher de Perthes, a Frenchman, first discoverer of flint implements. Although French scientists declared this find, known as the Moulin Quignon jaw, to be genuine, the view that it was false has prevailed among the English. Sir Arthur Keith and Earnest Albert Hooton are exceptions among Anglo-Saxons in showing sympathy toward the discovery, which, if real, would upset theories as to the antiquity of man in western Europe.

Reasons for considering the Moulin Quignon jaw as a plant: the workmen at the site previously had fooled Boucher de Perthes with some forged implements; it was discovered just eight days after a reward had been offered for osseous remains; it resembled a skeleton found fifteen miles away by a laborer known to be acquainted with the Abbeville workmen; its excellent state of preservation is not to be expected of a bone that old, and a trace of reddish sand was detected inside, whereas the gravel in which it was found was black.

Figures to show the great odds against which the Confederates contended during the Civil War have appeared from time to time as authentic works of Cazeone G. Lee, posing as an historian, D. I. Woods, clerk in the War Department at Washington, and others, and are pleasing to

Southerners who still are bitter about the conflict's outcome. Some of them were exposed by Major Thomas L. Livermore in *Numbers and Losses in the Civil War* (1901) and by F. C. Ainsworth, adjutant general of the army, in 1912.

According to Lee there were 600,000 men in the Southern army and 2,700,000 in the Union army. Official figures, according to W. J. Ghent in the *Independent* for September 11, 1913, show 2,898,304 Northern enlistments; but, he adds, "at no time did the Union have a million men on its rolls, and not more than two-thirds of the total were at any time available for service at the front."

The statistics of Woods, whom Ghent declares to be a fictitious authority, give, in a total of 2,278,588 who fought for the North, only 118,000 who were above twenty-one years of age. This statement, absurd on the face of it, is not substantiated by official figures. Nevertheless, the fiction has wide circulation.

One instance in which chauvinistic wishful thinking threatened to lead to serious international complications was the faking by Paris newspapers in the spring of 1927 of the successful landing in New York of the French aviators, Nungesser and Coli, now believed to have been lost in the Atlantic Ocean near Newfoundland. To understand the gullibility of French aviators, statesmen and citizens, according to Leland D. Case, editor of *Together,* who was then on the staff of the Paris *Herald,* it is necessary to remember the attitude of the French toward America after the World War.

For years unwise American tourists had mocked the French by lavish spending of the debased franc, by outbidding natives for taxicab and other services, and by raucous reminders that it was the United States that won the war. The desire to be ahead of America in some form of international competition was intense when the two French airmen took off for the east-to-west flight.

When a cabled report was received that the United States Naval Station at Portland, Maine, had sighted an airplane believed to be the *White Bird,* joyful editors waited neither for confirmation nor for more details. Instead, they rushed into print with headlines announcing the safe arrival of the national heroes in Manhattan. More than that, one journal went to the extent of printing an eyewitness account of the landing, part of which read as follows:

When Nungesser's airplane appeared above the roadstead of New York, Commander Fouillors, chief of the Navy air chaser service, flew out with a squadrilla to meet the aviators, and as soon as the plane was visible from the shore, ship sirens and whistles blew and flags flew from every mast. Numbers of pleasure craft went out to meet the incoming plane as well as many military and civil planes, the last-named hired by cinematograph undertakings and newspapers.

The descent to the water was made under excellent conditions, and the plane was immediately surrounded by a number of boats, whilst hydroplanes flew over it at a low altitude.

Nungesser and Coli, once their machine was safely on the water, remained a moment motionless, as though unconscious of the acclamation and salutes from boats around them. Then they stood up and embraced each other.

When this account was received at Villacoublay, where Nungesser and Coli were trained, aviators went up and dropped red flares over Paris. There was a celebration at Le Bourget field. At the restaurant where Nungesser played billiards with Georges Carpentier, the pugilist, and others, balls were thrown into the air and cues waved. Flags which had been flying a few days earlier in memory of Joan of Arc were put up again. Jubilant crowds milled through the streets, shouting, "We've beaten the Americans! France is first! Vivent Nungesser et Coli! Vive la France!"

When official confirmation of the story was not forthcoming, the crowds took up positions before the various newspaper offices, especially before those of the two American papers. A French girl, secretary to the editor, was sent out to tell the crowd before the Paris *Herald* office that the paper would post the report as soon as it arrived. Before the office of the French paper *Le Matin,* the crowd insisted that an American flag be taken down. It was, but all other flags were removed at the same time.

Seeking a scapegoat, someone began the rumor that cabled reports from the United States had been false. Also, it was said that if the Frenchmen actually had failed, fabricated weather reports from the other side of the Atlantic were the cause. Investigation in the sober days to follow proved that neither charge had any foundation in fact. It was revealed further that the French ministries of commerce, war and the interior themselves had verified the false reports.

The matter was debated in the Chamber of Deputies, and an investigation of the government's responsibility demanded. It was not forthcoming, and sober parliamentarians declared that the government itself had been too hasty in accepting as true what all wanted to believe.

Because of the anti-American sentiment aroused by the incident, Ambassador Myron T. Herrick advised Lindbergh and the other American fliers waiting to take off from New York to postpone their flights a few weeks. When the flying colonel made his sensational landing a fortnight later, all dudgeon against his country certainly had disappeared.

Among the cases of patriotism gone wild, others given so far in this chapter pale before that of an obscure Parisian clerk, Vrain Lucas, to whom was vouchsafed the sight of crowds milling in the streets, shouting, "Vive la France," and denouncing as a traitor anyone daring to suggest that his forged autographs might not be genuine.

Lucas's frauds were in the form of letters supposedly from the collection of "Count de Boisjourdain" which he sold to Michael Chastes, eminent French mathematician, astronomer and member of the Academy of Sciences. It was the formal approval April 12, 1869, by the French government of part of the collection of 27,340 documents which led to the popular street demonstration. These letters, purported to have passed from Blaise Pascal to Robert Boyle, proved to even an Englishman's satisfaction that the French scientist had anticipated Newton's discoveries in gravitation and the fundamental laws of physics.

Suspicion first began to be directed against Lucas when Breton, official at the observatory, discovered that sixteen of the letters were to be found in Saverien's *Histoire des Philosophes Modernes* (1761). Chastes, however, countered that Saverien stole the originals without acknowledgment. Sure enough, shortly afterwards Lucas was able to produce proof of this contention in the form of an epistle from Montesquieu to Saverien recommending him to Madame de Pompadour who had a vast collection of autographs.

Lucas's frauds began with a faked pedigree for the gullible Chastes. Learning his client's vanity and desire to become a popular hero as the discoverer of patriotic lore, the country-bred clerk reaped a financial harvest for ten years, supposedly receiving nearly 6,000 pounds for his labors. As a reward for bringing the letters to the public's attention, Chastes, in turn, was embraced warmly by Thiers and received the sanction of the Academy of Sciences.

The Pascal-Boyle correspondence was not the only one which caused Frenchmen to rejoice. Through Lucas, Chastes also obtained ample evidence of the fame of ancient Gaul. When Thales wanted political advice he wrote to King Ambigat of Gaul for it; the inhabitants of Gaul were praised by Alexander the Great in a letter to Aristotle; the Druids were mentioned by the risen Lazarus in a letter to St. Peter; Mary Magdalene corresponded with the King of the Burgundians; Jesus Christ received a communication from Castor, a Gallic doctor. And all of these early correspondents used perfect French! Some of them even used paper containing a fleur de lis watermark.

In 1854 Feuillet de Conches in his *Causeries d'un Curieux* unsuspectingly printed two Montaigne letters forged by Lucas. They are in Volume III, page 248, of the original edition. Had not a group of impartial Florentine scholars been invited to examine samples of Lucas's handicraft, there is no telling how many similar errors of scholarship might have resulted. Exposed by the Italian savants, Lucas was sentenced in February, 1870, to two years in prison and fined 625 francs. After the Franco-Prussian War he was not heard of again.

Of the ease with which Chastes was deceived, Charles Whibley wrote in the *Bookman* for January, 1917, that Lucas "plumbed the depths of human vanity. He saw with what ease a man may be deceived who wishes to believe in falsehood, and he acquired a keen insight into the credulous character upon which a literary forger must work."

CHAPTER IX

Incentives to Believe: Prejudices, "Pet" Theories

D R. FREDERICK A. COOK never changed his story that April 21, 1908, he led the first expedition in modern times to reach the mythical North Pole, nearly a year before Rear Admiral Robert E. Peary discovered it April 6, 1909. In 1936, at the age of seventy years, he abandoned his retirement to demand that the American Geographical Society conduct a complete and impartial investigation of his claims. He also became a prolific writer of letters in his own defense to newspapers and other periodicals, and brought libel suits unsuccessfully against the *Encyclopædia Britannica,* which says his claim is "universally rejected," and against the authors and publishers of books in which similar statements appear.

Since Philip Gibbs, eminent British journalist, in 1909 was the first to express doubts regarding Dr. Cook's contention, the Cook-Peary controversy has been kept alive to an extent unprecedented for one in which a large proportion of the participants are not affected directly. No example illustrates better the predilection of newspaper readers to take sides vehemently on a matter of popular interest, or of scholars to permit their judgments to be affected by personal factors.

The vicarious enthusiasm that such an incident creates is illustrated by the correspondence between two laymen, E. A. Stowe, editor of the *Michigan Tradesman,* and George Kennan, magazine writer, made public in the February 10, 1926, *Outlook.* After a University of Copenhagen commission had reported, following a thorough investigation, that Dr. Cook's evidence was inadequate and a National Geographic Society group had called Peary's records correct, the issue apparently was closed. Consequently, Stowe, who, to the last, had defended Dr. Cook and refused to believe Admiral Peary had reached the pole, contritely wrote to Kennan December 23, 1909, as follows:

I assume that you are very happy these days over the vindication of your position on the Cook-Peary controversy. You certainly have reason to feel happy, because your position was taken and maintained without any personal feeling either way.

On the other hand, my position was due largely to my personal feelings, although I have never met either Cook or Peary. I heard Peary lecture on the North Pole a couple of years ago, and was not at all impressed with either his modesty or sincerity. . . . My personal opinion of the two men was formed wholly from their own actions, and, while I am, of course, very much disappointed over the fiasco which has attended Dr. Cook's claims, I cannot consistently concede the claims of Mr. Peary until his proofs have been passed upon by the same tribunal that condemned Dr. Cook's proofs.

It is this tendency, which has persisted for more than five decades, to choose between Dr. Cook and Admiral Peary that casts significant light upon how bias, prejudice and preconceived attitudes affect human credulity. Statistical evidence of this fact was supplied by the Pittsburgh *Press,* which conducted a poll of its readers. The result—the numbers indicating the number of persons believing each statement—follows:

Cook discovered the North Pole in 1908	73,238
Peary discovered the North Pole in 1909	2,814
Peary reached the North Pole in 1909	18,043
Cook did not reach the North Pole	2,814
Peary did not reach the North Pole	58,009

Commenting upon these results, the editors of the *Independent,* in their issue of December 30, 1909, declared:

It is natural that more votes should have been cast for Cook than for Peary, because Cook had the happy faculty of making friends and inspiring confidence wherever we went, and, besides, the champions of the "under dog" in any crowd are always more vociferous. But the curious thing about it is that 58,009 persons should believe that Peary did not reach the Pole merely because he had treated ungraciously a man who was trying to rob him of his glory!

That even scholars are not immune to the human weakness of permitting desire to color rational judgment is the contention of some authorities who claim to have examined the Cook-Peary controversy impartially. For instance, in his *Peary,* William Herbert Hobbs says that the Norwegian explorer, Otto Sverdrup, was a Cook partisan because in 1898 Peary, in high dudgeon because another had invaded a part of the earth which he conceitedly considered his own special domain, snubbed Sverdrup in the Far North. The Americans, Greely and Schley, likewise attacked Peary because he had disproved the existence of an island which the former allegedly discovered and named for the latter, Hobbs contends. Captain Thomas F. Hall's *Has the North Pole Been Discovered?* and W. Henry Lewin's *The Great North Pole Fraud,* on the other hand, are friendly to Cook and unfriendly to Peary. Defenders of both men were enraged by J. Gordon Hayes' *The Conquest of the North Pole,* in which the author asserts neither claimant reached the pole, whose real discoverer he believes to have been Richard E. Byrd in 1926.

As the *Independent* declared:

> There will be a "Cook party" to the end of time, no matter how strong the evidence brought against him in the future, no matter if he made public confession of fraud. . . . This sentiment of personal devotion and championship once aroused is one of the most powerful and indestructible of human motives.

Of the ubiquitous tendency to persist in believing falsehood because to be incredulous would involve the embarrassing and psychologically difficult experience of abandoning a preconceived idea, or pet theory, there is no better illustration than that of the Würzburg stones by which the students of Johann Bartholomaeus Adam Beringer, early eighteenth century professor of natural philosophy, enabled him to ruin his own career.

At the time the most important subject occupying the attention of the scientific world was the nature of fossils, and Dr. Beringer, an intensely religious man, had advanced an original theory that they were merely "capricious fabrications of God," hidden in the earth for some inscrutable purpose, possibly to test the faith of man. So great an obsession did gaining acceptance of this theory become with him that his students at the University of Würzburg wearied of listening to its exposition. So, when one of them came across the account of a joke which the students of Athanasius Kircher, seventeenth century German mathematician and scientist, had played on him, they decided to emulate it.

On the side of a hill where the good professor took his classes in search of geological specimens, Dr. Beringer's students planted absurd clay tablets bearing inscriptions in Hebrew, Babylonian, Syriac and Arabic. Becoming bolder after a few preliminary successes, they inscribed the signature of God himself on one of the "fossils."

Beringer was astounded and elated. He saw in the finds proofs of his theory and immediately began preparation of a tome in Latin. At great expense he had engravings made of the finds and prepared an elaborate scholarly description and explanation of them.

The jokers uneasily began to realize they had gone too far and confessed to the professor. The result was entirely the opposite of that expected; Beringer refused absolutely to believe them. Instead, he accused them of attempting to rob him of the honor of a great discovery and went ahead with his book. It appeared in 1728, entitled *Lithographiae Wirceburgensis,* and contained an ingenious allegorical frontispiece, a title page devoted entirely to the author's previous scholarship, a nine-page dedication to Dr. Christopher Francis, prince bishop of Würzburg, a preface of about the same length, fourteen chapters forming the body of the book, and twenty-one plates of the figures.

The objections of his friends and the charge of a hoax, Beringer dismissed; and he demonstrated how the finds proved his previously announced theory as to the nature of fossils and refuted the idea that the inscriptions might be vestiges of early "pagan occupation of the land," meaning the Gauls.

The shout of laughter which greeted the book was too much even for Beringer. The remainder of his fortune went to buying back all existent copies. It is said that he died broken-hearted. After his demise Hobard of Hamburg, a bookseller, bought all available copies from the heir of the original publisher and reissued them. Then he compiled a second edition under a new title.

Another scholar, whose zeal to establish a thesis caused his downfall through the cunning of a student, was Dr. Gesenius, foremost Hebraic scholar of the middle nineteenth century. The hoaxer was Frederick Wagenfeld, who produced what purported to be a fragment by Philo of Byblos, a writer of the first century who was known to have translated the ancient history of Phoenicia by Sanchoniathon.

The fragment, which Wagenfeld said had been found in Santa Maria convent at Merinchão near Oporto, Portugal, by a Portuguese officer named Pereira, substantiated what Gesenius had conjectured regarding the succession of Phoenician kings and, in addition, gave incidents of the times of Solomon and Ezekiel, of whom Sanchoniathon was made to seem a contemporary.

Investigation revealed that the convent was fictitious and the manuscript a poor forgery, even containing a contemporary paper mill's stamp. Nevertheless, Gesenius was discredited because of his immediate uncritical acceptance of the specious evidence, as was G. F. Grotefend, leading philologist of the time, who wrote the introduction to a German translation of the alleged ancient history of Phoenicia.

High up in any list of literary leaders who have permitted their prejudices to warp their judgment would be Dr. Samuel Johnson, the crusty lexicographer, who, because of his intense dislike of John Milton, helped disseminate a shameful hoax intended to sully the Puritan poet's reputation.

The perpetrator of the hoax was William Lauder, who is said to have been enraged by Alexander Pope's unfavorable comparison in his *Dunciad* of Arthur Johnston's poems with those of Milton. Lauder at the time was attempting to persuade the schools to adopt his own edition of Johnston's work. In 1750 Lauder published *An Essay on Milton's Use of and Imitation of the Moderns in His Paradise Lost.* When exposed by Dr. John Douglas, Lauder was proved to have invented Latin poets and a number of literary authorities to show that Milton was a plagiarist. His principal bit of chicanery was the interpolation of eight lines in a Latin translation of *Paradise Lost* by Hogg to make the passage read the same as one by a fictitious Dutch divine whom he created.

In his biography of Johnson, John Hawkins says that when the doctor saw proof sheets of Lauder's work, he "seemed to exult in a persuasion that the reputation of Milton was likely to suffer by this discovery. That he was not privy to the imposture I am well persuaded, but that he wished well to the argument must be inferred from the preface, which indubitably was written by Johnson." The anonymous author of an article, "Literary Impostures of Lauder and Bower," in the June, 1849, *Eclectic,* reprinted from *Sharpe's Magazine,* similarly wrote:

It is to be feared that his latent hostility to Milton—his abhorrence of the "sour republicanism" of the great Puritan poet—prompted him to lend a readier ear to Lauder's assertion than can be justified on principles of fairness and candor.

After Douglas' exposé, Johnson allegedly wrote the confession which Lauder signed. The latter, however, had learned no lesson and, four years later, he wrote a pamphlet vindicating Charles I of plagiarism in *Eikon Basilike* which had been brought by Milton to show that the king had used as his own Pamela's prayer in Sir Philip Sidney's *Arcadia.* In his confession in this instance Lauder quoted a line from Virgil and credited it to Ramsay, a Scotch poet, "to improve Ramsay," he said. Then he left England for Barbados, where he issued a series of contradictory explanations of his career.

Another important instance in which Dr. Samuel Johnson displayed extreme gullibility was that of George Psalmanazar who, in the role of a converted heathen from Formosa, became the lion of British society.

Psalmanazar made his English debut by means of an introduction to the Bishop of London by the Reverend Alexander Innes, formerly of St. Margaret's, Westminster, who is reputed to have stolen a treatise on *Moral Virtue* from the Reverend Archibald Campbell to be published as his own. Innes, at the time he met his protégé, was an army chaplain at Sluys where the supposed Asiatic was in the service of the Elector of Cologne. He asserted that he had succeeded in converting the heathen after Jesuits, Lutherans and Calvinists had failed and, as a reward, was made chaplain-general of the British forces in Portugal.

The converted heathen caused a sensation in London, where he was dined, wined, and introduced to royalty. Dr. Johnson was fascinated by him, and the Archbishop of Canterbury received him. To complete his Christian education, so that he might return as a missionary to his native land, he was sent to Oxford by the Bishop of London. There he burned candles in his windows all night long to create the impression of being an ardent student.

An Historical and Geographical Description of Formosa appeared in 1704. It introduced the British to the religion, customs and manners of the natives of Formosa. An alphabet and grammar were included. In a second edition a few years later the author answered twenty-five objections to his original account.

After having "gotten by" Hans Sloane, secretary of the Royal Society, Lord Pembroke, the Prussian minister, and others, Psalmanazar met defeat at Oxford under the grilling of Halley, the eminent astronomer, and other savants who questioned him on the sun's position at noon, the duration of twilight and other astronomical phenomena in his supposed native land. These questions he could not answer. After repudiating one confession, he made another in a posthumous work.

Psalmanazar's real name never was known. He is supposed to have adopted his pseudonym from Shalmaneser, King of Assyria, mentioned in II Kings 17:3. It was established that he was a native of southern France, that he attended a Jesuit school, and that before assuming the role of a Formosan he had posed unsuccessfully as a vagabond Japanese convert. His story of a Father de Rode, a Jesuit who, disguised as a Japanese, had been his tutor in Formosa, was pure fiction.

Of Psalmanazar, Henry G. Hewlett wrote in the May, 1879, issue of *Cornhill:*

> The Tories, headed by the clergy, are delighted at such a signal demonstration of the superior claims of Anglicanism to any other form of Christianity, and the Whigs to find their suspicions of Jesuitry so strongly confirmed. The fashionable world is enraptured with the acquisition of a young man of noble birth, uncommon ability, good looks, and fair breeding, a Christian who was once by his own confession a cannibal.

No better opportunity to expound their theories ever was provided to linguists than that which followed the discovery in 1838 of a mysterious stone in the Grave Creek Mound at Moundville, West Virginia. Until one day in 1930 when Andrew Price, president of the West Virginia Historical Society, accidentally solved its riddle, its queer inscriptions had been examined and interpreted by so many different authorities in so many different ways that some of the man in the street's inveterate skepticism as regards academic authorities seems justified.

About 1890 the Bureau of American Ethnology published a summary of the attempts up to that time to decipher the bizarre inscription on the Grave Creek stone. One French scientist in 1856 had translated it as "The Chief of Emigration who reached these places has fixed these statutes forever." Another French scientist in 1872 read a paper at the Congress of Americanists at Nancy in which he said the writing was Canaanite and meant, "What thou sayest, thou dost impose it, thou shinest in thy impetuous clan and rapid chamoid." A third guess was: "The grave of one who was assassinated here. May God avenge him, strike his murderer, cutting off the hand of his existence."

Four linguists said the inscription was Etruscan; five held it was Runic; ten, Phoenician; fourteen, Old British; sixteen, Celtiberic, and one, ancient Greek. Whatever the language, the stone seemed to indicate a civilization in America before Columbus.

In explanation of his solution, Mr. Price said that a casual side glance at the inscription caused a part of it to form the figures, "1838." With this as a clue he used his printer's knowledge of type to translate the whole as "Bill Stump's Stone, October 14, 1838." Found a year after the publication of Charles Dickens' *Pickwick Papers,* the stone evidently was the work of a jokester or of someone merely attempting to amuse himself.

Decidedly on the humorous side, but significant in demonstrating how even the erudite mighty fall, is the story related by Wells Drury in *An Editor on the Comstock Lode* of "The Traveling Stones of Pahrangat Valley."

These remarkable rocks were the figment of the imagination of a pioneer journalist, William Wright, who assumed the nom de plume of Dan De Quille in his writings for the Virginia City *Enterprise*. Drury explains:

> With feigned scientific minuteness he showed how these traveling stones were by some mysterious power drawn together and then scattered wide apart, only to be returned in moving, quivering masses to what appeared to be the magnetic center of the valley. Upon these pretended observations he predicated a new doctrine concerning electrical propulsion and repulsion. "These curious pebbles," he averred, "appear to be formed of loadstone or magnetic iron ore. A single stone removed to a distance of a yard, upon being released at once started off with wonderful and somewhat comical celerity to rejoin its fellows."

Given wide publicity, this story reached Germany and caused a furor among scientists dabbling with the study of electromagnetic currents. The secretary of one of the societies wrote to Dan to demand further details. "In vain he disclaimed the verity of his skit. His denial was treated as an unprofessional attempt to keep his brother scientists in ignorance of the truth concerning natural laws, the effects of which they were convinced had been first observed and recorded by 'Herr Dan De Quille, the eminent physicist of Virginiastadt, Nevada.'"

From the "greatest circus man in America," probably P. T. Barnum, De Quille received an offer of "ten grand" if he could make his stones perform under a canvas tent.

Other De Quille hoaxes which found widespread credence included a new kind of perpetual motion machine and an ammonia helmet for use on the hot deserts.

The penultimate to which otherwise sober seekers after the truth can go in defense of their convictions occurred in 1928 when police had to be summoned to quell a disturbance during which bricks and stench bombs were thrown at the annual meeting of the College of France in Paris. The bone of contention was the identity of bricks, tablets and vases found by a peasant boy while plowing on his grandfather's farm near Glozel, a small village close to the famous spa at Vichy.

Acme

OUR ANCESTORS BELIEVED IN THESE

(Upper left.) Early picture of a porcupine which seventeenth century scientists believed to be a deadly animal, able to throw its quills like arrows. *(Upper right.)* An early conception of the American bison from Hennepin's *New Discovery in America,* published in 1698. The upside-down animal is an opossum. *(Middle left.)* Seventeenth century travelers were warned against the lamia, said to have a woman's face and to be prone to lure men to their death. *(Middle right.)* Early writers described an animal of "yellowish carnation," something like the familiar hyena, so wild that only one or two persons had ever seen it. *(Lower left.)* This was a seventeenth century artist's conception of the bright red mantichora, native of India, which he drew from the accounts of travelers. *(Lower right.)* This seventeenth century picture of a group of dogs contained one with a human face.

Courtesy, Dr. David Riesman, Philadelphia

SOME OF THE GLOZEL FINDS

Archaeologists nearly came to blows while debating whether these and many other relics, dug up near Glozel, France, were of antique or modern origin.

First and principal exponent of the Glozel finds as relics of a stone-age civilization in western Europe from ten to twenty thousand years ago, was Dr. Albert Morlet, a surgeon and amateur archaeologist of Vichy. He was especially impressed by an alphabet of 136 characters, as was Professor Salomon Reinach, conservator of the Museum of St. Germain-en-Laye, one of France's leading official archaeologists, long an exponent of the theory that civilization originated in the Mediterranean area.

To Morlet and Reinach the relics formed a link between palaeolithic and neolithic stages of culture. To Camille Jullian, widely known historian, they provided important knowledge of the Gallo-Roman period about the beginning of the Christian era. Jullian thought they probably were part of the equipment of a sorcerer of the third century after Christ.

Professor J. Loth, of the College of France, was most impressed by the stone death masks, one of which was called the Beethoven mask because it resembled the death mask of the great composer. Professor René Dussaud, an opponent of the antiquity of the finds, answered that it *was* a replica of the Beethoven mask. Dussaud further produced a modern dictionary in which there was an exact copy of the reindeer found as an anachronism among neolithic relics.

It remained for Edmond Bayle, director of the laboratory of legal identification, to settle the problem by chemistry and microscopy. Put in water the stones crumbled, cells of a tiny piece of grass were found to be intact, there were fragments of thread with aniline dye, bone instruments were filled with marrow.

Before this iconoclastic proof was forthcoming, however, an international commission, appointed by the International Anthropological Congress at Amsterdam, had condemned the finds as modern inventions, only to have its findings contradicted by another commission appointed by dissenters.

Arrested in England for the sale of some spurious relics of William Penn, a professional faker with a record which might well be the envy of any other hoaxer, made a complete confession of a number of impostures, of which the Glozel plants were the most important. He was Hunter Charles Rogers, who revealed that much of the confusion at Glozel resulted from his placing a few genuine articles among the fakes. According to the late Dr. David Riesman, of the University of Pennsylvania, who made a study of Glozel, no credence has been given Rogers' claim.

One interesting phase of the Glozel dispute was the verdict of 1,000 francs which Morlet won in a suit against the *Journal des Débats* and the French Society of Prehistory for accusing him of being a faker. On appeal the verdict was reduced to one franc and costs, but it was a moral victory for Morlet.

When a prejudice is widespread, any anecdote tending to fortify it finds credence among the general population, not alone among scholars. Early in the twentieth century one such prejudice was against supposedly hard-headed and hardhearted scientists; and because of it, supposedly, a garbled newspaper account of the valedictory speech in 1905 of Sir William Osler, upon his departure from the Johns Hopkins University, was believed, to the eminent surgeon's discredit.

To lighten his speech at the farewell dinner in his honor, Dr. Osler made a humorous reference to Anthony Trollope's *The Fixed Period* in which a chloroform club is advocated for men of more than sixty years of age. The next day a reporter's eagerness to make a good story, instead of restricting his account to the facts, was seen in the headline of a Baltimore paper, "Osler Recommends Chloroform at Sixty."

For weeks and months the controversy raged; newspapers received indignant letters, other scientists were interviewed, editorials were written, cartoons were drawn. The public, said Harvey Cushing, Osler's biographer,

knowing nothing of the whimsical reference to Trollope's novel interposed to mask his own pain at parting, nor of the rather pathetic allusion to his own advancing years . . . felt that it was the heartless view of a cold scientist who could condemn man as a productive machine.

Osler's wife and secretaries cooperated to keep him from reading threatening letters and unfavorable press comment. The surgeon's own mother and several other relatives were over ninety at the time. According to Hector Charlesworth, Dr. Osler's brother Britton Bath Osler, a lawyer, did commit suicide at sixty, by overwork. Although "oslerize" has not yet been added to dictionaries as a synonym for "to commit suicide," it has wide currency in the slanguage as such.

Similarly, despite the efforts of the Atlanta *Constitution* to put a stop to it, a story broadcast by the late Arthur "Br'er Rabbit" Brisbane in 1913 was widely believed as indicative of primitive conditions in the textile industries of the South. The story, which the Hearst syndicate writer said was obtained from the Covington (Georgia) *News* and through a private investigator, was of the holding of a funeral of a girl employee in a

Georgia cotton mill at night to permit fellow workers to attend, because the mill owners refused to allow their help to leave during working hours.

The *Constitution* proved: (1) that the girl, really a woman of twenty-five, never worked in the cotton mill; (2) that the funeral was held at night to meet a family exigency, with the burial the following day; (3) that many employees of the mill were present at the daytime interment; (4) that Brisbane's correspondent admitted being in error.

Brisbane, however, refused to back down. Instead, he chastised Editor Clark Howell for trying to avoid an uncomfortable situation. Howell retorted with signed statements from the minister who officiated at the funeral, the mayor of Covington, the editor of the *News,* the president of the cotton mill and many others.

In the same year the Atlanta *Constitution* engaged in an even more heated editorial war with other publications throughout the entire country over the facts in the case of Ollie Taylor, a thirteen-year-old boy whose father brought habeas corpus proceedings to get him out of Hopeville Reformatory, to which he had been sentenced at the age of nine years following the theft of a bottle of soda water. The Supreme Court of the state had held that the court sentence was legal.

The incident was interpreted to mean that Georgia permitted a life sentence for such a trivial offense as theft of a five-cent bottle of Coca-Cola. The *Constitution* immediately branded this interpretation as incorrect, and Howell conducted an investigation to show that, in reality, Ollie Taylor for years had been a juvenile court case; that his sentence had not been for life or until he reached his majority but was indeterminate, and that the child had been released once only to be returned to the reformatory upon his failure to become rehabilitated. It was after this second committal that the father started legal action.

The story got into the magazines in its distorted form. The *Saturday Evening Post* quoted from the *Journal of Criminal Law and Criminology.* The *Literary Digest* originally was misled but, when its attention was called to its errors, printed an article to correct the wrong impression of the first.

The Chicago *Tribune* encouraged the sending of letters and telegrams condemnatory of the Georgia court's action to the governor of the state, members of the legislature, congressmen and other influential citizens. After the *Constitution* had printed the facts, the New York *Evening Post* commented: "The facts in the case turn out to be about as nearly as is possible the exact opposite of the report."

No desire to believe the pleasant could be greater than that of a parent of a child whose safety is in doubt. Upon this paternal and maternal disinclination to abandon hope for a son or daughter, more than one impostor has imposed.

There was the mother of Roger Charles Tichbourne whom everyone else believed drowned in 1854 off the coast of Brazil. Although the young man's estate was settled in 1855, his bereaved mother refused to accept his death as proved, and advertised widely throughout the world for knowledge of her son. After ten years she believed her prayers to have been answered when, through an agency in Sydney, Australia, she learned of a man answering Roger's description.

When the impostor, Arthur Orton of Wagga Wagga, New South Wales, arrived in England, the eager mother took him to her bosom as her own flesh and blood; but others were skeptical. In 1871 trustees of the estate of Roger Tichbourne brought suit to expose the imposture. Because he had acquainted himself carefully with details of the family history, Orton made a plausible presentation on direct testimony and was identified by more than one hundred persons to whom he had been careful to relate anecdotes in the early life of the dead Roger Tichbourne. During cross-examination, however, he failed lamentably and, when it was shown he did not possess certain tattoo marks, he was convicted of forgery and sentenced to fourteen years in prison. In a second trial, which consumed 188 days by comparison with 102 days for the first, he was found guilty of perjury. As a consequence of public addresses he delivered after the case was ended, Orton's solicitor, a Dr. Kenealy, was disbarred for breach of professional etiquette. Elected to Parliament, he tried to obtain a royal commission to inquire into the case, but only his vote was cast in favor of it. Orton died April 1, 1898, and on his coffin was inscribed, "Sir Roger Charles Doughty Tichbourne."

The eagerness of a parent whose child has been kidnaped to believe any supposed clue which might lead to his return certainly is understandable. Cruelly taking advantage of it, when a kidnaping which receives more than the average amount of publicity occurs, psychopathic persons with a perverted sense of humor or victims of delusions often have caused unnecessary parental grief as well as handicapped law enforcement officers in their quest for the malefactors.

Best known of many such malicious incidents are the two cases connected with the notorious kidnaping and murder of the infant son of Colonel and Mrs. Charles A. Lindbergh in the spring of 1932. As a result of the aberration of John Hughes Curtis, Norfolk, Virginia, boat builder, Colonel Lindbergh made several trips on the ocean to seek a contact with the kidnapers. He was on the last of those excursions when word of the finding of his son's body reached him.

Curtis, in his confession to police and in his testimony during the trial, could give no satisfactory explanation except that he must have "become insane on the subject for the time being which caused me to make up the story in its entirety." The story was of a Sam, who came to see him at the Norfolk Country Club, of which Curtis was past president, about a week after the kidnaping. Through Sam, Curtis said he met others of the group and saw in their possession some of the bills included in the $50,000 ransom which Colonel Lindbergh paid in the vain hope that it would bring about the return of the baby.

The Reverend H. Dobson-Peacock of Norfolk believed Curtis' story as did Rear Admiral Guy H. Burrage, U.S.N., retired. Curtis went to Hopewell, New Jersey, to inform the state police. He was offered large sums for his story by two newspapers, the New York *Herald Tribune* and the New York *Daily News*—both offers contingent, however, upon the safe return of the child and the approval of Colonel Lindbergh.

Following a jury trial, Curtis was convicted of having knowingly given false information to Colonel Lindbergh and police. He paid a fine of one thousand dollars, but his year's sentence was suspended. The verdict indicated that the jury believed Curtis actually knew the kidnapers, although his confession was otherwise and both Colonel Lindbergh and detectives testified that they did not believe any part of his story to be true.

Much more fantastic than John Hughes Curtis' story of the Lindbergh kidnaping was that of the late Gaston Means, former Department of Justice investigator, by the time of his second trial in May, 1933. Already serving a term of fifteen years for theft of $104,000 as ransom money from Mrs. Evelyn Walsh McLean, estranged wife of the former publisher of the Washington *Post,* he and Norman T. Whitaker were found guilty of conspiracy to defraud because they persuaded Mrs. McLean to try to pawn jewelry to raise an additional $35,000.

The climax of Means' testimony in his second trial was that the body which Colonel Lindbergh identified as that of his son was not Charles A. Lindbergh, Jr., but a "plant." This he said he had on the authority of a Wellington Henderson, ringleader of the kidnapers and prominent Communist. He said he handed over the ransom money given him by Mrs. McLean to three strangers at Alexandria, Virginia, and followed the trail of the kidnaped baby from Aiken, South Carolina, to El Paso, Texas, thence to Chicago and back to Washington. Irving Fenton, another of the kidnapers, showed him some of the "Jafsie" (Lindbergh) money in Chicago and named some dead beer runners as also having been partners to the crime.

Partly because no other witnesses who ever heard of either Wellington Henderson or Irving Fenton could be found and partly because of the general incredibility of Means' story, the jury found him and Whitaker guilty. Means died early in 1939 in Atlanta federal penitentiary, however, without confessing.

CHAPTER X

Incentives to Believe: The Thirst for Vicarious Thrills

WITH the cooperation of three university and seven public libraries, a questionnaire was sent to 271 readers of books which have been proved to be spurious, either wholly or in part. Typical examples were the completely forged *Memoirs of Li Hung Chang,* composed in an Hawaiian prison by William Francis Mannix, and the highly romanticized *The Cradle of the Deep* by Joan Lowell, the first edition of which was publicized as an authentic adventure story.

As the 132 replies which were received began to come in, the writer realized with increasing intensity that, in the guise of scientific research, he had done a cruel thing, comparable to running around on circus day sticking pins into children's balloons. Only 41 of the 132 had known the true nature of the books they read, and only 29 more had either become suspicious or been enlightened later. That left 61 whose first disillusionment came with receipt of the letter accompanying the provocative questionnaire.

On the whole the iconoclastic information was received in a spirit of good sportsmanship; but a plaintive melancholy typified the efforts at scholarly bravery in the replies. While one reader of Miss Lowell's odyssey confessed to "keen disappointment" that it was not all sterling, another felt that he had been "swindled"; a third "admired the author for even the imagination to think of those happenings," and a fourth epitomized the attitude of the majority in the following words:

I changed my opinion of the book when I found out that it was not a true story. The literary qualities were not outstanding, but the facts it contained made the book. When these were found false, it took all the worthwhileness out of the book and thus left nothing worth reading. Miss Lowell must be credited, however, for her vivid imagination.

Although the entire study is open to suspicion because the sample unavoidably was small (the library records cover a few years only and only readers who withdrew books, leaving unreached an undetermined number of others who may have consulted them in reading rooms), the results unmistakably showed the following:

1. If a book is read with full realization of its spurious nature, it is likely to be enjoyed for what it is.
2. If a reader becomes suspicious, while reading a book that is not what it purports to be, his pleasure is diminished.
3. If a reader does not learn that he has been hoaxed, his pleasure is unaffected.
4. If a reader learns, after completing a book, that it was not what he believed it to be, he is indignant and displeased.

These conclusions, of course, merely are the "common sense" ones which anyone would imagine without going to the trouble of sending out a disturbing questionnaire. We can take our "escape" literature—our fairy tales, Santa Claus legends, detective yarns, ghost stories, Baron Munchausens, Paul Bunyans, Richard Halliburtons and Robert Ripleys—either as entertainment or as exciting fact. If the former, we receive from them vicarious thrills comparable to those given by a William Faulkner or Ernest Hemingway novel. If the latter, in addition, we have stirred in us the inspirational if irrational hope that, in emulation of our worshiped heroes, we too some day may lift ourselves above the commonplace and humdrum in a world in which they are proof such can be done.

The potentially greater "lift" to be derived from an authentic thriller is obvious; also, the sizable inherent disappointment when he with whom one has flown on wings of fancy "toward the horizon—toward the beyond the horizon—toward the beyond the beyond," as Corey Ford has put it, is proved unworthy of adulation. Consequently, the role of debunker of the exciting and adventurous is an unsympathetic and arduous one. In this, as in all other fields, men believe what they want to believe—what, in fact, some psychiatrists suggest, it is good for them to believe.

Consider, for instance, the comparatively recent case of *A Notable Lawsuit,* composed in 1899 by Franklin H. Head, a Chicago banker and corporation director whom Eugene Field once called the first literary figure of that city. Intended solely for the amusement of a feminine friend, once in printed form it circulated widely, impressing the Rowfant Club of Cleveland so much that, by popular demand of its members, the complete works of Head were published by it with the statement in the introduction that it was "the only publication of the Rowfant Club originating in what might be called the popular clamor of the members rather than the cooler considerings of the committee."

To epitomize, the story of *A Notable Lawsuit* is that of the discovery of a hole in a cave on Deer Isle, for more than a century the property of the Olmsted family, formerly of New York and now of Chicago. Through an advertisement in the New York *Tribune,* an iron chest is recovered from its present owner and is found to fit the excavation exactly. The initials "W. K." on the chest lead to the suspicion that it once contained the treasure of Captain William Kidd, the pirate. The longitude and latitude of the isle are found to correspond to the figures on a slip of paper which Kidd gave to his wife just before going to the gallows.

The bank accounts of the original John Jacob Astor, who rented the isle for trapping purposes, and of Jacques Cartier, an agent of Astor's about 1800, are investigated, and suspicion is created that the discovery of the Kidd booty was the foundation of the huge Astor fortune. The heirs of the original Olmsted bring suit against the Astor family for principal and interest. The leading lawyers of the day, including Elihu Root and Joseph H. Choate, are employed.

To attempt to put a stop to the flood of letters of inquiry with which they had been annoyed for more than two decades, the contemporary Olmsteds finally designated one of their number, Frederic L. Olmsted, to write a pamphlet, *Commentary upon "A Notable Lawsuit,"* to be used in the future instead of personal replies. This strategy undoubtedly worked to the convenience of the Olmsteds, but the Astor-Kidd-Olmsted legend persists. In its issue of July, 1931, *Forum Magazine* related it seriously with attractive layout and illustrations, appending an editor's note, however, to reveal the hoax.

Testifying regarding the point, to establish which this incident has been mentioned here—the avarice with which the Cinderella-like masses cling to belief in such a hair-raiser—*Outlook Magazine,* October 29, 1924, editorialized as follows:

And what is very curious is the undoubted fact that some who hear the truth utterly refuse to credit it, and prefer to believe in the cave, the iron chest, the lawsuit, and all the rest. . . . It has all the elements of a successful hoax. It awakens that strange delight which so many folk experience from being fooled, and it contains other elements which have contributed to its success and caused its grave acceptance even until today. It has in it a tale of buried treasure and of Captain Kidd. . . . It is in some odd fashion the kind of story which many of us like to believe, which we would cling to even if archangels should come to testify against it.

"People don't like to be fooled. But they love to fool themselves," commented a feature writer for the Philadelphia *Public Ledger* whose privilege it was to investigate another case in which the same human tendency to be carried away by the fantastic graphically was illustrated. That was the "Beauty and the Beast" press-agent stunt in which figured the same Norman Jefferies who caused the Jersey Devil, mentioned in Chapter III, to materialize.

More in disrepute than ever with Philadelphia's editors after the Jersey Devil hoax, Jefferies had to be really adroit when the manager of a hideous dwarf, appropriately named Quasimodo, appealed to him to revive interest in his charge's appearances throughout the East in carnivals. As worked out by this master of publicity, the story "broke" from a small city, Hornell, New York, where spectators were turning their backs in disgust upon the sight of the noseless, diminutive human with teeth from ear to ear. Disregarding entirely the consensus of her companions, a beautiful and wealthy young girl had become enamoured of Quasimodo and a public marriage had been arranged by the showmen.

Journalistic sob sisters and masculine tear jerkers were rushed to Hornell by the metropolitan press to send back minute play-by-play accounts of the spectacular but gruesome affair. When the show within a week moved to the Philadelphia Arch Street Museum, attendance records established by the Jersey Devil were broken. As long as business warranted it, Quasimodo and his bride were paraded before the gullible; then the marriage was annulled without difficulty inasmuch as the dwarf was an idiot.

Years later Harry W. Moore persuaded Jefferies to reveal the secrets of his career and commented as follows, in an article "A Master Hoaxer Tells All" in the December 8, 1929, issue of the Philadelphia *Public Ledger:*

But here is the strange part. People fooled themselves into believing what they wanted to believe. They wanted to believe that this girl was a wealthy heiress. So no one, not even the authorities, who were seeking a way to prevent the marriage, even thought of verifying the story of her identity. Quasimodo's manager did not even admit at the interview that she was wealthy or socially prominent. He was evasive and the reporters took this evasion for admissions.

People don't like to be fooled. But they love to fool themselves. Thousands fooled themselves in the recent stock market activities. Thousands fool themselves when a fake stock salesman approaches them. They are not listening so much to his patter. They are dreaming of the wealth which he dangles before their eyes and before they come out of the dream, they have signed on the dotted line. They love it. Press agents merely exploit a universal weakness.

Sometimes this "exploitation" is unintentional. Sir Thomas More, satirical sixteenth century idealist, was thoroughly amazed, according to the anonymous author of *Sketches of Imposture, Deception and Credulity,* to have his immortal *Utopia* accepted as the true account of a trip to a mid-Atlantic island. When the religious inquired regarding the possibility of sending missionaries to convert the Utopians to European standards, the great portrayer of a supposedly ideal commonwealth was downcast.

The late George Barr McCutcheon was no less annoyed and bewildered when the realism of his Graustark adventure stories caused travel agencies, steamship lines and others engaged in transporting the annual army of American tourists to Europe to curse his name.

According to Arthur Maurice, quoted in the *Literary Digest* for November 17, 1928, about 80 per cent of Mr. McCutcheon's own mail from strangers inquired about the best way to get to Graustark, the most suitable season to make a trip there, or criticized McCutcheon adversely for certain statements in his novels about the mythical kingdom:

He was expected to be friend, counselor and tourist information bureau in all matters relating to the Balkans in general and the Principality of Graustark in particular. It should have been perfectly obvious that Graustark and the surrounding states depicted in his novels were purely imaginary, but eight-tenths of his letters from strangers were written in the belief that these places had actual existence. There was a touch of decided pathos in some of these letters.

One correspondent wanted to settle a bet as to how to get there; a Cincinnati cynic took exception to the hour fixed in one of the Graustark stories for the dispatch of a train. "Such stupidity spoiled the book" for him, he wrote. Some suggested a relationship with the royal families of Graustark or adjacent states. One tried to establish a family connection with Beverly Calhoun, saying, "I am getting up a family tree so that I can join the Daughters, and it may be that you can help me some."

Sir Walter Scott's Waverley novels, Washington Irving's Knickerbocker tales, James Fenimore Cooper's Indian adventure stories, Edgar Allan Poe's accounts of mesmerism, especially "The Facts in the Case of M. Valdemar," and many of the adventure stories and historical novels of Daniel Defoe were believed by thrill-seeking readers.

When the second part of *Robinson Crusoe* appeared, Defoe expressed his own "doubts" as to the truth of all of Crusoe's narrative. Of his *Tour Through the Whole Island of Great Britain,* written without having left

London, he afterwards confessed that one of his informants had "fibbed a bit." Of Defoe's persistence in giving his writings the semblance of reality, Gerridina Roorda in his *Realism in Daniel Defoe's Narratives of Adventure* explained:

> Popular prejudice against fiction induced Defoe to give his tales of adventure the form of pseudo-authentic accounts. He strove to make these credible by vouching for their authenticity and by a peculiar method of narration which tended to realism.

"The Apparition of Mrs. Veal" has been suspected of having been a publicity stunt to promote the sale of Drelincourt's *A Christian Defense Against the Fear of Death,* which the ghost, in whose actuality readers were prone to believe, recommended.

No discussion of the "the public likes to be fooled" philosophy can be finished—or, in fact, more than begun—without mention of the originator of the aphorism, the "prince of humbugs," Phineas T. Barnum, master showman and expert psychologist. Space does not permit retelling here the multitudinous familiar anecdotes which biographers have related of him. Briefly, among the high lights of a career during which he attracted millions to his museums and circus tents were the following:

His first and perhaps most notable "contribution to science"—Joice Heth, whom he purchased from another showman with credentials proving that she was the 161-year-old nurse of George Washington. In her semi-paralyzed state she certainly looked all of that age, but an autopsy revealed that she probably was not over eighty. Nevertheless, she was well versed in Washington's boyhood before Barnum obtained her.

"The Light of Asia," a whitewashed elephant, was acquired to compete with a rival who had a genuine white elephant from Siam. Because it was too easily detected as a fraud it was shortly withdrawn. Jumbo, Barnum's famous exhibit, was a genuine giant. Likewise, Tom Thumb and his friends were real midgets.

The woolly horse was purchased in Cincinnati and was advertised as a find of Colonel John C. Frémont and his party who were lost in the snow of the Rocky Mountains.

The Feejee mermaid was obtained from Moses Kimball of the Boston Museum, and was said to have come from Calcutta in 1817. It was a skillful grafting of a monkey's uppers onto a fish's lowers. Illustrated advertisements showed it in its supposed native state alive.

The Dorchester mermaid was similarly constructed and, like Barnum's, came from the Orient where manufacture of mermaids seems to have been a profitable business for a time. It was exhibited by Melvin T. Freeman of Dorchester, formerly assistant water commissioner of Boston.

Barnum erroneously has been credited with authorship of the aphorism concerning suckers that "there's one born every minute."

Although critics of contemporary civilization have been inundating us for years with warnings that our industrialization and urbanization are destroying individuality to an unprecedented extent, thus multiplying the chances of success of the spinners of fictitious yarn for Coney Islanders, sober examination of the record of centuries reveals that as long as men have left home and returned, they have found wide-open ears awaiting them. Said an unknown feature writer in the Chicago *Inter-Ocean* for January 2, 1910:

The gentle art of travel faking as we know it began with the great migratory movement of the Middle Ages, the movement marked by crusades, olyphunts, silks, chess and Venetian caravans. From then on to the present there has probably not been a generation without its travel faker.

Antedating even the time cited by this commentator, however, were at least two peregrinators whose fantastic imaginations stimulated pens so eloquent that twentieth century students of composition and literature are assigned to study them, proper but superfluous warnings being issued, of course, regarding the credence to be given to the contents of their readings.

The first was a twelfth century Jew, Benjamin of Tudela, who came back to his native city in Germany with a description of the tomb of Ezekiel containing the libraries of the first and second temples of Jerusalem and of a nation of 400,000 independent Jews in the Euphrates Valley. With Benjamin's manuscript in tow, Wesselus of Groningen and several other scholars vainly sought these and numerous other wonders. According to Isaac D'Israeli in *Curiosities of Literature*: "The fictitious travels have been a source of much trouble to the learned."

Whereas Benjamin, oddly for his time, generally stayed within the limits of the plausible, the other early Munchausen, Sir John Mandeville, astounded his sycophantic coevals with accounts of devils belching flames on mountain tops, of men with heads of beasts, birds resembling the fabulous roc of Arabia which carried off elephants with ease, and of a Tree of Life with magic white and green leaves. Presented in a manner which has won for Sir John—or whoever their author really was—the title of "the father of English prose," the *Travels* appeared originally in the latter part of the fourteenth century in French as a supposed translation from Latin. Parts of John Bunyan's *Pilgrim's Progress* may have been inspired by the *Travels,* scholars hold.

When the era of exploration, which began late in the fifteenth century and continued for two centuries, did get under way, almost any kind of mariner's tale had considerably more than an even chance of success. Because of the superstition of centuries regarding the denizens of the uncharted oceans and beyond, little subtlety was necessary, and raconteurs of the epoch do not deserve a great amount of credit for the "whoppers" that they thought up for the amazement of the folks at home.

There was a predisposition to believe in the sea serpents, pilhannaw birds and other monsters reported by John Josselyn who visited the New World some time between 1638 and 1663. Captain John Smith of Jamestown didn't see any of them, but he was able to festoon later editions of his otherwise prosaic memoirs with the Pocahontas anecdote. Because the literate public came to expect its explorers both to see marvelous things and to experience the heroic, during this period there appeared scores of books which confounded scholars for centuries. Many of them were written by authors who never set foot on a boat but in their continental garrets concocted adventure tales to satisfy the public appetite. Prominent among such works were Jonathan Carver's *Travels Through the Interior Parts of North America in the Years 1766, 1767 and 1768,* Christian Frederick Damberger's *Travels Through the Interior of Africa from the Cape of Good Hope to Morocco Between the Years 1781 and 1797,* Thévenot's *Voyages and Travels,* Père Du Halde's *The General History of China* (1786), Gemelli Careri's *Voyage Around the World,* John Hill's *Grand Tour of Europe,* Charles Cochrane's *Journal of a Tour* (1830), credited to a fictitious Juan de Vega, and John Hunter's *Memoirs of a Captivity Among the Indians of North America.*

An early emulator of George Psalmanazar was Archibald Bower, who collaborated with him in writing *Universal History,* and on his own produced a tale similar to that which made Psalmanazar the hero of London society. It was a thrilling story of escape from a Jesuit college at Arezzo and of conversion to Protestantism about the year 1726. At least twenty-one pamphlets are known to have been published during the controversy which ended with a learned exposé by Dr. John Douglas, who also helped expose Psalmanazar.

The eighteenth century also was that of the real Baron Munchausen whose alleged adventures were told of him by one of his drinking companions, Rudolph Erich Raspe, in *The Surprising Adventures of Baron Munchausen*, which first appeared in 1786 in London and has been republished with additions many times since.

The real Munchausen was born in Bodenwerder of an ancient noble family in 1720 and became a Prussian officer, serving in the war against Turkey and retiring in 1750. In Bodenwerder, Weser, Germany, is to be seen a monument to him astride his famous half-of-a-horse doomed to perpetual thirst because of a body severed by a portcullis.

Many of the Munchausen stories which have delighted readers for a century and a half reach the height of the delightfully ridiculous. There is no record of anyone's ever having taken them seriously. They have, however, formed a norm with which many similar attempts at tall-story telling have been measured. A. G. L'Estrange suggested in his *History of English Humour* that they were intended as a satire on the marvelous travel stories of the time; they were dedicated to Bruce, a traveler whose account generally was discredited.

With the nineteenth century the existence of fabulous creatures in the remote parts of the earth was so thoroughly disproved that the emphasis in travelers' tales very definitely was upon unusual and thrilling experiences rather than upon the relating of amazing sights.

In 1898 a London magazine serialized the harrowing account of thirty years spent among the cannibals of Australia, of a fight with an octopus, of a shipwreck in which the narrator was rescued by a dog, of playing pirate with pelicans whom he robbed of their fish, and of a dwelling of pearl shells in which the adventurer enjoyed a shark-hide hammock. The British Association for the Advancement of Science, which invited the writer, Louis de Rougemont, to address it at Bristol, could discover nothing incredible about these anecdotes. Neither could experts of the Royal Geographical Society. Nevertheless, upon the magazine's own admission, the entire tale was a hoax. De Rougemont, following a public confession, revealed he really was a Swiss named Grin and departed with the proceeds of his fun.

The influence of increasing public knowledge of geography also was shown in Captain J. A. Lawson's *Wanderings in the Interior of New Guinea*, published in 1875 in London. Avoiding incredible exaggeration, it was a circumstantial day-by-day account "wonderful enough to cause the public to gape, yet not too fantastic," according to Albert Payson Terhune in a newspaper syndicated feature printed January 29, 1910, by the New York *Evening World.*

Captain Lawson's mountains, lakes and animals were larger than any others known to civilized man but not so large or grotesque as to be unbelievable, in contrast to the tales which Mandeville and others brought back from unknown regions in the earlier centuries.

Before the publishers called in copies, the book was accepted as a straightforward, plain narration of facts by an intrepid traveler. The strange monkeys of which he wrote were thought by some to be the missing Darwinian links, and Mt. Hercules, rising 25,314 feet, was accepted as surpassing Everest. Said Terhune: "The taste of the author's accurate and learned times urges him to restrict himself to marvels of an approved scientific nature . . . such as fairly high mountains and moderately large beasts, and to eschew such things as magic and monsters, in deference to the advanced stage of intelligence."

British publishers occasionally still call in copies of a travel book about the accuracy of which embarrassing questions have been asked, a recent example being Dr. Arthur Torrance's *Junglemania,* suspected of being a plagiarism of a novel, *Sepia,* by Owen Rutter. In the United States, especially during the skyrocketing twenties, however, the situation is that aptly described by Corey Ford in the July, 1929, issue of *Vanity Fair* as follows:

From a modest beginning the national appetite for Adventure has grown to such proportions that today the travel book is as standard to the American scene as corn flakes, radios, or Bishop Cannon; and in and out amid this summer harvest, the publishers scurry eagerly, grabbing up what windfalls they may find, offering travel books and more travel books without pause to investigate whether they are true or not, stirring up a lather of excitement like an insect whipping up its own spittle, swearing their heads off, never casting a weather eye to the future, never realizing that even the great American public can be stampeded once too often.

During the decade after this was written librarians continued to report travel books as the most popular type, despite an increased interest in works dealing with economic problems and world political affairs. In addition to this normal demand for "escape" literature, a liberal attitude on the part of critics is a boon to those who feel the urge to "stretch a point" here or there. In June, 1929, during the heights of the controversy over Joan Lowell's *The Cradle of the Deep,* the *Bookman* published a

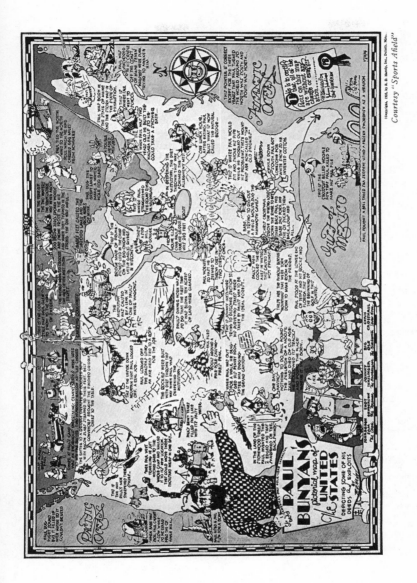

Chicago Historical Society

On fine linen stationery, with the engraved coat of arms of the British royal house, these invitations to the coronation of Edward VII and Queen Alexandra in 1902 caused several hundred of Chicago's "upper crust" moments of exultation. When, however, the recipients got around to reading the Instructions, on a separate card, they realized that they had been cleverly hoaxed.

The instructions read as follows:

"Those honored with invitations to the coronation are expected to give particular attention to their attire, and must be clothed according to their rank. Peers and peeresses of the realm, baronets, knights and their ladies, and members of the gentry are privileged to wear the royal crimson velvet, with coronets, tiaras, necklaces, rings, ear-rings, bracelets, epaulets, buckles, collarettes, sashes embroidered with strawberry leaves in silver gilt, girdles, stomachers, silver gilt crowns, and capes edged with twenty-five rows of minever. Titled nobility from America, such as merchant princes, coal barons, trust magnates, lords of finance with their ladies, must appear in costumes typifying the origin of their titles, and they may carry tape measures, coal scuttles, oil cans, stock tickers and other heraldic devices, and may wear stick pins, clothes pins, scarf pins, coupling pins, hair pins, rolling pins, cuff buttons, shoe strings, picture hats, turbans, handcuffs, overcoats, imitation lace scarfs, celluloid collars, hose or half hose as the case may be, rhinestones, collar buttons of silver gilt, and golf capes edged with two and one-half rows of rabbit skin.

"By special royal proclamation it is commanded and decreed that during and after the coronation when healths and toasts are to be drunk or thirsts are to be quenched either in high-balls, cocktails, sours or any other mixed drinks also by means of whiskey straights; old underhoof rye, manufactured by Chas. Dennehy & Co., of Chicago, U. S. A., shall be used, as it has been found by His Majesty to be the very best, purest and most ancient whiskey vended.

"By order of THE EARL MARSHAL.

"Verbum sapienti satis est."

revealing debate on the subject, "Are Literary Hoaxes Harmful?" The argument of Lincoln Colcord, who upheld the affirmative, was a lament, partly in the following words:

I believe that today, for the first time in literary history, we have the spectacle of a hoax of first proportions which has been fully exposed, while no one concerned in the fraud, either innocently or deliberately, seems greatly disturbed. . . . The critics who supported the book take refuge in the argument that it does not matter whether it is a hoax or not, so long as it is good reading; and criticism in general seems to lean towards this opinion.

Defending what Mr. Colcord admitted to be the majority point, Heywood Broun wrote that his first inclination was to demur to his opponent's arguments—to demur, he explained, being the legal way of saying, "What the hell!"—but to fill the space assigned him, he added:

In other words, Mr. Colcord would have us substitute the dull and dreary for the imaginative. He would abolish not only the last coast of Bohemia but its attendant ocean. I have no doubt that mankind could be cured of its romantic conception of long voyages beyond the equator if some hard-fisted writer insisted enough upon rubbing our noses in the brine. But would the world be any happier for its disillusion?

The world, encouraged by such a critical attitude, doesn't care. Instead, it has taken to its heart Joan Lowells, Richard Halliburtons and Trader Horns.

The only compromise by the publishers of *The Cradle of the Deep* with the book's critics was, when the tale reached the dollar edition stage, to quote Hugh Walpole on the jacket as believing, "Invention or not, it is a work of the most lively entertainment."

As to the late Richard Halliburton, his vigorous rejoinders to defamers leave one ready to believe that he actually followed the itinerary of his *Royal Road to Romance* and subsequent travelogues. Some of the exploits which he related and the swashbuckling aura with which he draped himself and his every vicissitude are still frequently questioned, however. For instance, his account of triumphantly swimming in the pool of the Taj Mahal has been robbed of much of its heroism by other visitors to the spot who declare the basin of murky liquid is hardly three feet deep.

Mrs. Ethelreda Lewis of South Africa, who collaborated with (that is, did all of the writing for) Alfred Aloysius Smith on *Trader Horn, Harold*

the Wedded, or the Young Vikings and *The Waters of Africa,* expressed
the majority point of view toward books of their kind in the following
words:

There is a footnote in *Trader Horn* which says, in effect, to the reader:
"Here is an old man who told a lie to me on his first appearance on my
doorstep. It was a lie about his birthplace, and there may be others in the
book. Here then is a book—take it or leave it on those conditions." Were
I to edit the book again, I should still add the footnote, for I still think
that although there are misstatements and exaggerations and the dates are
all muddled, what remains of value is not only remarkable but is *all that
matters* in a book so teeming with rich philosophy and rich and unique
love and knowledge of nature and human nature. It is not the facts of
Horn's life that matter to the literary reader for whom I wrote. It is his
fancies. Facts are common to all; but such fancies as Horn's are common
only amongst the rare souls and those touched with a certain quality of
genius.

Not only has the American public shown an increasing avidity for the
most recent in romantic adventure, but it has received enthusiastically
publishers' republication of some of the best of the old ones. For a time
Baron Munchausen jokes were "the thing." Then Paul Bunyan tall stories
became bigger and better. Scores of books about Bunyan's less known
counterparts appeared from all parts of the country: Tony Beaver, denizen
of the southern forests; Pecos Bill, from the Pecos River region of western
Texas; Dave Bunch, fabulous strong man of Shannon County, Missouri;
Gopher Bill, pioneer and plainsman; Allan Bradley, giant of Hedgehog
Harbor, Wisconsin; Kemp Morgan, oil worker of the Southwest; John
Henry, Louisiana Negro; Tom Quick, New York Indian killer; Solomon
Shell, Kentucky mountaineer, and many others. All possessed unparalleled
strength and capacity, their feats often approaching the miraculous. Most
of them had animals also capable of gigantic achievements rivaling those
of Babe, Bunyan's blue ox, or Lucy, his cow who once ate spruce and
balsam boughs and produced milk which Bunyan's loggers used for
cough syrup.

Popular among the "revivals" have been the romantic adventure tales
of Herman Melville, George Borrow and Edward Trelawny, all nineteenth century writers whose posthumous fame has exceeded considerably
that enjoyed by them during life because critics charged that they mixed
fact and fiction too freely in supposedly autobiographical accounts.

In this chapter, by argument and example, it has been demonstrated that the ubiquitous and eternal psychological necessity for vicarious adventure affords a lucrative opportunity for the imaginative wayfarer, to the distress of literary purists and often of sober scholars. Appropriate "clinchers" with which to conclude this section are two typical quotations from the questionnaires mentioned at the beginning:

I would like to travel if it were possible, and as it is not, I like to read books of as varied a country as possible.

I had read an article in the *Geographic Magazine* on the South Sea isles and the pictures in this magazine included the mountains described in *Typee*. I liked *Typee* because of its ideal country and climate, also including the happiness of the natives. To me *Typee* was more the way God intended us to live in the Garden of Eden before the fall of man.

CHAPTER XI

Incentives to Believe: Cultural Climate

INDIFFERENT, ignorant, vain, suggestible, awed by the real or feigned prestige of those who speak with authority, man believes what he wants to believe.

If this is so, as I have sought to demonstrate in the first ten chapters, the successful swindler, impostor, faker or forger—hoaxers all under the definition on which this study is predicated—is he who convinces his victims that he can supply that which is needed to make satisfactory belief plausible:

The means whereby health, wealth and happiness may be obtained;

The essential evidence that one's church, political party, race, city, state or nation is superior;

The fragments of knowledge to establish a scientific, literary, artistic, historical or other hypothesis;

The spectacular incidents to give sanctions to prejudices, attitudes and opinions;

The heroes to worship and the vicarious thrills by which to escape an otherwise dull and routine existence.

These "lacks" are basically ubiquitous and eternal. Throughout the centuries hoaxing has succeeded because of the same norms of social behavior. Nevertheless, fashions in hoaxes change with cultural conditions. The psychological thesis that men are prone to believe what most needs to be believed is established convincingly by an historical survey of the types of deception which have been most successful at different periods. Briefly, the evidence shows:

In highly creative periods there are few literary or artistic forgeries. When, however, writers, painters, sculptors and other aesthetes become sterile or imitative, buyers of first editions and old masters must beware.

When governments are stable and peace is maintained by a satisfactory balance of international political power, voters participate in orderly elections with a comparatively clear understanding of the issues involved, and diplomacy is more of the "open covenants, openly arrived at" nature. In times of great political stress and excitement, however, roorbacks abound, issues are beclouded by journalists and demagogues, chauvinism overshadows historical iconoclasm and atrocity stories multiply.

When migration and colonization are easy for the persecuted or economically underprivileged, swindles are at a minimum. As the rich get richer and the poor get poorer, however, Better Business Bureaus are overburdened, and there must be Barnums, Trader Horns and Douglas Corrigans to divert an increasingly large number of minds from their troubles.

When church and state are reconciled, the unconventional bit of religious lore is called heresy. When, however, ecclesiastical authority, either spiritual or temporal, wanes, apocryphal literature abounds.

During periods in which science is largely a matter of academic concern to mathematicians and laboratory logicians, the masses are unconcerned except when some theorist is so rash as to question Holy Writ. When, however, the results of experimentation begin to become evident in everyday life, through technological developments, labor-saving devices and mechanical recreational facilities, no supposed discovery made possible by the microscope or telescope is too marvelous to be believed.

To determine the extent to which cultural climate affects credulity, the investigator must refer to the scholars who have examined the fads and fashions of the different eras. He will make the significant discovery that each investigator who has studied the charlatanism of a particular period concludes his quest in the conviction that "humbuggery" then was "at its heights," "in a golden era," "rife" or "unrestrained." Nevertheless, the opportunity of which the hoaxer took advantage or the temptation to which he succumbed differed from century to century with cultural conditions, in the ways already indicated.

Professor Alfred Gudeman found: "The entire classical period of Greek literature furnishes us with no authentic instance of a literary fraud." He explained this circumstance in his essay "Literary Frauds Among the Greeks" in *Classical Studies in Honour of Henry Drisler,* as follows:

But this fact will no longer surprise us when we remember that this epoch marks the very culmination of the creative faculty of the Greek intellect, and as a consequence all the enduring monuments of genius which this era produced are characterized by originality of thought and expression, each author exhibiting an individuality quite his own. And if it be added that the only channel of publicity was a vast listening public, an audience in

the literal meaning of the term, the natural obstacles in the way of a successful perpetration of literary forgery will be seen to have been well-nigh
insurmountable. In fact, literary frauds cannot thrive in an era of intellectual productivity. It was not till a *reading* public had arisen in Greece,
the existence of which can hardly be said to antedate the days of Aristotle
and Isocrates, that such practices found more favourable conditions of
growth; for now the poet or prose writer no longer stood in full glare of
national publicity, and the reader had ceased to be in living touch, as it
were, with the author.

It was not until after the "golden era" of productivity ended, with the
almost simultaneous deaths of Alexander the Great, Aristotle and Demos-
thenes, that positive motives for fraud appeared. He continued:

There followed an age characterized by antiquarian research and
scholasticism. The foundations of originality being now exhausted, and
with no great objects to evoke enthusiasm or excite patriotic devotion,
scholars turned their attention to taking an inventory, so to speak, of their
glorious literary inheritance. The student and commentator succeeded the
creative artist. . . . This penetrating scrutiny in fields of research hitherto
entirely neglected must have soon revealed the fact that the writings of
many authors, having been eclipsed by the noonday splendour of some
greater genius, had been allowed to perish and that authentic biographical
information was in many instances utterly lacking. Now under the stim-
ulus of this curiosity, only the more enhanced by the obstacles thrown in
its way, it is not difficult to understand how anecdote and fable gradually
came to usurp the place of truth and facts no longer ascertainable and that
men of talent felt themselves induced to fill up some of these gaps by productions of their own.

The formation of big libraries and the generous prices paid for ancient
manuscripts are considered by all commentators on the period from Plato
to Cicero to have been stimulants to fraud. Richard Bentley in his *Dissertation upon the Epistles of Phalaris* wrote:

To forge and counterfeit books and father them upon great names has
been a practice almost as old as letters. But it was then most of all in
fashion, when the kings of Pergamus and Alexandria, rivaling one another in the magnificence and copiousness of their libraries, gave great
prices for any treatises that carried the names of celebrated authors. Which
was an invitation to the scribes and copiers of those times to enhance the
price of their wares by ascribing them to men of fame and reputation, and
to suppress the true names, that would have yielded less money.

J. A. Farrer began his *Literary Forgeries* with an almost identical statement and added, as does Bentley, that further confusion resulted from the custom, "in the schools of the sophists, of writing exercises on the imaginary speeches or letters of persons of celebrity: some of which came in time to pass as original works."

Either as the result of a deliberate intention to deceive, or innocently, gaps in the literature of the preceding centuries were filled by students of Plato and others who, according to Dionysius as quoted by Gudeman, "kindly lent their literary skill and learning to fill up a deplorable gap in Greek historiography."

Dionysius named, among those who supplied an unbroken series of tragic and comic poets from Thespis and Susarion down, representing every phase of Greek drama, Heraclides Ponticus, pupil of both Plato and Aristotle, who invented mythical predecessors of Homer, including Philammon, Linos and Amphion.

Speeches were invented for Pericles and other orators in whose audiences there probably were no stenographers, and still were accepted as genuine in Cicero's time. The Jews of Alexandria, during the reign of the Ptolemies, are said to have forged a number of Orphic hymns and to have interpolated the works of Hesiod and others to prove that much Hellenic wisdom was in reality stolen from the Pentateuch. Homer was made to appear as staunch advocate of stricter observance of the Sabbath. Major interpolations of Homer were intended to glorify Greece.

To Aristotle is given the credit for being among the first to express misgivings concerning much apocryphal material. Aristotle himself, like Plato and others, later was forged to trap unwary bibliophiles. Many of these attempts, however, were too crude to deceive, as, for instance, the so-called *Orphic Argonatria* in which Orpheus is made to say seriously that he expects to reach Ireland, probably landing at Queenstown and continuing to Liverpool. Likewise, a poem, "De Vetula," attributed to Ovid but probably written in the thirteenth century, makes Ovid talk of algebra, which was then not known by name.

The detailed story of the part religious forgeries have played in establishing the church has been reserved for Chapter XIV. The statements of a few authorities on the early Christian era, however, will provide a preview of what that chapter contains.

"Any expectation of an increasing regard for truth with the coming of the Christian era is doomed to disappointment," declared H. M. Paull in *Literary Ethics*. "The word 'truth' has not the same significance for the

Oriental as for ourselves," according to Renan as quoted by Henry G. Hewlett in the February, 1891, *Nineteenth Century,* to explain the incessant manufacture of apocryphal material which the church was forced, at the end of the second century, to halt by attempting to discriminate between what was genuine and what specious.

"It must be kept clearly and constantly in view that what we understand by a literary and historical conscience simply did not exist in the early Christian environment," wrote J. M. Robertson in *The Jesus Problem.* According to Hewlett in the article mentioned:

> Bearing in mind that it was from the eastern churches these fabrications usually proceeded we may justly make a large allowance for the difference which has always subsisted between the western and eastern mind with regard to the value of truth. . . . In estimating the culpability of a particular imposture, the difference which has always existed between the moral standards of various races must be taken into account.

Of the medieval period T. F. Tout in *Medieval Forgers and Forgeries* discovered:

> It was almost the duty of the clerical class to forge. If it did not always commit culpable forgeries for its own particular interest, it forged almost from a sense of duty for the benefit of society, the community, the house whose interest it represented.

> For in medieval eyes forgery in itself was hardly regarded as a crime. . . . Forgery hardly comes within the modest list of offenses within which the medieval mind limited its conception of a crime. It was natural to look indulgently upon an offense to which so large a proportion of the educated population was addicted. . . . Accordingly all practitioners of forgery had the "benefit of clergy."

The change, Tout explained, began with the prohibition of forgery of the king's seal and the counterfeiting of money.

The centuries from the fall of Rome to the Renaissance are called the Dark Ages because of the absence of critical scholarship and of anything approximating what we know as the scientific spirit. Virtually all literary and historical works produced during the period are unreliable. According to Paull, credulity was considered almost as a virtue, legends were accepted as true and traditions arose with absolutely no basis in fact. Historians even accepted without question such stories as that Brutus visited England. Bishop Stillingfleet in his *Origines Britannicae,* page 50 (as quoted in the *Portfolio,* September, 1816), said of this type of forgery:

It is well known that it was no unusual thing in that age [about the beginning of the sixteenth century] to publish books under the names of ancient authors. For about that time men began to be inquisitive into matters of antiquity, and therefore some who had more learning and better inventions than others, set themselves to work to gratify the curiosity of those who longed to see something of the antiquities of their own country; and such things were so easily and implicitly received by less judicious persons that it proved no easy matter to convince them of the imposture.

To explain the legends which grew up about the Emperor Constantine, first Christian Roman emperor, Professor Christopher B. Coleman wrote in his *Constantine the Great and Christianity*:

The early and luxurious growth of legends about Constantine is explained partly by the relative weakness of the investigative and historical spirit of the Romans. History among them never reached the position of an independent science.

The victory of Constantine and Christianity over persecution and paganism, Coleman believes, fired the imaginations of those who were to make the legends and history of the future.

After indicating the unreliability of the writings of Orosius, F. J. C. Hearnshaw, in the August 1, 1923, *Fortnightly Review,* wrote of the Middle Ages:

In deploring, however, this medieval prostitution of history to propaganda, we must be careful not to judge the conscience of that primitive and semi-barbaric age by the loftier standards of either ancient or modern times. It is probable that the monastic chronicler as he recorded imaginary marvels and the papal lawyer as he concocted fictitious donations and decrees had no more sense of wrongdoing than had Thucydides when he put supposititious speeches into the mouth of Pericles, or than has Mr. Drinkwater when he invents dialogues for Oliver Cromwell and Abraham Lincoln. . . .

The Dark Ages lightened as the Renaissance of the fifteenth and sixteenth centuries developed. With the revival of learning there began a fervent search by scholars for lost or hitherto unknown manuscripts. After the capture of Constantinople by the Turks the learned Greeks had been scattered all over the southern part of Europe, with the result that literary and artistic masterpieces which they had salvaged began to appear in many places when interest in them renewed. Because there had not yet developed an historical and scientific spirit by which to evaluate these finds, however, many forgeries were mixed with them.

Of the attitude of scholarship during the Renaissance, Andrew Lang wrote in the December, 1883, *Contemporary Review*:

> As yet scholars were eager rather than critical; they were collecting and unearthing rather than minutely examining the remains of classic literature. They had found so much, and every year were finding so much more, that no discovery seemed impossible. . . . This was the very moment for the literary forger; but it is improbable that any forgery of the period has escaped detection.

The anonymous author of "Literary Impostures—Alexandre Dumas," in the April, 1854, *North American Review,* expressed a similar view:

> In the sixteenth century it seems to have been considered as a regular and laudable amusement to circulate forged fragments of the classics. [Printing was still in its infancy and all the masterpieces were in manuscript form.] Scholars all over the land were busied in collating and comparing together different readings of the same piece, and in preparing it for the press. . . . This greedy appetite was often the cause of no little confusion to the too confiding editors, whose credulity led them to accept for genuine relics of antiquity such fraudulent imitations as the love of practical jokes might induce less grave and sober students to palm off upon them.

The deceptions of Michelangelo, mentioned in Chapter IV, were typical of the period. To obtain reputations and customers, Fra Filippo Lippi, Andrea del Sarto, Botticelli and other masters faked the ancients. Gardner Teall wrote in the December, 1908, *Cosmopolitan*:

> A study of the antique came so quickly into fashion, and in the train of it such efforts to collect ancient objects of art that skillful artists and artisans of the time could scarcely refrain from the temptations held out by the ease with which clever art forgeries were palmed off upon the gullible, who paid enormous prices for them.

The passage in the preceding chapter which dealt with fabulous tales of adventure might well have been inserted here to show the effect of public interest and information. Impetus was given the faked travelogue by the explorations of the fifteenth and sixteenth centuries, which included the discovery of the New World. Beginning with accounts of stupendous forms of animal and plant life, similar to nothing found in the known world, the mariners' yarns changed, with the development of geographic knowledge, to tales of thrilling experiences by intrepid adventurers.

A similar development may be noted in the field of literature. With the invention of printing and the consequent increase in literacy, authorship flourished. Characteristically, the eighteenth century, in which the novel developed, is known as "the golden era of the literary fraud." It was this period which Andrew Lang had in mind when he wrote in the December, 1883, *Contemporary Review*:

> In the whole amusing history of impostures, there is no more diverting chapter than that which deals with literary frauds. None contains a more grotesque revelation of the smallness and the complexity of human nature, and none . . . reveals more pleasantly the depths of mortal credulity.

Commentators on this period of literary history almost parody the apologists for early Christian writers. Forgery was still practiced freely and was condoned, and a popular prejudice against the new literary form, fiction, led authors to attempt to pass off their works as genuine narratives. Virtually every leading writer of the period appears, occasionally at least, among the ranks of hoaxers: Jonathan Swift, Samuel Johnson, Daniel Defoe, William Lauder, Horace Walpole, to mention only a few. James Lyman Whitney's *A Modern Proteus* is a sizable catalogue of books which were published under more than one title, each representing at least one literary theft.

A description of the period is given by J. S. Smart in *James Macpherson: An Episode in Literature* (a study of the poems of Ossian, mentioned in Chapter VIII):

> The classical literature of the early eighteenth century had passed its prime and was dying. . . . The reaction against it which led to the romantic movement was beginning. If it were possible to describe the poetry of Pope's age in a single phrase it might be called "which had its roots in criticism rather than imagination." It aimed at a revival or emulation of Latin and Greek literature by using the work of antiquity as models and its critics as law-givers. The taste of the rising generation now demanded something less studied, more spontaneous and more exciting.

One hundred years later, however, the situation was changed, Henry G. Hewlett states in the February, 1891, *Nineteenth Century*:

> In the present century, though the literary forger has been far from inactive, his successes, owing to the general spread of culture, and the special development of critical discernment, have happily been few and short-lived.

In a comparatively minor quasi-intellectual field, autograph collecting, the influence of cultural conditioning is demonstrable. The fad developed on the Continent during the eighteenth century, and according to *Harper's* for October, 1870, in each country the forged autograph conformed to the taste of the natives. In Germany, for instance, the forger wrote in Greek or Latin; in France he fabricated correspondence and memoirs; in England he became a poet and invented supplements to Shakespeare, Shelley and Byron. According to Farrer, between 1822 and 1835 more than 12,000 autographs were sold in France; from 1836 to 1840 some 11,000 were auctioned; between 1841 and 1845, about 15,000; and between 1846 and 1859, as many as 32,000. He remarks:

Whence came this enormous supply? Direct theft from public libraries undoubtedly would account for many, but the greater part were the offspring of forgery. The demand gave rise to the supply.

Born in the eighteenth century as an adult, the United States during the nineteenth century felt the lack of a childhood with its rich memories and cherished traditions. How it went about supplying this lack will be the main thesis of the next chapter, to be followed by another in which will be considered the effect a catch-as-catch-can democracy has had upon hoaxes connected with politics and government. The impact of contemporary civilization upon scientific, literary, journalistic faking also will be dealt with in later chapters. For a bird's-eye view of the present century the following from the pen of J. C. Funk in *Hygeia* for December, 1932, is apropos, even though his subject matter was the limited field of medical charlatanism:

Now the peculiar thing is that the modern faker is little changed either in method or in manner from his forerunner of a hundred years ago. While incantations, amulets and charms have been discarded, practically all the rest of it survives. The onward rush of scientific achievement in medicine, chemistry, bacteriology, sanitation and disease prevention in no wise dampens the brazen effrontery of this seductive gentry. To them the significant fact remains that some of the then incurable and stubborn diseases are as yet in these classes; and inasmuch as hundreds of thousands of people suffer from them or imagine that they do so, the harvest remains ripe for plucking as in the days of yore, with the added advantages that accrue from increased population, easy communication and richer purses.

To summarize all that the first part of this book has revealed, the following sage observation of an anonymous writer in the *Dublin University Magazine,* quoted in the *Eclectic* for July, 1868, may be recalled:

If we are to judge by the avidity with which men in all ages have swallowed and still continue to swallow the most palpable deceptions, we must conclude that the aphorism we have prefixed to our present article is not, as the satiric poet intended, a mere jest, but a positive fact.

The aphorism, taken from *Hudibras,* was as follows:

> Doubtless the pleasure is as great
> Of being cheated as to cheat.

PART II

HOW THEY SUCCEED

CHAPTER XII

Historical Hoaxing

A GENERATION ago, and for many preceding generations, school boys and girls believed not only in Santa Claus, the Easter Bunny and the stork but also in Helen of Troy, Robin Hood, William Tell, King Arthur, Robert Bruce's spider, the Pied Piper of Hamelin, Lady Godiva and Peeping Tom, Paul Revere's ride and George Washington's cherry tree.

Today, our historical debunkers assure us, all is changed. Not only have modern youngsters lost their faith in legendary figures, but they also poke fun at mother and father for not knowing that no law was passed in 1228 in Scotland to permit women to propose marriage to men every four years; that witches were not burned at Salem; that Priscilla did not tell John Alden to speak for himself; that Pocahontas did not save John Smith's life; that the heroic picture of Washington crossing the Delaware was not painted on the spot; that America was not named for Amerigo Vespucci; that Louis XIV never said, "L'Etat, c'est moi," that Wellington never shouted, "Up, guards, and at 'em," that Nelson at Trafalgar never signaled, "England expects every man to do his duty," that Theodore Roosevelt's unorthodox scramble up San Juan Hill did not win the Spanish-American War; that Pershing never said, "Lafayette, we are here," that there is nothing secret about the Pyramids and that probably a lot of other things we think happened never did.

Maybe so. Nevertheless, a high-school history teacher whom the writer knows—in a school system which for years has selected its textbooks with the greatest possible care so as to eliminate the unreliable, particularly the chauvinistic anecdotes—was baffled by her inability to inspire a scientific attitude in her students, and made an attitude test according to the most approved methods, which she had authorities on the faculty of one of the nation's leading universities check. Here is what she found her class to believe:

1. American foreign policy always has been wise and unselfish.

2. All wars in which our country has been engaged were necessary and glorious.

3. The affairs of foreign countries are of little interest to us.

4. Americans are superior to other people, and the United States is a leader in nearly all forms of social and political activity.

5. Freedom of speech has been practiced since the writing of the Constitution.

6. The Constitution is above criticism.

7. Equality of opportunity has been won and is maintained in the United States.

8. The common man may expect to be comfortable and secure in the United States.

With the rightness or wrongness of these or any other attitudes the present study is not concerned; but it is significant that a single competent teacher cannot dissipate the stereotypes regarding her own subject obtained from parents, other teachers and other textbooks. "Since history has been the target of investigation," she remarked, "other courses in the high-school curriculum have come through with the very thing which has been suppressed in the field of social science. Many books used in foreign language departments are colored. French and German readers written at the time of the World War adroitly tell their side of the story. Again, in some English courses we find evidences of instilling ideas having to do with hero worship, patriotism and morals."

In other words, historical beliefs attain cultural sanctions which do not change in a generation. Furthermore, even historians who condone glorification of heroes and events in the interest of patriotism are bewildered by conflicting interpretations of identical periods of history by equally eminent scholars. Their dilemma was explained in part by F. J. C. Hearnshaw in the *Fortnightly Review* August 1, 1923, as follows:

History has, from early times, been the happy hunting ground of the propagandist. Every kind of zealot has felt that the appeal which he makes to abstract principle will be immeasurably strengthened if he can supplement and reenforce it . . . by a demonstration based on accomplished fact. History is the memory of the human race, but it is a memory artificially created and sustained. It is the historian who determines, by his method of selection and rejection, what facts or legends are to be perpetuated and in what light they are to be regarded.

Much—for the sake of clarity regarding the point of immediate concern let us say, all—of this incessant rediscovery and reinterpretation of history in accordance with contemporary opinion, is unintentional. Our great historians, from Herodotus to the present, have not been deliberate hoaxers. The scholarly confusion which their best, honest efforts has caused, however, complicates the task of the sincere truth seeker and, through him, of the masses for whose attitudes and opinions he is responsible to a large extent. If objective historical research is an impossible ideal, the harm that the good men of historical bent may do may be as extensive and intensive as that caused by the renegades who consciously distort and confuse.

One more quotation to elucidate the point, taken from an article by C. E. Ayres in the March, 1929, *Bookman*:

What do we know of the past? The greatness of Greece? That was the invention of Plutarch. The fall of Rome? That was Gibbon's idea. Magna Charta was reconstructed, almost invented, by Coke. The Industrial Revolution was coined by Arnold Toynbee. The English "people" was devised by Green. Tacitus was not aware that Rome was falling, Gibbon saw nothing of the Industrial Revolution. Macaulay never heard of the English people. Bancroft was entirely ignorant of the significance of the frontier in American history, as he died two years before Turner "saw" its extraordinary significance.

The historians just mentioned are among the greatest of all time, and we cannot believe their sins to have been deliberate. On the lesser lights the *New Republic* editorialized May 9, 1923:

They wrote, too often, with a political purpose, more or less subtly concealed, and political purposes seldom square with truth. One wrote the history of Greece with a view to bolstering parliamentary institutions. Another wrote the history of imperial Rome in justification of Bismarckian imperialism. And when nationalism went mad, toward the end of the century [the nineteenth], every country developed its corps of historians along with its guns and ships, as a weapon of national defense or aggression. Every political party, every social class, came to have its official manipulator of history. The historians who remained steadfast in their loyalty to the truth were helpless to check the flood of spurious historical ideas. The public preferred the debased coinage in its daily trafficking and came to regard it as standard. History had become present politics.

It is with these charlatans that this chapter is concerned. While the quotation is fresh in mind, consider the experience of Dr. William E. Barton, who devoted a lifetime to distinguishing legend and myth from fact so that the unadulterated greatness of Abraham Lincoln might be understood. In the Boston *Herald* in 1925, Dr. Barton declared:

Several years ago I made a careful investigation of the matter of President Lincoln's letter to Mrs. Bixby, and wrote an article which I sent to one or two periodicals, but it was returned unprinted. The editors thought the public did not care to have its faith in that letter disturbed.

The Bixby letter, every schoolboy knows, allegedly was written to the mother of five sons who died fighting for the Union cause. Although the original of the letter is lost and the many supposedly authentic facsimiles of it contain noticeable differences, Dr. Barton did not say that Lincoln could not have written it. However, he did learn that not all of Mrs. Bixby's sons enlisted in the army, and that not all of those who did were killed. If Lincoln wrote the beautiful prose credited to him, "it was a beautiful blunder and well worth while for the sake of the letter," he concluded.

Another precious Lincoln anecdote which it is considered almost sacrilegious to question is that which first appeared in poetic form from the pen of Francis de Haes Janvier and was included in the *Personal Reminiscences* of L. E. Chittenden, register of the Treasury under Lincoln, published in 1891. It has the sympathetic president making a frantic dash from Washington to stop the execution by a firing squad of William Scott, a soldier caught asleep while on sentinel duty.

This story, "true in spirit if not in fact," Dr. Barton completely disproved by discovering the actual pardon, signed by General McClellan, not President Lincoln. The latter, Dr. Barton admitted, might have approved McClellan's action, which followed the presentation to him of a petition signed by seven captains of Scott's regiment and Brigadier General W. F. Smith asking that the young soldier's life be spared. Existence of this petition disproves the myth that Lincoln was the only humanitarian among those who directed the military tactics of the northern army. There is no record, Dr. Barton found, of any soldier's having faced the firing squad for falling asleep while on duty during either the Civil or any other American war.

As one of his reasons for writing *The Life of Abraham Lincoln,* Dr. Barton gave: "All the extant biographies of Lincoln contain inaccuracies, some of them trivial, others important, and few of them grave." In his *Myths After Lincoln,* Lloyd D. Lewis explained this avidity for Lincoln apocrypha as an understandable attempt to give the United States what it lacked during the first ninety years of its existence: a hero-god to worship. Because Tom Lincoln seemed too unromantic a figure to have sired the Great Emancipator, there even have been scandalous whispers about

Abraham's legitimacy and also about that of his mother, Nancy Hanks. All brands of Christians have vied with one another to prove that Lincoln, who never joined a church, favored this or that denomination. For the superstitious there is the tale that he had a premonition of death through a dream which he related to his cabinet the day of his assassination. Ida M. Tarbell thinks the Herndon story of Lincoln's failing to appear on the first day set for his marriage to Mary Todd is apocryphal.

To bolster the Greenback-Populist movement during the last quarter of the nineteenth century a mosaic of quotations from Lincoln's speeches, addresses to Congress and inaugurals was edited, with interpolations to indicate that he had prophetic vision regarding the monetary problems of a generation after his death. The most pertinent paragraph, denunciatory of the money powers and their increasing control over the nation's natural resources, was pure fiction. It follows:

I see in the near future a crisis approaching that unnerves me, and causes me to tremble for the safety of my country. As a result of war, corporations have been enthroned and an era of corruption in high places will follow, and the money power of the country will endeavor to prolong its reign by working upon the prejudices of the people until all the wealth is aggregate in a few hands and the republic is destroyed.

Despite the decline of the Greenback movement this quotation continues to pop up. During the 1936 presidential campaign the columnist, Herbert Agar, used it. In its issue of November 4, 1936, the Kansas City *Times,* which used Agar's column, editorially reprimanded its author and gave a list of important Americans who have been misled into repeating it as genuine. George Seldes used it in his book *You Can't Do That* to open the chapter "The Fascist Pattern: Money," and also referred to it later in the book.

During the 1936 campaign, the Republican National Committee quoted an even more important Lincoln forgery as Number 1 of an illustrated series of short items, called "The Strange New Deal": "If we buy a ton of steel rails in England for $90 America gets the steel rails but England gets the $90. If we buy the steel rails in the United States we have the steel rails and the $90 too." As numerous authorities have pointed out, the first steel rails were not rolled in the United States until May 24, 1865, a month after Lincoln's death. After Senator L. J. Dickinson of Iowa used the fictitious quotation in a speech in Boston in February, 1935, the Boston *Herald* credited it to Robert G. Ingersoll about 1894. The quotation appears in George L. Chase's *Industrial Development of Nations* and has been used many, many times, frequently with some other commodity substituted for steel rails.

One of the most recent important attempts to complicate the research for true Lincolniana was that of a Miss Wilma Frances Minor who convinced the editors of the *Atlantic Monthly* that a collection of weather-beaten love letters she produced actually passed between Lincoln and Anne Rutledge, his sweetheart. Miss Minor said her mother obtained them from Frederick Hirth who got them from his sister, Elizabeth Hirth, who got them from Sally Calhoun, who got them from Matilda Cameron, friend of both the alleged correspondents.

Upon their appearance in the *Atlantic Monthly* beginning with December, 1928, they were pounced upon by scholars. The brief but stormy controversy ended with a critical review by Paul M. Angle, executive secretary of the Abraham Lincoln Association, and an admission of their probable spuriousness by the editors of the *Atlantic* in April, 1929. Mr. Angle applied five tests: (1) ink and paper; (2) soundness of pedigree—line of reliable owners; (3) handwriting; (4) general content, and (5) how incidents check with historical fact. He found them faulty in all five respects.

Into the land of myth and legend, along with Abraham Lincoln, has gone his assassin, John Wilkes Booth. Because of many circumstances—such as the ease with which he gained access to the president's box at the theater, his unimpeded escape and the secrecy enforced by Secretary of State Seward in disposing of his body—there is ample ground for disagreement among historians regarding some of the details. When a collection of Lincoln's letters in the Library of Congress was examined in 1947, however, the hopes of many that new light would be shed on the problem were not realized. It is unlikely, however, that better evidence will be submitted than that assembled by Francis Wilson in his *John Wilkes Booth: Fact and Fiction of Lincoln's Assassination* to disprove the widely held belief that the man who was shot April 14, 1865, in a barn on the Garrett farm in Virginia either by Boston Corbett, a cavalry sergeant, or by himself was not in reality John Wilkes Booth.

Still on display at carnivals is a mummified body of a man who committed suicide in 1903 at Enid, Oklahoma. Known as David E. George, he was one of about forty persons who "confessed" shortly before death that they were Booth. The sensation of the remarkably embalmed body results from the assiduousness of a Memphis lawyer, Finis Bates, who obtained it after it had remained unclaimed for several years and identified it as that of a John St. Helen who, years before, believing he was about to

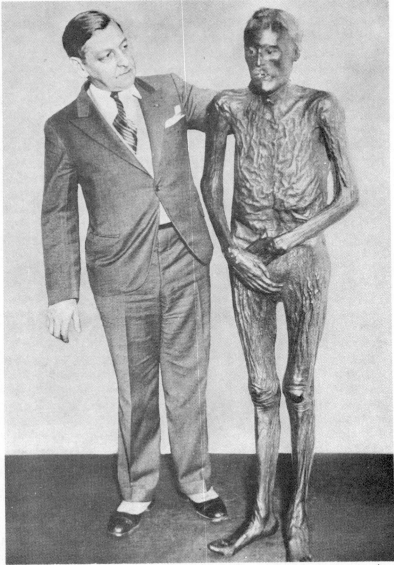

Acme

IS THIS JOHN WILKES BOOTH'S MUMMY?

This is the mummy which has been shown for years in side shows as that of the assassin of Abraham Lincoln. It is that of a man, known as John St. Helen, who died in Enid, Okla., in 1903. X-rays reveal he suffered fractures and wounds similar to those of Booth and that his stomach contains a signet ring inscribed with either a "B" or an "S."

Nicolet Chapter, Daughters of the American Revolution, Green Bay, Wis.

HONORING A FRENCH PRINCE?

Miss Marian Skenandore, whose family came to Wisconsin from New York with Eleazar Williams, who claimed to be Louis XVII of France, is shown unveiling a marker Oct. 27, 1927, to indicate where the supposed dauphin lived. Below is a close-up of the inscription, reading: "This tablet marks the landed estate of Eleazar Williams who served in the U.S.A. during the War of 1812 and who was reputed to be Louis XVII, dauphin of France. This tract of land extending from Little Rapids to Kaukauna was deeded by the Menominee Indians to Madeline Jordain, a daughter of the tribe and wife of Eleazar Williams. Erected by the Jean Nicolet Chapter, Daughters of the American Revolution, 1926."

die, confessed his "identity" to Bates. Bates told his story in *The Escape and Suicide of John Wilkes Booth.* Although the mummy bears a resemblance to Booth, even to bodily scars, impartial authorities never have accepted it as genuine. In 1910 the *Dearborn Independent* examined its record carefully with negative results.

According to Franklin J. Foster of the University of Alabama, there are in existence about 200 pistols of which each owner believes he has the one that killed Abraham Lincoln. On the anniversary of Lincoln's birthday in 1925 the Minneapolis *Star* printed an interview with Blanche de Bar Booth, niece of the assassin, to the effect that her uncle called upon her in the eighties. This she denied in a letter to Francis Wilson.

According to Burke McCarty in *The Suppressed Truth About the Assassination of Abraham Lincoln,* Booth was merely the tool of a Catholic pro-southern organization which plotted the crime. Other historians insist that cabinet members and other high officials were among the conspirators. In 1938 Izola Forrester wrote a book to say that she is the granddaughter of Booth, who escaped and married. To all of this, the serious scholar who thinks it matters displays either grievously iconoclastic attention or skeptical disdain; and he who thinks it does not matter throws up his hands in dismay.

Long before the myth makers had a chance to go to work on Lincoln material, George Washington was of course the favorite for those who felt the young nation must have apotheosized heroes. Among the books which the young Lincoln is said to have treasured was Pastor Weems' *Life of George Washington,* which was assigned to its proper place in Chapter VIII. That chapter also took care of Paul Revere's Ride, the Mecklenburg Declaration of Independence, Betsy Ross, the "shot heard 'round the world," Barbara Fritchie and a number of other historical legends.

Another probably apocryphal tale, still widely believed regarding the first president, is that he was overheard by a Quaker, Isaac Potts, praying loudly at Valley Forge. In 1891 the discovery at Mount Vernon of an autographed prayer was said to substantiate this story. In a privately printed edition the Reverend W. Herbert Burk in 1907 presented the copy book prayer as confirmation of the belief that Washington was a religious man. William J. Johnson used the prayer in *George Washington the Christian.* Its genuineness was disproved by Rupert Hughes in the first volume of his biography of Washington.

In March, 1935, the Freethinkers of America unsuccessfully sued the rector, warden and vestry of Trinity Church, New York, for $5,000.20 damages on the imputed ground that the Washington prayer inscribed on a plaque and sold on postcards for ten cents each at St. Paul's Chapel is a "religious fraud." This prayer purports to be taken from George Washington's "circular letter addressed to the governors of all the states on disbanding the army," June 8, 1787, at Newburgh.

What Weems and others did for Washington other writers did for many another Revolutionary and later hero. The chief biographer of the naval hero John Paul Jones was Augustus C. Buell, whose *Life of John Paul Jones* was examined critically in 1906 by Mrs. Reginald de Koven and found to be "the most audacious historical forgery ever put out upon a credulous public."

Suspicions that Buell's account was not altogether reliable began with the attempt to trace the books included in his bibliography. Some, such as the memoirs of Adrien de Capelle and the papers of Joseph Hewes, never were found; nor are there any records that these writers ever existed. Likewise, the Robert Morris, Gouverneur Morris and Livingston papers never were in the possession of the New York Historical Society, where Buell said he consulted them.

One of the main incidents in Buell's biography concerns John Paul's adding Jones to his name. Professor Albert Bushnell Hart gives Junius Davis credit for disproving the statement that this was at the request of a William Jones who, in return, promised Paul that he would remember him in his will. Davis made a long list of points: (1) William Jones never left John Paul a penny; (2) Paul never qualified as Jones' heir; (3) Paul never inherited anything, etc.

Willis J. Abbot in his autobiography tells the story of Alfred Henry Lewis, who also wrote a life of John Paul Jones. After the exposure of Buell's book Abbot congratulated Lewis on having the only authentic life of Jones. Lewis responded: "The hell, that's the only book about Paul Jones I ever read. I just took it and translated it into my own language. If it's all wrong, so's my book."

In general histories of the early periods of America's existence, the same unreliability is encountered. For instance, for more than one hundred years the best first-hand, eyewitness account of the American War of Independence was supposed to be *The History of the Rise, Progress and Establishment of the Independence of the United States of America,* by William

Gordon, printed in England in 1788 and in this country the following year.

In the preface the author innocently acknowledged his indebtedness to the *Annual Register,* an English publication founded in 1758 by Robert Dodsley and edited for thirty years by Edmund Burke. After Bancroft, Channing and other historians for a century had quoted from Gordon's account without taking the trouble to investigate his references, Orin Grant Libby decided to look up the files of the *Register.*

The result showed that Gordon merely copied, virtually word for word, from a series of articles under the title *History of Europe* which described the chief events on both sides of the Atlantic leading up to the Revolution. Summarizing his findings for the American Historical Association in 1899, Dr. Libby said:

> To sum up our conclusions thus far, we may say that Gordon was neither a man of unimpeachable veracity nor a great historian, and that his history must be rejected wholly as a source for the American Revolution.

Likewise suspect is one of the earliest works to deal with the history of colonial Puritanism in New England, *The General History of Connecticut,* published in 1829 by the Reverend Richard Peters and drawn upon heavily ever since by historians. It attracted popular as well as scholarly interest by its list of laws enacted by the Puritan lawmakers enjoining their constituents not to kiss their children on the Sabbath, nor to make mince pies or play any musical instrument except the drum, trumpet or jew's-harp and, in general, invoking similar drastic restrictions upon liberty of action on week days.

That no such laws ever existed, and that Mr. Peters was "a lying Episcopalian parson," is believed by most historians today. That he gave a fairly good picture of the unwritten moral code of the time is the most anyone says for him. It is agreed that at least one-fifth of the "laws" never were codified. Of the others it is contended variously that Mr. Peters invented them, or that he took them from *The History of New England,* by Daniel Neal (London, 1747), which, as far as I know, never has been attacked.

Neal also printed twenty-eight of the same laws, and therefore Professor Walter F. Prince believed that, if they were forged, Mr. Peters was not the guilty author. Professor M. S. De Vere, of the University of Virginia, author of *Americanisms* (1872), considered all of them authentic, and many churchmen have come to their support. On the other hand, Albert Bushnell Hart refuses to accept them because of the failure of any historian to find them in records of the time. James Hammond Trumbull of Hartford, Connecticut, denounced them vehemently, as did Harold Underwood Faulkner.

"History will be sought in vain for a more extraordinary growth of fame after death," wrote Professor Edward G. Bourne in *Essays in Historical Criticism* of Marcus Whitman (1802–1847), American pioneer and missionary, who in 1900 polled as many votes as George Rogers Clark, William Lloyd Garrison, Wendell Phillips and James Monroe for a place in America's Hall of Fame. The Whitman legend, as Bourne calls it, was that it was he who saved Oregon Territory for the United States by a trip in 1843 from Walla Walla, in the Territory, to Washington, D. C.

Bourne, whose conclusions have been accepted by historians, believed the real purpose of Whitman's return East was to obtain a reversal of the decision of the American Board of Commissioners for Foreign Missions to terminate the Northwest missions. The first claim that he also visited Washington, interviewing President John Tyler and Secretary of State Daniel Webster, was made in 1864 by the Reverend H. H. Spalding, a missionary associate. Whitman and his wife were massacred by Indians in 1847.

Amplifications of Spalding's story have been multitudinous. The controversy did not end with Bourne's scholarly documentary study in 1901. It is continued today by lay historians in special works on the subject, but the story is rejected by careful writers, many of whom never accepted it.

Whitman College at Walla Walla was founded in 1859 by Cushing Eells as a memorial to Marcus Whitman.

Summarizing his point of view on why the soul of John Brown (1800–1859) has kept "marching on," Leland H. Jenks wrote in the March, 1924, *American Mercury*:

Like many other Americans of mediocre talent, Brown has come to enjoy a posthumous fame that is grossly disproportionate to his actual facts, and often at variance with them. So wide, indeed, is the disparity between what he did and what he is venerated for, that it may be fairly argued that the Brown of American legend is not the real Brown at all, but merely the hypostasis of an idea, the personification of that remote ideal which the Nineteenth Century called Liberty.

Of the hero of the attack in 1859 on Harpers Ferry, James Truslow Adams says in his *The Epic of America*:

Perhaps no man in American history less deserves the pedestal of heroism on which he has been raised, but the North at once enshrined him as a saint, and more than ever convinced the South that there could be no peaceful solution of the conflict . . .

With these opinions the *Encyclopædia Britannica* and James Ford Rhodes and other historians agree.

Stephen D. Peet in *Prehistoric America* (Vol. II, p. xix) dismisses *Traditions of Decoodah and Antiquarian Researches,* by William Pidgeon, written in 1858, as follows:

It purported to be a description of mounds and earth works which the author had discovered, the explanation of which was given to him by the last prophet of the Elk nation, called Decoodah. This book has been quoted extensively by writers upon archaeology, and the cuts have been used as correctly representing the groups of mounds and effigies. The localities in which Mr. Pidgeon stated there were extensive groups of emblematic mounds have, however, been visited by various gentlemen who are in the field, but so far, not a single group has been identified and it is exceedingly doubtful whether any of them will be. Mr. T. H. Lewis and the author of this book have sought for these groups but have failed to find them. There are so many marvelous things about the book, and such a misty shadowy way of describing the mounds that many have doubted whether any of the descriptions could be relied upon, for they are so vague and uncertain. We consider the work as of no value to science.

Charles E. Brown, director of the Wisconsin State Historical Museum, was one of those who have searched for the mounds. He told the writer that not one could be found.

When we come to the twentieth century we find both myth makers and debunkers hard at it. Ferdinand Lundberg in his *America's Sixty Families* says Theodore Roosevelt decidedly was not a trust buster but the genial William Howard Taft was; Mrs. Woodrow Wilson, wife, and Joseph Tumulty, secretary, of the World War president, fail to agree on the part he played in many matters of state; the taciturnity of Calvin Coolidge is denied by many who knew him intimately; John Hamill's *The Strange Career of Mr. Hoover Under Two Flags* has been disproved but still believed by many; it did no good in many quarters for President Roosevelt to deny that his family name was Rosenfeldt and his ancestry at least part Jewish, that his mother obtained a large rent for the use of the family estate at Hyde Park, New York, as a summer White House, and that he spent more federal money than Congress allowed for travelling expenses.

Prime latter-day presidential mystery of all, however, is just what happened in the national capital during the short time Warren G. Harding was in the White House. How much credence can be placed in any of the several books on the Harding administration which have been published to date is difficult or impossible to say. Because they contradict one another, all cannot possibly be authentic.

Nan Britton's *The President's Daughter* was among the first of these books and contained the charge that President Harding was the father of Miss Britton's daughter, Elizabeth Ann. In November, 1931, Miss Britton lost a $50,000 libel suit against C. A. Klunk of Marion, Ohio, author of *The Answer to the President's Daughter,* who called her book a lie.

Another equally sensational book was Gaston Means' *The Strange Death of President Harding,* with its insinuation that Mr. Harding was poisoned by his wife, Florence Kling Harding, at San Francisco. In *Liberty* for November 7, 1931, Mrs. May Dixon Thacker, who did the actual writing of the book upon information supplied by Means, repudiated it. It must be admitted, however, that Mrs. Thacker gave no convincing reasons for coming to the conclusion, nearly two years after the book appeared, that it was a hoax. She seems merely to have been irritated by Means and to have decided that what she had formerly believed was not true at all.

Revelry, a novel by Samuel Hopkins Adams, easily was recognized as a story of the Harding administration. It suggested the president's death was suicide to escape the results of scandal about to break. It was debated in Congress following its appearance in 1926.

In 1932 appeared *The Inside Story of the Harding Tragedy,* by Harry M. Daugherty, Harding's campaign manager and attorney general. Thomas Dixon in the introductory "Historical Note" said: "This book will certainly discredit three scurrilous attacks entitled *Revelry, The President's Daughter* and *The Strange Death of President Harding."* The book is, truly, almost a complete denial and whitewash. It ends with the following two paragraphs:

If Harding had lived!

It is yet too early to see him in true full perspective—a modern Abraham Lincoln whose name and fame will grow with time.

Who the hoaxer was, the future may tell.

Despite the impression which up to this point this chapter may have created, not all, or even the best, historical hoaxing has been done on this side of the Atlantic. The *New Republic* in its issue of May 9, 1923, remarked:

For 2,000 years and more Herodotus was honored with the title of Father of History. Then came the nineteenth century with its passion for truth. Herodotus was weighed line by line and found light. It was proved that he had falsified events, in passages without number. His old title gave way to a new one, Father of Lies. . . . Herodotus lied, but for the sake of the Muse. History, as he conceived it, was an art, as exacting as tragedy or sculpture. If the facts did not observe the proper proportions, fall into the desired rhythms, he mended them, in good faith. He never lied to advance any selfish personal or political purpose. The best thing we can do is to return to his methods.

High up in the list of spurious documents which caused scholarly confusion are the Epistles of Phalaris which for more than fifteen hundred years were accepted as genuine and formed the basis for many other writings until 1695 when Richard Bentley exposed them in *Dissertation on the Epistles of Phalaris.*

The one hundred forty-eight epistles allegedly were composed by the Tyrant of Agrigentum in Sicily between 570 and 544 B.C. Contained in them was a fascinating description of the life, civilization and culture of the Greek colonies in the Mediterranean. Although Erasmus suspected they were an invention of the second century, it remained for Bentley to prove that the supposed Phalaris mentioned places nonexistent during his lifetime and also spoke of the art of tragedy, then unknown. Bentley also pointed out plagiarisms of Herodotus, Democritus, Callimachus and others. Today authorship of the epistles generally is ascribed to Adrianus of Tyre in A.D. 192. Of them Andrew Lang wrote in *Books and Bookmen:*

These illustrate, like most literary forgeries, the extreme worthlessness of literary taste as a criterion of the authenticity of writings.

Perhaps no great writer confounded both his contemporaries and their descendants more than Daniel Defoe. His satirical *The Shortest Way with Dissenters* resulted in his being sentenced to the stocks when it was taken seriously; his *Robinson Crusoe* was one of the most successful literary hoaxes of all time. His *History of the Great Plague in London* was advertised as written by "a citizen who lived the whole time in London"; but Defoe was four years old at the supposed time of writing of the "eyewitness" account which Dr. Richard Mead, famous historian, and many others quoted as authentic. His *Tour Through the Whole Island of Great Britain* and *New Voyage Round the World* were written without their author's having left home.

These works and others, including *The Apparition of Mrs. Veal, Moll Flanders, Colonel Jack* and *Captain Singleton,* were disturbing to the literary purists among his coevals. Posthumously, however, it was *The Military Memoirs of Captain Carleton,* which he may not have written, which upset the historical applecart.

Although this book appeared in 1728, according to Arthur Parnell, it excited little or no interest among historians until Boswell quoted Dr. Samuel Johnson as believing the memoirs contained the best account of the achievements of the Earl of Peterborough. It was this endorsement which inspired Sir Walter Scott, an admirer of Peterborough, to reedit the forgotten work.

From then on, Parnell relates, all subsequent writers on the wars of Queen Anne, with three exceptions, made the memoirs the basis of their accounts. Scott's glowing preface, claiming undoubted authenticity for the book, was accepted at its face value until 1830, when there arose a school of skeptics who believed Defoe was the author. It is included in the editions of Defoe's work by William Hazlitt, John Lockhart, Henry Bohn, Dr. Tegg and others, editions still to be found in modern libraries.

Says Parnell in *The War of the Succession in Spain*:

The upshot of the matter is the remarkable fact that, whilst every nineteenth century English history (hitherto written) treating of the War in Spain is based on the Carleton "memoirs," every nineteenth century edition of Defoe's works includes them among his fictions. . . .

As to Peterborough being the person who conceived its production, paid for its publication, and inspired its central portion, there can be little reasonable doubt. And in regard to its actual writer, all the circumstantial testimony as yet obtained (which is of some extent) points unswervingly to a master of libellous literature who was one of the few intimate friends of the projector, a close associate of Dr. Freind, and a bitter enemy of Lord

Galway; in short, to Dr. Jonathan Swift, Dean of St. Patrick's. That Defoe was the author is a theory of the most irrational nature. All the available information (general and special) completely dispels such an idea.

Another and more important instance in which the error of an eminent scholar in sanctioning as genuine historical material that was specious led to confusion for centuries, was the championing by Dr. William Stukeley of De Situ Britanniae, supposedly by Richard of Cirencester, "discovered" by Charles Julius Bertram.

Even today schoolbooks and atlases have not been purged of the influence of the former fake whose real author at the time, 1747, was a twenty-four-year-old teacher of English at the Danish Royal Naval Academy at Copenhagen. It was not, in fact, for one hundred and one years that the disastrous hoax was discovered; in the meantime, Bertram (1723–1765) had died covered with glory.

De Situ Britanniae was a description of Roman Britain and was accompanied by an ancient map. Stukeley, first secretary of the London Society of Antiquaries, apparently was overzealous in his desire to obtain credit for giving it to the world. Thus, when Bertram presented to him the "ancient" manuscript reputedly discovered by the youth in some archives, he negotiated for its prompt publication.

Among the results were the following: the British Royal Ordnance Survey copied the sites of Roman stations and these were still on its maps at the close of the nineteenth century; the keeper of the Cotton Library assured Stukeley that the handwriting on the manuscript was genuine fourteenth century; Henry Hatcher of Salisbury translated the book from Latin into English and vouched for it; John Whitaker, historian of Manchester, used it as the chief authority for his Antiquarian Romance; the great Gibbon said of its supposed author: "Although it may not seem probable that he wrote from the manuscript of a Roman general, he shows a genuine knowledge of antiquity very extraordinary for a monk of the fourteenth century." Gibbon also accepted the names and locations of the ninety-two Roman towns mentioned in the new "find."

The document was included in Bertram's Britannicarum Gentium Historiae Antiquae Scriptores Tres (1757) which corrected and supplemented Antonus' Itinerarium. A genuine work by Richard of Cirencester, Historical Mirror, was edited by J. E. B. Mayor following the popularity which that otherwise unimportant writer enjoyed after publication of Bertram's spurious discovery.

Exposure came in 1866 when Karl Wex, a German critic, showed that the quotations in the manuscript from Tacitus were from a late sixteenth century edition and that the entire work was a mosaic of extracts from Tacitus, Selinus, Caesar and others, some of them paraphrased.

Today we have the "new" type of biography, in reality posthumous psychoanalytical diagnoses in the best Freudian tradition. A century ago we had "memoirs," autobiographical accounts which were even more unreliable. As Albert Bushnell Hart wrote in *Harper's* for October, 1915:

> We expect from writers of personal memoirs and autobiographies that they shall refresh their memories from diaries and letters and other data. Yet in the whole list of American historical liars none are more distinguished than some of these autobiographists. A shelf of literature might be filled with so-called memoirs which are full of what a genial journalist has called "habitual facticides."

What was true of American memoir writers also was true of European autobiographers of the early nineteenth century, with this difference: most of their stories were ghost-written for them without their knowledge or consent. Augustine Thierry is authority for the statement that a majority of the memoirs appearing between 1825 and 1840, dealing with the Napoleonic period, were forgeries. Two writers, Baron de Lamothe-Langon and Maxime de Villemarest, are said to have conducted a veritable factory to produce spurious manuscripts.

De Lamothe-Langon, whose real name was Etienne Léon, produced in his own name twenty novels. He was one of the most notorious forgers of alleged works of Ann Radcliffe. Among the characters for whom he wrote "memoirs" were the Duchesse de Berry, Richelieu, Marie Antoinette, Talleyrand and Frederick the Great. Among the pseudonyms which he used were the Comtesses d'Adhemar, the Vicomte de Vandery, the Comtesse Ordu C-, and Louis Julien de Rochemont.

He also is suspected of having been the author of *Recollections of the Private Life of Napoleon* by Constant, premier valet de chambre, the English translation of which, by Walter Clark, appeared in 1895. In the preface the translator admits that Napoleon's nephew in *Napoleon and His Detractors* bitterly assailed the book, attacking both its authenticity and its genuineness. "But," wrote Clark, "there appears no good reason to doubt its genuineness, and the truthfulness of many of its details is amply supported by other authorities."

To the "credit" of Maxime de Villemarest are memoirs of Mlle. Avrillon concerning the Empress Josephine; of Blangini, famous Italian composer; of Adele Boury, and of De Bourrienne, celebrated minister of state.

Souvenirs de la Marquise de Créquy was published by an author who called himself Jean L'Evangéliste-Marie-Pierre O'Rourke. He claimed to be descended from a King of Ireland and to belong to the Legion of Honor. Lenôtre accepted the book as "one of the best and truest pictures of Parisian society during the reign of Louis XV and Louis XVI." The real author is said to have been M. Cousin, Comte de Courchamps, whose seven volumes of the work appeared in Paris in 1834. Under the title, *The French Noblesse of the Eighteenth Century* by Mrs. Colquhoun Grant, it was abridged and published in England in 1904.

Unwary historians still are liable to accept statements which first saw light in *Histoire des Sociétés Secrètes de l'Armée,* by Charles Nodier. The fiction was written in the character of a retired officer of Napoleon's army and is a full account of a secret society called the Philadelphes. This, according to the narrative, had as its purpose the restoration of the Bourbon line. When Bonaparte learned of it he caused the leader, Colonel Cudet, to disappear mysteriously. After several of his contemporaries accepted the work seriously, Nodier confessed it had no basis in fact.

In the Rare Book Room of the Library of Congress is a copy of *Lettres de Monsieur le Marquis de Montcalm,* published in 1777. The supposed author was Pierre Joseph Antoine Roubant, who was born in 1724. The letters were quoted as authentic by Chatham in parliamentary debate and were accepted for more than a century.

Among the legends connected with the French Revolution is that the inventor of the guillotine was the first to suffer death through its use. On the two hundredth anniversary of his birth (May 28, 1738) a columnist in the London *Daily Telegraph* wrote that not only did Dr. Guillotin not die by the guillotine but he did not even invent it. In the Cluny Museum, this authority declared, is a death certificate proving that Guillotin died peacefully in bed just a few days before he had rounded out a century of life. Further:

Known as the "manaia," the guillotine had existed in Italy for centuries before the French Revolution.

All Dr. Guillotin did was as a member of the States-General to propose a uniform way of carrying out the death sentence in France. Under the ancient regime there were various methods, from simple hanging to

the refined breaking on the wheel, according to the custom of the individual Province.

The talk of introducing uniformity was entrusted early in 1792 to Dr.
Louis, the permanent secretary of the Academy of Surgery.

He chose the guillotine. The instrument was designed under his
supervision by a German craftsman of the name of Schmit, whose normal
business was harpsichord-making.

As might be expected a similar legend persists regarding the electric
chair. Despite tradition, Charles Justice, who was electrocuted October
27, 1911, in the Ohio Penitentiary, did not invent the chair. Rather, it was
invented by Harry Glick in 1896. Glick was a murderer serving a life
sentence, but he died of heart disease in the prison.

For audacity, ability to survive repeated exposés and success in hood-
winking experts, an American journalist, William Francis Mannix, had
few if any equals. Public and college libraries still have many copies of
Memoirs of Li Hung Chang, the great Chinese statesman, which Mannix
wrote to pass the time as a prisoner in a Honolulu jail. The original edition was published in 1913 by Houghton Mifflin after it was approved by
John W. Foster, secretary of state under Benjamin Harrison, who served
with Li Hung Chang at a peace conference in 1897, and others who knew
him well. E. B. Drew of Boston, formerly an official of the Imperial
Chinese Customs, discovered discrepancies in it, and in 1923 the publishers
issued another edition with an introduction in which Ralph D. Paine told
the interesting story of the hoax. Unfortunately for scholarship, the 1913
edition was the better seller.

Mannix's remarkable career as a hoaxer began in his youth, when he
earned large checks from several metropolitan newspapers by sending
fictitious lists of 'guests at Adirondack summer resorts. Discovered when
he carelessly repeated the same names too often, he next became a reformed drunkard and lectured in the vicinity of Watertown, New York,
on his alleged harrowing experiences fighting John Barleycorn.

The outbreak of the Cuban insurrection against Spain found Mannix
in Havana as correspondent for the New York *Times,* Philadelphia *Press*
and other newspapers to which he syndicated atrocity stories which outdid
even the best efforts of the young men of Messrs. Hearst and Pulitzer.
Arrested and deported by the Spanish authorities, he returned to the
United States and lectured on his expulsion and enjoyed the distinction of
having his case debated in Congress. After the *Maine* was destroyed it

was revealed that the majority of his interviews with Cuban rebels had been invented in the café of the Hotel Mascotte, Havana.

Discharged by the Philadelphia *Press* for involving it in a million-dollar libel suit, Mannix obtained a position with the Honolulu *Advertiser* in November, 1911, under the name William Grant Leonard by means of faked recommendations from pastors in Portland, Oregon, and San Francisco. Six months later he began a year's term in Oahu jail for forging his employer's name to a small check.

Governor Frear sent Mannix the typewriter on which he composed *Memoirs of Li Hung Chang*. Friends brought him the historical works on China from which he paraphrased chapters. Prior to book publication parts appeared in the New York *Sun* and the London *Observer*.

Pardoned by Governor Frear after eight months, Mannix founded the Pacific Associated Press, inventing a list of fictitious directors. Through it he syndicated stories and interviews, including one with the Chinese President Yuan Shih-kai which appeared in the July 26, 1916, issue of the *Independent*. Mannix used the names of his "directors" in answering Houghton Mifflin's letters when suspicion began to grow. He even asked for expenses to go in search of himself in China and invented a number of scholars to vouch for the memoirs.

Mannix's last hoax seems to have been a form letter which he sent to several manufacturing companies suggesting articles on the use of their products in the ancient imperial palace in the Forbidden City of Peking. Samuel Hopkins Adams, who conducted a newspaper column, "Ad-visor," exposed the fraud.

This chapter by no means has covered the entire field of known or strongly suspected historical fakes. If to the complete list of exposed myths and legends were added those which an omnipotent authority would include, how much that has escaped the debunkers and is considered sound historical knowledge would be found in it?

CHAPTER XIII

Governmental Hoaxing

CROWDS have milled and rioted, governments have been threatened and overthrown, both peacefully and by violence, international relations have been strained and wars have been fought, all as a result of hoaxes.

The record as regards the very oldest of the old-timers is, of course, woefully inadequate, but on the basis of it the title of "Father of Fakers" goes to a Greek of the seventh and sixth century B.C., Onomacritus. As chief of the Orphic succession it was his responsibility to obtain oracles for the guidance of the tyrant Pisistratus, whose friend and counselor he was, and for his successor, the tyrant Hipparchus.

Eager to please, Onomacritus built up a reputation for his ability to elicit auspicious messages from the gods. At one time he was caught interpolating some passages of his own in Homer's account of the visit of Odysseus to Hades, but was forgiven. Finally, however, he was caught red-handed by Lasus of Hermione inscribing on a thin sheet of lead in old Cadmean letters a prophecy that one of the isles near Lemnos would disappear under the sea.

This lapse was Onomacritus' undoing, and he was banished. Luck, however, was with him. Hippias, younger brother of Hipparchus, also in enforced exile, had become attached to the court of Darius the Persian. Hearing of Onomacritus' misfortune, he persuaded Darius to invite the seer to join his entourage. The faker was put to work at his old job of extracting advice from the unseen powers that be. The results were gratifying and complimentary, and the climax was a series of oracles stressing the advisability of a military campaign against Athens. After the disastrous Battle of Marathon, which some historians have called the turning point of history, Onomacritus was heard of no more.

From Onomacritus to William Randolph Hearst the names of many famous persons have been associated with attempts to shape the course of human events by hoaxes perpetrated through or upon government. The great lawgiver, Solon, for instance, forged a line in Homer's catalogue of ships to prove that Salamis belonged to Athens. To win popular support for the trip of Vasco da Gama around the Cape of Good Hope, a stone with an inscription addressed "to the inhabitants of the West" supposedly was dug up. It contained a prophecy that its finding would predate by a brief period the discovery of a new trade route to the East.

Considerable credit for an important victory in the long struggle for freedom of the press—the opening to reporters of the gallery in the British House of Commons—goes to Dr. Samuel Johnson because of his *Reports of the Debates of the Senate of Lilliput*. With the assistance of an unknown member he published daily these minutes of a supposedly fictitious legislative body. Although camouflaged, the debaters and issues easily were identified by readers.

Prominent in any compilation of historical mysteries is whether Mary Queen of Scots was an accomplice of her third husband, James Hepburn, Earl of Bothwell, in the murder of her second, Henry Stewart, Lord Darnley. The evidence by which an authoritative answer might have been given—the contents of a silver casket—was destroyed shortly after its alleged discovery in Darnley's effects on the defeat of Mary's army at Carberry Hill.

The mysterious Casket Letters, of which supposed copies but not the originals exist, were accepted as genuine at the time and turned public opinion further away from Mary, already suspected of being a murderess. That Bothwell was responsible for the explosion February 9, 1567, in the cottage near Edinburgh when Darnley was recuperating from smallpox, is accepted by historians as proved. Within three months Mary married Bothwell; but she went to the block nineteen years later without confessing any complicity in the crime.

"It may be doubted whether any book in the world's history ever had so decisive an effect on the tide of events," wrote J. A. Farrer in *Literary Forgeries* of the spurious memoirs of Charles I, known as *Eikon Basilike*. Had it appeared a few weeks before instead of after the monarch's execution, that event might not have occurred. As it was, circulation of about 90,000 copies is credited with having contributed as much as anything else to the downfall of the Commonwealth of the Cromwells by creating the impression that the dead king's benevolent Christian impulses had not been understood by his subjects.

After the Restoration, Dr. John Gauden proved that he was the author of *Eikon Basilike* and was rewarded with appointment as Bishop of Exeter. The best that John Milton, delegated by the Council of State to discredit Charles' alleged story, could do was to prove that a prayer had been purloined from Sir Philip Sidney's *Arcadia.*

Many "immediate causes" for the French Revolution have been given, and historians do not agree as to what was the final incident to discredit the Bourbons with the masses. All agree, however, that the episode of the Diamond Necklace was an important factor, and some even go so far as to conjecture that, had it not occurred, Louis XVI and his queen, Marie Antoinette, might not have gone to the guillotine.

Historians, from Carlyle to Zweig, have called the Diamond Necklace episode fantastic, incredible. The necklace was one which Louis XV had ordered for his mistress, Madame du Barry. Reputedly worth about a half-million dollars, it still was in the possession of the jewelers, Boehmer and Bassenge, when Louis died suddenly. Marie Antoinette refused to buy it and never did. The jewelers and the gullible Cardinal Prince de Rohan, however, were duped into thinking she would, and possession of the valuable trinket passed to a group of extremely clever impostors headed by a Comtesse de Lamotte-Valois.

That lady convinced De Rohan that she could restore him to favor with the queen, who hated him because, as ambassador to Austria, he had insulted her mother, Maria Theresa. She even produced an impersonator of Marie Antoinette to tell De Rohan in the moonlight that all was forgiven, and that he was authorized to purchase the diamond necklace for her. When De Rohan advanced a quarter of the price, delivery was made to another conspirator, a palace secretary named Latreau, who presumably was to deliver it to the queen.

When the jewelers called for payment of the second installment, Marie Antoinette disclaimed all knowledge of the deal. Years later Napoleon said her greatest mistake was to demand a public trial in the Parliament of Three Estates to clear her name and convict the conspirators. After six months the Lamotte woman, who was born Jeanne de St. Remy de Valois, descendant of an illegitimate son of Henry II, was convicted and sentenced to the Bastille. Cardinal de Rohan was acquitted, as was the self-styled Count Alessandro di Cagliostro, master mountebank of the time, who had urged the cardinal to enter upon the negotiations. Letters which had been presented to the infatuated De Rohan as from the queen easily were proved to be forgeries. Nevertheless, as is always the case, public opinion divided and remained unaffected by the official verdicts.

Among the many disputable phases of the incident is the part played by Cagliostro, revealed after his death in a papal prison to have been Giuseppe Balsamo, son of a poor peasant of Palermo, Sicily. Through magic and prophecy this master impostor captivated one European capital after another and made a handsome living through hypnotic cures of the sick and sale of his elixir of life. As proof of the potency of this "wine of Egypt" he pointed to his wife, apparently a beautiful girl in her early twenties, who he said actually was an old woman with a son of fifty years. He himself, he declared, had been alive since the days of Jesus, being, in fact, the Wandering Jew. Using what would today be called "kingfish" methods, he founded the Grand Egyptian lodge, a modified form of Freemasonry, of which he became Cophte and his wife Grand Princess.

Of pretenders to every European throne there always have been and still are many. To tell about all of them would require a book larger than this. A few, however, have been more annoying than others, and at least one, a thorough impostor, almost succeeded in ascending the throne of England.

He was Perkin Warbeck, a seventeen-year-old living model of a Breton merchant when he first attracted the attention of the Yorkists, still rankling over the defeat, five years previous, of the army of another "Duke of York," exposed as a simple subject named Lambert Simnel. Because of his regal bearing as he displayed the clothing of his master, Perkin often had been suspected of possessing royal blood. He is known to have sworn under oath before the mayor of Cork that he was not the Earl of Warwick, son of the Duke of Clarence who had been put to death by Richard III, and also to have denied he was the bastard of Richard III himself.

His protests that he was not Richard, Duke of York, second son of Edward IV, however, were of no avail. Once prevailed upon to play the part, he did it well. Insisting that he had not been killed in London Tower, he visited the French king, Charles VIII, in Paris and received a delegation of English Yorkists who crossed the Channel to offer him their swords. He was acknowledged by Margaret of Burgundy as her nephew, attended the funeral of Frederick III in Vienna, corresponded with Queen Isabella of Spain and traveled with Maximilian to Flanders, where he was acknowledged by the new emperor as the lawful king of England.

Had Perkin's followers been content merely to parade him before the crowned heads of the Continent, Perkin never might have come to regret his unsolicited role. However, what they wanted was action, and so, July 3, 1495, the rebel forces attempted to land on the coast of Kent. From shipboard Perkiñ saw his followers entrapped and annihilated by Henry VII's men.

A later assault, which seemed for a time likely to result in the capture of Exeter, ended instead in Perkin's capture by enemy reenforcements. His attempt to escape from London Tower in 1499 was used as an excuse to hang him. The same year a third pretender, Ralph Wilford, who claimed to be the Earl of Warwick, met the same fate; an Augustinian friar, Patrick, his chief backer, was imprisoned for life.

Three hundred years later the British succession again was endangered seriously, not through revolutionary threat but as a result of one of the queerest lawsuits in history. Complainant was the self-styled Princess Lavinia of Cumberland, the daughter of Olivia Wilmot Serres and, in ordinary life, Mrs. Anthony T. Ryves, wife of a portrait painter. The case she took to court in 1866 grew out of the pretensions and forgeries of her deceased mother.

Mrs. Serres, after two earlier stories, in 1820 publicly announced herself as the legitimate daughter of Henry Frederick, Duke of Cumberland, and Olive Wilmot in 1767, five years before the Royal Marriage Act which nullified any marriage contracted with anyone in the succession to the Crown without the monarch's consent. She produced a doctor's certificate that the child born April 3, 1772, to Robert Wilmot and Anna Maria, his wife, at Warwick, was still-born; she alleged that the Duke of Cumberland substituted his own child to avoid scandal.

Mrs. Serres also invented a noble parentage for her mother, who she said was the child of a Princess of Poland, sister of a Count Poniatowski, and the Reverend James Wilmot. The forgeries exposed in court, Mrs. Ryves lost her case, and the British throne ceased tottering.

Although Eleazar Williams, Wisconsin and New York Indian who decided in middle life that he was Louis XVII, left no one able or willing to press his claim, in France the descendants of many another lost dauphin caused almost as much trouble as the offspring of Olivia Serres did in England.

Among the most persistent were the son and grandson of a Prussian locksmith, Charles William Naundorff, on whose tomb in Delft, Holland, is inscribed: "Here lies Louis XVII, Duke of Normandy, King of French courts." The original Naundorff tale was that he, the dauphin, was drugged by friends, officially declared dead in his coffin, and then rescued. In Vienna, he was captured by his enemies and incarcerated in Strasbourg fortress, but again was assisted to escape to Germany where he worked as a watchmaker and assumed the name of Naundorff.

In 1851 Charles Naundorff, a son, brought suit in France to recover property belonging to Louis XVI and Marie Antoinette, his alleged parents. He lost but tried again twenty-three years later with the same result. In a Parisian wineshop a grandson for years held court as King John IV. In July, 1954 the Paris Court of Appeals ended the 103 year-old lawsuit by declaring the real dauphin died at the age of ten.

Two other events occurring between the establishment of the Third Republic and the outbreak of World War I were much more important to Frenchmen. They were the Franco-Prussian War, 1870–71, and the Dreyfus Affair, 1894–1906. With each is associated some of the worst diplomatic skulduggery of history.

Historians are wary about accepting Prince Bismarck's ego-biographic account of how, in the presence of Generals Moltke and Roon, he dramatically altered a message he had received from the King of Prussia before releasing it to the press, to make it read as though Wilhelm I had insulted Count Vincent Benedetti, the French ambassador. There is no question, however, that this interpolated message, the famous Ems dispatch, was what Bismarck intended it to be—"a red rag upon the Gallic bull." Both sides were ready for war and just waiting for an excuse to begin it; the Ems dispatch supplied the excuse.

The most important forgery in the celebrated Dreyfus case was a letter signed "Alexandrine," apparently Colonel Panizzardi, attaché of the Italian embassy in Paris, clearly implicating Captain Alfred Dreyfus of the French army in a conspiracy to sell military secrets to the Germans. The persistence of several believers in Dreyfus' innocence, however, led to the discovery, four years after Dreyfus' first conviction and sentencing to notorious Devil's Island, of the real author of the letter: a Colonel Henry, head of the French Intelligence Department, who cut his throat to escape living disgrace. The next year, Dreyfus, who had twice been tried and found guilty, was pardoned. The guilty conspirator quite certainly was Major Esterhazy, who, however, was tried and acquitted while anti-Jewish sentiment kept Captain Dreyfus in exile and caused Emile Zola, author of *J'Accuse,* to be sentenced to two years' imprisonment which was reversed on appeal. Because of public hatred against him, Zola had to leave France for England; but when he died in 1902 he had been vindicated and was given a state funeral.

The Ems dispatch had the effect in France which Bismarck intended because public sentiment had been whipped up against Germany. Dreyfus was convicted, and those who actually committed the crime were acquitted largely because anti-Semitic feeling was intense at the time. Across the Channel, during the decade between the two events, the readiness to believe the worst about an unpopular troublesome member of Parliament accounted for the success of what has been called the boldest political hoax of history: the attempt to ruin Charles Stewart Parnell, Irish leader.

The forgeries, which nearly accomplished their purpose, were serialized in the august London *Times* under the title "Parnellism and Crime." They consisted of letters which Parnell supposedly had written to express his pleasure at news of the murder in Phoenix Park, Dublin, of the newly appointed secretary for Ireland, Lord Frederick Cavendish, and a petty official. Parnell publicly deplored the crimes, but in the forgeries was made to explain that he did so merely for strategic purposes.

Nothing that the valiant Irishman could say in the House caused anything but incredulous laughter. Accepting the truth of the *Times* articles, Lord Salisbury, the prime minister, denounced Gladstone for his friendship for Parnell.

Upon the advice of friends Parnell did not bring legal action, and the incident might have ended had not a former member of Parliament, F. H. O'Donnell, considered himself damaged by the libel. He lost the suit he brought against the newspaper, but during his trial a number of new letters, credited to Parnell and more damaging than those that had been published, were introduced into evidence.

Again Parnell's denial was received frigidly. In vain did he request appointment of a select committee to inquire into the authenticity of the correspondence. Making what it considered a magnanimous gesture, however, the House finally consented to appoint a commission of judges with statutory power to investigate.

Once in court Parnell, with his friends' assistance, was relentless in tracing the forgeries to their source. An important witness was a Richard Pigott, among those responsible for the letters' reaching the *Times*. He was subjected to a blistering cross-examination by Sir Charles Russell. Required to write some words, he committed errors in spelling similar to those in the letters. The following day Pigott did not appear in court, but

Henry Labouchère and George A. Sala, friends of Parnell, were there with his signed confession. Eight days later Pigott committed suicide in a Madrid hotel when informed a policeman wanted to see him. Parnell received 5,000 pounds from the *Times* in a settlement out of court.

In colonial America one of the first attempts by a government to stampede the people into overt behavior through a deliberate hoax was a complete failure. Known to historians as the Philadelphia Alarm, it was engineered by Governor John Evans, either to test whether the Quakers were as pacific as they claimed to be or to frighten the provinicial assembly into passing a militia law.

On the day of the annual fair in 1706, with sword drawn, Evans frantically dashed on horseback amid the crowd, entreating the people to prepare to protect the city, against which the French and Indians, he shouted, were about to march. Although many fairgoers returned home, leaving unpaid the debts it was customary to take care of on that occasion, only Evans' militia and a few non-Quakers stood guard for two nights at the wharves and along the water front.

According to Thomas F. Gordon in *The History of Pennsylvania*:

This experiment on the principles of the Quakers was wholly unsuccessful; the greater part attending their religious meeting, as was their custom on that day of the week, persisted in their religious exercises amid the general tumult instead of flying to arms as the governor had anticipated. Four members only repaired with weapons to the rendezvous.

A century and a half later, in 1862, a similar scare, origin unknown, resulted quite differently in Milwaukee, then a city of 45,000. It was during the Civil War and the army of General Robert E. Lee had just begun a successful invasion of Maryland. Likewise, the Sioux Indians were on a rampage in Minnesota. So, when wild-eyed refugees began streaming into the Wisconsin metropolis from the direction of Waukesha, with a story that an army of Confederates had reached the state by way of Canada and, augmented by Redskins, was about to scalp everyone in the vicinity, near panic resulted.

"Eyewitness" accounts of scalpings in Waukesha; of Hartland, Pewaukee and West Bend in flames and of marauders in the outskirts were listened to and believed. The Chamber of Commerce recommended that every boat in the harbor be seized to convey the population far out into Lake Michigan; only one man who stole a rowboat and spent the night in the open in the rain is said to have acted upon the advice. After the local militia reconnoitered over a three-hundred-mile area, the frightened populace began to breathe normally again.

The gold market advanced, and two leading New York City newspapers were suspended for four days as the result of what is called the only deliberate and mischievous political hoax of the Civil War period.

The *World* and the *Journal of Commerce* were the papers involved. They printed as authentic an alleged proclamation by President Lincoln which reached their offices at three o'clock on the morning of May 18, 1864, on regulation manifold paper customarily used for Associated Press dispatches. The proclamation arrived too late for careful editorial supervision but not before the printing offices closed. Other newspapers in New York receiving the same story were suspicious and withheld publication.

The forged proclamation called for four thousand new recruits between the ages of eighteen and forty-five and also announced a day of fasting and prayer. It was the work of Joseph Howard of the Brooklyn *Eagle,* who was arrested and imprisoned at Fort Lafayette.

Although both papers printed immediate retractions and called in as many copies of their early editions as possible, a military guard was established in their offices and publication was suspended for four days. The owners and editors were arrested but were released shortly.

The New Orleans *Picayune,* which copied the dispatch, was suppressed for more than two weeks by General Banks. Opposition papers saw in the suspensions evidence that the president was opposed to free speech. Secretary Stanton was charged with malice toward the *World,* leading opposition paper to Lincoln's policies.

The already unhappy Andrew Johnson was harassed further by a journalistic fake similar to the specious Lincoln Proclamation, but more malicious in its intent. As published in the Philadelphia *Public Ledger* October 11, 1866, and subsequently sent out by the Associated Press, the dispatch, supposedly originating in Washington, purported to summarize five questions which the president had submitted for answer to his attorney general. "Political dynamite" at the time, the Johnson queries were in substance: (1) Is the present Congress a legal one? (2) Would the president be justified in sending his next annual message to an unconstitutional assembly? (3) Has a Congress like the present a right to exclude representatives from ten states? (4) Is the president required to enforce those provisions of the Constitution which give to each state an equal right to representation? (5) What steps should the president take to secure the assemblage of a constitutional congress?

The premium on gold went up 3 or 4 per cent when the story reached Wall Street. A quick denial from Washington, of course, followed.

Ulysses S. Grant, Johnson's successor, had his troubles too. Not the least was the persistent attempt of the developing Greenback-Populists to pin the Wall Street label on anyone and everyone in Washington. In addition to the specious Lincoln statements mentioned in Chapter XII, there were the Luckenbach Affidavit, Banker's Circular, Hazard Circular and other surreptitious pamphlets intended to prove that big moneyed men conspire to create panics and industrial disturbances so as to be able to buy heavily on a falling market and later sell on a rising one.

Ranking first among the anticapitalistic hoaxes of the period was that which took advantage of the vehement opposition of a sizable minority to the act demonetizing silver which it called the Crime of '73. That the act was "a dastardly scheme of the gold ring of New York" was substantiated by the story that an Englishman, Ernest Seyd, had come to America with $50,000 to induce members of Congress to abolish free coinage of silver. It was pointed out that the sum specified was rather inadequate to accomplish much with a legislative body of four hundred.

A fantastic account of a fake newspaper story, invented by five Denver reporters, that was the immediate cause of the Boxer rebellion was given by Harry Lee Wilber in the spring, 1939, *North American Review*. The quintet concocted a yarn about five American steel magnates on their way to China to supervise the tearing down of the ancient Chinese Wall as a gesture of good will and to facilitate trade. When the story was cabled to China it caused the seething revolutionaries to hasten their plans to drive out the hated foreigners.

Bitter as the animosities engendered by a strictly domestic issue may become, when a foreign element is interjected into a controversy hatreds may approach panic proportions.

In 1924 Britain's first Labor government, having recognized Soviet Russia, faced the country in a general election on the specific issue of entering into a commercial treaty with her. It cannot, of course, be said authoritatively that Labor would have won had the campaign been normal. There is no doubt, however, that a cleverly executed roorback, timed so as to make impossible adequate rebuttal, caused Labor's defeat to be not nominal but overwhelming.

The hoax was an alleged "very secret" letter from Zinoviev, high Soviet official, to members of the British Communist party advising open violence, sedition and subversion in the British army and navy as the first steps in a British proletarian revolutionary movement.

The effect it was intended to have is derived from the following editorial comment of the London *Mail* in which the forgery appeared:

That such a document should have been held back until the very last minute of the election campaign is another sign that the government has a bad conscience in the matter. And well it might have! The country now knows that Moscow issues orders to British Communists and they are obeyed by Communists here. British Communists, in turn, give orders to the Socialist government, which it tamely and humbly obeys.

Many of the innumerable efforts to blacken Bolshevik Russia in the eyes of the rest of the world originated with exiled White Russians. For others, newspaper correspondents and their superiors, realizing what their readers wanted to believe to be true, were responsible.

After the revolution but before the end of World War I, the counterattack of the White Russians began with an attempt to prove that the Bolsheviks, who had deserted the Allied cause, were aligned with Germany. The most notable evidence to that end became known as the Sisson documents because they were accepted as valid by Edgar Sisson, formerly editor of the *Cosmopolitan,* then a member of George Creel's wartime Committee on Public Information, after Raymond Robins, head of the American Red Cross in Russia, and others had denounced them as forgeries.

Vouched for by a committee of historians appointed by Creel, the documents were published in the United States. They were proved spurious by the New York *Evening Post* in its issues of September 16 to 21 inclusive and November 11, 1918. The British War Office previously had turned them down as not being material for propaganda.

After the war public hatred in this country for the new regime in Russia was both the cause and the result of grossly inaccurate handling of news concerning it in the American press. According to Professor Edward A. Ross of the University of Wisconsin, in his *The Russian Soviet Republic*:

In the course of a little over two years the New York *Times* reported the fall of Petrograd six times, announced at least three times more that it was on the verge of capture, burned it to the ground twice, twice declared it in absolute panic, starved it to death constantly, and had it in revolt against the Bolsheviks six times, all without the slightest foundation in fact.

A thorough and scholarly study of the New York *Times,* an extremely bold venture at the time, was that of Walter Lippmann and Charles Merz. They selected the *Times,* not because they believed it to be more deficient or unfair than other newspapers but, on the contrary, because of its outstanding reputation for accurate reporting. Their conclusions appeared in a supplement to the *New Republic* of August 4, 1920. A significant paragraph was the following:

The news as a whole is dominated by the hopes of the men who composed the news organization. They began as passionate partisans in a great war in which their own country's future was at stake. Until the armistice they were interested in defeating Germany. They hoped until they could hope no longer that Russia would fight. When they saw she could not fight, they worked for intervention as part of the war against Germany. When the war with Germany was over, the intervention still existed. They found reasons then for continuing the intervention. The German Peril as the reason for intervention ceased with the armistice; the Red Peril almost immediately afterwards supplanted it. The Red Peril in turn gave place to rejoicing over the hopes of the White Generals. When these hopes died, the Red Peril reappeared. In the large, the news about Russia is a case of seeing not what was, but what men wished to see. This deduction is more important, in the opinion of the authors, than any other.

Although, with the rapid improvement of our foreign correspondence everywhere, including Soviet Russia, during the decade after the World War, the grotesqueness exposed by Ross, Lippmann, Merz and others disappeared, the fear of Communism inspired and directed from Moscow persisted and grew. Even to receive a letter with a Russian postmark was to be suspect, and the quickest way to destroy a political opponent was to pin the red label on him.

In November, 1926, the American Department of State made the stupid mistake of "planting" with the Associated Press (the United Press and International News Service refused it) a story that a strong anti-American Bolshevik plot was brewing in Mexico. Undersecretary Olds explained that no statement regarding the plot could come from the government, but he wanted the report to go out. The plot had been a long time in reaching fruition.

An even balder attempt to discredit both Socialist-inclined Mexico and several liberal members of Congress, publicists and clergymen was that of the newspapers owned by William Randolph Hearst in the fall of 1927. The first batch of copy contained facsimiles of documents supposed to have been filched from the confidential files of President Plutarco Elías Calles of Mexico to prove that $1,250,000 had been withdrawn from the Mexican national treasury for use as bribes.

The four senators involved, Borah, Heflin, Norris and La Follette, naturally demanded and obtained a Senate investigation. Mr. Hearst himself took the stand and confessed that no attempt had been made to ascertain the validity of the documents, and that even he doubted they were genuine. Handwriting experts, including those selected by Hearst, detected errors in Spanish spelling and grammar which indicated that the composition was by someone better acquainted with English than with Spanish.

In *You Can't Print That!* George Seldes revealed that the identical documents had been offered to him shortly after he arrived in Mexico City as correspondent for the Chicago *Daily Tribune,* and that, over a period of years, virtually every other American newspaperman of importance had had a chance to purchase them from their owner, a Miguel Avila, who trafficked in all sorts of spurious literature. It was from Avila that Hearst obtained them for $20,000.

After publication of this colossal hoax, according to John Winkler in his *William Randolph Hearst,* ill feeling between the two countries, already intense, became so much worse that the administration felt compelled to send a member of the J. P. Morgan firm, Dwight Morrow, to Mexico City as ambassador, and to persuade Colonel Charles A. Lindbergh, then at the height of his popularity, to sacrifice his Christmas holiday to make a good-will tour of Mexico and South America.

While investigating the Hearst Mexican documents, the Congressional committee, headed by Senator David A. Reed of Pennsylvania, received without comment photographs of other documents supposed to show alleged payments of Soviet Russian money to Senators Borah and Norris. They were supplied by an American living in Paris who wanted $50,000 for the originals—for which, however, he refused to vouch.

Payment of $100,000 to each senator was supposed to have been made through the Russian ambassador at Paris, either directly or through Dudley Field Malone, liberal American attorney who had offices in Paris.

Senator Borah's signature was forged to a letter to the Soviet minister.

Assistant Secretary of State Olds also testified to the Reed committee that he destroyed an alleged receipt by Senator Borah for bribes received from the Mexican government. An expense credit was authorized for Ivy Lee, public relations counsel, by M. Rakovsky, a former Soviet ambassador at Paris. About two hundred and fifty documents submitted to George Barr Baker, who accompanied President-elect Hoover on his goodwill tour of Latin America, were denounced by the committee as of no authenticity.

Two years later, after Senator Borah had had the courage to be among the first members of Congress to advocate diplomatic recognition of Soviet Russia, a new batch of forgeries appeared to prove that he had received Moscow gold in exchange for his efforts. Learning of the hubbub in Berlin, where he already had earned a reputation as a great correspondent, H. R. Knickerbocker recalled that similar documents had been offered to him a few weeks before. Single-handed he found the forger, a White Russian named Orloff, and obtained the evidence on which he and his accomplices were tried and convicted.

The American parallel to the British Zinoviev case occurred in 1930 in New York. The documents, supposed to have been stolen from the Soviet embassies in Berlin and Paris, convinced Grover Whalen, police commissioner, that the Amtorg Trading Corporation, the Soviet commercial agency in the United States, was engaging in propaganda activities on behalf of Communism and American recognition of Bolshevik Russia. Most of the thirty agents mentioned in letters signed by an equally unknown A. Fedorov, however, could not be traced. It was pointed out that the Russian abbreviation for ambassador, *polpred,* had been used as the name of a city in New York state, that only one of the letters was on Amtorg stationery, and that there were numerous misspelled names and errors in Russian grammar.

In the totalitarian states official explanations of both internal and foreign policy all are suspect. Individuals are brought home, after mysterious absences, in coffins, often sealed, and their families are told they either committed suicide or were killed while attempting to escape punishment for alleged offenses against the state. The most dastardly Jewish and Communist conspiracies are given as justification for purges and pogroms; in Russia, of course, it is the capitalist devil that inspires the high officials who periodically make virtually unbelievable public confessions before facing the firing squad.

Although the truth never may be known, strong circumstantial evidence has been produced to indicate that the destruction by fire of the German Reichstag building February 27, 1933, a month after Adolf Hitler became chancellor and a week before a general election, was the work of the Nazis themselves and not of the half-witted Dutchman, Marinus van der Lubbe, who paid with his life for the crime. At any rate, by placing the responsibility upon the Communists, the Hitlerites came close to obtaining a two-thirds majority of the Reichstag in the election to enable *der Führer* to win dictatorial powers for five years.

To discredit Adolf Hitler more than he himself did by his writings, words and actions, the usual crude stories were circulated. At one time he had been considered homosexual and a woman hater; at another, the secret possessor of a veritable harem. The wishful thinkers had him dying on more than one occasion from a throat ailment; and in March, 1939, appeared *The Strange Death of Adolf Hitler,* allegedly written by one of four doubles who took his place after his mysterious poisoning on the eve of the Munich conference September 29, 1938, to obtain the transfer of the Sudetenland to Germany. Not until the summer of 1938 was an alleged baby picture of Hitler, which Acme Newspictures insists originated in Austria, revealed to be a retouched snapshot of a Lakewood, Ohio, child.

A victim of his ignorance and his prejudices, the average reader is virtually helpless when it comes to distinguishing fact from fiction regarding men and events. Only prompt exposure can prevent the wildest kind of fake from exerting widespread influence. One incident in which, happily, such prompt exposure occurred was the simultaneous publication in England and the United States of *Whispering Gallery,* a compilation of startling glimpses behind the scenes of European political life. The book was published anonymously but the publishers insisted they knew the author and vouched for his integrity. This, it later was revealed, was not the truth, as they had received the manuscript from Hesketh Pearson, who refused to tell where he got it. Chagrined by the uproar that resulted, the publishers forced Pearson finally to confess authorship.

Among the chapters most calculated to make *Whispering Gallery* a best seller was that relating the fabricated details of an interview between King Edward VII of Britain and Kaiser Wilhelm II of Germany during which Edward led Wilhelm on to disclose his plans for conquering the world. There were too many living persons mentioned in the hoax to permit it long life, and within a few weeks the publisher called the book in.

An old stand-by which crops up at international conferences and fails

BABY PICTURE OF ADOLF HITLER A HOAX

In May, 1938, Acme Newspictures, Inc., reissued this picture with the following cut lines: "Still unexplained after nearly four years is the mystery of the hoax through which an unauthentic picture of Adolf Hitler as a baby was circulated through the United States and widely printed. Deepening the mystery, if anything, has been the recent revelation that the picture purporting to be that of Baby Hitler actually was a photograph of 2-year-old John May Warren, then of Westport, Conn., now residing in Lakewood, O. The mystery began when the German consul branded as a 'fabrication' a Hitler baby picture printed in this country in 1933. Inquiry at the time showed that the photograph had originated in Austria, made its way to London through regular, legitimate news channels and thence to the United States. Recently, Mrs. Harriet M. W. Downs noticed the false picture reprinted in a magazine and recognized it as a photo of her son by a former marriage, John May Warren, now grown into a strapping, freckled schoolboy of eight years, who looks nothing like Hitler. The original snapshot had been retouched so that a baby cap was painted out and the features distorted so that what had been a babyish squint in the true picture appeared as a particularly unpleasant grimace. Discovery of the origin of the photo, however, still does not explain how it got to Austria, or who perpetrated the hoax. Photo shows (_left_) the original photograph purporting to be Baby Hitler, (_right_) the original snapshot of John May Warren. Note how the features were transformed by a retoucher's brush."

THE KENSINGTON STONE

A side (*left*) and front (*right*) view of the Kensington Stone which some authorities believe contains runic characters to prove the Vikings reached what is now Minnesota in 1362.

to impress either diplomats or correspondents is documentary proof that the cost by which a British subject may become an American citizen has been reduced to a mere fifty-three cents, and the time required for naturalization to nine days, three hours and six minutes.

This forgery, supposedly obtained in 1919 for David Lloyd George by Sir William Wiseman, head of the British Intelligence Service in the United States, is so absurd that it is almost incredible anyone ever should fall for it. Nevertheless, William B. Shearer, "observer" at Geneva disarmament conferences for certain American munition manufacturers, seriously submitted it to a Senate investigating committee as an example of what a fellow can pick up if allowed to travel freely.

The document was traced to Dr. William Maloney, a widely known nerve specialist. Under suspicion as a British agent in 1919, he composed the travesty which then was published as a joke by the Friends of Irish Freedom.

In October, 1939, the fake became the subject of congressional debate as part of a long letter which Colonel Edward M. House allegedly wrote to President Wilson to explain how the United States again could become a British colony. The letter was introduced into the *Congressional Record* by Representative Jacob Thorkelson of Montana, who later withdrew it in the face of ridicule.

In contrast, is an anecdote which may be considered humorous. In 1926 Lieutenant Commander R. T. Gould, an Englishman, wrote *Oddities* and included the exact bearings of Thompson Island in the South Atlantic, where it "would be found if it exists." Inasmuch as the tiny spot had been discovered in 1825 by Captain Norris of the *Sprightly* and had not been settled by the English, the Norwegian government became interested.

The British government proved cooperative, granting permission for the expedition which set sail under the command of a Captain Larsen. Around and around sailed Larsen and his men before turning homeward to find Gould and his publishers and determine what was the matter. The satisfaction they got may be deduced from the letter which Gould's publishers sent to the *Publisher's Circular*:

In the cause of international peace we are offering a modest prize to any reader of *The Publisher's Circular* who, proceeding to latitude 54 minutes 26 seconds south, longitude 3 degrees 24 minutes east, should discover and locate Thompson's Island and deposit thereon, as a token of his achievement and for the benefit of the natives, if any, a complete set of *The Reader's Guides.*

CHAPTER XIV

Religious Hoaxing

W HEN Jesus of Nazareth was crucified, only one man recognized the importance of writing the biography of this despised and rejected man while those able to supply the facts regarding his words and deeds still were alive. His name was not Matthew, Mark, Luke or John, but Joseph of Jerusalem. The pains that he took to preserve his priceless manuscript were not realized until 1927, when Luigi Moccia, a municipal clerk of Cerignola, Italy, revealed to the Christian world the debt it owed to this hitherto unknown zealot.

Moccia had kept the parchment Gospel according to Joseph secret for eight years. It was necessary to have the biblical Greek translated and to check on the probability of the written record of the manuscript's peregrinations, since its composition shortly before the destruction of Jerusalem by Titus in A.D. 70.

This record, skipping centuries during the Middle and later ages, was clear for the important first few hundred years. On what he predicted would be his last day alive, with Roman soldiers sacking and burning the city, Joseph wrote: "Therefore, I hide my document, hoping to save it from inescapable destruction. Whoever of you finds it let him pass it on without delay."

It was none less than Helen, mother of the Christian Emperor Constantine, who recovered the precious manuscript from its hiding place in a small house near the site of Solomon's Temple. Subsequently she sold it to some unknown Israelites, but about A.D. 332 it came into the possession of the National Library at Alexandria, Egypt. When that monument to ancient learning was destroyed in A.D. 640 by the Caliph Omar, the Gospel of Joseph miraculously was salvaged. From then on the history of the document is incomplete and uninteresting. The old pilgrim, just returned from Palestine, from whom Moccia obtained it, refused to explain how it had come into his possession.

More important to theologians than the pedigree of Moccia's treasure was the part of Joseph's preface which read: "Fearing that this writing may be modified and destroyed by some of our opposers, I have left four copies to our excellent brothers: Matthew of Capernium, Mark of Jerusalem, Luke of Antioch and John of Thesda." In this sentence is seen the historic significance of Joseph's work.

This Fifth Gospel of Joseph is, of course, a fake. According to the biblical scholar Edgar J. Goodspeed of the University of Chicago, "The Fifth Gospel is simply a running together of the four canonicals with very few imaginative additions. All a perfectly obvious fake, by a man quite ignorant of first century manuscripts, and ways of writing, as well as of the development of Christian ways of thought."

Experts consulted by the Manchester *Guardian* and the New York *World* pointed out that the gospel was written in the Greek of the Renaissance, not of the Roman Empire. The parchment also was proved to be of modern origin. Nevertheless, a few years after the discovery, the Reverend Salvatore Riggi of Schenectady, New York, printed the Italian translation privately in this country and set to work on an English translation. Professor John R. Van Der Veer of Union College became convinced of the genuineness of some of the parchments which he examined and, with Father Riggi, is hopeful that some day Joseph will be included in authorized versions of the New Testament.

Luigi Moccia lived altogether too late. As recently as four hundred years ago, and at any time during the preceding fifteen centuries, he would have been revered for his spectacular addition to the Apocrypha, and Joseph would have had a more than even chance of being accepted at its face value. During the struggle of the Christian church to dominate the western world, many "missing links" were needed. Especially desired was proof, other than that supplied by theologians, of the historicity of Jesus, more nearly complete details of His life, particularly His early years and, in later centuries, the legal history of the church itself.

Not that Luigi Moccia lacked predecessors: he had thousands. As early as the end of the second century, the church was compelled to designate which of the multitudinous scriptures were genuine, and which spurious. Unfortunately, the criteria followed are unknown, and there is hardly a book of either Old or New Testament that has not been questioned, either wholly or in part, by some reputable scholar in an earnest attempt to separate the reliable from the untrue.

Today the Old Testament Apocrypha proper, still included in some editions of the Bible, include I and II Esdras, Tobit, Judith, Additions to

Esther, Wisdom of Solomon, Ecclesiasticus, Baruch, Epistle of Jeremy, Additions to Daniel, Prayer of Manasses and I and II Maccabees. The best known among the books whose spuriousness is seldom questioned are: History of Johannes Hyrcanus, Book of Jubilees, Ascension of Isaiah, Pseudo-Philo's Jambres, Joseph and Asenath.

Criticism of the orthodox books of the Old Testament centers about the Pentateuch, Daniel and the Psalms, although the authorship of virtually every other book has been questioned. Scholars who have studied the style of the books named in the original Hebrew, comparing them with documents of known historical worth, have shown by internal evidence that these and other parts of the Old Testament are comparatively recent inventions. Wrote William Robertson Smith in *The Old Testament in the Jewish Church*:

All the books of the Apocrypha are comparatively modern. There is none of them, on the most favorable computation, which can be supposed to be older than the latest years of the Persian empire. They belong to the age when the last great religious movement of the Old Testament under Ezra had passed away—when prophecy had died out, and the nation had settled down to live under the law, looking for guidance in religion, not to a continuance of new revelation, but to the written Word, and to the interpretations of the Scribes.

Criticism of the Mosaic origin of the Pentateuch includes the fact that it contains an account of Moses' own death and such anachronisms as references to the later kings of Israel and to the time when the Canaanites no longer inhabited Palestine. Recently discovered tablets of the Persian king, Cyrus, show that the Book of Daniel is unauthentic and could not have been written during the Babylonian captivity. Professor James H. Breasted showed that Psalm 104 is a plagiarism of the Egyptian Akhnaton's *Hymn to the Sun*.

Deuteronomy is believed to have been written in the seventh century before the Christian era; parts of Zechariah have been proved to be later additions; Isaiah could not have written parts of the books assigned to him, nor could Micah have been the author of all of that book. Important interpolations of the four gospels, according to the *Encyclopædia Britannica*, include the whole story of the woman taken in adultery between John 7:52 and 8:12; the long insertion after Matthew 20:28 (61 words); the story of the face in the sky after Matthew 16:2-3 (31 words); and the story of the angel and the bloody sweat in Luke 22:43-44 (26 words).

New Testament material generally discarded as spurious, in addition to that already mentioned, includes: Gospels according to the Egyptians, Gospel according to the Hebrews, the Protevangel of James, the Gospel of Nicodemus, Gospel of the Twelve, the Gnostic gospels of Andrew, Apelle, Basilides, Cerinthus and twenty others, the Abgar epistles passing between the King of Edessa and Jesus, the epistles of Clement, Barnabas, Polycarp, Pauline epistles to the Laodiceans and Alexandrians and a third Pauline epistle to the Corinthians.

One of the earliest attempts to establish the life of Jesus historically was the interpolation of a widely known passage of Josephus (Antiq. Lib. 18 c. 3). Orosius, St. Augustine, St. Thomas Aquinas and virtually every other important theologian of the early Christian era were confused by forgeries intended to substantiate the facts contained in the four gospels and the historic claims of the church to spiritual and temporal power. The situation, touched upon in Chapter XI, was well summarized by F. J. C. Hearnshaw in the August 1, 1923, *Fortnightly Review*:

During this long period of ecclesiastical domination, history as a science was unknown. It was the hand-maid of theology—a subordinate whose duty it was to supply the anecdotes by means of which the moralists pointed their sermons, the examples by way of which the religious philosophers conveyed their teaching, and the data on the basis of which the politicians of the Church founded their claims to world dominion.

As the church grew in size and influence so also did the incentive to establish firmly the authority of the bishopric of Rome, both internally and in relation to the empire. Two bold forgeries, long recognized as such by lay and religious authorities, accomplished the result. They were the False Decretals and the Donation of Constantine.

The authorship of the spurious Decretals never has been established. Upon their appearance in the tenth century they were credited to a bishop named Isidore who lived at Seville, Spain, between 590 and 636. They consisted of a new canonical code based upon papal letters, canons of council and decretals hitherto unknown, and included seventy letters attributed to the popes of the first three centuries up to the Council of Nicea, acts of council classified by regions, and a series of thirty decretals attributed to the various popes from Sylvester to Damasus. To conceal their worthlessness they were accompanied by some genuine decretals, the oldest of which dates from 385.

The effect was instantaneous and tremendous, for the discovery established the antiquity of the supreme authority of the Bishop of Rome, added strength and cohesion to the churches, enforced the rights of the bishop and his comprovincials, gave greater stability to the diocese and ecclesiastical province and protected the clergy in property as well as person against the encroachments of temporal power. By showing that each bishop was amenable only to the immediate tribunal of the pope, one of the most ancient rights of the provincial synod was abrogated.

Pope Nicholas I gave formal authority to all of the new decretals, without exception; and so they passed into later canonical collections. The first doubts were expressed in the fifteenth century, by Cardinal Nicholas of Cusa and Juan Torquemada. It was a full century later, however, that the Centuriators of Magdeburg in *Ecclesiastica Historia* virtually decided the matter with a scholarly criticism. Since then it has been accepted that the genuine documents in the collection are far in the minority.

What the False Decretals did for the spiritual authority of the bishopric of Rome within Christendom, the Donation of Constantine attempted to accomplish for the church's temporal position in Italy. The Donation (of the crown and other insignia of sovereign dignity, the Lateran Palace and all the provinces of the Italian peninsula), supposed to have been made by the converted Emperor Constantine to St. Sylvester, Bishop of Rome, was in gratitude for his miraculous recovery from leprosy as a result of Sylvester's ministrations. The emperor then abandoned Italy and returned to the East to rule his empire there.

The story of the Donation first appeared in a letter from Pope Adrian I to Charlemagne petitioning him to emulate the first Christian emperor by making a generous gift to the Catholic Church. Authorities differ as to whether Adrian manufactured the story himself, or had a ghost writer. At any rate the revelation of the supposed magnanimity of Constantine was not questioned for more than two hundred years: late in the tenth century Leo of Vercelli, chancellor for Otto III, expressed doubts. Another four hundred and fifty years passed before Laurentius Valla reopened the controversy, which then lasted until near the end of the eighteenth century.

As Christianity spread, the emulators of the authors of the False Decretals and the Donation of Constantine became legion. To give greater weight to their own essays and homilies, churchmen thought nothing of attaching the names of holy fathers whose authority was recognized. Erasmus was known to have complained that he possessed not a single work of the fathers upon the genuineness of which he could depend.

To strengthen the hands of the popes "by agencies of spiritual terrorism," and to narrow the pale of the church to exclude those who dared exercise the right of private reason and conscience was the purpose of the Athanasian Creed, of which the *Encyclopædia Britannica* says: "The so-called 'Athanasian Creed' is universally admitted to be later than the time of Athanasius." By most scholars Athanasius' *Eleven Books Concerning the Trinity* are attributed to Vigilius, a colonial bishop of Thapsus in North Africa. The creed still is an integral part of the Anglican Prayer Book.

Of the vital Apostles' Creed, Alvan Lamson wrote in *The Church of the First Three Centuries:*

The Apostles' Creed is sometimes referred to as the "primitive creed" of Christians; and it is still sometimes insinuated that it was of apostolic origin. That it was not the production of the apostles, however, is a point which has been long universally conceded by the learned, both Protestant and Catholic; and to go into a discussion of it would be a mere waste of time and labor.

As the rivalry between church and state developed, holders of church property, especially monasteries, forged royal and private charters to prove their right to possession. An outstanding example occurred in England about 1414 during an internecine dispute between the monks of Spalding and Croyland over some real estate. It was the spurious *History of Croyland,* credited to Ingulf, a monk who died in 1109, that clearly established the claim of the Croyland monks. There were many repercussions of this ecclesiastical forgery, according to T. F. Tout, who wrote as follows in his *Medieval Forgers and Forgeries:*

The early history of the fraud is obscure, but from the sixteenth century onward it became generally accepted. It was quoted under Elizabeth to prove that Cambridge University was flourishing in Norman times. In the seventeenth century it deceived most of the antiquaries and the historians including such great scholars as Dugdale and Spelman. The note of warning was sounded by the learned Henry Wharton and Hickes, the English Mabillion, declared strongly that the charters were forgeries. Gibbon sneered at the statement that Ingulf studied at Oxford books of Aristotle, not known at that time in Europe. But all the literary historians, from Hume downward, eagerly adopted its picturesque purple patches. While good chronicles have not to this day found an English translator, the pseudo-Ingulf was done into the vernacular time after time. The long series of apocryphal charters are solemnly set forth in the last edition of the *Monasticon.* The local historian, the guide book writer, the text book maker, all made Ingulf his own. When the nineteenth century found him out, and a crowd of scholars, Palgrave, Riley, Lieberman, Searle, published conclusive demolitions of his statements, the pseudo-Ingulf still kept some conscious and unconscious disciples. Less than forty years ago a scholar, officially attached to the British Museum and supposed to be enough of an expert to edit the whole corpus of Anglo-Saxon charters, maintained that, though spurious in form, Ingulf's charters were reconstructions of original deeds, and therefore contained much true history. It requires a faith greater than the faith that moves mountains to clear away the lofty pile of lies that has overwhelmed the good faith of the monks of Croyland.

Another kind of forgery was to link an important name with a church or monastery's founding. Of such character was *The History of Charles the Great and Orlando* which appeared in 1121 and purported to be a personal narrative of Turpin, private secretary of Charlemagne. It related the story of the founding by Charles of the shrine of St. James at Compostella. Detected, the work became known as *Le Magnanime Mensonge*.

In the nineteenth century the Bishop of Le Mans was convicted of forging charters to the detriment of the rights of the Abbey of St. Calais. Lanfranc, Archbishop of Canterbury in 1072, was exposed as the author of an elaborate series of forgeries. Exposed myths concerning apostles and saints are included in *Enthusiasm of Methodists and Papists Compared,* by Bishop Lavington, and in Henry Stephens' *Apology for Herodotus.* Typical of them was the anecdote of the birds that warbled and stretched their necks while listening to St. Francis preaching in the desert.

Reminiscent of the attempt of fascist Germany to rewrite the Scriptures and church history to prove that Jesus was non-Jewish, was the order of Martin Luther to the Magdeburg centuriators to rewrite the story of Christianity. "Their history was, of course, almost as false and entirely as prejudiced as that which they assailed," wrote F. J. C. Hearnshaw in the August 1, 1923, *Fortnightly Review.*

The Jews also have had their troubles. The most important religious hoaxer of that faith in recent history was M. W. Shapira, who unsuccessfully attempted to sell an alleged ninth century B.C. version of Deuteronomy to the British Museum for one million pounds.

Shapira, a Polish Jew, conducted an antiquity shop in Jerusalem in the middle half of the nineteenth century. His "find," which he credited to Moses, was prepared on fifteen strips of sheepskin cut from the ends of three-hundred-year-old synagogue rolls treated with chemicals to give them the appearance of even greater age.

Previously Shapira sold forged Moabite pottery to the Prussian government following discovery of the Moabite stone in 1868. Clermont-Ganneau, who deciphered the stone, exposed him. He also inspected the Deuteronomy manuscript and declared it a forgery. Shapira committed suicide in 1884 at Rotterdam.

The sins of the Jews, of course, are infinitesimal by comparison with those committed against them. Most contemporary anti-Semitism, however, is based on psychopathic prejudice or upon generalities like Adolf Hitler's in his monomaniacal *Mein Kampf*, in which there is a paucity of documentary proof of the alleged heinous designs of world Jewry.

"Bible" of the Father Coughlins, Fritz Kuhns and others who wish to quote chapter and verse in their diatribes accusing the Jews of responsibility for most if not all that is wrong with the world, is the moth-eaten *Protocols of the Elders of Zion* which has been explained and exposed so many times that further comment seems terrifically anticlimactic.

To those who, despite the overwhelming evidence to the contrary, persist in believing in the Protocols, they provide proof that international Jewry is conspiring with Freemasonry to overthrow all the governments of the world and replace them with an international Jewish tyranny. First published in their present form in 1905 as an appendix to *The Great in the Little*, by a Russian, Sergei Nilus, the twenty-four protocols purport to be a verbatim account of the secret sessions of the first Zionist Congress in 1897 at Basle, Switzerland. To bring about the decay of Christian civilization, the elders plan to "corrupt the young generation by subversive education, dominate people through their vices, destroy family life, undermine respect for religion, encourage luxury, amuse people to prevent them from thinking, poison the spirit by destructive theories, weaken human bodies by inoculation with microbes, foment international hatred and prepare for universal bankruptcy and concentration of gold in the hands of the Jews."

In 1921 a committee of prominent New York Jews proved that the most frequently circulated edition of the protocols at that time was the work of General Rachkowsky, head of the Russian secret police in Paris, assisted by a Matthew Golowinsky. In 1934 a group of Swiss Jews successfully brought suit against the Swiss National Socialist league for circulating the protocols and introduced evidence tracing the forgery's history to its source.

It has been established without a possibility of a doubt that the protocols originally were a plagiarism of the pamphlet *Dialogues in the Under-world Between Machiavelli and Montesquieu,* written in 1865 by Maurice Jouly as a satirical attack on Napoleon III. In 1884, in their interpolated form, they were published in Russia to divert suspicion from the real conspirators to the Jews after the assassination of Czar Alexander II.

Since then they have been republished at different times in virtually every nation. To his interpolation of Jouly's pamphlet, Nilus added an extra chapter, "In the Jewish Cemetery of Prague," lifted from a novel, *Biarritz,* written in 1868 by Hermann Josedsche.

For years Henry Ford believed in the protocols and, through his Dearborn *Independent,* conducted one of the most important anti-Semitic campaigns ever attempted in the United States. It ended when Aaron Shapiro, a Jewish lawyer, brought suit, whereupon Ford retracted and apologized publicly. In 1938, when the Reverend Charles E. Coughlin published the protocols in his *Social Justice,* he quoted Ford as believing that "they fit in with what is going on" even though in themselves false. Coughlin also stressed their "factuality."

Coeval with the rise of fascism was an increase in attempts to prove the existence of the spirit if not the letter of Protocols Nos. 3 and 5: "We will represent ourselves as the saviors of the laboring classes who have come to liberate them from this oppression by suggesting that they join our army of Socialists Anarchists, Communists, to whom we always extend our help under the guise of the fraternal principles of the universal solidarity of our social masonry . . . We will adopt for ourselves the liberal side of all parties and all movements and provide orators who will talk so much that they will tire the people with their speeches until they turn from orators in disgust."

Father Coughlin reproduced almost verbatim in the article "Background of Persecution" (in *Social Justice* for December 5, 1938), as his own editorial composition, a speech delivered September 13, 1935, by Dr. Paul Joseph Goebbels, German minister of propaganda and public enlightenment. It was a long recitation of wholesale murders in many parts of the world by Jews. Father Coughlin also charged that wealthy American Jews helped finance the Russian Revolution, giving as his source *The Mystical Body of Christ in the Modern World,* by Professor Denis Fahey of Dublin, Ireland. Father Fahey declared that the proof of the assistance was contained in a secret report of the American Secret Service to the French high commissioner and later was incorporated in a British white paper.

Denials of Father Coughlin's charges were immediate and overwhelming from every possible source. The original white paper referred to, discovered in the British Library of Information, did not mention any such report. Alexander Kerensky, head of the Russian government which succeeded that of the czar only to be deposed by the Bolsheviks, said in Chicago that there was not a single Jew in the first Red Russian government, and that no American Jews helped in any way.

In Mexico City, the exiled Leon Trotsky, co-leader with Lenin of the revolution, denied that any assistance was received from American Jews. In New York Kuhn, Loeb & Company vigorously denied Father Coughlin's charge that the late Jacob Schiff, director of the company, had helped the Bolsheviks. Most convincing refutation of all came from Frank J. Wilson, chief of the United States Secret Service, who issued a formal statement denying the existence of any such report.

Steadily gaining in popularity since its appearance in the February 3, 1934, *Liberator* (American pro-Nazi publication printed at Asheville, North Carolina), is a fictitious quotation from a speech which Benjamin Franklin is said to have made to the Constitutional Convention in 1788, warning against the Jews. A diary kept by Charles Pinckney, later governor of South Carolina, is given as authority for Franklin's anti-Semitic attitude.

Several eminent historians, including Charles A. Beard, searched diligently but unsuccessfully for any such Pinckney journal or for any Franklin remarks which might be interpreted as anti-Jewish. The Franklin Institute showed, on the contrary, that Franklin contributed to a building fund of the Hebrew Society of Philadelphia and signed an appeal for contributions by others.

As the international struggle between totalitarianism and democracy becomes more intense, there will be more and more propaganda and lies to link the Jews with Communism and to undermine the influence of organized religion as a threat to a state's power over its people. More than at any other time for two centuries or longer, the church is in politics, whether or not it wants to be. It is, furthermore, decidedly on the defensive, and its supporters' interest in religious hoaxes in the immediate future doubtless will be more and more toward exposure of those directed against it.

CHAPTER XV

Scientific Hoaxing

THE MIND READER who appears in your local theater or high-school auditorium and, with or without blindfold, identifies concealed objects and answers intimate queries regarding your past, present and—most important—future, is an entertainer. The more successful he is, the readier he is to disclaim any supernormal ability and to assist in the exposure of those who publicly practice palmistry, crystal gazing, X-ray eyeing, table tapping, trumpet blowing and the like as lucrative applied science.

Unfortunately, it takes more than the standing offer of a Harry Houdini or Joseph Dunninger to reproduce by mechanical means any phenomenon of a fortune teller or spiritualistic medium, to convince millions of the ordinarily gullible that the part of the amazing exhibition hidden from them in a darkened room ever could have been seen, even if the eye were quicker than the hand.

What is not generally known is that frequently the mind reader has the same difficulty. As his skill develops he becomes less and less dependent upon the mechanical devices which are its basis, or he minimizes their importance. It is especially easy for him to begin believing in himself when he begins giving individual seances, the success of which may depend upon facial or muscle reading. If a few guesses are lucky, he may be well on the way toward paranoia.

The writer knows what he is talking about, because he once was a professional mind reader. He was not a very good one, but the experience was invaluable because he reached the stage at which his own power began to "get" him. It left him wondering how many of those who see horoscopes in the stars, tell character by feeling bumps on the head, or go into trances to converse with someone else's grandmother and sell perfumed bicarbonate of soda as a cure for cancer are conscious charlatans, and how many actually believe in what they are doing.

Certain it is that the vast majority of the superstition, mysticism and quackery that have confounded true scientists throughout the ages has been perpetuated, if not originated, innocently. Consequently, it is difficult to determine what unscientific beliefs and practices began as hoaxes. In *The Story of Human Error,* edited by Joseph Jastrow, distinguished scientists of every type relate how the search for truth has been impeded by colossal mistakes by the most honest investigators.

Nevertheless, it is indisputable, as A. A. Roback wrote in his article "Quacks" in the May, 1929, *Forum,* that

every new science, every fresh discovery, every invention has been capitalized to serve the needs of the universal and ubiquitous charlatan. . . . In order to trade upon the ignorance and—worse than ignorance—the utter lack of discrimination of the masses, quackery always takes its cue from developments in the world of knowledge. For this reason quackery may serve as a sort of barometer to reveal the "precipitation" of knowledge in any given period.

Thus, we have had and, in many instances, continue to have both astronomy and astrology; chemistry and alchemy, divining rods and searchers for the philosopher's stone; anthropology and theories of Nordic or Aryan supremacy; neuroanatomy and phrenology; religious faith and cultist faith healing, incantations, sorcery, witchcraft and inquisitions; psychoanalysis and mesmerism, dream books, handwriting analysts and no end of "free" lecturers on personal problems; endocrinology and the goat glands of Dr. John R. Brinkley; calories and vitamins and a host of food faddists with sure-fire health and reducing diets, mineral salts and radium waters; plastic surgery and a legion of face lifters, dimple makers, paraffin injectors and fingerprint erasers; ophthalmology and the Natural Eyesight Institute of Los Angeles (until the Post Office Department got busy); cardiology and a nation-wide heart-disease racket to swindle the insurance companies; physics and gold extractors, perpetual motion machines and no end of energy-producing contraptions whose inventors need only a little capital to make themselves and scores of others wealthy; physiotherapy and a flooded market of electrical fat-removing belts, neck and leg stretchers and X-ray machines; pathology and an army of quacks with cures for baldness, cancer, diabetes and tuberculosis, Dr. Mahlon Locke of Williamsburg, Ontario, who twists feet, Dr. Alpheus Myers' tapeworm trap, and so many other ways of losing your health while trying to improve it that it is a wonder the editors of *Today's Health* don't commit suicide in despair.

In "To the Pliocene Skull" Bret Harte immortalized one of the most innocently intended scientific hoaxes which, nevertheless, incited a scholarly controversy from the effect of which researchers stumbling upon a number of books dealing with prehistoric North America still suffer.

The skull, which Professor James D. Whitney, California state geologist, inspected and declared to belong to the Pliocene period, was a "plant" in Marson's Mine, Calaveras County, California. It was put there by John C. Scribner, a Wells Fargo agent, druggist and keeper of a general store at Angels camp where the miners lived, merely to confound his friends.

When Professor Whitney made his startling statement, other authorities flocked to the scene. Because the find was made beneath hard rock, Professor Le Conte of the University of California was skeptical. W. H. Holmes, curator of the Department of Anthropology of the Smithsonian Institution, was certain that the relic was modern and its discovery a hoax. While these two and others exchanged scientific pleasantries, Scribner continued to shove his drugs and groceries across the counter without saying a word. To his sister and the Reverend Mr. Dyer, rector of the Episcopal Pro-Cathedral of Los Angeles, however, he told the truth; and upon his death they revealed it. Not, however, without difficulty, for the Los Angeles *Times,* to which they first took their story, refused to print it, explaining: "History seems to stick to the delusion."

There are several other cases of scholarly confusion as a result of the discovery of artifacts difficult of comprehension. In 1838 near Neroc, France, was discovered a stone with the inscription, "Similiter causa-que ego ambo te fumant cum de suis." The secret of understanding it, someone finally realized, was in giving proper emphasis to its pronunciation. Properly read it was, "Six militaires casaques égaux en beauté fumant comme deux Suisses," which, translated, is: "Six Cossack soldiers, equally handsome, smoking like two Swiss." An old resident recalled that the stone was from a building which in 1814 was occupied by Russian troops who probably did the best they could with a strange language.

Seventy-seven letters so skillfully divided into apparent words, syllables and abbreviations as to give the impression of a Latin inscription relating to Emperor Claudius, for a long time baffled antiquarians. Properly arranged the letters spelled in perfectly good English: "Beneath this stone reposeth Claude Coster, tripe seller of Impington, as does his consort, Jane." It had been cut on a flat stone in 1756 by a professional engraver, upon the order of a London practical joker.

According to William Bridgman, in the August, 1913, *Munsey's,* a convention of antiquarians at Banbury was puzzled for days by a worn and ancient block of stone, said to be the cornerstone of an old building which had been razed. Finally, its inscription was translated to read: "Ride a cock horse."

Vallancey, Irish antiquary, is said to have found on a hillside of Tara a sculptured stone with six letters inscribed. He included an engraving of it in a costly publication, translating it to read: "To Belus, God of Fire." Later it was proved to be the letters in the name of an Irishman who, lying down to rest, had incised them lazily with a knife or chisel.

Because of an ancient Hindu superstition that bad luck can be averted by spreading a rumor about some evil condition or grotesque discovery, foreign correspondents in India fell victim early in 1935 to a report that fossil remains of a pygmy race had been found near Bombay. The story was printed seriously throughout the world.

In the same year the United Press sent out the account of the discovery of Sasquatch men, remnants of a lost race of "wild men" who inhabited the rocky regions of British Columbia centuries ago, roaming the province again. The hairy giants were reported to be disturbing residents of Harrison Mills, fifty miles east of Vancouver, with long, weird wolf-like howls and to be showing scant respect for private property.

Unfortunately, no specimen of this primitive tribe was captured, so it still is unknown whether they are the long-sought "missing link" between the anthropoid apes and man. However, in the June 15, 1929, *Illustrated London News,* appeared the picture of a strange specimen which its discoverer, Francis de Loys, said, in an accompanying article, filled an important gap in the succession of forms ranging from the anthropoids to man. He said it was an Amer-anthropoid, a new member of the family of platyrhinians.

On his difficult return trip from the Tarra River in the Motilones districts of Venezuela and Colombia, where he trapped and killed the beast, De Loys was compelled to part with the skin, skull and jaws, retaining only the picture as evidence. This photograph, furthermore, is from the front and does not show the chief feature of the specimen—its lack of a tail; and no scale is given to indicate proportions. The written description is of a female ape about 157 centimeters high, 112 pounds heavy, with thick, coarse, long, grayish brown hair, having thirty-two teeth without any protuberances of the back portion of the mandibles.

Because of the uncertain value of the record and because De Loys waited twelve years before presenting it, Earnest A. Hooton in *Up from the Ape* refused to attach any value to Amer-anthropoid. Ralph Linton, another outstanding anthropologist, believes the animal was a spider monkey.

It is not always possible to chuckle over the mighty scientist whose overzeal in seeking fame caused him to fall from fame and fortune. Johann Beringer died of humiliation after his students tricked him with the Würzburg stones, and French anthropologists nearly came to blows defending their positions. Most tragic of all, however, is the story of Paul Kammerer, "the modern Darwin," who committed suicide when his career was ruined by a drop of ink beneath the skin of a toad's thumb.

Who injected the India ink into the specimen, Kammerer, in his suicide note, could only conjecture; it might have been a former laboratory assistant. Its presence was the evidence upon which the noted scientist based the conclusions of his *The Inheritance of Acquired Characteristics* which appeared in 1924.

Kammerer's experiments had been conducted with midwife toads, so named because of the male's habit of carrying the female's eggs on his legs until the young hatch under water. The Viennese scientist divided his toads into two groups. One he raised entirely out of water, forcing the specimens to hatch their eggs in the air; the other he kept in tanks in which the only ground available consisted of small islands on which the temperature was maintained at a point calculated to cause the creatures to seek the water to cool off.

As a result of this experiment with several generations of toads, Kammerer declared, the male toads raised on land gradually lost their egg-carrying habits. Those forced to live in the water developed, after a few generations, what is known as nuptial pads, little horny pads on the thumbs, which are common among water frogs and are used to hold on to their mates in the water.

When Kammerer took his specimens to London to lecture on them, Dr. Thornley Garden, professor of zoology at Cambridge, said: "Kammerer begins where Darwin left off." Dr. G. H. F. Nuttall, professor of biology at Cambridge, opined: "He has made perhaps the greatest biological discovery of the century."

It was Dr. G. K. Noble, of the American Museum of Natural History of New York, who, in an article in the English magazine *Nature* for August 7, 1926, announced the results of chemical, histological and dissection tests on one of Kammerer's specimens brought to this country by

an associate. Noble noticed at once that the little blackened thumb pads
lacked certain characteristics of such pads. These were smooth and bore
no trace of the epidermal spines which should have been apparent. Also,
the coloring appeared under the microscope to be below the epidermis, or
outer skin, rather than in it. The left wrist of the specimen he found to
have been lacerated; the black ink readily washed out in the dissecting
dish water.

In his farewell letter, addressed to the Communist Academy, Moscow,
with which he had been affiliated only a short time before his death, Kammerer wrote:

Who besides myself was interested in perpetuating such falsification of
the test specimen can only dimly be surmised. There is no doubt, however, that thereby almost my whole life work has become dubious. Consequently, although I didn't participate in this fraud, I feel I am not
entitled any more to accept your nomination. Moreover, I find it is impossible to survive my life work's destruction. I hope to find tomorrow sufficient courage and fortitude to end my wretched life.

Had the hoax on Dr. Kammerer succeeded, it might have confounded
the scientific world for a generation. Exactly that is what happened as
regards a "most elaborate and carefully prepared hoax" in the field of
anthropology, to quote those who exposed it in 1953: Dr. K. P. Oakley of
the British Museum and two Oxford professors, Dr. J. E. Weiner and Dr.
W. E. LeGros Clark. These scientists proved that the jaw of the fabulous
Piltdown Man is that of a modern ape and does not belong with the top
part of the skull which Charles Dawson, lawyer and antiquarian, dug up
in 1911 in a gravel pit on the Piltdown Common in southern England.

For forty years the Piltdown Man confused anthropologists. If genuine
it would mean modern man has existed on earth for 500,000 years. It didn't
"fit" on the evolutionary tree constructed from other discoveries. The
scientific method by which the exposé was made was discovered during
World War II by Dr. Oakley while studying the use of fluorine to protect
teeth. He learned that the longer a bone lay in the ground exposed to
fluorine-bearing waters, the more fluorine it would absorb. Tests based
on this knowledge proved the Piltdown skull to be about 50,000 years old
and the jaw a fake. In his book, *Piltdown Forgery,* Dr. Weiner presented
evidence that Dawson was known to stain bones and otherwise fabricate
ancient finds. Nevertheless he died in 1916 known as the "wizard of
Sussex" where a monument commemorates his famous discovery.

CHAPTER XVI

Literary Hoaxing

DESPITE the tenacity with which he resists the efforts of iconoclasts to destroy the pleasure he derives from myths, legends and old wives' tales, in an abstract vote the average person doubtless would express a preference to have his histories, historical novels and motion pictures, biographies and autobiographies, antiques, art treasures, autographs, first editions, travelogues and adventure stories "on the level."

When, however, it comes to such erudite matters as whether Homer or a half-dozen other fellows wrote the *Iliad,* whether *Hamlet* was the composition of Shakespeare or Francis (or Roger or Leonard) Bacon and whether Edward N. Westcott or Rudyard Kipling was the author of *David Harum,* he is equally certain to feel that they are the concern of scholars only. The ordinary playgoer concentrates on what happens on the stage and may not even read, much less remember, the small type on his program giving the playwright's name. Likewise, he recalls Scarlett O'Hara long after he has forgotten Margaret Mitchell.

This probably is as it should be. Nevertheless, to scholars who decide what is and what is not a classic, and who influence our own literary taste and writing styles more than we realize, it is of vital importance to know who actually wrote what and all the attendant circumstances. This chapter is concerned with their problems.

Literary scholars have been confounded by forgeries of virtually every literary master, by the creation of fictitious authors, by plagiarisms, thefts, dishonest handlings of material, fabricated biographical data regarding authors and a great deal of plain, ordinary tomfoolery which has turned out to be serious.

It is natural that the biggest names should be those most often forged, and the best work that most frequently plagiarized or stolen. If the complete story of literary hoaxing were told, there would be hardly a name familiar to students in the literature survey course which would not appear in it. To the layman, the revelation would be distressing that, as often as not, these names would be included among the hoaxers rather than among those whose material was defiled.

Christopher Marlowe, for instance, stole from Edmund Spenser—in one case an entire stanza from *The Faerie Queene*; Thomas de Quincey in his essay on Samuel Taylor Coleridge charged that the latter appropriated the work of Schelling for an entire chapter of his *Biographia Literaria*; to Burton Rascoe, Milton's *Paradise Lost* was the "baldest plagiarism" of literature, being taken largely from Salandra's *Adamo Caduto*; Voltaire stole ideas and works promiscuously, and the elder Dumas conducted a veritable factory to transform the works of others to his own use; Sir Walter Scott took for his own two poems sent him by Surtees for *Minstrelsy of the Scottish Border*; Edmund Burke wrote *Vindication of Natural Society* in the character of "a late noble writer"; Benjamin Disraeli stole from Macaulay, Pope, Balzac, Dryden and many others, his famous oration at the funeral of Wellington having been taken bodily from a review article by Thiers, French historian, on Marshal Saint-Cyr; Edward Robert Bulwer-Lytton plagiarized George Sand's *Lavinia* to produce his *Lucile* and also pilfered from Musset, Heine and others; Thomas Hardy took an entire chapter from *Georgia Scenes* by a forgotten American humorist for his *Trumpet Major*; Charles Reade's *Picture in My Uncle's Dining Room* came from a forgotten magazine story, *The Old M'sieu's Secret*; a part of Tennyson's *Home They Brought Her Warrior Dead* is a duplicate of Scott's *Marmion,* and so on through the entire history of English literature.

Much nearer the top than the bottom of any compilation of inveterate literary thieves and plagiarists would be William Shakespeare himself. Because he helped himself to so many of Marlowe's "mighty lines," some critics contend that Marlowe was the author of some Shakespearean plays, notably *Pericles* and *Titus Andronicus*. A scene in *The Tempest* was taken bodily from an essay by Montaigne, and many and many another masterpiece had its counterpart in some earlier work which the immortal bard transmuted into melodious verse.

Turning for the nonce from the sins of the giants to those committed against them, Shakespeare's name again goes to the head of the list. According to William Jaggard, in his *Shakespeare Frauds,* a "new and great revival in honor of the bard [which] was springing up" was responsible for a series of early eighteenth century forgeries. In his *Literary Ethics,* H. M. Paull says the first of these occurred about the turn of the century when Nahum Tate, poet laureate, wrote a happy ending for *King Lear.*

In 1707, Paull says, Tate produced another drama which he signed, "By N. Tate, author of the Tragedy called *King Lear*."

According to Jaggard, however, the first deliberate forgery of the Stratford bard was in 1728, when Lewis Theobald "discovered" a lost play, *The Double Falsehood; or The Distrest Lovers*. This was performed at Drury Lane and passed through two editions. Critics who refused to accept it as by Shakespeare nevertheless failed to guess the real author. Dr. Richard Farmer thought it was by James Shirley, a contemporary of Shakespeare, and Edmond Malone credited it to another early seventeenth century writer, Philip Massinger. Theobald was exposed by Isaac Reed.

The next Shakespearean revival followed the 1769 jubilee in his honor. Since then Shakespeare's mulberry tree has been mentioned in a joking manner, as virtually every visitor to Stratford-on-Avon that year was given a souvenir said to be from it. Said Jaggard: "The very Forest of Arden could scarcely have grown enough wood for all the things that came from that one small mulberry tree."

Peter Cunningham, a neighbor of John Payne Collier, enjoyed a brief period of popularity in 1840 when he announced the discovery of original court records of the time of Elizabeth and James I with references to Shakespeare. A microscopic investigation revealed the forgery which Cunningham, a government audit clerk, had not found it difficult to perform.

The most dramatic of all forgers of Shakespeare was William Henry Ireland, during another revival period. The great James Boswell went down on his knees and kissed what is popularly called "the immortal hoax of Ireland" or "Ireland's sin." Richard B. Sheridan purchased the supposed long-lost play, *Vortigern and Rowena*, and produced it at Drury Lane with one of the best actors of the day in the leading role. Dr. Joseph Warren solemnly declared of Shakespeare's newly discovered confession of faith, an accompanying manuscript: "We have very fine things in our church service, and our litany abounds with beauties; but there is a man who has distanced us all."

The "man" in reality was an eighteen-year-old boy, the son of a respected bookseller whose part in the affair never has been clearly established. The boy's skill at emulating the style of the great Shakespeare was surpassed only by his ability to think up breath-taking relics to discover and his gift for reproducing documents and other mementos with all the appearance of age and authenticity.

Ireland's story reads like a novel, which it became in James Payn's

The Talk of the Town. Whether or not he wanted to imitate Thomas Chatterton (see Chapter IV), it is certain that on a visit to Stratford he met John Jordan, forger of the will of John Shakespeare, William's father.

He began his own career with a crude pen-and-ink drawing of the Droeshut portrait in a letter purporting to be from Shakespeare to his friend Cowley, the comedian. This portrait, it is known, was neither drawn nor engraved until seven years after the poet's death, but no one seemed to remember.

When Ireland's offering was complete it contained two complete plays, *Vortigern and Rowena* and *Henry II,* letters to Anne Hathaway, in one of which was enclosed a lock of the poet's hair, legal contracts, autographed receipts, and—climax of all—a deed of property as a gift to a William Henry Ireland, who had saved Shakespeare from drowning in the Thames.

It was to his ability to prove his descent from this namesake that young Ireland gave credit for his being able to obtain the treasures from a "gentleman of property" at Stratford in whose home they allegedly were discovered.

A committee of the most outstanding literary scholars of the time, professional antiquarians, the poet laureate and others came to the humble shop of Samuel Ireland, the father, to examine the finds. One and all acclaimed the relics as genuine, and for some time Edmund Malone, leading Shakespearean critic of the day, stood alone in disbelief, and George Chalmers answered him with two bulky volumes of *Apology.* The poet laureate collaborated with Sir James Bland Burgess in writing the prologue for *Vortigern.*

Another who became skeptical before the April 2, 1796, Drury Lane performance was John Kemble, the actor. Forbidden by his contract to withdraw from the cast as Mrs. Siddons had done, he prepared to make the production as much of a burlesque as possible. The writer has found four different versions of the line in Act V which he is supposed to have delivered with mock emphasis; the most popular rendering of it seems to be, "And when this solemn mockery is o'er." At any rate, led by "plants" whom Kemble had instructed how to act, the audience got the point, and by its reaction expressed agreement with the sentiment. It is said that Kemble tried to get the production scheduled for April Fool's Day, and, failing that, to have a farce, *My Grandmothers,* as an afterpiece. Again critics do not agree as to whether he was successful in the latter attempt.

As Malone's scholarly criticism of the forgeries began to gain adherents, Ireland confessed publicly in 1805, and again in the preface to the 1832 edition of *Vortigern*. Before he died, however, he repudiated his confession. He also at one time exonerated his father of any complicity and at another accused him of being equally culpable.

"The point of the joke is," wrote Andrew Lang in the December, 1883, *Contemporary Review*, "that after the whole conspiracy exploded, people were anxious to buy examples of the forgeries. Mr. W. H. Ireland was equal to the occasion. He actually forged his own or (according to Dr. Ingleby) his father's forgeries, and, by thus increasing the supply, he deluged the market with sham shams, with imitations of imitations. If the accusation be correct, it is impossible not to admire the colossal impudence of Mr. W. H. Ireland."

The latest outstanding Shakespearean forger was John Payne Collier, whose "Old Corrector" resulted in a protracted squabble among critics, to whom the emendations in a second edition second folio were a sensation.

The famous Perkins folio, so called because of the name on the flyleaf, appeared in 1852 and formed the basis of Collier's *Notes and Emendations to the Text of Shakespeare's Plays* and of changes in his edition of Shakespeare's plays the next year. Collier's story was that he came on the folio in Rudd's bookshop just after it was sent in from the country by a Mr. Perry. That gentleman later failed to identify the copy in Collier's possession as the one which he previously had possessed.

The Duke of Devonshire, to whom Collier presented the treasure, loaned it to the British Museum for examination in 1859. Experts declared the emendations forgeries of a modern date. They discovered, beneath the ink, penciled notes in a modern hand. Collier was exposed by Nicholas Hamilton in his *Inquiry*, published in 1860.

Another Collier forgery was Shakespeare's signature to a genuine letter at Dulwich. He also made spurious entries in *Memoirs of Edward Alleyn*, it was revealed when his library was sold in 1884. A folio discovered by Collier in Bridgewater House in 1835 also came under suspicion.

In literature "the Puck of Commentators" was George Steevens who, when he disliked a writer, forged in order to embarrass or wound him; and when he had no grudge he kept on hoaxing anyway. To his credit were his contributions in exposing both Chatterton and Ireland, but, as Isaac D'Israeli wrote of him in *Curiosities of Literature*:

If we possessed the secret history of the literary life of George Steevens it would display an unparalleled series of arch deception and malicious ingenuity. He has been happily characterized by Gifford as "the Puck of Commentators." Steevens is a creature so spotted over with literary forgeries and adulterations that any remarkable one about the time he flourished may be attributed to him. They were the habits of a depraved mind, and there was a darkness in his character many shades deeper than belonged to Puck; even in the playfulness of his invention, there was usually a turn of personal malignity, and the real object was not so much to raise a laugh as to "grin horribly a ghastly smile" on the individual.

The critic Malone incurred the dislike of Steevens. D'Israeli quoted Boswell as relating that Steevens frequently wrote for an afternoon newspaper notes on Shakespeare purposely to entrap Malone and to obtain for himself an easy triumph in the next edition.

Among his forgeries of the dead was a letter from George Peele describing a "merry meeting at the Globe" attended by Shakespeare, Ben Jonson and Ned Alleyn. The date given was 1600, two years after Peele's death. Steevens attempted to get Dr. Berkenhout to use the letter in his history of English authors.

Best known of Steevens' tricks was the anecdote on the life of Milton, which he borrowed from Vanderbourg's *Clotilde,* itself a leading fake (see Chapter IV). As rendered by Steevens it had Milton asleep under a tree near Cambridge when two foreign ladies stopped, admired his beauty and left a few verses from Guarini's *Madrigal* in his hand. Milton's famous trip to Italy was said to have been to search for the donor. The story appeared in the *General Evening Post* during the spring of 1789.

Steevens' joke on Gough, celebrated archaeologist, is credited to a grudge. On a piece of chimney slate, he inscribed rude letters, "Here Hardcnut drank a wine-horn dry, stared about him and died." Steevens arranged to have a curiosity dealer display it where Gough would see it and to "remember" that the spot where it was found was in Kennington Lane near the supposed palace of Hardcnut or Hardicanute. The inscription was described by Gough before the Society of Antiquaries and was engraved for the *Gentleman's Magazine.*

London Magazine printed a purported extract from a Dutch Traveler on a Javanese upas tree whose noxious effluvia killed all vegetation and animal life for twelve or fourteen miles around. In one edition of his works Steevens inserted some obscenity for which he said he was indebted to two respectable clergymen whom he named. His *Boke of the Soldan* is said to have been written to impose on "a literary friend." At one time he charged that Shiells, amanuensis of Dr. Samuel Johnson, was the author of almost all of Theophilus Cibber's *Lives of the Poets*.

The two most frequently forged writers of the early nineteenth century probably were Mrs. Ann Radcliffe and Sir Walter Scott. In the appendix to *Mrs. Radcliffe: Her Relation Towards Romanticism,* Alida A. S. Wieten lists eighteen novels falsely credited to her, and names three more about which there are doubts.

The leading forgery of Scott resulted from a wager which a German, G. W. Haring, won by producing a novel which passed as a genuine number of the Waverley series. Called *Walladmor,* it appeared in 1824 at Leipzig as a translation from the supposed original English. Impressed, De Quincey undertook to translate it "back" into English, whereupon he found it so unworthy of Scott that he substituted a version of his own which he dedicated to Haring. Scott, by that time used to having novels put out in his name, showed no spleen in disclaiming *Walladmor* in the introduction to *The Betrothed*.

Among the many other faked Scott novels, most of which were published in Paris, were the following: *Allan Cameron, La Pythie des Highlands, Ayme Verd, Le Proscrit des Hébrides, Morendum, a Tale of the 1210s,* and a series, Tales of My Landlord, containing *Pontefracte Castle* in three volumes.

Although Macpherson's Ossian was the most ambitious and, from a strictly literary point of view, the best attempt to produce a fictitious library of literature for the Scotch, it was by no means the only such attempt. In fact, it is difficult today to tell which of any collection of Scotch ballads actually were sung by the old-time Highlanders, and which are recent imitations, mostly from the early eighteenth century.

The celebrated "Hardyknute" is foremost among those about the authorship of which there was protracted dispute. It appeared in 1719 in Edinburgh as a "discovery" by Lady Wardlaw, who later was proved to be the author. In 1781 John Pinkerton knowingly included it as genuine in *Scottish Tragic Ballads*; but in 1786, in the preface to *Ancient Scottish Poems,* he candidly confessed that it and most of the other poems in the former volume were faked. In the meantime Ritson violently attacked "Hardyknute," which is to be found in Thomas Percy's *Reliques of Ancient English Poetry,* Series the Second, Book the First, No. 17, even in editions appearing as late as 1873.

Inasmuch as Robert H. Cromek previously had criticized as poor some of the poetry of Allan Cunningham, it is not clear to what extent he really was hoaxed when he included in his *Remains of Nithsdale and Galloway Song* contributions which Cunningham submitted as genuine ballads.

Likewise, the lenient attitude toward literary faking taken by Sir Walter Scott in the preface to *Border Minstrelsy* causes one to wonder if he really was fooled by "Slaying of Anton Featherstonhaugh" and "Bertram's Dirge," written by Robert Smith Surtees and contributed as genuine pieces. The same Surtees is known to have sent Hogg a number of spurious Jacobite ballads which also were published.

The most innocent of all authors of ancient lays seems to have been the nineteenth century Reverend R. S. Hawker who generally is exonerated of any intention to deceive with "Song of the Western Men." It is related that he was amused to have it accepted as genuine by Scott, Macaulay, Dickens and others and to find it in 1832 in Deacon's *Ancient Poems, Ballads, Songs of the Peasantry of England Taken Down from Oral Tradition,* although he publicly had confessed to its authorship in 1825.

The poem is to be found in Volume II of *Scottish Traditional Versions of Ancient Ballads,* edited by J. H. Dixon, which is part of Volume XVII of the Percy Society publications, printed in 1846 in London. In his preface Dixon swears that all the contents are authentic, affirming, "They are, indeed, not such compositions as a literary impostor would think it worth while to produce."

Introducing "Song of the Western Men" as the thirty-sixth poem, he says: "This spirited song was written at the time of the committal of Bishop Trelawny to the Tower in 1688 for his defense of the Protestant religion."

The name of Voltaire was forged to a quarto edition which appeared at Geneva and later in Holland as *Private Lives;* he himself helped to confuse literature by first publishing *Candide* anonymously as a translation from the German of a fictitious Dr. Ralph.

In 1633 William Prynne attacked the stage in *Histriomastix.* Parliamentary action closing the theaters in 1649 was followed by the publication of *Mr. William Prynne, His Defence of Stage Plays, or a Retraction of a Former Book of His Called Histriomastix.* Prynne disclaimed this in a pamphlet. Henry Walker ten years later issued *A Terrible Outcry Against the Loitering Prelates* under Prynne's name, and again Prynne published a formal denial. What happened to Walker when he was summoned to appear before the House of Commons is not recorded. It is known that he also forged a declaration of Charles I under date of August 27, 1647, and that king emulated Prynne in making public denial.

Thomas Carlyle endorsed thirty-five letters of Oliver Cromwell that William Squire of Norwich proved to be forgeries, forty years after his death. John Ruskin once called a forged Carlyle letter "not the least significant of the utterances of the master." Ruskin himself saw alleged letters of his own given newspaper publicity.

Although Lord Byron denied authorship of a number of works credited to him, *The Vampyre* and *An Account of My Residence in Mitylene* appeared in an edition of his works published in 1825, the year after his death, and again seven years later, together with an explanation of how Byron composed them. Much more important mishandling of the name of Byron was by the outstanding autograph faker who posed on both sides of the Atlantic as Icodad George Gordon Byron, illegitimate son of the great poet and a Spanish lady of noble family.

The Byron forgeries got under way when a beautiful lachrymose lady, posing as the daughter of the surgeon who attended Fletcher, Lord Byron's valet, on his deathbed, appeared in 1848 at White's Pall Mall bookshop. Her weeping tale of being forced to support an invalid and impecunious sister "took in" White, who purchased from her a large packet of correspondence, most of which presumably passed between Byron and the poet Shelley.

Moxon, the publisher, purchased most of the Shelley letters from White and persuaded Robert Browning to write his only prose of any length or consequence as an introduction to them. Unfortunately for Moxon but fortunately for letters, one review copy was sent to Alfred Lord Tennyson, at whose home it was seen by Robert Palgrave, editor of *The Golden Treasury*. As he read them some of the letters seemed so familiar to Palgrave that he returned home and rummaged through the effects of his father, Sir Francis Palgrave, the historian. In an article written by Sir Francis twelve years earlier for the *Quarterly Review,* the son discovered the source of most of the Shelley material.

When the alleged Miss Fletcher appeared again she was followed, and the trail led to the bogus Icodad, her husband. Together they fled to New York, where the pretender announced he would publish a biography of his "father" based in large part upon more than one thousand of the poet's unedited letters and his journal. Icodad was repudiated by Mrs. Leigh, Byron's sister, and most of what he produced easily was proved to be specious.

Ambitious and clever as was Icodad George Gordon Byron, he was a rank amateur by comparison with Constantine Simonides, the master forger of them all (with the possible exception of Vrain Lucas, whose story was told in Chapter VIII). Because it would have been impossible for him to fabricate all the twenty-five hundred manuscripts which he peddled to collectors in all parts of Europe, scholars agree that some, including those purchased by Sir Frederick Madden for the British Museum, are genuine, and that others were only faked copies of originals found in the monasteries of Mount Athos where Simonides said he made most of his "discoveries."

Simonides began by producing fragments of many widely known writers, including Hesiod, Homer and Anacreon, which he said had been bequeathed to him by an uncle. Unable to pay the full $10,000 for a lotus-leaf Homer, the King of Greece suggested that the directors of the University of Athens share the expense. Only one of a dozen experts appointed to investigate suspected a fake. He, however, finally proved his point by showing that the new Homer reproduced all the misprints of a recent edition by a German editor, Wolff. The same manuscript was turned down by the British Museum but later was purchased by Sir Thomas Phillips.

Following his exposure in Greece, Simonides began his wanderings. At Constantinople he announced a Sanchoniathon, then an ancient Greek work on hieroglyphics, then a history of Armenia. In a garden of Ismail-Pasha, Khedive of Egypt, he dug up a box of manuscripts. The Duke of Sutherland paid $4,200 for a forged letter from Alcibiades to Pericles. When Tischendorff discovered at Mount Sinai a Sinaitic Codex, recently sold by the Russian government to the British Museum, Simonides said it was a transcription of one he found at Mount Athos. Scholars, however, discredit his claim. A Greek copy of *Shepherd of Hermas,* purchased by Dindorf, still is in the library of the University of Leipzig.

Simonides' most notable attempt, the one which led to his downfall, was a palimpsest history of Egypt by Uranius. The original writing was supposed to be beneath four others: (1) a work of Flavius Josephus; (2) a history of the Virgin Mary; (3) a work of the Emperor Constantine, and (4) a history of St. John the Baptist. Dr. Dindorf, foremost classical scholar of the day, was convinced of the authenticity of the palimpsest and induced the King of Prussia to purchase it while he made preparations for its publication by the Clarendon Press at Oxford. Microscopic and chemical tests revealed that wherever the writing of the so-called palimpsest was crossed by twelfth century writing, the ink of the supposedly older letters in reality overlay the allegedly later writing. Certain anachronisms also were noted. In Simonides' room after his arrest were found materials and history books by which it was possible for him to produce the work.

Simonides failed because scholars already had begun to make use of chemistry to detect frauds among the hundreds of thousands of "discoveries" which, undetected, would have been accepted to fill gaps in literary history, especially of the Greek and Roman periods. Lacking modern tools, throughout the preceding centuries, the equivalent of libraries of specious classics was produced. Scores of hands, some of them before the Christian era began, scholars believe, helped convert the *Iliad* and the *Odyssey* into their present forms. Pseudo-archaic words, tenses and expressions and references to iron, a metal virtually unknown before the sixth century, are clues by which to determine the parts Homer did not write. In a similar manner a poem, "De Vetula," credited to Ovid, was proved a thirteenth century production because it made the Latin poet talk of algebra, unknown by name during his lifetime.

The man who, according to J. A. Farrer in *Literary Forgeries,* "contributed more to the confusion of literature, whether innocently or not, than any man of his own or of any other generation," was Annius of Viterbo, a fifteenth century master of the Vatican. In his *De Comentariis Antiquitatum* he published the allegedly rediscovered works of eleven writers that had been lost to the world. Included were the lost writings of Cato and Xenophon and those of Berosus, Antoninus Pius, Manetho, Philo Judaeus, Caius Sempronius and Myrsilus, all of which, Annius contended, he had found buried in the ground. It is reported that Leandro Alberti died disconsolate after discovering that much of his *Description of Italy,* published in 1568, was worthless because taken from Annius.

Of the innumerable forgeries of Cicero two are of particular interest. The first occurred in 1583 when Charles Sigonius of Modena announced the discovery of *De Consolatione,* in which the great Latin orator consoled himself upon the death of his daughter, Tullia. It was not until 1783, exactly two hundred years later, that Terabosilii found, among Sigonius' papers, an incriminating letter confessing that he reconstructed the entire essay after finding only a fragment.

The other Cicero forgery appeared in 1811 at Bologna and was an alleged fourth book of *De Natura Deorum,* taking up the subject where the genuine third book left off. It purported to be edited from an ancient parchment manuscript found by P. Seraphinus. According to Farrer: "He had resolved to print it in order to show the similarity of its doctrines to those of the Catholic Church; the editor being convinced that, had Cicero been born in the Christian era, he would have conformed to the orthodox faith." Anachronisms in style easily proved it a forgery.

One of the "hottest" controversies among literary scholars was that which followed the discovery by Martinus Statilius, about the middle of the seventeenth century, in a library at Trau, Dalmatia, of a fragment to be added to the thirty pages of Petronius Arbiter's famous *Satyricon* known to exist at that time. Although Roman experts overlooked grammatical errors which caused others to consider the Trau fragment a forgery, and in 1668 attested to its genuineness, scholarship ever since has been divided.

Regardless of the authenticity of the Trau fragment, the great work of Petronius Arbiter, "the friend, minister and finally the victim of Nero," still obviously was incomplete. Two outstanding attempts have been made to supply the missing parts. The first was that of a French soldier, François Nodot, in 1693 and was a complete Petronius allegedly found in Belgrade while Nodot was engaged in a campaign against Turkey as a member of the Austrian army. Nodot failed to convince because of his inability to produce more than a copy of the supposed original. More than one hundred years later, in 1800, a Spanish writer, Joseph Marchena, for a time fooled critics with several alleged Petronius fragments which he said he found in a Swiss monastery. Professor Heinrich Eichstädt of Jena proved that both the fragments and some others supposedly by Catullus, published in 1808 by Marchena, were interpolations of an ancient manuscript in the library at his university.

Although, as previously noted, because of the development of scientific means of detection, literary forgeries have decreased, plagiarisms and thefts persist. As recently as June, 1935, *Esquire* printed a short story by Alvin B. Harmon, "The Perlu," which a pageful of "The Sound and the Fury" readers informed the editors was a bold paraphrase of Ambrose Bierce's familiar "The Damned Thing"; and this in turn had been suspected of being a plagiarism of Guy de Maupassant's "The Horla."

Fresh to memory also is the case of Lloyd Lewis, fifteen-year-old farm boy of Plattsburg, Missouri, who, in 1936, won a $5,000 prize essay contest on peace sponsored by Eddie Cantor, noted comedian, by copying the article "How Can We Stay Out of War?" by Dr. Frank Kingdon, president of the University of Newark, from the December, 1935, issue of *Peace Digest*. Before the exposure, however, Lloyd had a memorable trip to New York; he was sincerely amazed to learn he had done something reprehensible.

Whereas Dr. Frederick A. Cook is best known for his North Pole claims, as related in Chapter IX, he also was accused of having stolen the lifetime work of the Reverend Thomas Bridges, a missionary among the Onas and Yahgans, two barbarian tribes of Tierra del Fuego. While a member of the Belgian Antarctic expedition in 1899, Dr. Cook borrowed a Yahgan grammar and dictionary which Mr. Bridges had compiled. Subsequent efforts of the missionary and his son to obtain return of the manuscripts failed, and in time announcement was made of the impending publication of a Yahgan grammar and dictionary by Dr. Cook. Charles H. Townsend, of the New York Aquarium, saw the publication notices and advised the Belgian Commission to cancel publication plans, which it did.

For fifteen years Rostand's famous *Cyrano de Bergerac* was not played in the United States because of an amazing plagiarism suit won by a Chicago real estate man, Samuel Eberly Gross, in 1900. Although Richard Mansfield, who was touring in *Cyrano* at the time, friends and critics were skeptical, a jury decided that Rostand had stolen from Gross' unproduced *The Merchant Prince of Cornville* which, in 1899, he left for several weeks with Constant Coquelin, director of the Porte St. Martin Theater in Paris, and also once showed to A. M. Palmer, American producer. In 1915 a New York federal court decided against the Gross estate which tried to enjoin the production of Walter Damrosch's opera on the Cyrano story, and in 1923 Walter Hampden revived the play itself.

In the July, 1926, *International Book Review,* Charles Hanson Towne described the care which the average magazine editor must exercise to avoid accepting a plagiarism as an original composition. When editor of *Smart Set,* Towne published a short story which had appeared three years earlier in the *Atlantic Monthly,* and once had submitted to him a poem of his own composition.

When, in 1935, the late Oscar Odd McIntyre published *The Big Town,* a collection of pieces which had appeared previously in his widely syndicated newspaper column, "New York Day by Day," Christopher Morley pointed out thirty examples of plagiarism of his own "Bowling Green" column in the *Saturday Review of Literature,* ranging over a fifteen-year period.

No leading figure in English literature has been connected with more faked literature of the general nature indicated than the eminent Jonathan Swift, eighteenth century dean of St. Patrick's Cathedral, Dublin. Because he generally wrote anonymously, he perhaps has been credited with the authorship of much of which he was innocent. Nevertheless, there is sufficient evidence to prove that Dean Swift was a persistent practical joker, and that some of his humor verged on the malicious.

Perhaps the best known of the dean's hoaxes was played on Partridge, editor of an almanac. Under the pseudonym of Isaac Bickerstaff, Swift issued *Predictions for the Year 1708,* in which he forecast the death of Partridge March 29. When that day came and went, he soberly published a letter, supposedly from a revenue officer to a lord, describing the astrologer's last hours and demise.

Awakened by the sexton who wished to inquire if there were any orders for the funeral sermon, Partridge, it is said, tried in vain to prove himself alive. His wife was called a widow, and old friends met him on the street and apologized for their stares, explaining that he resembled a deceased acquaintance.

The publishers with whom Partridge dealt struck his name from their rolls and sought legal action to prevent further publication of an almanac in his name. In Portugal, it is said, the works of Bickerstaff were placed under the inquisitorial ban because the success of his predictions indicated association with the devil.

In desperation Partridge published a pamphlet asserting he was not dead. Swift countered with *A Vindication of Isaac Bickerstaff, Esq.* With such arguments as that no man alive could have written such stuff as appeared in Partridge's almanac, he "proved" that, despite his denial, Partridge was dead.

The result should have been satisfactory to the dean, for Partridge was forced, because of ridicule, to cease publication for six years. He resumed in 1714 after the demise of the *Tatler,* in which Steele wrote under the name of Bickerstaff which he borrowed from Swift. Believing that it was Steele who played the trick on him, Partridge, in his first number, pointed out that he actually had outlived Bickerstaff.

Somewhat similar was Swift's method of defending his name against Edmund Curll, author of a collection of indecent stories which he published as *Dr. Swift's Miscellanies.* Swift retorted with *The Poisoning of Curll,* which included a deathbed confession by his libeler.

Another hoax credited to Swift was a pamphlet containing the alleged dying confession of a common robber, named Elliston, in which appeared a fictitious list of other criminals and of receivers of stolen goods. Street robberies, it is said, declined noticeably for several years after its publication.

Swift was a member of the Scriblerus Club, to which Gay, Pope, Parnell and Arbuthnot also belonged. This group conceived the idea of prolonging "the memory of that learned phantom which is to be immortal," Martinus Scriblerus, by means of a burlesqued biography intended to ridicule false learning. Swift had been called Martin by Oxford scholars because both swifts and martins are forms of swallow; hence the name Martinus. Because Arbuthnot was the leader of the group, the name Martin came to be applied to him alone.

Arbuthnot wrote Scriblerus' early life, and the account of his travels was assigned to Swift. Says Craik, biographer of Swift:

> The literary monuments of Scriblerus are not to be found in anything that proceeded directly from this ineffective partnership of wit, but in the isolated efforts of the two greatest of the group—in *Gulliver's Travels* and the *Dunciad*.

Sterne later pilfered Arbuthnot's contribution for material for *Tristram Shandy*.

Swift's last and, according to Carl Van Doren, greatest hoax was a poem on his own death which was "between an abridgement and a burlesque" of a genuine eulogy to himself seriously intended not to appear until after his demise. After publishing anonymously the burlesqued poem under the date of All Fools' Day, 1733, Swift declared someone had memorized the original and played a trick on him. "But even this trick shall not provoke me to print the true one, which indeed is not proper to be seen till I can be seen no more," he wrote.

Because of the practice of writing anonymously or under a nom de plume, many another prominent author has been victimized. Numerous nonentities claimed to be the author of Mary Ann Evans' outstanding novels, published in the name of George Eliot to avoid the prejudice against feminine writers. Charles Lamb flew into a rage when another announced himself to be the real Simon Pure, demanding, "Is there no law against these rascals?" This was strange language from one who, according to H. M. Paull in *Literary Ethics,* confessed, in a letter to a Miss Hutchinson in 1825 regarding his *Memoir of Liston*: "Of all the lies I ever put off, I value this the most. It is from top to toe, every paragraph, Pure

Invention, and has passed for gospel; has been republished in newspapers and in the penny handbills of the night, as an authentic account."

William Sharp confused biographers for many years by publishing both under his own name and under that of Fiona Macleod for whom he supplied biographical data, still to be found in some books of reference.

Among the many books which have troubled both the literati and historians was *The Athenian Letters,* which appeared in 1741 in a private edition of only eight or twelve copies and was given to the world in general in 1798. According to the author, Charles Yorke, eighteenth century eccentric, the letters were found in a library in Fez, Morocco, by a learned Jew who willed them in 1688 to the English consul at Tunis. The complete title indicates their nature: *Letters from an Agent of the King of Persia Residing at Athens During the Peloponnesian War to the Minister of State, Translated by Moses ben Meshobab from a Manuscript in the Old Persic Language Preserved in the Library at Fez.*

When he visited the monks at Palermo in 1782, Joseph Vella, chaplain of the Knights of Malta, sympathized with their hope of some day finding Arabian writings to complete their histories. Seven years later, under the editorship of Vella, appeared the first volume of *Codice Diplomatico di Sicilia sotto il governo degli Arabi, pubblicato per cura e studio di Alfonso Airoldi.* Other volumes, all dedicated to the King of Naples, followed until the sixth appeared in 1793. In the aggregate they purported to be an Arabic translation of seventeen of the last books of Livy, containing a substantial history of Sicily.

Unfortunately for Vella, a German orientalist named Hager visited Sicily and, after cursory examination, declared his work to be spurious. To give Vella a chance to explain, the King of Naples appointed a commission of five. In preparation for his appearance before it Vella memorized a few passages from his Italian translation of the alleged original Arabic and, because none of the five could understand Arabic, he got away with it. Later, however, a group of Arabic scholars examined the so-called originals, which Vella had had printed with a font of Arabic characters obtained from the typemaker Bodoni, and announced that they contained, not the history of Sicily but the simple story of Mahomet. In 1796 Vella confessed and was sentenced to prison for fifteen years.

The existence of an institution to restore Latin as the spoken language of the Italian peninsula was the startling revelation of *Relazione del Collegio Petroniano della Balie Latino aperto in Sienanel, 1719,* published at Siena by Gigli, widely known scholar. According to the fictitious yarn the children of the "best families" were cared for by nurses and teachers imported from Poland, Hungary and Germany because of their fluency in the language of Caesar. A cardinal of the thirteenth century was given a spacious mansion by the governor of the school, according to this piece of fiction which, for a time, passed as fact.

Best letter writer in the early decades of the eighteenth century was supposed to be Horace Walpole, whom Lady Craven (Margravine of Anspach) accused of capitalizing upon the current avidity for gossip to start a scandal about her as a practical joke. Walpole also produced a forged letter from the King of Prussia to Rousseau and *The Memorial,* signed by various noblemen and gentlemen. His best known work, acclaimed by Scott as "the first modern attempt to found a tale of amusing fiction upon the basis of ancient romance and chivalry," was *The Castle of Otranto.* This he first published as of foreign origin and a true narrative; in the second edition he confessed his own authorship.

As serious to scholars as forgeries, plagiarisms and inventions are fallacious biographical anecdotes regarding their authors and attempts to confuse the record as to who wrote what. Early in the nineteenth century, actuated by what he called "high spirits," Francis Mahony, as "Father Prout," started a lively argument by publishing a clever French translation of Wolfe's "The Burial of Sir John Moore" which he pretended to regard as the original of the English poem which was first published anonymously.

In recent years William Allen White, eminent Emporia, Kansas, editor, innocently started a controversy still waging regarding the authorship of *David Harum.* It happened when White found a copy of Edward N. Westcott's masterpiece misplaced in the city library on the Kipling shelf. He wrote a facetious paragraph about his discovery, and the humorless took it seriously.

In the December, 1934, issue of the *Pacific Weekly,* Ella Winter declared that James Stephens, Irish author, was the real author of George Moore's *A Story Teller's Holiday,* for which Moore had paid him $500. In the United States at the time, Stephens vehemently denied the story but added that his denial probably would not stop a protracted controversy. In the fall of 1935 Simon & Schuster denied a report, which appeared in several western newspapers, that Josephine Johnson, author of the Pulitzer prizewinning novel, *Now in November,* really is one Sally Sue Allen, a former Seattle girl.

The same year a silly prank by one Cy Perkins of Melbourne, Florida, helped rather than hurt sales of Kenneth Roberts' best-selling *Northwest Passage*. Before the gullible Kiwanis Club of Titusville, Florida, Perkins impersonated Roberts in the delivery of what the Titusville *Star-Advocate* said was "a most interesting and instructive talk on the subject of 'Rogers' Rangers,' recently published in the *Saturday Evening Post*." The imposture was revealed when a Titusville Roberts fan wrote to the *Post* for further information and was told that Roberts was then on his way home from a trip to Italy.

It is by no means uncommon for a leading writer, especially one who uses a nom de plume, to be impersonated by lecturers, check cashers, amorous suitors, social lions and others. It is related that once impersonators of Edna Ferber and Octavus Roy Cohen appeared on a platform together, neither knowing that the other was a faker.

Although the apocrypha regarding the authors of all times are prodigious, no other wholesale creation of faked pedigrees compares with that of an unknown contributor or contributors to the 1886 and 1888 editions of *Appleton's Cyclopedia of American Biography*. Fifty years later scholars still were discovering new fakes, the count in 1936 being eighty-four. First discoveries, however, did not come until thirty-three years after publication, when Dr. John Hendley Barnhart, bibliographer of the New York Botanical Garden, denounced fourteen of the biographies of scientists who, he said, if they existed at all never wrote the works with which they were credited. Since then Dr. Barnhart has added fifteen botanists to his list of fictitious entries; the staff of Sabin's *Dictionary of Books Relating to America* has found sixteen spurious biographies in one section of the *Cyclopedia*; and numerous other investigators have debunked others. Inasmuch as many of the biographies were contributed and the integrity of their authors not questioned, the way was open for the unscrupulous. Who took advantage of the opportunity is unknown because he records were lost before Dr. Barnhart's first investigation.

From all of which the layman, as intimated in the first paragraphs of this chapter, turns in disgust and says, "Anyway, it's a good story."

CHAPTER XVII

Journalistic Hoaxing

THE featured article of June 20, 1937, in the Chicago *Daily Tribune* began as follows:

Timed to lend the greatest possible support to the waning communistic C.I.O. movement in the United States, three Russian flyers were speeding tonight toward Oakland, Cal., goal of their 6,000 mile nonstop flight from Moscow.

That such a flight was attempted none can doubt; later the same day the trio was forced down after 63 hours and 17 minutes at Vancouver, Washington. A careful definition of that much-abused adjective "communistic," however, is necessary before its use by the "world's greatest newspaper" to describe the Committee for Industrial Organization can be accepted. Furthermore, at this time, in the opinion of almost everyone else, instead of "waning," the C.I.O. was in its heyday, and only Colonel R. R. McCormick's writers saw any connection between it and the aviation feat.

Because this blatantly colored story was based on an actual news event, it does not qualify as a hoax as defined for the purpose of this study. It is staggering to imagine the size this book would attain if such a restriction were not invoked. For an idea the reader is referred to William Salisbury's *The Career of a Journalist,* Silas Bent's *Ballyhoo,* the chapter on the press in Ferdinand Lundberg's *America's Sixty Families,* and George Seldes' four reminiscent volumes, *You Can't Print That! Can These Things Be! Freedom of the Press* and *Lords of the Press.*

In reply to a question from a Columbia University student preparing a graduate thesis as to whether they concurred in "the theory of American journalism that news is separate from opinion," the editors of the New York *Post* wrote:

DEAR MR. E. K. MERAT: We're surprised at you. We don't know who has been handing you this line. . . . The theory that the news columns of a paper are solely reserved for the facts and the editorial columns held sacred for opinion is one of the hoariest pieces of bunk ever peddled to a class in journalism.

Even with colored and distorted stories ruled out, the complete list of journalistic hoaxes would be interminable. Any newspaperman or former newspaperman can entertain for an evening with anecdotes eligible for inclusion in a complete compilation. More than a hundred newspaper hoaxes already have been mentioned in this book, chiefly in Chapter I; about fifty more are reserved for succeeding chapters. The thirty-odd selected for this chapter are typical of those which had a strong effect upon some newspaper itself instead of or in addition to another institution or the general credulous public.

Every history of American journalistic hoaxing properly begins with the celebrated moon hoax which "made" the New York *Sun* of Benjamin Day and with it the entire penny press of New York. It consisted of a series of articles, allegedly reprinted from the nonexistent Edinburgh *Journal of Science,* relating the discovery of life on the moon by Sir John Herschel, eminent British astronomer, who some time before had gone to the Cape of Good Hope to try out a new type of powerful telescope.

So fascinating were the descriptions of trees and vegetation, oceans and beaches, bison and goats, cranes and pelicans that the whole town was talking even before the fourth installment appeared August 28, 1835, with the master revelation of all: the discovery of furry, winged men resembling bats. Said Herschel, according to his unknown amanuensis:

We counted three parties of these creatures, of twelve, nine and fifteen in each, walking erect towards a small wood . . . Certainly they were like human beings, for their wings had now disappeared and their attitude in walking was both erect and dignified. . . .

About half of the first party had passed beyond our canvas; but of all the others we had a perfectly distinct and deliberate view. They averaged four feet in height, were covered, except on the face, with short and glossy copper-colored hair, and had wings composed of a thin membrane, without hair, lying snugly upon their backs from the top of the shoulders to the calves of the legs.

The face, which was of a yellowish flesh color, was a slight improvement upon that of the large orang-utan . . . so much so that but for their long wings Lieutenant Drummond said they would look as well on a parade ground as some of the old cockney militia. The hair on the head was a darker color than that of the body, closely curled but apparently not woolly, and arranged in two curious semicircles over the temples of the forehead. Their feet could only be seen as they were alternately lifted in walking; but from what we could see of them in so transient a view they appeared thin and very protuberant at the heel. . . .

We could perceive that their wings possessed great expansion and were similar in structure to those of the bat, being a semitransparent membrane expanded in curvilineal divisions by means of straight radii, united at the back by the dorsal integuments. But what astonished us most was the circumstance of this membrane being continued from the shoulders to the legs, united all the way down, though gradually decreasing in width. The wings seemed completely under the command of volition, for those of the creatures whom we saw bathing in the water spread them instantly to their full width, waved them as ducks do theirs to shake off the water, and then as instantly closed them again in a compact form.

When this appeared Day was able to announce that the *Sun* possessed the largest circulation of any newspaper in the world: 19,360. Rival editors were frantic; many of them pretended to have access to the original articles and began reprinting the *Sun*'s series. It was not until the *Journal of Commerce* sought permission to publish the series in pamphlet form, however, that Richard Adams Locke, one of Day's bright young men, confessed authorship. Some authorities think that a French scientist, Nicollet, in this country at the time, wrote them.

Before Locke's confession a committee of scientists from Yale University hastened to New York to inspect the original articles; it was shunted from editorial office to print shop and back again until it tired and returned to New Haven. Edgar Allan Poe explained that he stopped work on the second part of "The Strange Adventures of Hans Pfaall" because he felt he had been outdone. So many writers have perpetuated the legend that Harriet Martineau in her *Retrospect of Western Travel* said a Springfield, Massachusetts, missionary society resolved to send missionaries to the moon to convert the bat men that a complete quotation of what the celebrated traveler really wrote is in place:

I happened to be going the round of several Massachusetts villages when the marvelous account of Sir John Herschel's discoveries in the moon was sent abroad. The sensation it excited was wonderful. . . . A story is going about, told by some friends of Sir John Herschel (but whether in earnest or in the spirit of the moon story I cannot tell) that the astronomer has received at the Cape a letter from a large number of Baptist clergymen of the United States congratulating him on his discovery, informing him that it had been the occasion of much edifying preaching and of prayer meetings for the benefit of brethren in the newly explored regions; and beseeching him to inform his correspondents whether science affords any prospects of a method of conveying the Gospel to residents in the moon. . . .

In the midst of our amusement at credulity like this, we must remember that the real discoveries of science are likely to be more faithfully and more extensively made known in the villages of the United States than in any others in the world. The moon hoax, if advantageously put forth, would have been believed by a much larger proportion of any other nation than it was by the Americans; and they are traveling far faster than any other people beyond the reach of such deception.

After a number of his competitors, humiliated because they had "lifted" the series and passed it off as their own, upbraided Day, the *Sun* of September 16, 1835, admitted the hoax.

The *Sun* also was the vehicle for the second noteworthy American newspaper hoax. On April 13, 1844, it headlined an important story as follows: "Astounding News by Express via Norfolk; the Atlantic Crossed in Three Days; Signal Triumph of Mr. Monck's Flying Machine." This outstanding bit of fiction posing as fact, known as the balloon hoax, was composed by Edgar Allan Poe. Although there was considerable excitement for several days, it easily was ascertained that Monck and eight passengers did not land near Charleston, South Carolina, after seventy-five hours in the air.

The same Richard Adams Locke who was the author of the moon hoax wrote the news story of the autopsy which revealed that Joice Heth, one of P. T. Barnum's most famous exhibits, was not 161 years old and therefore probably not the nurse of the infant George Washington. He had been present at the post mortem, and his article was in the nature of an exposé.

What purported to be an exposé of Locke's exposé appeared in the New York *Herald* the next day, February 27, 1836. The story, inspired if not written by James Gordon Bennett himself, began:

Annexed is a long rigmarole of the dissection of Joice Heth, extracted from yesterday's *Sun* which is nothing more than a complete hoax from beginning to end.

This charge the *Herald* made on "reliable information"; and it substantiated its story by several fictitious certificates that the Negro on whose body the autopsy was performed was an "Aunt Nelly" of Harlem. Joice

Heth herself, according to the article, was still being exhibited in Connecticut.

Bennett was not the author but rather the victim of this hoax. It was Levi Lyman, Barnum's assistant, who supplied the "facts." After he came to realize how he had been duped, Bennett upbraided Lyman upon a casual meeting; whereupon Lyman, ostensibly to make amends, offered to tell Bennett the real story of the discovery and training of Joice Heth.

Beginning with the issue of September 8, 1836, therefore, the *Herald* published a series of six articles entitled, "The Joice Heth Hoax." Lyman's fiction was that Barnum discovered the old Negro on a Kentucky plantation, that he had all her teeth extracted, taught her the Washington story, exhibited her in Louisville as 110 years old, in Cincinnati as 121 years old, in Pittsburgh as 141 years old and finally in Philadelphia as 161 years old. The whole tale, Barnum revealed in his autobiography, was Lyman's invention.

Ranking perhaps second to the moon hoax in the annals of American newspaper hoaxdom is the Wild Animal Hoax which appeared in the New York *Herald* of November 9, 1874. It must have run at least five full newspaper columns, and purported to be an eyewitness account of the escape of all the animals in the Central Park zoo. Forty-nine persons were said to be dead, of whom twenty-seven were identified (the names were given). Two hundred were injured, sixty seriously.

Twelve animals were still at large, and a proclamation by the mayor warned citizens to stay at home. Chester A. Arthur, Samuel J. Tilden and other prominent New Yorkers were mentioned as having taken part in the animal hunt up and down Broadway and Fifth Avenue, into and out of important churches (the story supposedly "broke" on a Sunday), and before leading business establishments.

The hoax was given away in the last paragraph, which had the subheading, "The Moral of the Whole," which revealed that Thomas B. Connery, managing editor, who had ordered the story written, had a serious motive: to direct attention to the zoo's shortcomings. Few readers, of course, reached the last give-away paragraph. James Gordon Bennett, owner of the paper, collapsed in his bed while reading the story, and stayed there all day. A member of the *Herald* staff, Dr. George W. Hosmer, celebrated war correspondent and later Joseph Pulitzer's secretary and doctor, appeared in the office with two big navy revolvers, shouting as he entered, "Well, here I am." Other newspapers were taken in. Major George F. Williams, city editor of the *Times,* frantically drove to police headquarters to berate the officials for giving a rival paper a scoop.

One of the most successful newspaper hoaxes of the period which the contemporary journalists mean when they talk about the "good old days," was that by which the New York *Tribune* stirred editors from Maine to California to retort angrily to the alleged comments of Matthew Arnold, famed English critic, who toured the United States triumphantly in 1883. According to Lucius Beebe in the New York *Herald Tribune* for June 25, 1933, Arnold "left behind him a positively blazing saga of erudite culture, the American people felt that at last it had drunk well and deeply of true Pierian waters, and the stage was set for one of the most fabulously successful newspaper hoaxes ever perpetrated."

It appeared April 6, 1884, in the New York *Tribune* in the form of an article by "Mr. Arnold" in the *Pall Mall Journal.* Under the headline "A Solid Basis of Philistinism—a Varnish of Culture," and a London date line, Dr. Arnold was reported to be disdainful and patronizing about everything in this country. Chicago in particular got a terrible scoring.

According to Beebe, just about every paper in the country rose in editorial wrath against Arnold. The Chicago *Tribune* reprinted the dispatch under its own correspondence credit line as from the *Pall Mall Gazette* and charged that Arnold was seeking retaliation because his Chicago visit had been a financial failure. The Chicago *Inter-Ocean* hailed the message as "the usual disgusting insolence characteristic of people who think it aristocratic to pay politeness with imposition and courtesy with impudence."

The New York *Tribune* kept its secret about a week when it ended the matter with an editorial paragraph as follows:

A good many journals with that sort of enterprise which consists in appropriating what they find in the *Tribune's* columns without acknowledgement, are gravely commenting about Mr. Arnold's paper about Chicago given to the world in our issue of last Sunday. They attribute it to Mr. Matthew Arnold and quote it from the *Pall Mall Gazette.* This is beyond the record. The *Tribune* gave it to them simply as "Mr. Arnold's" paper and from the *Pall Mall Journal,* a publication only issued, so far as we know, on the first of April. Moral: It is better to follow the *Tribune* exactly and also to give credit.

Two dominant figures in the good old days were Mark Twain and Eugene Field, several of whose written and other practical jokes already have been related. Twain's most successful journalistic whopper related an imaginary murder of a wife by her insane husband who dashed into Carson City, Nevada, "with his throat cut from ear to ear and bearing in his hand the reeking scalp from which the warm, smoking blood was dripping." Twain, incidentally, did not originate the saying, "Everybody talks about the weather but nobody does anything about it." The author of that widely quoted sentence was Charles Dudley Warner.

During his Denver period Field's most outstanding joke was to ruin the much advertised lecture by Oscar Wilde by announcing in his paper that the great English writer would arrive a day earlier than previously announced. Then the humorist donned knee breeches and a monocle and simpered and giggled for the crowd which met him at the station and crowded the streets along his itinerary to his hotel. Arriving there, Field changed clothes and hastened to his office to write the story of Wilde's supposed reception. The next day the real Wilde arrived in Denver unnoticed and lectured to only a handful of auditors.

At least one journalistic hoaxer of about this time seemed to have second sight. In 1883 shortly before authentic news came of the explosion of Krakatoa, greatest volcanic eruption of modern times, the assistant telegraph editor of the Boston *Globe* invented an interview with an old South Seas captain which obtained wide circulation on both sides of the Atlantic. Based on encyclopedia accounts of such eruptions in the past, this yarn told of an island's being blown into the sky, of a shower of ashes darkening the sunlight, of blocks of ice in the midst of streams of red-hot lava, of the ocean bubbling with heat and of tons of dead fish floating on the water's surface. So Florence Finch Kelly tells us in *Flowing Stream*. The critics of the young writer, Soames, were dismayed and silenced when it became apparent he miraculously had imagined just about what happened in Sundra Strait.

William Salisbury's *The Career of a Journalist* is a veritable encyclopedia of fakes in which the author participated or of which he had intimate knowledge. Interviews were faked, aldermen were induced to introduce ordinances in exchange for favorable publicity, shirts of the friends of publishers and publishers' wives were stuffed, directors of corporations in competition with those in which owners were interested were given bad mention or none at all, every detail of a nonexistent hoboes' convention was dramatized, warning was given of a nation-wide Carrie Nation brigade of which none but the writer had knowledge; prominent persons were given the opportunity to deny outlandish rumors without any circulation outside of the news room, and doubt was created in readers' minds when their denials were printed.

The leeway allowed reporters in the halcyon days just before the turn of the century also was demonstrated by an incident reported by Charles Chapin in his *Charles Chapin's Story*. Refused passes to Hooley's Theater in Chicago, Frank Wilkie, reporter for the old *Times*, wrote five or six columns about a fictitious panic at the show place. Included was a list of dead and injured among whom were numerous prominent citizens. The final paragraph was: "This is what may happen."

Lest it be believed incorrectly that the journalistic hoax was an invention of the nineteenth century, it should be recalled that no American editor ever dumfounded readers more than the versatile Benjamin Franklin, with whose name are associated more "firsts" than are ascribed to any other denizen of the New World, perhaps of the Old as well.

Franklin's *Poor Richard's Almanac* was the precursor of the "Believe It or Not" type of journalism in which posers are put one day and answered the next. The difference, however, was that whereas modern readers have to wait only one day, or may even turn to another page of the same issue for the answers, Poor Richard's public had to be patient for an entire year.

Examples of Franklin's wit are his "Enigmatical Prophecies" for 1736 that many of America's greatest cities soon would be under water, that a power with which the country was not at war would take great numbers of vessels fully laden out of our seaports, and that an army of musketeers would land in this country to annoy the inhabitants.

The answers included in the 1737 almanac revealed that the water was that of the sea and rivers, raised in vapor by the sun to descend as rain; the power with which we were not at war was the wind; the army of musketeers was composed of mosquitoes, armed only with a sharp sting. "Everyone knows they are fish before they fly, being bred in the water; and therefore may properly be said to land before they become generally troublesome," he concluded.

On the other side of the Atlantic, also, harmless faking got an early start. Once during the first decades of the nineteenth century, just before edition time in the office of the Leicester, England, *Herald*, a tray of type upset. Instead of delaying the presses Sir Richard Phillips, the editor, is reported to have gathered up the pied type, assembled it as best he could, and printed it. Attached was a notice that the Dutch mail had arrived too late to be translated and therefore was being printed as received. A story, probably apocryphal, is told that thirty years later Phillips met a Nottingham reader who said he had preserved a copy of the paper hoping some day to have the Dutch letter explained.

In Volume II of his autobiography, John Francis, publisher of the *Athenæum,* says of the London *Gazette*:

The most famous incident connected with the paper during the last century was the forgery of one number issued in May, 1787. No police acuteness was acute enough to lay hand on the inimitable rogue who played that perilous joke.

This laconic notice is all that the writer could find regarding this incident.

The story of a similar forgery, this time in France, was related by John Augustus O'Shea in his *Leaves from the Life of a Special Correspondent.* Paris was at first aghast and then laughed at news of the appointment of known bitter enemies of the government to cabinet positions which appeared in an apparently regular edition of *Moniteur,* the official governmental paper.

Editors of foreign newspapers were having the story translated when the issue was revealed as a concoction by *Figaro,* anti-imperialist publication edited by De Villemessant. The style and typography of the genuine *Moniteur* had been imitated exactly. O'Shea comments:

The strangest feature in this freak of the inventive M. de Villemessant was that his grotesque perversion was a foretokening of what did come to pass not long after. Paris laughed at his mock cabinet, but Paris laughed at the wrong side of its mouth when the commune uprose with its debauched prefect of police and its swaggering general from the cabarets and would gladly have welcomed the imagined ministry it once derided.

To the credit of Charles Langdon Clarke, who fooled a fundamentalist into accepting a fabricated account of the finding of the fossil of a whale which could have swallowed Jonah (as related in Chapter VII) and convinced an inveterate enemy of the clan Maclean that a nonexistent Stranways had written a book to prove the Macleans deserted Bonnie Prince Charlie (as related in Chapter III) are several other amusing and successful fakes according to Hector Charlesworth in *More Candid Chronicles.*

When the tomb of the Egyptian King Tutankhamen was opened,

Clarke wrote a serious article "King Tut's Golden Typewriter" for the Toronto *Mail and Empire,* in which he described the discovery of such an article among the other treasures. After a rival editor assigned a reporter to interview Dr. C. T. Currelly, curator of the Royal Ontario Museum and a renowned Egyptologist, Clarke revealed the hoax.

One of Clarke's escapades which Charlesworth understandably did not mention was his attempt to demonstrate that the prize version of the words for "O Canada" was a plagiarism of a poem by Alexander Hume of the sixteenth century, of Dr. Sprat, Bishop of Rochester during the reigns of James II and William III, and of John Langhorne who wrote "Owen of Carron." Charlesworth himself was the judge who was ready to cancel the award when Clarke confessed.

Another Canadian hoaxer of whom Charlesworth also wrote in his *Candid Chronicles* was Louis P. Kribs of the Toronto *News.* His most successful venture was a faked interview with Sir John A. Macdonald announcing his retirement from public life. Readers were struck with consternation at Macdonald's remarks until they were shown to be taken verbatim from Washington's Farewell Address.

While running a country newspaper at Barrie, Canada, Kribs caused half the population to walk over to view the results of a train accident at Allandale in which one T. H. O. Mascat had been killed. The victim turned out to be an ordinary cat.

A wrong guess proved fatal to the reputation of a third Toronto newspaperman, Charles T. Long, whom New York newspapers thereafter referred to as "the Toronto Liar."

Long's story, which almost every other newspaper in Canada and the United States except his own, the Toronto *Empire,* printed, pertained to the mystery created by the disappearance of a Dr. Cronin of Chicago. Long, while engaged in newspaper work in Chicago, had been acquainted with Dr. Cronin and knew of his sympathies with the Irish movement. He therefore announced that the missing man had been seen in Toronto on his way to London to testify at the Parnell inquiry (see Chapter XIII).

Chicago detectives traveled to Toronto to investigate. The next day came the announcement of the discovery of the murdered doctor's body in Chicago.

Although it helped circulate World War I atrocity stories most of them did not originate in the press: poisoned French wells, Belgian children with severed hands, raped Rumanian women, crucified Canadian soldiers and the like. For the most colossal journalistic blunder of all, furthermore, the United Press Associations have been exonerated completely. That was the false report that the Armistice had been signed November 7, 1918.

The official explanation is that someone, now commonly believed to have been a German secret agent, telephoned both the French and the American intelligence offices that the armistice was signed. According to Colonel Edward House, President Wilson's personal representative in Paris, in a communication November 8, 1918, to Secretary of State Robert Lansing, everyone eagerly believed the report. A naval attaché in the American embassy, a Captain Jackson, sent a telegram to Admiral Henry B. Wilson, commanding officer of the American naval force who was stationed at Brest, to announce the happy news.

Admiral Wilson, naturally having no reason to doubt the report, showed his wire to none other than Roy W. Howard, president of the United Press, who was about to embark for home. Believing he had the scoop of the century, Howard acted as any other newspaperman would have done in similar circumstances: accompanied by a naval aide dispatched by Admiral Wilson, he went to the censor's office and filed a cablegram to the United States. Then he began to "follow up" his sensational story and learned that it was premature. Within an hour he sent another cable ordering the first one killed; however, the cables were jammed, and his second message was delayed twenty-four hours in transmission.

When newspapers from coast to coast subscribing to the United Press service appeared with the false report beneath gigantic headlines, the public response was what might have been expected. Factory whistles blew, church bells rang, parades were organized, public leaders addressed jubilant crowds, and bonfires were lighted. It was a wild nation-wide demonstration which proved what the German hoaxer (if there was one) desired: that the people of the victorious Allied nations preferred immediate peace to revenge inflicted by a ravaging army from the Rhine to Berlin.

The war over, the leading topic of discussion for a decade and a half became prohibition, and the most sensational newspaper hoax of the period capitalized upon public interest in the subject. That was a story concocted, not by a publisher or editor to increase sales but by a youthful reporter to keep his job. It "broke" in the August 16, 1924, issue of the sedate New York *Herald Tribune* under a four-column headline: "New Yorkers Drink Sumptuously on 17,000-Ton Floating Café at Anchor 15 Miles Off Fire Island."

Illustrated by a three-column map to indicate the ship's location, the story was a sensation. It was written in the first person by the cub, Sanford Jarrell, as an eyewitness account of "millionaires, flappers and unemployed chorus girls" enjoying themselves at an old-fashioned American bar, dancing to a Negro jazz band and drinking toasts to a crude reproduction of the Statue of Liberty on the poop deck. Although the liner flew the Union Jack, it had no name on its hull; a possible clue to its identity, however, was silverware and napery marked "Friedrich der Grosse."

Although scooped, other newspapers could not ignore the story. Fuming editors sent reporters in cutters up and down the coast, and Washington ordered the Coast Guard to join the search. Conjectures regarding the Rum Row phantom's identity were legion. Somebody recalled the rumor that such a boat had served as headquarters for the entire Atlantic rum fleet; others said it probably was the *Von Steuben,* formerly the *Kronprinz Wilhelm,* a German raider during the war, sold by the United States Shipping Board and recently resold for scrapping. A third guess was that the entire story was a press-agent stunt to advertise a motion picture.

As the plot thickened, Jarrell was hard put to it by his superiors to produce more evidence than his own hang-over story. He left the news room promising to return with irrefragable proof. Instead, he sent back a confession by messenger. Abashed, the *Herald Tribune* published an apology addressed to all other New York newspapers and the public.

The hoax was not entirely without profit. By the most exceptional chance Universal Pictures Corporation was just about to release a film, "Wine," centered around just such a cabaret as Jarrell had described. It is possible the young hoaxer received his inspiration from advance notices of it, but it seems certain that the motion picture company had nothing to do with his story. It capitalized, however, upon the unexpected publicity by means of an advertisement in the form of a letter to the public signed by the "captain of the 12-mile-limit café." Readers were advised to "go to the manager of your favorite picture theater and whisper, 'Show me Wine.' He will do the rest."

In an article "Three-Cents-a-Day Dreams," in the December 15, 1938, issue of *Ken,* John F. DeVine told of two newspaper hoaxes of the early twenties which, he said, had not previously been exposed. One was the story, given wide publicity during the marathon dance craze of 1923, that a Homer Morehouse of North Tonawanda, New York, dropped dead after dancing eighty-seven hours. Mark Sullivan seriously retold the anecdote in the second volume of *Our Times*. The other yarn, which fooled Walter Lippmann, then chief editorial writer for the New York *World*, was the concoction of a Newark (N. J.) *Star-Eagle* reporter regarding a mechanical bull operated by a control board with which picadors and matadors battled while Spanish-American citizens of Newark applauded and jeered as their skill merited. Lippmann compared the mechanical bull to President Coolidge's electric horse, and the Associated Press sent the story to newspapers all over the country.

Another sensational story given wide circulation by press associations in January, 1927, was unique in providing the only known example of a number of newspapers' being hoaxed into thinking they had been hoaxed by a competitor. It began with an account in the Chicago *Journal* of a predatory chicken hawk which had been preying upon the pigeons which swarm about the Art Institute and downtown elevated platforms. It ended a week later with advertisements for an imminent *Journal* serialized story, "The Pigeon and the Hawk."

Nobody but the author of the original *Journal* article apparently ever saw the hawk. Nevertheless, the search for it was front-page news in every Chicago newspaper for a week. In the Chicago *Tribune* alone the hawk hunt was the inspiration of two front-page political cartoons by John McCutcheon, for front-page stories for five consecutive days, for at least one serious editorial, for an avalanche of contributions to the "Voice of the People" column, for a question by the Inquiring Reporter and for a picture of a hawk holding a dead pigeon in its claws. Superficial examination of the picture, presumably taken at night and showing the bird on top of the Art Institute, is sufficient to bring out that it was faked. So probably were similar pictures in other papers.

Thoroughly aroused, the Lincoln Park Gun Club appointed a committee to kill the hawk; Walter J. Greenebaum, an investment banker, offered a fifty-dollar reward for the public enemy, dead or alive; Boy Scouts organized to conduct a search, and many volunteers appeared with a wide assortment of weapons to take part. As it began to appear that the nocturnal visitor had no reality outside of the news, the skeptical came to consider the entire business a frame-up. This Richard J. Finnegan, at the time editor of the *Journal*, denies. He says that the reporter who wrote the original article at least believed he saw a hawk. Mr. Finnegan's account of how he capitalized upon the public interest it created is a better story than if a hoax had been planned from the story.

Mr. Finnegan's inspiration was to rush into print with a serial, "The Pigeon and the Hawk." Finding himself completely out of fiction, he tried to persuade one member of his staff after another to write it. Failing, he undertook the job himself. "It was trash," he said later; but, once started, it had to be continued. "I found myself just one installment ahead of the composing room and never knew what the next episode was to be. Something had to be written, so I wrote it," he reminisces. The appearance of the first announcement of the series was the signal for all other papers to drop the story in the belief they had been hoaxed into giving advance publicity to a competitor's feature.

Halfway through Mr. Finnegan spent a very profitable social evening, others in the company being Oliver Barrett, member of the law firm representing the Samuel Insull interests, and Henry Horner, then a judge and later Democratic governor of Illinois. Barrett was an autograph collector and an authority on Abraham Lincoln and Andrew Jackson. Despite his scholarship he was an avid reader of "The Pigeon and the Hawk" and tried to persuade the editor to tell him how it would come out. Mr. Finnegan could not do so because he didn't know himself.

After Barrett retired Judge Horner expressed amazement at the interest shown by such an erudite person in such cheap reading. To the judge Finnegan then told his secret, and the difficulty he was having keeping the story alive. Together they went to work on the installments to come, introducing mutual acquaintances under assumed names. Chief of these was Barrett, who was given the name of Oliver Bartlett, which many of his friends came to call him. Plot incidents were veiled but not so as to be unrecognizable by those acquainted with them.

After 1927, Finnegan, who later became editor of the tabloid *Sun-Times* never was without an assortment of serial fiction upon which to draw in an emergency.

How a newspaper hoax brought an end to the prohibition era in 1933, four hours earlier than had been expected, and spoiled the plans of a number of Utah politicians to enjoy a few minutes of nation-wide fame was revealed by Don Howard, news editor of the Salt Lake City *Telegram*.

Thirty-five states already had voted for repeal of the Eighteenth Amendment, and Utah was to be the thirty-sixth. Delegates to the repeal convention were assembled but had postponed voting to permit a nation-wide radio hook-up "with a lot of long-winded speeches they imagined would be good publicity for the state," according to Howard.

"It was a case of my paper going to press without the repeal story unless something was done," Howard explained. What he did was to fake a news story that delegates to the Maine repeal convention had decided to move the clock ahead to enable them to beat Utah to the thirty-sixth place. The effect upon the Utah delegates, to whom Howard read this fictitious report, was as he had hoped. Plans for the evening session, broadcast and all, were abandoned; arrangements hurriedly were made for the best radio hook-up possible on short notice; speeches were cut and edited, and the prohibition era came to an end four hours ahead of schedule. The *Telegram* had the story in time.

Also in 1933 were demonstrated the serious consequences which may result from a well intentioned journalistic deception. James ("Gentleman Jim") Corbett, one-time heavyweight boxing champion of the world, was dying from cancer. His doctors had told him he had heart disease and, because Corbett was an avid newspaper reader until the last, prevailed on the press to falsify the nature of his illness until after his death.

The result, according to the late Marlen Pew, editor of *Editor and Publisher,* was indicated by a letter he received from a prominent physician which he epitomized as follows:

Following the publication of the story showing how Corbett was given false hope of recovery, the physician writes, he was called by a patient who had read the article and who had grave fears she was suffering from cancer of the liver and was also being deceived. Another patient with heart trouble sought assurance that she did not have a cancer. A third patient, suffering from intestinal and liver condition, was found in a state of "anguish" through fear that she was being misinformed as Corbett had been.

When they write their reminiscences American foreign correspondents usually cast new light on many stories which previously thrilled readers of international news. Several reporters who covered the Italian invasion of Ethiopia, for instance, have told how both news and pictures were faked by newspapermen who wearied of being kept hundreds of miles from the front. In *Covering the Far East,* Miles Vaughn exploded the Japanese human bomb story, which had three Japanese soldiers committing suicide so that an important sector of the enemy line might be blown up with them. Vaughn said that actually the three were killed accidentally while attempting to bomb the Chinese.

Webb Miller in *I Found No Peace* revealed that the story from the French Riviera of a British millionaire who embarrassed his guests by inducing them to swim in bathing suits which dissolved in salt water was a pure fake. The reporter inventing it was ordered by his managing editor to ship several of the suits to the United States; he complied with an hermetically sealed box containing some finely pulverized breakfast food to create the impression that, despite precautions, the suits had dissolved in the salt air.

In the April, 1940, *Goldfish Bowl,* publication of the National Press Club of Washington, D. C., the famous Lacon, Illinois, cat-and-rat ranch of about 1875 was revealed to have been a hoax instigated by Willis B. Powell, Lacon editor, who supplied the Associated Press with details which were printed by newspapers in all parts of the country. The spurious prospectus on which the news accounts were based read as follows:

Glorious Opportunity to Get Rich—We are starting a cat ranch in Lacon with 100,000 cats. Each cat will average 12 kittens a year. The cat skins will sell for 30 cents each. One hundred men can skin 5,000 cats a day. We figure a daily net profit of over $10,000. Now what shall we feed the cats? We will start a rat ranch next door with 1,000,000 rats. The rats will breed 12 times faster than the cats. So we will have four rats to feed each day to each cat. Now what shall we feed the rats? We will feed the rats the carcasses of the cats after they have been skinned. Now Get This! We feed the rats to the cats and the cats to the rats and get the cat skins for nothing.

Another journalistic "classic" was debunked by Arthur Robb in his "Shop Talk at Thirty" column in the February 19, 1938, *Editor and Publisher.* It was the "See God" news story which Dick Beamish, then a reporter of the Philadelphia *North American,* and later Richard J. Beamish, public utility commissioner of Pennsylvania, wrote of the Harwick coalmine disaster near Pittsburgh in 1904. Tradition has it that Beamish wrote as his lead: "God sits on the mountains of Harwick tonight while below in the valley Death and Sorrow lurk." The night editor supposedly tore his hair and wired his reporter: "See God. Get Interview. Rush Picture."

A characteristic of the mine run of newspaper hoaxes is their good humor. Many of them may originate or perpetuate unscientific attitudes, but, because they are intended to build circulation, most of them are on the funny and generally harmless side. Notable exceptions are the myths and legends on which the Hearst newspapers thrived for forty years.

Many of William Randolph Hearst's multitudinous hoaxes were hate producers. Through distortions and outright lies he fomented trouble between this nation and several others and augmented internal political bitterness. Books have been written about his versatile career as a whole and about segments of it. No period has received greater attention than that of the Spanish American War; some writers have gone so far as to declare that it was the atrocity stories in Hearst's New York *Journal* which were responsible for Congress' decision to intervene in Cuba.

No denial has ever been made of the authenticity of the telegrams between Hearst and Frederic Remington, artist whom he sent to Cuba in 1896 to sketch Spanish atrocities. Remington cabled: "Everything is quiet. There is no trouble here. There will be no war. I wish to return." Hearst replied: "Please remain. You furnish the pictures; I'll furnish the war."

Among the most revolting of the drawings which Remington thereafter sent back was one showing a young Cuban girl stripped naked so that three Spaniards could search her clothes. The New York *World*, which for a time tried to outdo the *Journal* in the manufacture of atrocities, scotched that one by producing the young woman in question. She was humiliated by both the story and the illustration, declaring that the search was conducted in private by matrons.

Leading Hearst heroine of the period was Evangeline Cisneros, a Cuban girl imprisoned for conspiring against the Spanish government. Hearst petitioned the Queen of Spain and the Pope and then sent reporters to effect her release. It is strongly suspected they bribed prison officials, but they staged a prison break to produce a sensational story. Afterwards Señorita Cisneros triumphantly toured the United States, stirring up anti-Spanish sentiment wherever she appeared.

When the *Journal* obtained a purloined personal letter from Depuy de Lome (Spanish minister to Washington) to a friend, in which he referred to President William McKinley as "a low politician catering to the rabble," it went into a frenzy over the insult. Later, however, it sarcastically apologized to the minister because, it said, he had told the simple truth. When President William McKinley was shot fatally at Buffalo, his assassin, Leon Czolgosz, was found to have in his possession inflammatory Hearst editorials against the president.

The Spanish governor of Cuba was "Butcher Weyler" to the Hearst press, and it used the mysterious sinking of the *Maine* as a deliberate provocation to war. In *Imperial Hearst,* Ferdinand Lundberg allows his well founded hatred for William Randolph Hearst to overwhelm him to the extent of insinuating Hearst himself had a hand in the destruction of the *Maine.*

As related in Chapter XIII, Hearst's persistent campaign to bring about American intervention in Mexico culminated in 1927 with the publication of spurious documents purporting to show that American senators and other leaders had been bribed with Mexican money. That was merely the worst of many steps whereby Hearst attempted to stir up anti-Mexican hatred. Lundberg tells of a picture which the New York *American* published December 22, 1913, allegedly of a number of Mexican children with hands upraised, being driven into the water before being shot. The English traveler who took the picture indignantly explained that the children had been bathing peacefully and had raised their arms at his request to make a better picture. Furthermore, the scene was British Honduras, not Mexico.

An object of even greater Hearst venom became the Soviet Union which Hearst had constantly on the verge of counterrevolution and incessantly plotting for the overthrow of the United States and the rest of the capitalistic world, in pre-World War II days. A favorite stunt was to reprint as of recent origin pictures of the actual Volga famine of 1921, or of similar suffering in some other country. Most vicious series of this sort appeared in 1935 signed by Thomas Walker. Not only did a reputable Hearst foreign correspondent, Lindsay Parrott, innocently contradict it by a self-inspired series of articles on the richness of the Russian harvest that year, which Hearst's editors were careless enough to publish simultaneously with the hoax articles and pictures; more important, Walker was arrested when he arrived in England, and revealed to be Robert Green, an American forger who had broken out of the Colorado state prison in 1921.

Another Hearst Russian famine series was signed by Fred Beals, a former labor leader who led the Gastonia textile strike in 1929. Indicted for murder, Beals jumped bail and escaped to Russia. He was employed there but was discharged. One document, of which the Hearst papers printed a facsimile, revealed a Russian legend to indicate the cause of discharge was "loafing." Mr. Hearst's stooges, however, translated the legend "left on vacation."

In 1928 Hearst was ousted from France for having directed an employee to steal a copy of a secret treaty between France and Britain. He returned to the United States and upbraided the Department of State for not making a vigorous protest. In 1932 the New York *Mirror* ran a picture allegedly of hunger marchers storming Buckingham Palace in London. It was revealed that the scene actually was of a 1929 crowd gathered anxiously during the illness of King George V.

At home Hearst became a political imponderable. He resembled the old woman in the familiar joke who didn't know which side she was on but was certain that when she decided she would be "awfully bitter." In his early days Hearst gained a reputation as a champion of labor; after the depression he became the most bitter opponent of New Deal and any other attempts to pass protective labor legislation. In 1935 Hearst personally looked over Governor Alfred M. Landon of Kansas and thereafter took the credit for having "discovered" the Republican candidate for president. The 1936 campaign, as far as the Hearst papers were concerned, however, was an anti-Roosevelt rather than a pro-Landon one. The November landslide over, Hearst hastened to get on the band wagon by giving the president's third son a position with one of his radio stations and by naming the president's son-in-law publisher of his strike-ridden Seattle *Post-Intelligencer*.

The Hearst press backed Chicago's clownish mayor, William Hale Thompson, in his campaign to keep King George out of Chicago; it gave the Rev. Charles E. Coughlin his fascistic ammunition and became a persistent red baiter for many years. About 1935 the heaviest Hearst guns were turned on the schools. Reporters wrote letters to leading liberal educators declaring that they were interested in getting "the real stuff about capitalism, socialism and communism." Personal interviews followed, and then articles about the leftist leanings of many prominent scholars. At Teachers College of Columbia University, however, Professors William H. Kilpatrick and George S. Counts proved more than a match for the Hearstling, who considered his assignment an extremely distasteful one. They got him to admit he would not be allowed to quote them fairly and that anything they said which might be interpreted to substantiate the fact the Red Menace actually existed would be played up, because "Hearst wants material along this line." Aided and abetted by the Hearst press, Charles R. Walgreen withdrew his niece from the University of Chicago, which he accused of communistic leanings. The resulting investigation by the state legislature was a farce, and a year later Mr. Walgreen atoned somewhat by making a substantial grant to the university to promote the teaching of Americanism.

In 1936 the liberal New York *Post* exposed a series of articles in the

Mirror, allegedly based on a reporter's interview with a confessed murderer, John Fiorenza, as being faked. If authentic they would have blackened the reputation of the woman whom the weak-minded Fiorenza had raped and strangled. In 1937 Max Lerner, then an editor of the *Nation,* told a Washington, D. C., audience President Roosevelt's plan to reorganize the Supreme Court did not go far enough; the Hearst Washington *Herald* headlined its account of his speech: "Editor Hits Court Plan." During the Spanish War the Hearst newspapers published pictures of alleged Loyalist atrocities which were proved to be scenes of acts committed by the rebels.

In 1954 the Honolulu *Star-Bulletin* abandoned its annual practice of using a fake story, usually scientific, on April Fools' Day (see illustration opposite page 9) because of the adverse reaction to a radio hoax to the effect that Congress had passed the Hawaii Statehood bill with an amendment to enable islanders to get income tax refunds. Many other American and European newspapers and magazines, however, continue the April 1st hoax tradition. Likewise, the Harvard *Lampoon* continues its tradition of putting out occasional fake editions of the Harvard *Crimson.* In 1946 such an edition announced the imminent demise of varsity football. In 1951 the *Crimson* itself was taken seriously by the commercial press when it printed a letter from "Radcliffe Mother" suggesting that Harvard men should be drafted as a protection to New England girlhood.

Everybody got a good laugh out of the success of a group of practical jokers in a Wall Street brokerage firm who invented a fictitious college football team, the Flying Figments of Plainfield Teachers College, and succeeded in getting accounts of its winning games into most New York newspapers each week. A fictitious press agent, using an impressive letterhead, sent out stories of the prowess of the team's star halfback. He was half Chinese, Johnny Chung, and kept up his strength by eating wild rice during intermissions. He was credited with scoring 63 of Plainfield's 117 points in seven games, all of which it won against mythical opponents. A friend of the pranksters finally exposed them to the press, raising hopes that truth always will be revealed in the end.

CHAPTER XVIII

Public Relations Hoaxing

THE late John D. Rockefeller promiscuously hands out shiny new dimes! A circus midget sits on the lap of J. P. Morgan! A leading home-run slugger visits a boy fan in a hospital and autographs a baseball for him! Two Hollywood idols elope to Yuma, Arizona! Charlie McCarthy is kidnaped!

Were these publicity stunts hoaxes? If so, why not every reluctant appearance of a celebrity at a place where it is beneficial to be seen? every speech delivered by a statesman or tycoon but composed by a ghost writer? every philanthropy by a millionaire whose reputation needs a boost? every photograph of an attractive air-line hostess? In fact, what about almost every news-worthy action of anyone?

Because shirt stuffing has become a recognized legitimate and lucrative business, it is impossible any more to include in the same category as the crude publicity stunts of the immediate past the comings and goings of the great and would-be great dictated by public relations counsel. Only amateurs or psychopaths today sit on flagpoles, kiss babies, give away cigars or swallow goldfish. Professionals know that newspaper space-grabbing has been developed into a science, and that to keep in the public eye requires the year-round advice of a trained adviser.

The trick today is not to try to crash the front-page with a stunt but to become and to remain news by a continuous and consistent program of action which editors cannot ignore, or at least with regularity to be where legitimate news is occurring. If this is hoaxing the public, it is because the public fails to understand that those in the journalistic limelight sedulously seek its glare rather than wait for it to shine upon them.

A contemporary publicity hoax can be considered to occur only when an editor or his readers or, as often happens, both fail to recognize the publicity seeking back of any unusual occurrence. For instance, a few years ago at Excelsior Springs, Missouri, a supposedly lovesick swain,

Harold Hulen, chained himself to a radiator outside the apartment of the object of his affections, Miss Florence Hurlbut, and said his sit-down strike would continue until she consented to marry him. While he dozed she escaped and traveled, via transport plane, to New York, where she almost landed a well-paying job until it leaked out that Harold was in cahoots with her from the start to help her crash Broadway.

This was a story which could and probably would have been ignored, despite its human interest, had the truth been revealed early enough. In other cases, however, the editor who hates to be taken in is helpless. For example, what could he do when even the president of the United States traveled to Dearborn, Michigan, to take part in what was ballyhooed as Light's Golden Jubilee to commemorate the fiftieth anniversary of the invention of the incandescent lamp by Thomas A. Edison? The jubilee was a publicity stunt thought up by Edward L. Bernays, nephew of Sigmund Freud and dean of American public relations counsel, at the time representing the electric light industry. Regardless of the motive, the jubilee was held, Mr. Edison was honored, President Herbert Hoover and a large number of other notables attended. The newspapers couldn't ignore the story; the publicity stunt worked, and it hardly can be called a hoax.

For the purest examples of out-and-out publicity fakes by big-time operators, it is wise to go back to the days of P. T. Barnum, patent medicine shows, carnivals and circuses. Let the time, for instance, be 1876; the place, Philadelphia; and the occasion, the centennial celebration of the signing of the Declaration of Independence. The cynosure is the main exhibition building, where an unprecedented collection of the world's foremost treasures is to be seen—priceless jewels, the finest specimens of the art of gold and silver smiths, wonderful enamels, engraved gems and the world's largest sapphire.

Imagine the horror with which you pick up a Sunday morning newspaper and read that part of this display, several million dollars' worth, has disappeared overnight. The police give the encouraging assurance that the identity of the thieves is known, as well as the method used to enter the building: a tunnel under Elm Avenue leading from the hall to a temporary hotel. Even though you read the story through the last paragraph, which contains a tip that its writer might be misinformed, is not your interest in the precious relics stimulated? If not, you are unusual, for thousands of extra visitors flocked to the fair grounds during the days immediately following publication of just such a story.

At the Cotton States Centennial in New Orleans eight years later, there were no dazzling stones but a much more precious show piece: the Liberty Bell itself, brought from Philadelphia under careful guard. The slogan of the exposition was "No North; no South; but an Undivided Country," and it was upon the patriotic feelings it engendered that the publicity hoaxers capitalized with their story of a masked mob which overpowered and drugged the custodians of the leading exhibit, after which they laboriously loaded it onto a truck and carried it to a near-by levee. From then on the story, fabricated in its entirety, is told beautifully by the late Willis J. Abbot in *Watching the World Go By,* as follows:

The soft ground was said to show the ruts of the truck on which the heavy burden had been carried, and so many footprints as to indicate that a large mob had been concerned in the outrage. There were no interviews with the police who guarded the bell—it was hinted that their physical condition made it impossible. With true journalistic skill the story was brief, lacking in detail and sounding as though it had been telephoned in from the distant fair grounds just in time to catch the last edition.

When I went out to the Exposition that morning, it seemed that all New Orleans was in a state of wild excitement. A former managing editor of the New York *World* was on the street car with me and was violent in his denunciation of the unreconstructed and unrepentant Southerners. "Don't tell me they are loyal," he cried. "They hate the North as much today as they did before Appomattox. Any good, loyal American would reverence the Liberty Bell, but these infernal traitors have thrown it into the Mississippi. If I were President, I'd order a warship here today, anchor it off the spot where the bell sunk, and compel them to dredge for it and raise it."

The crude publicity fakes of the nineteenth century are typified by one mentioned by Henry Watterson, eminent editor-publisher of the Louisville *Courier-Journal* in his autobiographical *Marse Henry:*

With the opening of every Monte Carlo season the newspapers used to tell of the colossal winnings of purely imaginary players. Sometimes the favored child was a Russian, sometimes an Englishman, sometimes an American. He was usually a myth, of course.

Just as anachronistic parallels of such space-grabbing persist today, so shortly before World War I the press agent for Mme. Modjeska, the Polish actress, was ahead of his times when he engineered a riot in the lobby of a Washington, D.C., theater, presumably by drama lovers unable to obtain tickets. The press associations gave the account nation-wide publicity.

P. T. Barnum never has been equaled as an inventor of fakes, but his publicity methods, though effective, were crude. A typical stunt was to have a sartorially correct gentleman arrange and rearrange a series of bricks, one to a block, until he reached the entrance to Barnum's Museum, whereupon he collected them all, purchased a ticket and disappeared inside. The crowd, intent upon his mysterious eccentricity, followed in the hope of satisfying its curiosity.

Even without physical lures, countless other crowds have "gone inside" as a result of publicity stunts which are a tradition with the entertainment business. Unequaled in the art of packing them in, the man who is given credit for having hastened the success of the motion picture industry, was the late Harry Reichenbach whose autobiography, *Phantom Fame,* was completed after his death by his collaborator, David Freedman. In spite of the fabulous character of some of the tales included, the truthfulness of the book has been affirmed by many persons mentioned therein or otherwise in positions to know.

When Reichenbach took hold, the motion picture industry was floundering along as a five-cent attraction. How he helped elevate it is illustrated by the way in which he made Americans Tarzan-conscious. To direct attention to the first Tarzan picture, Reichenbach caparisoned a live ape in evening clothes and turned him loose in a leading New York hotel. When the sequel, *The Return of Tarzan,* was about to be released, he became even more daring. A mousy pianist registered for a room on a lower floor of a Manhattan hotel and had his own piano drawn up through a window from the outside while quidnuncs watched. With his eccentric appearance and actions already under discussion, the guest became the object of special investigation by the management when he ordered a breakfast of fifteen pounds of raw meat. The result was the discovery that the piano box contained, not a musical instrument but a full-grown lion at liberty in the long-haired one's room.

Reporters found that the unusual pet's owner was registered as T. R. Zan. He explained that, because of his devotion to the Tarzan tales, he had changed his name to that from a more common one. His choice of animal companions also showed the Tarzan influence.

To advertise *Trilby,* Reichenbach had a personable young woman feign a trance at the end of a performance. Because, a few minutes before, she had run around the theater a number of times, her respiration and pulse baffled physicians. For days the press ran accounts of interviews with psychologists on the possibility of a person's being hypnotized by a motion picture, and thrill seekers packed the theater to see if they could be.

When *The Virgin of Stamboul* was in the offing, Reichenbach collected a group of Turkish cooks, arrayed them in native costume and took them to Schenectady, where it leaked out they had been sent to the United States by their wealthy master to search for an American marine who had eloped with his comely daughter. The story they told before a prying reporter discovered a costumer's label on their outfits, paralleled the plot of the picture which was released shortly afterwards.

Outside of motion pictures Reichenbach's record also was impressive. Once he won a bet by elevating an obscure singer to fame within seven days. By directing the attention of Post Office Department officials to a row of asterisks following a love scene in Elinor Glyn's *Three Weeks,* he got that book much needed advertising through its being banned from the mails. When the ban was lifted, the third-rate novel became a best seller.

Harry Reichenbach's masterpiece was one for which he never received just due, either in pay or in reputation. That was his engineering of the investigation by none other than Anthony Comstock of an obscure, not very artistic and, according to present standards, thoroughly innocuous nude painting which became the talk of the world. The painting was the celebrated "September Morn" by the minor French artist Paul Chabas, which Reichenbach found on display in the window of a second-rate art shop in Brooklyn. For forty-five dollars Harry incurred the wrath of the great reformer by bribing a small gallery of urchins to gather before the window and point, grimace and remark. Summoned by an anonymous telephone call, the austere Comstock took one look and marched off to police headquarters.

Chabas and the art dealer were, of course, acquitted and "September Morn" became the rage. Copies appeared in homes in the most out-of-the-way places. There were "September Morn" dolls, statues, calendars and umbrella and cane heads; sailors had the modest, shivering damsel tattooed on their hairy chests and amateur artists drew their versions on barroom floors. In all, more than seven million copies were sold.

Shortly before he died in 1937, at the age of sixty-eight years, Chabas spiked the legend that the model of his masterpiece then was starving in a Parisian garret. He refused to reveal her identity but said that at forty-one she was married happily to a wealthy French industrialist and had three lovely children. This, an anonymous writer for the Hearst press shortly denied in an article syndicated by King Features to the effect that he had found the matured model in a Parisian café acting as a hostess. She was a childless divorcée, he wrote, named Suzanne Delve. It probably would be safer to believe Chabas.

September 1, 1957, forty-five years after it was painted, the most controversial nude of modern times went on public exhibition in the Metropolitan Museum of Art, to which it was donated by William Coxe Wright of Philadelphia.

On the other side of the Atlantic the most ambitious attempt to "pull a Reichenbach" failed because the British government understandably became too interested for its promoter's good. To stimulate interest in a forthcoming cinema based on the life of Lord Kitchener, who was lost mysteriously at sea in May, 1916, Frank Power (real name, Arthur Vectis Freeman) announced that the great Briton's body had been found in Norway.

The stunt of bringing back a coffin supposedly containing Kitchener's body was a sure-fire one inasmuch as all sorts of rumors had circulated for years regarding the *Hampshire,* on which he was bound for Russia on a secret mission when the vessel struck a mine and sank. Foremost rumor was that the British government itself was guilty of the hero's death for having sent him on a ship known to be unsuitable for service and about to be scrapped when World War I broke out.

All this, Power recalled in a signed article in the London *Referee,* August 8, 1926, in which he also announced finding Kitchener's grave in a Norwegian cemetery and removal of the body for shipment to England. Because of the tremendous interest this story naturally created, the British Admiralty hastened to issue its long overdue report on Lord Kitchener's Russian mission. The Norwegian government, furthermore, assured the British that no grave had been opened nor body removed, and that all British sailors buried in that country had been identified as victims of the Battle of Jutland.

Nevertheless, preparations for return of the coffin progressed. Newsreel men were on hand when it was loaded onto a London-bound boat. However, British bobbies were waiting August 14, 1926, when it arrived in London, brushed Power aside, and immediately turned the cargo over to the coroner. In the presence of authorities, the coffin was opened and found to be empty. Power, proved to have purchased it in Kirkwell, in the western part of England, insisted that the coffin had been robbed after seizure. Few believed him, and not many went to see the film he had hoped to boost.

Of the undignified antics to which stars themselves resorted before there were enough smart public relations men to teach them better, the following incident is typical. Struggling vigorously and shrieking, "Mister, mister, let me alone," an acrobatic dancer in a Manhattan night club, Mlle. Simone Roseray, was dragged out of a Central Park pool in midwinter, 1928, and taken to Washington Avenue Hospital. In her handbag was found the photograph of a man with an illegible endearment scribbled across it. In much larger letters the New York newspapers outdid themselves to acquaint their readers with the near-tragedy.

The picture was that of the proprietor for whom the girl worked; the press agent was Irving Strouse. When Mlle. Roseray recovered from her slight cold, an advertisement announced: "Roseray, fully recovered from her recent indisposition . . ."

A burlesqued aftermath of this stunt was the ingenious idea of the late Mary Louise "Texas" Guinan, widely known night-club entertainer. She appeared at the same Central Park puddle and watched while several men recovered a dummy from the water. In answer to reporters' inquiries, she replied: "It's me. I did it because I love him."

Somewhat similar was the stunt by which the motion picture version of *Poor Butterfly* was advertised. Found near a Central Park lake were the clothes of a Japanese woman with the identification, "K. Watsumi, Hotel Pennsylvania." Search of her room brought to light a suicide note with a Madame Butterfly story: the handsome American whom she had followed to New York was married to another. Because the police had been dragging the lake for the supposed body, they subjected the press agent to several uncomfortable minutes.

To advertise the circus for which he labored forty years, to become the world's leading circus publicity man, the late Dexter Fellows once marched Old John, oldest elephant in captivity, forty miles from New York City to Somers, New York, to visit the grave of the first elephant brought to America. The German midget, Lya Graf, who sat on J. P. Morgan's lap during a Senate investigation in 1933, got there through the ingenuity of Frank Braden, also a circus press agent, although neither party to the ruse knew it at the time. Morgan, not many days earlier, had demonstrated his hatred for news photographers by smashing a camera; more recently he had given the country a good laugh by testifying he had not paid a federal income tax the year before. As the midget tells her story, she was lured to the Capitol on a ruse, grabbed from behind by someone who said he wanted to introduce her to the richest man in the world and lifted onto the great one's knee by an unknown. She slipped off but was replaced promptly. Then the knee's owner relented, smiled and conversed with her about his grandchildren while, almost unnoticed, the flashlights flashed.

Coney Island's Luna Park once received a fortnight's continuous publicity by ferrying an elephant seventeen miles to Staten Island and freeing her on the shore where her appearance led to speculation as to whether she had swum all the way from Africa. After three days, during which the police vainly attempted to determine the animal's owner, the park's press agent showed up to claim her. He said the beast, whom he identified as the amusement place's Stella, had been despondent since the death of her mate and undoubtedly had attempted to commit suicide. Upon hearing this, city editors knew they had been duped but, because they already had played up the mystery so strongly, were compelled to print the solution, suicide theory and all.

For the Charlie McCarthy kidnaping of 1939, the dummy's owner, Edgar Bergen, was exonerated. Two newspaper friends faked the abduction with the assistance of a bellboy who related a harrowing tale of having been bound and thrown out of a car. Bergen himself declared he didn't desire that kind of publicity; he and Charlie disappointed their Sunday evening fans by making no mention of the episode.

The pecuniary advantage of having a sea serpent just over the horizon from where you want to rent rowboats, lease cottages or sell refreshments was explained in Chapter II. There also are other variations of the sea-serpent publicity business. One was worked successfully in several Great Lakes and Gulf of Mexico cities in 1931 by two visitors who identified themselves as Clifford Wilson and Francis Bagenstese, cement salesmen.

The stunt apparently worked best at Sandusky, Ohio, where the two regaled reporters and other auditors with a recitation of a desperate struggle in Sandusky Bay with an eighteen-foot monster who reared his head and emitted a cloud of blue-white vapor from his tail before being overcome. On exhibition for a nominal price in a Sandusky garage, the sea serpent was viewed by scientists who pronounced it an ordinary python. Nevertheless, the suckers shoved their way into the exhibition place.

In August, 1937, two widely separated places, Nantucket, Massachusetts, and Newport, Arkansas, vied with each other for the honor of producing the year's No. 1 sea serpent. In both cases the press cooperated perfectly, stories of the "armadas" hunting the monsters appearing throughout the nation. On the testimony of Captain William Manville, the New England monster was revealed to be about one hundred feet long with a head like a barrel and red-rimmed glaring eyes the size of dinner plates. Two business men were named as having discovered huge webbed-foot prints, sixty by forty-five feet on the shore at Madaket Beach. The legend of a Nantucket serpent which appeared one hundred and sixteen years earlier, and was sought one hundred and six years before by a special party aboard the sloop *Fame,* was revived from Maine to California.

After receiving untold front-page space, the Nantucket beastie was revealed to be an inflated rubber creation of the type used in the R. H. Macy Thanksgiving Day parades in New York City. Its designer, in fact, was Tony Sarg, who has charge of Macy's annual festival. It was exposed by the New Bedford (Mass.) *Standard-Times,* whose editor thought it unfair to frighten vacationists merely to advertise a metropolitan department store. When the rubber monster was beached, representatives of the press, radio and newsreels were present, and it was announced that the serpent would be seen again in that year's Thanksgiving Day parade.

The Newport, Arkansas, White River Monster petered out much faster. The scare began when a plantation owner, Bramlett Bateman, was reported to have seen a big gray Thing emerge from a place where the river is known to be sixty feet deep. It floated for a few minutes on top of the water and then disappeared, leaving behind plenty of bubbles. The local weekly was first with the story, but then the press associations took it up and the 4,547 residents of Newport enjoyed a brief but profitable opportunity to dispense their home cooking to the thousands of visitors who followed the signs to the fenced-off area and paid twenty-five cents each to get inside.

Hoping to intensify interest, the Newport Chamber of Commerce really killed business by hiring a Memphis diver with an eight-foot harpoon to descend to the bottom of the eddy and see what he could see. After

"Life," Pictures Incorporated, "Editor & Publisher"

THREE PROOFS OF GULLIBILITY

(Upper left.) A list, containing the names of 1,600 people who invested $5,000,-000 in a worthless gold mine, was displayed by William Dan Bell, promotion manager of the Cleveland Better Business Bureau, at the 1937 convention of the Better Business Bureaus at Mackinac Island, Mich.

(Upper right.) A stranger told Earl Baker, 11, of Coatesville, Pa., that he could obtain an artificial leg by collecting 50,000 match box covers. Later Earl, who lost his leg when he took a dare to hop a moving freight train, learned it was a hoax. Sympathetic neighbors took up a collection to buy him an artificial substitute.

(Below.) Nantucket Islanders were frightened by this "sea serpent" which was a balloon creation of a New York department store.

Wide World and International

THREE OUTSTANDING PUBLICITY STUNTS

(Above left.) "Ladies in black" appear every year at the tomb of Rudolph Valentino in Hollywood.

(Above right.) Harold Hulen, of Excelsior Springs, Mo., chained himself to a radiator outside the apartment of Miss Florence Hurlbut and said he would stay there until she married him. She flew to New York to try to get a night-club job on the strength of the publicity.

(Below.) Four hundred Italian women knelt and prayed on the sidewalk in front of the New York home of Governor Herbert H. Lehman to obtain executive clemency for some condemned murderers. It was a publicity stunt to advertise the theater of Clemente Giglio, shown standing in the picture, which newspapers printed seriously.

seventy-five minutes he was compelled to confess that he saw nothing, and those who had bet it would be a sturgeon or a catfish or an alligator gar or a cousin of the Loch Ness serpent had to be content to call it even.

Who profited by one of the earliest attempts to direct attention to lighter-than-air travel the writer does not know. Although revealed by the New York *Sun* to be inspired by a press agent, it is difficult to believe that someone on the editorial staff of the New York *World* was not in on it.

The story, together with a sizable artist's interpretation of the incident, appeared in the *World* for May 14, 1897. It was the disastrous end of an unidentified balloon which had crashed into the water near the pilot boat *Joseph Pulitzer,* three miles southwest of Sandy Hook. Two days later the *World* had the story that two passengers on the balloon were rescued by the sloop *Mary Jane.* Then the *Sun* got busy and, on the testimony of one of the principals who gave everything away while "in his cups," it declared:

The *Sun* learned yesterday morning that the two "aeronauts" reported by the *World* and *Journal* to have been "probably lost" after making a balloon ascension from somewhere, had been on solid earth all the time since the report that they were "missing" was coupled with the alleged discovery of a small balloon adrift off the Jersey coast, and that they would doubtless be "rescued" in time for the Sunday editions of the fly-gobbling newspapers. Sure enough, they were. Early last evening Mrs. Wand, the janitress of the house at 361 W. 25th Street where the men lived, received the following telegram from them, dated from Long Branch:
"We are not drowned and will be home tonight. Balloon lost."
The only person now missing is the press agent who invented the fake.

Contrasting the example just related with another, also in the field of aviation but of modern origin, is a good way to comprehend what public relations counsel have accomplished. In February, 1935, the late Amelia Earhart Putnam, the nation's leading woman flier, soloed from Honolulu to Oakland, California, in eighteen hours. Although the true character of her escapade was exposed in advance, the far-flung press followed her progress hour by hour, minute by minute, especially during the last half hour or so when she became lost in a fog over San Francisco Bay and nearly missed her landing.

Miss Earhart received $10,000 for her flight from the Pan-Pacific Press Bureau, an organization synonymous with Bowman, Deute, Cummings,

Inc., which handled the advertising accounts of the Hawaii Tourist Bureau, the Hawaiian Sugar Planters Association, the Hawaiian Pineapple Company and others interested in advertising Hawaii or in obtaining its admittance into the Union as the forty-ninth state. When she began signing articles about her exploit for the North American Newspaper Alliance, as expected, she was made by her ghost writer to refer to "the alluring southwest corner of the United States that is Hawaii."

That phrase and others like it, such as "Hawaii, an integral part of the United States," were ubiquitous in the newspapers and magazines of America in 1934 and 1935. Credit certainly is due to the Pan-Pacific Press Bureau for getting them into the writings of many of the nation's leading authors and over the signatures of movie stars and other public heroes. The campaign failed of achieving its major objective, however, because the Costigan-Jones tariff, which does not operate as though Hawaii were an integral part of the United States, was not revoked or modified.

One of the most successful stunts of the Pan-Pacific Press Bureau was to supply newspapers with illustrated articles on the anniversaries of their states' admittance into the Union. Each article told of the hardy pioneers who endured Indians, buffaloes and other hardships to carve out a new and subsequently famous state; the last two-thirds of each story was an argument that the stalwart business men who opened up Hawaii for trade with the mainland should be rewarded with statehood as were their intrepid predecessors.

"Planting" rumors that newspapers will print is an "old one." In *Science* March 8, 1907, an indignant correspondent complained of a story, which originated in St. Louis and was carried by the press associations, to the effect that an earthquake in Jamaica had caused an increased flow of oil in the wells of northern Texas and Louisiana and a corresponding diminution of the flow in the wells in the southern parts of those states.

Another much utilized clever device to conceal the identity of an advertiser or his agency or counsel is to create a high-sounding "institute" or "league" having all the appearances of a disinterested organization devoted to public service. A few years ago the entire country was exhilarated by the announcement of one of these, the American Patriotic League, that it planned to finance a bath, using a newly invented soap, for the Statue of Liberty. When the Department of War, which has jurisdiction over Bedloe Island, disclaimed any knowledge of the momentous event, inquiry revealed that the American Patriotic League's address was identical with that of an advertising agency handling a soap manufacturer's account.

That press agentry fakery is one phase in which the little business man often can compete successfully with the big was demonstrated late in 1935 when newspapers subscribing to the United Press service thrilled millions of readers with the account of a New York taxi driver whose bibulous fare paid him $900 to drive to Los Angeles. There the chauffeur sold his cab and departed for home by bus.

Because the driver's name was given, the truth was ascertained. It was that the man had driven to the coast with his children in search of a better job. Not finding it, he sold his cab and returned to New York. The press agent of the junk yard which bought the cab was responsible for the press association's version of the incident.

Another small business man's stunt was a New York Turkish-American Week, ostensibly to promote better relations between Turkey and the United States with the endorsement of official Washington and the Turkish embassy. Actually, the week, which came to a climax with a riotous banquet, was to benefit Libby's Hotel and Turkish baths.

To advertise his theater, Clemente Giglio, in early January, 1937, engaged Samuel Berg, unemployed press agent, to stir up public sentiment in favor of commutation of the death sentence of six young thugs who, two years earlier, had murdered a New York subway collector during a hold-up. Giglio posed as a humanitarian who offered his theater as a rendezvous for the mothers, other relatives and friends of the condemned half-dozen.

When Berg urged sympathizers to write to Governor Herbert H. Lehman, Giglio objected because the appeals were not made over the radio, in which he also was interested. He instructed Berg to have all letters sent to him for forwarding to the statehouse at Albany. When Berg suggested trying to get Clarence Darrow, famous Chicago criminal lawyer, into the case, Giglio remarked: "Why should we get Darrow? It's me who needs to be on the front page, not Darrow."

The climax of the stunt, which put Giglio into the news where he wanted to be, was a sidewalk prayer meeting of about two hundred men and women, in front of Governor Lehman's Park Avenue home in New York, the day before that set for the executions. A plan to transport several hundred women to Albany fell through, but the chief executive granted last-minute commutations to four of the six. After the other two were out of the way, Berg brought suit against Giglio to collect $2,000 in fees.

In Hollywood, scene of more practical jokes and birthplace of more myths and legends than any other American city, a press agent's stunt which got way out of hand was the mysterious "lady in black" who left a tear and a flower on the grave of Rudolph Valentino each August 23, the date of his death in 1926.

Russell Birdwell, later head publicist for Selznick International Studios, says that the first lady in black was an unknown girl whom he hired in 1928 to kneel at the resting place of the great portrayer of the "sheik" while a one-reel short, "The Other Side of Hollywood"—one of several Birdwell was making at the time—was being filmed. The narrator, Birdwell revealed ten years later, created the myth of the mysterious mourner who arrived at dawn each August 23 and departed shortly without a word.

To the amazement of Birdwell, in many of the succeeding years there actually was a lady in black. In 1938 the tradition was so firmly established that reporters and photographers took up the watch before daybreak. They were rewarded, not by one forlorn figure but by three. Because the first was too plump and the second too scrawny, they were passed up; Number Three was just right, blond and comely and escorted by a chauffeur. Furthermore, she talked, explaining that she had first met Valentino when he was a waiter in a New York restaurant and spilled soup down her neck. The next day Birdwell told how the whole thing began. In her syndicated column of February 14, 1940, Hedda Hopper, Hollywood reporter and critic, gave a different version of the "lady in black." She wrote that a florist, who retired recently, began the hoax to encourage the annual practice of placing flowers at Valentino's grave.

The object of the publicity stunt, legitimate or hoax, it should be clear by now, is to get someone's name before the public. Generally, but not always, the beneficiary of the publicity wants to be presented in a favorable light, but it is an axiom that any attention is better than none. A small town, for instance, considers that it has been "put on the map" if an attention-getting newspaper account is printed under its date line. "Do something worth talking about, and they'll talk," is the rule which press agents, publicity directors and public relations counsel follow.

With the professionals the desideratum is to make the news-worthy incident seem to be a normal occurrence rather than inspired with an eye on the front page. With the less experienced, and consequently more open-handed, the bigger the splurge the better. The method of superior finesse calls for money and persistence in the belief that a brief moment in the limelight is not enough; the seeker of quick fame and fortune counts on a gigantic moment not only to land him on top but to keep him there. Occasionally a Douglas Corrigan succeeds with this technique, but for every wrong-way flier there are thousands of wrong-guessers who either fail to win the dizzy importance they crave or sadly discover it to be short-lived. As in an army at war, however, there always are replacements. So daydreamers go on hoping and expecting to get in some newspaper reporter's way on some happy occasion, while men like Edward Bernays and Carl Byoir work silently behind the scenes.

Within a decade after the end of World War II, public relations was "the thing," meaning that there hardly was a business, labor union, entertainer, politician or other individual or group in the public eye without employed counsel to advise and direct their relationships vis-à-vis others. It became virtually impossible to distinguish between those actions which were natural results of personal interest and inclination and those motivated by a desire to build good will in some way. "Worry" literature began to appear, notably Frederick Wakeman's *The Hucksters*, Jeremy Kirk's *The Build-Up Boys*, John G. Schneider's *The Golden Kazoo*, Vance Packard's *The Hidden Persuaders* and others. Warnings were sounded against the new technique called "subliminal projection" whereby split-second advertising messages are flashed on television screens to influence the subconscious minds of viewers. It became more and more difficult to distinguish between what was hoax and what normal procedure in this field.

CHAPTER XIX

Hoaxes of Exposure

THE way to fight fire is with fire.

As regards the present subject this old bromide means that hoaxes have been perpetrated not only to swindle but also to catch swindlers, to expose unscrupulous newspapers as well as to build circulations, to show up pomposity, arrogance and false learning as well as to confuse reputable scholars, to deflate as well as to stuff unworthy shirts.

In their intriguing *The Run for Your Money,* E. Jerome Ellison and Frank W. Brock relate several instances of baiting by the National Better Business Bureau of different kinds of "talent bureaus," which offer to write music for poems, rewrite short stories, novels, plays and motion picture scenarios and obtain dramatic and radio tryouts for amateurs. To three "literary bureaus" was submitted a synopsis of *Home from the South Sea Islands,* deliberately the worst composition that its author could make it. All sent congratulations on the originality of the plot material and the literary handling. One called it "original, dramatic, colorful," and all offered improvement for a fair-sized fee.

What Willard E. Hawkins, editor of *Author and Journalist,* called "probably the nadir of literary hopelessness" was achieved early in 1933 by his nineteen-year-old daughter in *Her Terrible Mistake,* a motion picture scenario, and *The Missing Twin,* a 30,000-word novel, written in the name of Lottie Perkins. Two agencies fell for the former and five for the latter. Both compositions were the worst kind of drivel. The plot of *Her Terrible Mistake* concerned the proverbial small-town belle rescued by her swain from "a villain in sheepe's clothing . . . a traveling salesman." The novel was unspeakably ungrammatical. To achieve fame, Lottie Perkins was assured, her short story would have to be rewritten at a price which varied from $10.00 to $21.50, and her novel copyrighted and printed at a cost of from $360 to $375. To protect themselves under the law, Hawkins pointed out, these "vanity" publishers print a few copies for the author to give to his friends.

With the cooperation of *Metronome,* magazine for musicians and music lovers, the National Better Business Bureau exposed eleven song publishing houses as willing to publish a thoroughly rank popular song —for a substantial fee, of course. William Arms Fisher, editor of Oliver Ditson Company, music sheet publishers, also submitted a ridiculous poem to a number of musical agencies, all of which assured him he had discovered "a gold mine" and submitted contracts. According to the copyright office at Washington more applications are made in a single year by one of these companies than by all four of the largest high-class musical companies together. Many of the songs have music virtually the same. Since the average cost per victim is about forty dollars, the song-sheet racket must yield more than one million dollars annually. In 1936 W. C. O'Brien, Post Office Department solicitor, attempted to put a crimp in the business by submitting "The Girl of the Dale," an impossible libretto, to Universal Song Service whose director, Henry Cohen, admitted on the witness stand he had been agent for 3,735 songs in five years but had sold only forty-five of them to the motion pictures or a reputable publisher.

Walton C. John writes in the March, 1938, *School Life* that in recent years the United States Office of Education has had its attention directed to "nearly fifty institutions of questionable character, many of which were 'diploma mills' pure and simple, as well as others whose courses were of relatively little educational or professional value." In 1936 the Ministerial Association of Los Angeles became so disgusted and alarmed at the ease with which mail-order ministers were being graduated that it hired investigators to gather evidence. Their crowning achievement was obtaining, for ten dollars, a certificate of ordination for Rev. Drake Googoo, a "Persian clairvoyant with some stage experience." The recipient, the Ministerial Association disgustedly but gleefully informed the press, was Comedian Joe Penner's theatrical duck.

In the golden days of American journalism, when moon, balloon and wild-animal hoaxes were helping the newspaper giants of today get their start and press associations didn't amount to much, publishers who paid out real money for cable and telegraph news constantly had to contend with the widespread practice among their competitors of appropriating it entirely without credit.

To put a stop to this larceny the hoax was an effective weapon. During the turbulent days just before and during the Spanish-American War, the outstanding New York rivals, William Randolph Hearst's *Journal* and Joseph Pulitzer's *World,* set traps for each other. In a list of Spanish casualties during a naval bombardment of San Juan, the former included the name of an alleged Austrian artilleryman, Colonel Reflipe W. Thenuz. When the *World* copied the list, Editor Arthur Brisbane of the *Journal* revealed that the name meant "We pilfer the news," the initial and first name backwards being the first two words and the last supplying the rest in phonetics. On its part the *World* proved that its rival had been tapping its wires by "planting" in a story the name Lister A. Raah, anagram for "Hearst is a liar."

Also during the Spanish-American War the *News-Record* of Fort Smith, Arkansas, was humiliated by falling into a similar trap laid by the Cotton Exchange of that city. The object was to put a stop to the use of news flashes arriving over the exchange's wire before they were transmitted directly to the newspaper by its press service. The hoax was a short news bulletin of the sinking of a Spanish gunboat, the *Drocker-swen*. The name, of course, was *News-Record* in reverse.

During the Polish War the New York *Courier and Enquirer* printed a denial of the fall of Warsaw, supposedly obtained from papers recently arrived on the ship *Ajax*. Without acknowledgment, the *Journal of Commerce* rewrote the story from a copy of the limited edition containing it, which the *Courier and Enquirer* made certain it obtained.

In 1910 the little town of London, Ohio, was excited by the account in its *Times,* edited by Harry F. Harrington, later director of the Medill School of Journalism of Northwestern University, that a distinguished Brazilian coffee operator, Lirpa Loof, was about to pay it a visit. In a few days rival papers were running voluble accounts of interviews with the great man and were insinuating that local merchants were interested in forming a new coffee importing company. Harrington waited until one of them asked to borrow a picture of Lirpa Loof before revealing that its subject's name spelled backwards was April Fool.

During the Balkan troubles of 1912 the Jacksonville (Fla.) *Metropolis,* now the *Journal,* one day appeared with a front-page spread concerning an important engagement near a town named Temehtmorfnelots. The Jacksonville *Star* plagiarized the account before realizing the unpronounceable name really was "Stolen From the Met," inverted.

Not to this day has the United Press recouped the position it occupied in North Carolina before 1914 when the Raleigh *Times* revealed that it had been stealing Associated Press news. In an edition of not more than four copies, the *Times* carried a story that the cruiser *North Carolina* had been sunk by a mine in the Mediterranean while transporting refugees from Smyrna to Alexandria. It was made certain that the U.P. messenger had one of the copies containing the fictitious story and, after it had been sent by that service to all subscribers in the state, the *Times* revealed the trick. The Associated Press insists that it had no part in the incident, but publishers taking the rival service held an indignation meeting and quit the United Press en masse. Josephus Daniels, famous North Carolina publisher and statesman, confessed in *Tar Heel Editor* that he once was caught lifting a planted story of a shooting in Nash County.

After Walter Howey, brilliant managing editor of the Chicago *Tribune*, fell out with Colonel Joseph Patterson and went to the rival *Herald-Examiner*, he delighted in trapping his former associates into appropriating sensational but untrue feature articles, according to Burton Rascoe in *Before I Forget*. One stunt was to register an actress at a leading hotel as a South Bend, Indiana, girl suddenly become rich. After the *Tribune* interviewed her to learn how she expected to dispense her money in the big city, Howey thanked it for advertising a forthcoming *Herald-Examiner* serial, "The Ten Million Dollar Heiress."

Howey also faked a cable from Helsingfors regarding the escape of the monk Iliodor of the Russian royal house. When the *Tribune* rewrote the item he again thanked it for promoting the impending serialization in the *Herald-Examiner* of the monk's memoirs.

That journalistic thefts persist was proved in 1937 by the Los Angeles *Times* which long had suspected Hearst's *Examiner* of reprinting its pictures without credit. When District Attorney Buron Fitts was wounded by an unknown assailant, the *Times* retouched an exclusive picture of him as he was about to be taken to the operating room by painting out a cigarette in his hand. Surely enough, the retouched picture appeared in the *Examiner*.

In a letter to *Publishers' Auxiliary*, which that publication printed in its issue of February 10, 1940, Richard G. Taylor, publisher of the Kennett Square (Pa.) *Kennett News and Advertiser*, revealed how he caught local correspondents for metropolitan newspapers "lifting" news from his sheet. He did so by faking a story of a visit to Kennett by Chief Yrotss Ihte Lotsi, one of the few surviving full-blooded members of the Delaware tribe of Indians and a direct descendant of the great Indian chieftain, Ffutsse Lpoepre Htognil Aets. Taylor advised spelling the Indians' names backwards which, however, the West Chester *Daily Local News* failed to do before rewriting the article for its January 27, 1940, edition.

Not to catch a rival but to ridicule readers who are a ubiquitous irritation to editors because of the picayunish criticisms they make of newspaper inaccuracies, in 1938 the Huntsville (Ala.) *Mercury* printed a cor-

rection to end all corrections which, however, was taken so seriously that
like Robert Quillen's fabulous blessed-event wedding story, mentioned in
the Introduction, it was reprinted widely as fact. The correction:

The report in this paper last week on the death of Gil Jones was hur
riedly written and some errors crept into it which the *Mercury* cheerfully
corrects.

The *Mercury* said Gil Jones and his name was Gilbert and that his age
was 93 and it was only 39. His wife's name was printed as Hannah and
Susannah was correct.

That he had two sons and both the boys were girls—and that he lived
at Madison Cross Roads and it was Owens Cross Roads; that he left many
friends that mourned his death.

Now that that is over this paper does not propose to be browbeaten any
more for "dern" his hide not even his family are mourning his death—
they are all glad the mean old cuss has gone and where he has gone the
Editor of this paper hopes he will not have to go.

In the field of art several attempts to show up modern cults whose adherents have high-sounding Freudian explanations of how they put their
souls into their work have been such as to make lowbrows chortle. At
the 131st annual exhibition of the Pennsylvania Academy of the Fine Arts
in 1936 in Philadelphia, for instance, Margaret Gest won a prize for her
painting "Pink Lilies," despite the fact that it was hung upside down.
In the same year B. Howitt-Lodge, portrait painter, smuggled "Abstract
Painting of Woman" into the International Surrealist Exhibition in London. Signed D. S. Windle, it was a phantasmagoria of paint blobs, varie-
gated beads, a cigarette stub, Christmas tinsel, pieces of hair and a sponge.
The composer explained that he had painted the worst possible "mess" as
a protest against "one of the most warped and disgusting shows I ever
attended." The stock answer of the so-called modernists who believe in
the Emersonian principle that art is its own excuse for being, even though
it communicates nothing because its vocabulary is gibberish, was: "He
may think it's a hoax but he's an artist and unconsciously he may be a
surrealist. Aren't we all?"

To the 1938 spring exhibit of the Art League of Springfield, Massachusetts, a local conservative painter, J. P. Billings, sent "Opus No. 1." When
it was accepted he promptly resigned, explaining that he had attempted
deliberately to paint the worst picture of which he was capable. In *Time*
for April 11, 1938, a correspondent, Paul L. Nothstein of Chicago, pointed
out that Billings really copied a modern stained-glass window design by
Georges Desvallières, modern French artist, and that "the jurors showed

more discernment than anyone supposed; they saw the good of Desvallières shining through the bad of Billings."

Way in front as the most outstanding hoax perpetrated upon modernists and futurists in painting was that of Paul Jordan Smith, widely known author of *Nomad, Cables of Cobwebs* and other books. He was disgusted with Picasso, the distortionists, Dadists and other innovators, and disgruntled because some portraits by his wife, Sarah Bixby Smith, had been described by futurist critics as "distinctly of the old school"; and in the role of a scrofulous Russian named Pavel Jerdanowitch he founded the Disumbrationist school of art in 1924.

How what began as a mere pleasantry developed into an international hoax is best told in the words of the "artist" himself as follows:

Coming in from a game of golf one afternoon I was shown the new painting done by my wife, amiable soul; and while it was by no means as bad as the real modernists, its loud colors offended me. I asked for paint and canvas and said I'd do a real modern—I'd never tried to paint anything in my life. Given the oldest tubes of red and green paint and a worn brush I took up a defective canvas and in a few minutes splashed out the crude outlines of an asymmetrical savage holding up what was intended to be a star fish, but turned out a banana. I labeled it "Yes We Have No Bananas," took it to the dinner table for the delight or disgust of the family, and thought that was the end of the matter. However, a few days later one of my boys brought in a young art critic from one of the local papers. He was shown the painting but not told its origin. He pronounced it extremely interesting. I told him I thought it rotten; whereupon he said that one had no right to judge unless one knew what was in the soul of the artist!

That gave me the idea. He seemed a wholesome, intelligent youth, and I judged that his reaction was born of deference to current opinion. So I made up my mind that critics would praise anything unintelligible. But knowing that the critics have a weakness for things foreign I decided to take a foreign name—Pavel Jerdanowitch for Paul Jordan. Then I heard of the coming exhibit of the spring of 1925. I joined the group and sent my painting, framed and now named "Exaltation." Nothing happened until April 6, when le Comte Chabrier saw and reported the painting to the *Revue du Vrai et du Beau* at Paris. They wrote asking for photographs of my other work. I was silent. They wrote again, and I replied protesting that I was too poor to afford photographs of my work, but would furnish them with one of myself. I likewise furnished them with a sketch of my life (born in Moscow, emigrated with parents, lived in Chicago, became tubercular and went to the South Seas, then returned to the United States). That journal in Paris printed an estimate of my work, based on the picture "Exaltation." Then two other journals from Paris wrote me—*La Revue Moderne* and *Les Artistes d'Aujourd'hui.*

I was asked to exhibit in Chicago the next year, at Marshall Field's galleries where the No Jury people had their show. Over 400 paintings were exhibited and the *Art World* of Chicago, January 26, 1926, praised the exhibition in glowing terms. They reproduced but one of the paintings in their pages—it was my second masterpiece, called "Aspiration." Then the next year I exhibited in New York again—at the Waldorf—this time two small paintings, "Adoration" and "Illumination." *La Revue Moderne* praised these in the issue of June 30, 1927. A little later a biographical sketch of Pavel with high praise of him as a pathfinder was published in a book called *Livre d'Or* (1926) with a full page reproduction of "Aspiration."

After three years the author of Disumbrationism tired of the double life he was living. He confessed to a feature writer for the Los Angeles *Times,* which printed the first "exposé" of Pavel Jerdanowitch August 14, 1927. The story, according to Smith, was augmented and exaggerated by the Los Angeles *Examiner* and broadcast all over the world. Upton Sinclair tells the story in his *Mammonart.*

Revelation of their true nature did not mean the end of interest in the four paintings. Robert C. Vose, of the Vose Galleries, Boston, exhibited them in 1928 and writes: "It was the most widely noticed exhibition I have ever heard of." A serious catalogue was prepared for "those who realize that real art depicts not what we see but what we feel, hear and smell; these soul revealing creations will be sources of ecstatic, moronic rapture." There also was contained a portrait of Jerdanowitch which showed an emaciated bearded Russian with a corrugated brow; it had been posed by Smith himself who grew a real beard and made up for the camera.

A serious painter who enjoys doing frequently what Smith proved it is not difficult for an amateur to do, is Hugo Ballin of Pacific Palisades, California. To the 1934 show of the National Academy of Design in New York he submitted two paintings: one, a serious portrait of Dolores del Rio, motion picture actress; the other, "Mrs. Katz of Venice, Cal.," in the "modern" vein.

This hoax was a trap into which the intended victim, Edward Alden Jewell, art editor of the New York *Times,* fell. Ballin disliked Jewell because he had called him "one of a number of superannuated muralists

THE DISUMBRATIONIST
SCHOOL

In the name of Pavel Jerdanowitch, Paul Jordan Smith, Latin scholar and bibliophile, established the modernistic art school of Disumbrationism. The portrait at the left shows how he made himself up to represent a scrofulous Russian. Above is "Exaltation," first of the Disumbrationist paintings. Smith explained that it represents the breaking of the shackles of womanhood. The lady has just killed the missionary, represented by a skull. She is hungry. Women are forbidden to eat bananas on that island; she has just taken a luscious bite and is waving the banana skin in triumphant freedom.

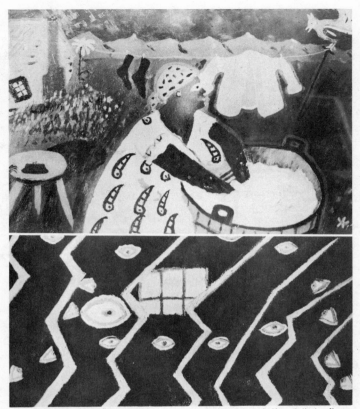

THESE FOOLED CRITICS

These are three of the Disumbrationist school paintings of Paul Jordan Smith in the name of Pavel Jerdanowitch: *(Top)* "Aspiration," which one art critic called "a delightful jumble of Gauguin, Pop Hart and Negro minstrelsy, with a lot of Jerdanowitch individuality." *(Center)* "Illumination," of which Jerdanowitch explained: "It is midnight and the drunken man stumbles home, anticipating a storm from his indignant wife; he sees her eyes and the lightning of her wrath. It is conscience at work." *(Below)* "Gination," of which he said: "It depicts the appalling effects of alcohol on Hollywood women of the studios. It is a moral picture. Note the look of corruption on the lady's skin. Everything is unbalanced. While good gin might not have just that effect, boulevard gin brings it about in short time. The picture is painted in bold strokes and with a sure hand. I believe it is the most powerful of my works."

long out of the running." When Jewell praised "Mrs. Katz" highly and reproduced it in his column, and wrote of the del Rio portrait, "Such vulgarities had best be forgotten as quickly as possible," Ballin was delighted.

First he wrote to Jewell in the name of Antonio Gamio, with which he had signed the painting, and received a congratulatory reply. Then he revealed the entire plot to the Academy. Finally, when that body suppressed the facts, he revealed them to Arthur Miller, art critic of the Los Angeles *Times,* who exposed the hoax and described Mrs. Katz as follows: "She is ugly, aging and wears blue slacks and spectacles. She has been reading a 'Romantic Love Secrets' magazine and sits idly dreaming of love."

Because he carelessly left his address on the back of another canvas, Ballin failed in an attempt similarly to hoax the judges of the Biltmore show in Los Angeles with "The Keeper of the Zoo," showing a libidinous-appearing man holding a mother ape whose baby plainly wishes to nurse, while his wife stands by. In 1936, however, he did stir up quite a bit of trouble with a sketch for a mural for the proposed new Inglewood post office. The subject for the competition was early California life and the gold rush of 1849 and, in addition to the hoax drawing, Ballin submitted six serious sketches. He was dumfounded when Washington informed him the fake had been selected, and he retorted angrily that he refused to complete anything which would be a disgrace. The sketch in question showed only the worst side of pioneer California: a bawdy barroom scene and a "bloated bond holder and his corpulent wife" contrasted with a begging Negro and weary miners.

Ballin also reports that he once "had a grand time doing a very bad novel about very bad people and a New York publisher, being under the impression that I was a female, fell for me."

Almost as old as literature itself is the controversy over the value of literary criticism. Editors and publishers deny that the mediocre work of an established writer receives greater attention than the first-class production of an unknown; but the avidity with which scholars accepted William Henry Ireland's forgeries of Shakespeare, Riley's forgery of Poe, the poems of Ossian, Edmund Lester Pearson's *Old Librarian's Almanack* and innumerable other fakes mentioned in preceding chapters proves that superior acumen is not always sufficient insurance against error.

Late in the sixteenth century a scapegrace named Muretus duped the foremost classical scholar of the day, Joseph Scaliger, into including in his

De Rustica, a commentary on Varro, some ancient Latin verses which he ascribed to the old comic poet, Trabeus. After the book appeared, Muretus confessed that he composed the verses to demonstrate the small dependence that can be placed upon the sagacity of anyone so prejudiced in favor of the ancients as Dr. Scaliger.

Disappointed because he did not win a prize in a literature contest sponsored by the French Academy, Desforges Maillard adopted the pseudonym of Mlle. Malerais de la Vigne and took in Voltaire, Destouches and, especially, Editor de la Roque of *Mercure de France.* The last named, who previously had rejected several of Maillard's poems, became enamored, through correspondence, with the supposed new and charming contributor.

In 1843 a heap of old hymn books and parish accounts supposedly yielded a seventeenth century chronicle of Abraham Schweidler, Lutheran pastor of Coserow, called *Marie Schweidler, The Amber Witch.* Dr. Johann Meinhold, the author, revealed that he conceived the hoax to trap supercilious critics; and he succeeded until he chose to make a voluntary confession.

During the heyday of his fame William Cullen Bryant's name was forged to a badly written poem, "A Vision of Immortality," which several newspapers accepted as genuine. According to a writer in the August 2, 1873, *Chambers's Journal:*

> When the editor [who first published the poem which others copied] was some time afterwards asked for an explanation, he boldly avowed that his purpose was to establish the fact that, no matter how atrocious an effusion might be, the name of a poet who had established a reputation would make it true poetry in the eyes of a large majority of poetry readers.

One of the most ambitious and successful attempts to "show up" critical scholarship occurred in the last decade of the nineteenth century with the "discovery" of *The Poems of Bilitis,* still enjoying popularity under the name of their real author, Pierre Louys.

The hoax began, according to an article in the New York *Journal* for January 27, 1898, by Henri Pene du Bois, a classmate of Louys', in the resentment of the two youths for the disdain with which German scholars regarded all things French. As conceived by Louys, Bilitis was a Greek poet of the sixth century B.C. who lived in the mountains east of Pamphylia, in Lesbos and in Cyprus. The poems which, Greek or French, are beautiful, were found in a subterranean Phoenician grave. Bilitis herself was buried at Palaco, Limisso, by the side of an ancient road; the stones of the house in which she lived now pave the quays of Port Said, according to the imaginative Louys.

Not only German scholars but also those of several other nations accepted the bait. Richard Dehmel translated twenty-six songs of Bilitis and published them at Leipzig as genuine; Dr. Paul Goldmann translated twenty songs and published them at Frankfort; Professor von Wilamovitz-Moellendorff translated thirty and published them at Göttingen; Alexander Backowsky translated eight and published them at Prague; Gustav Uddgren translated four and published them at Stockholm; Claude Debussy wrote music for four of them.

What should have been the literary hoax to end all literary hoaxes was *Spectra: A Book of Poetic Experiments,* by Anne Knish and Emanuel Morgan, published in 1916 by Mitchell Kennerley. The motive was similar to that of Paul Jordan Smith in establishing the Disumbrationist school of art, and the result was just as soul-satisfying to those who find it impossible to swallow such literary fads of the last half century as Vorticism, Imagism, Gertrude Stein and e. e. cummings.

On his way to Davenport, Iowa, to visit Arthur Davison Ficke, a fellow poet, Witter Bynner stopped off in Chicago to attend a performance of the Russian ballet, *La Spectre de la Rose.* During the evening both the idea of a colossal hoax to embarrass if not ruin the poetic faddists and the name for the new "school" occurred to him. Ficke readily and enthusiastically agreed to the plan, and for a frenetic fortnight the two firmly established poets experimented with opus after opus until they had enough for a sixty-six-page collection.

Kennerley, the publisher, had to be taken into the secret, but he was the only one. On Bynner's desk at Cornish, New Hampshire, an editor of the *New Republic* observed proof sheets and became enthusiastic. He accepted Bynner's explanation that he had been sent the proofs so that he could prepare a review prior to publication. For fifteen dollars Bynner was persuaded to send it, when finished, to the *New Republic.* Thus encouraged, Anne Knish (Ficke) and Emanuel Morgan (Bynner) wrote a panegyric, "The Spectric School of Poetry," which *Forum* published in June, 1916.

That article contained the substance of the preface to the published volume of which Don Marquis remarked: "Say what you will about the verse, the explanation is a corking explanation." Critics generally were so dumfounded that all a majority could do was to announce a new school of poetry, quote from the preface and cite an opus or two by way of illustration. The verse-reading public, however, was enthusiastic, and amateurs hastened to join the new school which held in its first sense "that the theme of a poem is to be regarded as a prism, upon which the colorless white light of infinite existence falls and is broken up into glowing, beautiful and intelligible hues," which, in its second sense, "relates to the reflex vibrations of physical sense and suggests the luminous appearance which is seen after exposure of the eye to intense light," and, in its third sense, "connotes the overtones, adumbrations or spectres which for the poet haunt all objects both of the seen and unseen world."

Their book as close to being a best seller as poetry ever reaches, Bynner and Ficke were confronted with the sizable and vexatious problem of what to do about the enormous fan mail which Anne and Emanuel began to receive and about the hero worshipers and interviewers seeking a glimpse of them in the flesh. Both had been advertised as residents of Pittsburgh, Morgan being said to be a native who had returned after twenty years abroad and Miss Knish an immigrant from Budapest. When the trail became hot the alleged modest pair had to be kept constantly on tour, and a few friends of Bynner and Ficke had to be admitted to the conspiracy to post letters in far-away places.

When a poet near the top of American letters, a Pulitzer prize winner in fact, wrote, "Whereas the Imagists merely prick at the surface, you probe to the core," the two original Spectrists were elated and tossed dice to determine who should have permanent possession of the letter. Bynner won and Ficke thereupon had a copy certified by a notary public to convince anyone to whom he showed his files that the praise of the serious-minded poet was genuine.

By the time the January, 1917, issue of *Others* appeared, filled with Spectric contributions and criticism, Marjorie Allen Seiffert had been let into the plot. Other Spectrists were sincere dupes. Alfred Kreymborg, editor of *Others,* was taken in completely. So was Lloyd Morris who, in *The Young Idea,* dismissed Ficke and Bynner with comparatively brief mention but published serious letters from Anne Knish and Emanuel Morgan explaining their outlook on the existent state of American poetry.

Perhaps the strangest story of all connected with the hoax is that related by Ficke in an unpublished manuscript:

One day during the war, in Paris, I, then a mere captain, trembling with awe, was greeted by a brigadier general of the regular army whom I had known slightly in peace days. The general and I took breakfast together; and he turned our talk to literary matters and asked me whether I thought the recently announced Spectric School was serious or a hoax. I said I imagined it must be a hoax. The general congratulated me smilingly on my acumen, and said I was right. "But how do you know, Sir?" I asked. "Because," he said with great good humor, "I myself am Anne Knish!" I expressed proper astonishment, and voiced my admiration for such versatility in a great military man. I also asked a number of questions—how the general first happened to write the Anne Knish poems, and why he chose that name—all of which he answered with engaging frankness and with obvious pride in his clever literary achievement. He pledged me to secrecy about all this. One thing only he refused to disclose to me: he said he was under solemn oath not to reveal the true name of "Emanuel Morgan" . . . I suppose that that hour was one of the most deliriously happy hours I have ever spent! . . . The general is still alive, though post-war demotions have reduced him from his dizzy rank of general. I have not seen him since; but if he does not treat me mighty handsomely next time I meet him I shall disclose his name to posterity. . . .

Had the war not intervened it was the intention of the authors to extend their school by inviting Edna St. Vincent Millay, Edgar Lee Masters, Edwin A. Robinson and others to join. George Sterling was invited, but his productions were considered too off-color for publication.

After Ficke went to France, Bynner included mention of the Spectric School in his public lectures. Suspicion had been growing as more and more people had to be let into the hoax. The climax was reached one night in Detroit when a heckler publicly challenged the speaker. Writes Bynner: "A direct and large lie was too much for me. To the high amusement of the audience, I thereupon told for the first time the complete story." Ficke confesses to having given the secret away to Maurice and Ellen Van Volkenburg in Chicago. They in turn told Horace Kallen, who goaded on the Detroit heckler.

Once it was exposed, those who had sponsored the Spectric School were hard put to retire gracefully. William Marion Reedy, who had been especially enthusiastic in *Reedy's Mirror,* backed out by means of an article written by Arthur J. Eddy, "Bynner, Ficke and Freud," in which it was said that "both Bynner and Ficke simply 'broke loose' in their burlesque and, for the first time in their lives, abandoned their literary pose under the cover of pseudonyms." This view is partly substantiated by an examination of Bynner's subsequent *The Beloved Stranger,* which the author admits derived directly from *Spectra.* Both authors sometimes wonder if, after all, they were not the victims of their own hoax.

What Witter Bynner and Arthur Davison Ficke did for the asinine vogue of hodgepodge verse masquerading as poetry, George Shepard

Chappell and Corey Ford attempted to accomplish for the deluge of romantic adventure tales which paved the Royal Road to Royalties for Joan Lowell, Richard Halliburton, Trader Horn and a galaxy of others.

Although Edmund Lester Pearson perhaps overstated the success of Chappell's *Cruise of the Kawa* when he called it "the most influential hoax of history" which "absolutely put an end to the flood of amorous South Seas books" because "nobody dared write in that vein afterwards," there is no question *Kawa* was a howlingly successful burlesque.

The groundwork was done by George Palmer Putnam, publisher, who submitted serious announcements to newspapers of the landing of Dr. Traprock in San Francisco after a Polynesian voyage on which he discovered a new group of islands which he named Filbert because of the extrordinary quantity of filbert nuts found upon them. The publisher's note to the published volume contains one of the newspaper stories which led to a prompt invitation of the explorer by the editorial board of the *National Geographic Magazine* to come to Washington for a conference.

The illustrations in *Cruise of the Kawa* taken alone were more than enough to indicate the writer's purpose. One showed the alleged Dr. Traprock, "of Derby, Connecticut," with his native wife; another was a view of a bird's nest containing dice, supposedly laid by a native bird. Nevertheless, Chappell writes: "Far and wide, *Cruise of the Kawa* was accepted as genuine, frequently even *after* it had been read."

About a dozen readers applied to be taken along on the next cruise of the *Love Nest,* the sailing dates of which were advertised in the back of the book. A garage mechanic in New Haven wanted to sell out for $2,500 and invest the entire amount in Chappell's venture. After the author had ignored one letter from this person, he received a last-minute telegram demanding instructions and offering to bring along an old Ford car.

The combined boards of trade of Derby and Shelton, Connecticut, where Dr. Traprock was supposed to have "hailed from," invited the "doctor" to deliver an address. "You have put Derby on the map," the invitation said. Comments Chappell: "Boy, were they sore when they found out it was a fake!"

Upon receiving copies of filing cards from the Prints Division of the government, Mr. Chappell was "delighted to know that all my travel books are filed right alongside Henry M. Stanley, Livingstone, Stefansson and all those guys. So maybe they're true after all. The government evidently thinks so, and who am I, etc."

Corey Ford, in the name of John Riddell, continued what Chappell started—with *Coconut Oil,* the supposed story of June Triplett, daughter of Captain Ezra Triplett of the *Kawa.*

During the course of her South Seas peregrinations June met Hairy Ape, the tender-hearted gorilla, visited the tribe of Itsi-Bitsi pygmies, learned about African spooks from O-Yeah and had other thrilling and bizarre experiences, all amply illustrated in the book.

The intrepid June also was credited with authorship of *Salt Water Taffy,* Ford's parody of Joan Lowell's *The Cradle of the Deep.* This book appeared shortly after Miss Lowell's overdrawn autobiography, and Mr. Ford writes: "Certain impartial observers claimed to have detected a good deal of similarity between her book and mine."

In an article, "The Adventure Racket," in the July, 1929, *Vanity Fair,* Ford also cast doubt on many another adventure story. Because he accompanied Eugene Wright on part of his travels, he is authoritative when he declares: "It is no secret now that *The Great Horn Spoon* is almost two-thirds false." Ford praised the literary merits of Wright's book, ridiculed reviewers who accepted it as genuine without adequate investigation and blamed book publishers for the flood of exaggerated tales which engulfed the literary world within the 1920's.

For the same reasons that the sight of pomposity slipping on a banana peel is funny, a number of hoaxes to expose the demagoguery, little learning and lack of cleverness of prominent figures in public life have been applauded as acts of public service.

After listening to a French cabinet member on the same day dedicating two statues, one to a musician and the other to a philosopher, Paul Birault, reporter for *L'Eclair,* Parisian newspaper, concluded that men seeking the public eye know little and care less about those whom they are thus called upon to honor.

To test his theory he issued attractively printed invitations to all the members of the radical wing of Parliament to become honorary members of a committee to celebrate the 150th anniversary of Hégésippe Simon, and to speak at the unveiling of a monument to the memory of this "precursor of modern democracy and martyr to the tyranny of the ancient régime." Each invitation contained a portrait of a bearded patriot of the French Revolution and his immortal quotation: "When the sun arises the darkness vanishes away."

Fifteen senators and nine deputies accepted the opportunity to "render homage to the great democrat," to "rescue from oblivion the memory of the precursor," to "pronounce the eulogy on this educator of democracy," etc. These letters were published in full in *L'Eclair*.

On the Hégésippe Simon case, the American *Independent* commented February 23, 1914: "Whether such a hoax could succeed in this country is doubtful. The members of our government would probably refuse an invitation of this kind unless they got at least one hundred dollars down and a percentage of the gate receipts."

That was in 1914. In 1930, following a number of celebrations of the birth anniversary of the Republican party, at Ripon, Wisconsin, Jackson, Michigan, and other towns which claim the distinction, invitations were issued for a testimonial dinner to commemorate the 150th birthday anniversary of Hugo N. Frye, of Elmira, New York, "father of the Republican party" in that state.

The Cornell University *Sun* sponsored the banquet. Among those who received invitations were Vice President Charles Curtis, Secretary of Labor James J. Davis, Congresswoman Ruth Pratt of New York, Senator Joseph Grundy of Pennsylvania and Claudius N. Huston, Republican national chairman. None of these could come; but all sent messages, of which Secretary Davis's was typical:

It is a pleasure to testify to the career of that sturdy patriot who first planted the ideals of our party in this region of the country. If he were living today, he would be the first to rejoice in evidence everywhere present that our government is still safe in the hands of the people.

The following day the maker of the slogans, "Protection for Our Prosperity" and "Freedom in the Land of the Free," was disclosed by Edward T. Horn and Lester A. Blummer, the student editors, to be "You-Go-and-Fry." Newspaper accounts of the prank were read in the Senate by Democratic Senator Pat Harrison of Mississippi while Vice President Curtis grinned sheepishly.

A third case, similar to the two just cited, partook of the features of both its predecessors. Similar to the Simon hoax, it had as its victims members of the French House of Deputies. Similar to the Frye hoax, it was perpetrated by students, this time of the famous Sorbonne.

While French statesmen were discussing payment of war debts to the United States, three undergraduates organized for their purposes the Ethnical Defense League of Newfoundlanders and Guatemalans, with a New York address. Seventy-two deputies were selected to receive a copy of the petition, which began, "You know that two states of the Republic of the United States are deprived of a majority of the privileges enjoyed by the forty-two others. They are the states of Newfoundland and Guatemala."

The deputies also were enlightened by the information that Newfoundland's 2,000,000 inhabitants are of Spanish origin, that they have spoken Spanish ever since Cortes conquered the country from the Incas, that the Guatemalans have spoken Portuguese since Don Pedro of Syracuse conquered the country in 1456, that these two states have only one senator each whereas the others, as New York, have twelve.

Nine of the seventy-two hastened to promise undying support to the league; two others tried to get in touch with the officers. Among the nine were several of importance. The students, who deserve mention by name, were Andrew Sarved, Paul de Rivaudier and Lucien Hoch.

The Philadelphia *Public Ledger*, January 29, 1933, editorially interpreted the hoax as indicative of the average French legislator's knowledge about all things in America, including war debts, the issue of the moment.

In *Days of Our Years*, Pierre Van Paassen related that students of Action Française, a royalist group, once sent a letter to all members of the French Parliament in the name of the Bureau of the National Representation of the Republic of Terrania. Thirteen deputies promised to plead with the foreign ministry in behalf of the Terranian people, "ground to pieces under the cruel tyrant's heel," and sixty-three others pledged moral support. Sisley Huddleston related in *Europe in Zigzags* that a large number of French deputies also once pledged support to the Committee for the Defense of Poldavia. According to several authorities five Italians once were admitted to sessions of the League of Nations Assembly as delegates from "Zembla."

Still well remembered is the Veterans of Future Wars, which originated at Princeton and swept collegiate America. Saluting with "hand outstretched, palm up and expectant," the young men of near draft age amused everyone but American Legionnaires by demanding their bonuses and pensions before rather than after risking their lives. Without mentioning the Legion's congressional fight at the time to obtain payment of World War adjusted compensation earlier than contemplated, Lewis J. Gorin, Jr., founder of the movement, seriously announced: "History shows that all bonuses have been paid long before they are due, and we are only asking for ours now." Gorin was an artillery captain in World War II.

To dramatize the extent to which indirect or "hidden" taxes contribute to the cost of living, the undergraduates of Rensselaer Polytechnic Institute quietly cornered all the pennies in Troy, New York. After bankers and business men somehow survived several changeless days, hundreds of students suddenly began to make purchases with the 250,000 coppers. For a week the community and the nation became thoroughly conscious of hidden taxes.

As propaganda for peace, on Adolf Hitler's birthday anniversary in 1939, the undergraduate newspaper at St. John's University, Collegeville, Minnesota, printed a casualty list including the names of many prominent students under the headline, "Battlefields Red With Alumni Blood." The same day, at Manchester College, North Manchester, Indiana, a fake radio broadcast of a European war caused at least one student to faint. At Cornell College, Mount Vernon, Iowa, students were called from their classrooms to the chapel to hear an army officer read an announcement that war had been declared. Someone who cried, "You'll be fools to enlist," was shouted down. A few minutes later the young people, much given to pacifistic talk, sheepishly realized how completely they had forgotten themselves in an hysterical setting. In March, 1940, several University of Pennsylvania students reported to register for the "draft" after the *Daily Pennsylvanian* announced: "All Universities Mobilized on Wartime Basis." Widespread indignation was the response of Northwestern University students to a fake story in the April 9, 1940, *Daily Northwestern,* at the beginning of Peace Week on the campus, which was headlined: "America at War—F. D. R."

Halbert A. Hoard's brassieres petition hoax got the most publicity of any of its kind, but there have been several other amusing examples of the scant attention some of us give to a document before signing it. In March, 1933, for instance, two Omaha, Nebraska, attorneys, aided and abetted by a gentleman of the press, obtained more than three hundred signatures to a petition to nominate Giuseppe Zangara for the Omaha city council.

Zangara, it will be recalled, was the crazed naturalized alien who fatally shot Mayor Anton Cermak of Chicago at Miami, Florida, while aiming at President-elect Franklin D. Roosevelt. His name was in almost every edition of every newspaper continuously for weeks. By intentionally giving the date of the primary election as April 8, 1934, instead of April 8, 1933, the hoaxers invalidated the petitions. Nobody who signed

the papers (many prominent citizens did) of course, felt any obligation to vote for the candidate in whose behalf they were circulated, or even to remember his name.

As a protest against attending a psychology lecture during the football season on a Saturday afternoon in the fall of 1938, a group of freshmen at the University of Michigan circulated a petition asking that the class be shifted to Wednesday. When a number of upper classmen read the undergraduate newspaper the next day, they discovered they had attached their signatures to the following:

We, the undersigned, hereby petition that the lecture in Psychology 2 be changed from Saturday to Wednesday afternoon. By signing this document without reading it we cheerfully disqualify ourselves as candidates for any degree conferred by this university. We furthermore declare that the freshmen are our superiors in wit and wisdom, and that our stupidity is surpassed only by the mental lethargy of the underpaid faculty that teaches us.

In May, 1939, sixty-two seniors of the Carrick High School in Pittsburgh, without first reading, signed a paper headed Petition for the Elimination of Weekly Guidance Programs. Actually the petition demanded that the school provide guns so that the students could shoot one another before being graduated.

Indignant because Ben Gitlow, vice presidential candidate of the Communist party in 1928, was refused permission to deliver a speech in the Dallas City Hall auditorium, Richard Potts, liberal editor of the *Common Herd,* set a trap for the city commissioners to prove that they were opposed to freedom of speech.

In the Dallas *Morning News,* October 18, 1928, appeared a news story with the following lead:

Holding that the time has come to begin active propaganda for the conversion by orderly processes of the American government into a monarchy, Richard Potts, self-styled secretary-general of the Royalist League of America, announced Wednesday that a mass meeting will be held Sunday afternoon in the City Hall auditorium.

Frightened by the publicity given the new party by press associations and the radio, the city fathers revoked Potts' permit to use the auditorium, whereupon he appealed to the district court for a writ of mandamus.

Nation-wide interest was aroused, and the American Civil Liberties Union offered its assistance.

According to Potts he was in constant fear that the commissioners would see the joke and allow him to hold his meeting. "But," he wrote, "they were as blind as blind Tom, and bit with open mouth at the bait and swallowed it bait, hook, line and sinker. So day by day the farce continued to the merriment of thousands who had sense enough to see and appreciate the joke."

After the writ of mandamus was refused on a technicality and the commissioners had again refused to grant a permit, Potts confessed his purpose, printed the speech he had intended to deliver had the meeting been held, and wrote: "Taking the case from beginning to end I am convinced that I won a moral victory for free speech in Dallas and in Texas."

At the next election Potts stood for city commissioner and was voted overwhelmingly into office.

To put an end to, or at least expose the promiscuity with which the Rhode Island Senate granted one-hundred-dollar bonuses to World War veterans who failed to apply for them during the specified period which ended in 1923, a Republican member in 1936 introduced in the Democratic-controlled legislative chamber a bill to pay a bonus to Sergeant Evael O. W. Tnesba of the Twelfth Machine Gun Battalion. Unanimous consent for its immediate consideration was granted, a Democratic senator seconded it and the bill was passed. It was reconsidered after someone read the machine gunner's name backwards.

No doubts ever have been expressed regarding the achievement of Gertrude Ederle, American girl who in 1927 was the first of her sex to swim the English Channel. Dorothy Cochrane Logan, a young English woman physician, however, the same year cleverly demonstrated how someone could fake such an exploit and the need for supervision.

She did it by disappearing into the water one evening at Cape Gris Nez, France, and appearing thirteen hours thirteen minutes later, at Folkestone, England, apparently having beaten Miss Ederle's record by one hour nineteen minutes, to win a one-thousand-pound prize offered by the *News of the World*.

As newspapers the world over acclaimed Dr. Logan, her friends prepared a celebration in her honor. Explaining that she was indisposed because of her exertion, she did not appear. The next day, after receiving the prize money, she promptly went to a bank where she deposited it to the credit of the *News of the World* and then went to the editor's office to confess. She led him to a hotel where, from a deposit box, was recovered a sealed letter, written before her escapade, to explain that, if she proved unable to complete the swim, she expected to spend the night in a boat and then pretend to have been in the water all the time. Because the Channel was rough she actually swam only the first and last few miles.

Commented the *News of the World*:

Americans claimed her as one of themselves. The Scots were proud of their countrywoman. The Welsh were delighted with her Cymric associations. Medical and other bodies were enthusiastic in doing her honor.

The civil authorities took a different attitude and fined both Dr. Logan and her trainer, Horace Corey, one hundred and fifty pounds respectively.

Almost without exception the perpetrators of the kind of hoaxes dealt with in this chapter, have been amateurs at that sort of thing. That is, they have concentrated their energies on exposing one or at most two or three situations which have "gotten under their skin" to such an extent as to compel action. Then they have laughingly rested on their laurels. There was, however, at least one professional bubble buster: Brian G. Hughes, New York paper-box manufacturer and founder of that city's Dollar Savings Bank, who died in 1924 at the age of seventy-five years. Wealthy, Mr. Hughes enjoyed spending his money in no way better than by exposing inflated egos.

The owner of numerous pieces of property, he erected "Not for Sale" signs on all of them. Instead, he posed as a public benefactor by offering supposedly valuable gifts of real estate to official and semi-official bodies. On one occasion he appeared before the Board of Aldermen to announce he wished to donate a plot of ground in Brooklyn as a public park. After accepting the offer and extending gracious thanks, the board appointed a committee to inspect its acquisition. It turned out to be a two-by-eight-foot rectangle which Hughes had purchased for thirty-five dollars near Sixth Avenue and Sixty-third Street. Several historical societies accepted from Hughes a mansion which Lafayette was supposed to have occupied during the Revolutionary War, actually a dilapidated shack at 147th Street and Concord Avenue in the Bronx, tenanted by tramps.

Hughes is credited with having been the first to drop a package of imitation jewels in front of Tiffany's. He also distributed tickets to banquets and other functions which never were held. Once he caused a frantic search of the Metropolitan Museum of Art by leaving a set of burglar tools and some empty picture frames on its doorstep. Disguised ornately as the Prince of Amsdam, Cyprus and Aragon, he presented an old policeman's badge to the actress, Lavina Queen, who sat on an improvised throne in the old Waldorf-Astoria in the belief she was being made a Princess of the Order of St. Catherine of Mount Sinai.

All of Hughes' vans bore the mysterious letters, L.P.B.M.I.T.W., which stood for "Largest Paper Box Manufacturer in the World." Hughes delighted in hanging expensive umbrellas in public places and then watching their thieves, upon opening them, become showered with signs reading, "Stolen from Brian G. Hughes."

Best remembered of Hughes' pranks were those involving animals. For an entire year, through newspaper publicity, he kept alive interest in the South American Reetsa expedition which he said he had financed. Finally word came that one rare reetsa had been captured; quidnuncs lined North River to watch its arrival. Down the gangplank came an ordinary steer. Spell "reetsa" backwards.

Purchasing an alley cat for ten cents, Hughes belittled the ability of some of the world's leading cat judges by entering it in an important animal show as of the famous Dublin Brindle breed named Nicodemus by Broomstick out of Dustpan by Sweeper. Almost unbelievably, the carefully groomed feline won a first prize.

Hughes' only outstanding failure was his own fault because he spilled his secret before judges at the Madison Square Garden horse show had a chance officially to pass on the horsy merits of Orphan Puldeca, Sire Metropolitan, dam Electricity, purchased by Hughes for eleven and a half dollars, from the Metropolitan Street Railway Company which was changing from horse to electric power. The animal could not be started until Miss Clara Hughes, its rider, jingled a little bell. Its name meant "Often Pulled a Car."

To demonstrate that all voters who "come to the aid of their party" don't know what they're doing, Mayor Simmons of Milton, Washington, promoted his mule, Boston Curtis, for Republican precinct committeeman. The animal won.

CHAPTER XX

Hoaxes on the Wing

OF THE enormous amount of ingenuity and energy which has gone into the making of many hoaxes there can be no doubt. Let the perpetrator of one repent, however, even immediately, and the effort he has expended heretofore becomes insignificant by comparison with that necessary to undo even what he has done.

A hoax, that is to say, is much easier to start than to stop. Confessions are not seen or heard by all or the same persons who were affected by the original stories, or they are forgotten, or they are not believed. If there is a written record, furthermore, months, years, or even centuries later someone is bound to find it, innocently resurrect the untruth and start it on its way again.

This chapter is concerned with the life cycles of hoaxes: the typical ways in which they receive their impetus, are disseminated and achieve a longevity of influence. All of the principles herein set forth have been illustrated amply throughout the preceding chapters, but fresh examples are used for the sake of variety and interest.

Although it is customary for the originator of a hoax to make certain that it is related or published at the proper time and place, not infrequently it is someone else who is most responsible for its becoming widespread. That, for example, was the case in 1906 when John Meyer, city editor of the Appleton, Wisconsin, *Crescent,* who later became secretary of the Inland Daily Press Association, earned quite a little "on the side" by successfully querying metropolitan newspapers all over the country regarding an unusual story related to him by a reputable undertaker and friend of the paper.

The yarn concerned a farmer who was too soft-hearted to shoot an old horse no longer useful to him and so placed in the animal's mouth a stick of dynamite which blew the faithful equine to bits as he galloped about the pasture. Meyer did not receive a single refusal from the editors to whom he offered the story; they all took from 150 to 500 words, with Chester Lord of the New York *Sun* wanting the most. It was not until several days later that Meyer learned it was a hoax which had earned him his checks.

The case of Israel Rouchomovski and the tiara of King Saitaphranes proves that the manufacturer of a hoax may not even know what he is doing. Rouchomovski, a humble goldsmith of Odessa, was used by two swindlers to produce a faked antique for which the Louvre in 1895 paid 20,000 francs in the belief it was a relic of the third century B.C. It was an exquisite job in gold constructed according to a design supplied by the hoaxers who paid its creator a mere pittance. To prepare the way for their subsequent sale they instigated newspaper accounts of the discovery of a remarkable collection of antiques by some Crimean peasants. Because they feared their treasure would be confiscated, the finders had fled their country, it was reported. The almost perfect state of preservation of the tiara aroused the suspicions of Henry Rochefort, editor of *L'Intransigeant.* An investigation led to discovery of the truth.

A hoax which the principal party involved did not know he was creating is the following typical case of a joke's being taken seriously. In "Inside Stuff," which he described as an "allegedly funny column" in the Scottsboro, Alabama, *Jackson County Sentinel,* P. W. Campbell in 1935 told a story of a four-eyed rattlesnake, seven feet long, with twenty-seven rattles. He thought he was poking fun at people who tell snake stories; but someone sent the story to several metropolitan dailies, and it got nation-wide circulation. It kept Campbell busy answering inquiries, including some from first-rate naturalists, from all parts of the country.

Hoaxes, as Campbell and many another have found out, travel fast. Former Governor Gifford Pinchot of Pennsylvania said he received letters "from every quarter of the globe, denouncing my inhuman cruelty" after an imaginative newspaper story to the effect that a Chesapeake Bay retriever which, in 1924, he gave to the Eastern Penitentiary in Philadelphia had been sentenced to prison because it killed a cat. "I never saw a better illustration of the impossibility of catching up with a lie—harmless as this lie was intended to be," Pinchot declared.

How such a story gathers momentum is illustrated by 127 clippings in the files of M. D. Hinshaw, editor, and Edward Richardson, publisher, of the now defunct *Rusk County Journal* of Ladysmith, Wisconsin. The story, with which these clippings are concerned, appeared originally in the *Journal,* January 21, 1926, as the second of a series of wondrous tales intended to increase circulation. The first was about a local man who extracted static electricity from the air to run a large motor and wood saw. The one which achieved nation-wide importance was of the discovery by two woodsmen in a hollow tree of the body of Pierre D'Artagnan, lost member of the Marquette-Joliet expedition of 1675, which had been petrified by the tree's sap.

First known reprint was by the Prairie du Chien, Wisconsin, *Courier*. Giving that paper credit, the Muscoda, Wisconsin, *Progressive* used it. Seeing it there, the editor of the Evansville, Indiana, *Courier* wired Ladysmith for more details. The Eau Claire, Wisconsin, *Leader,* February 7, 1926, declared that the *Wisconsin State Journal* of Madison had reprinted the story from a Marshall, Minnesota, newspaper. The Duluth, Minnesota, *Herald* queried Richardson for details about the same time, and the mayor of Ladysmith received a letter from Dewey A. Ganzel, schoolteacher at Albion, Nebraska, stating that he had seen the story in a Nebraska newspaper and asking, "For the benefit of our students who have taken up this discussion in current events, will you inform me whether or not this story is credible?"

Within a month the story had reached the large city dailies. A former resident of Ladysmith, then living in Portland, Oregon, received a copy of his home-town paper and gave it to the Portland *Oregonian* which wrote up the mummy story on page one. Other Pacific coast papers saw it there and rewrote it.

About March 1 the *Rusk County Journal* received a letter from the Rev. Francis Borgia Steck, C.F.M., of Washington, D.C., who asked for more information about the finding of the body, in which he was interested because of a dissertation he was writing on the Joliet-Marquette expedition.

It took a special bulletin of the Wisconsin Historical Society to apply any kind of brake to the spread of the absurd tale. In it Joseph Schafer, superintendent, pointed out that it is impossible for the sap of a tree, which contains mineral matter, to replace the liquid contents of the cells of a human body and that, even if it were possible, the clothing and slip of paper containing an account of the expedition would not be preserved.

Following the appearance of this iconoclastic evidence, the *Rusk County Journal* pointed out what had been obvious to some skeptics all along, that the original story was credited to the *Rusk County Lyre.*

It is unusual, almost phenomenal, for a hoax—or any other type of story for that matter—not to change form upon being retold more than once. It is through distortion, in fact, that many hoaxes are born. Two illustrative examples are the following:

(1) Familiar anecdote about President John Quincy Adams is that Mrs. Anne Neport Royall, editor of *Paul Pry*, once sat on his clothes while he was swimming in the Potomac River until he consented to give her an interview. In the April, 1939, issue of the *Quill*, Cedric Larson (Mrs. Royall's biographer) said there is no direct evidence to support the incident except the fact that President Adams was accustomed to bathing in the Potomac, and that Mrs. Royall was a journalist. She did not start *Paul Pry* until Adams had been out of office nearly three years. Nevertheless, the anecdote appears in many books and feature articles. John Hix used it in his syndicated cartoon feature, "Strange As It Seems," January 15, 1938. President Truman related it as true on at least one occasion.

(2) In 1827 a visitor from the East in Clark County, Ohio, gave an extemporaneous talk on railroads one evening at a meeting in a schoolhouse. A few days later Harvey Scott, secretary of the local debating society and later historian of Lancaster and Fairfield counties, received a letter from several "solid" citizens, stating, "You are welcome to use the school house to debate all proper questions, but such as railroads are impossibilities, and are impious and will not be allowed."

As related not infrequently today, what happened was that the Board of Education of Lancaster (not Clark) County passed a resolution forbidding the use of a schoolhouse for a public debate on the future of railroads because, "if God had designed that His intelligent creatures should travel at the frightful rate of fifteen miles an hour by steam, He would have foretold it through his Holy prophets. It is a device of Satan to lead immortal souls to Hell."

Although, in the January, 1928, issue of its *Quarterly*, the Ohio State Archaeological and Historical Society made known the truth, the interpolated version has been used more recently by Arthur Brisbane in an article in *Liberty*, by Dr. George W. Crane in his syndicated feature, "Case Records of a Psychologist" for March 2, 1936, by the *Tusculum Record* in its September, 1935, issue and undoubtedly by many other innocent believers who wish to demonstrate how essential it is to be open-minded about things.

Another cardinal truth about hoaxes is demonstrated by the Lancaster school board anecdote: they survive a great deal of debunking. In addition to all the historical misconceptions already mentioned, especially in

Chapters VIII and XII, Americans persist in believing that it was George Washington rather than Thomas Jefferson who warned us to avoid entangling foreign alliances and against electing a president for a third term. With our Scotch cousins we also cherish the memory of the indefatigable spider which inspired Robert Bruce and, with liberals the world over, we quote the supposed *bon mot* of the great Voltaire: "I do not agree with a word you say, but I will defend to the death your right to say it."

Numerous scholars searched through Voltaire's writings in vain for this quotation, which became popular after E. Beatrice Hall, in the name of S. G. Tallentyre, included it in *The Friends of Voltaire*, published in 1907. In a letter which Christopher Morley used in his "Bowling Green" column in the *Saturday Review of Literature*, August 17, 1935, Miss Hall confessed that she invented the phrase

as a description of Voltaire's attitude to Helvetius—and more widely, to the freedom of expression in general. I do not think and did not intend to imply that Voltaire used these words *verbatim,* and should be surprised if they are found in any of his works. They are rather a *paraphrase* of Voltaire's words in the Essay on Tolerance—"Think for yourselves and let others enjoy the privilege to do so too."

The Brooklyn *Eagle* commented aptly on this confession: "One might make a pretty sound bet that what M. Voltaire is mostly remembered for is the quotation he didn't make, which is an irony that François Marie Arouet would have cackled over in the full savage misery of his old age."

An "old standby" which persists, despite exposure that it was invented by a newspaper feature writer, is the letter of resignation a civil service employee of the United States Patent Office is supposed to have written about 1837:

I have been greatly interested in American invention, and have been happy to serve in the Patent Office, which service has made me familiar with the discoveries of our wonderful inventors. But I am now moved to resign, since all the great fundamental inventions have been made, and I am not willing to endure the drudgery of dealing with unimportant matters.

Another is the last will of Charles Lounsbury, written for *Harper's Weekly* in 1898 by Williston Fish, who died December 19, 1939, at Western Springs, Illinois, aged eighty-one. In Item 1 the testator supposedly left "all good little words of praise and all quaint pet names" to fathers and mothers, whom he charges to use them "justly but generously as the needs of their children shall require." To children exclusively were left "the dandelions of the fields and the daisies thereof, the yellow shores of creeks," "dragon flies," "the long, long days to be merry in," and "the Night and the Moon and the train of the Milky Way." All the other items were in similar mellow vein.

Similar in behavior to the story related in Chapter II of the wedding guests who were sacrificed to the wolves so that the happy pair might survive, are a large number of what Alexander Woollcott calls "fair specimens of folklore in the making." These are delightful or frightful little thrillers which keep cropping up as true accounts in widely separated settings. Says Woollcott in his *While Rome Burns*:

For such a story to travel round the world by word of mouth it is necessary that each teller of it must believe it true, and it is a common practice for the artless teller to seek to impart that belief to his listeners by affecting kinship, or at least a lifelong intimacy, with the protagonist of the adventure related.

Outstanding example of such a tale which has been given a long life, not only by word of mouth but in printed form, is that of a long absent son who returns to his parents' inn and retires for the night without revealing his identity. While he sleeps he is murdered by the old folks who believe he has great riches concealed on his person or in his luggage. Too late they discover who he was.

This plot has been traced to a pamphlet published in 1618 and may be much older. It was the basis of a play, *Guilt Its Own Punishment, or The Fatal Curiosity* by George Lillo, produced in 1736 in London. The German playwright, Werner, adapted it for use in one of the "fate plays" which became popular in Germany during the nineteenth century. It became the subject of a popular song about the turn of the century and was the plot of one of the first motion pictures ever made. In the 1911 edition of Dunlop's *History of Fiction* it is included as told by a minor Italian writer, Vincenzo Lota (1703–1794), and as having been first printed in 1794. In recent years amateur players have presented it as *The Surprise*.

During the past quarter century the anecdote has been the basis of a supposedly authentic news item about every six months. Each time it is given a different setting, usually some obscure town in Poland or the Balkans. In 1934 the Associated Press used it as coming from Warsaw and, a few weeks later, as from Oravisa, Yugoslavia. The latter story had a new twist, the suicides of the mother and sister who did the fatal stabbing. King Features syndicate followed it up by an illustrated feature article, including photographs of Mother Marie Petrak and Sister Kate, and insisted fiction had at last become fact.

One of the best of this type of tale whose genealogy Alexander Woollcott has investigated, is that of the English widow and daughter who arrive in Paris from Bombay, India, during the Paris Exposition. The mother is ill, and the hotel physician sends the daughter to his home to obtain a special medicine. After two torturously long taxicab rides and an agonizing wait while the doctor's wife prepares the formula, the daughter returns to the hotel to find that her mother has disappeared. The room in which she left her has been entirely repapered and refurnished, and there is no record of her having been registered. The solution is that the mother was found to have the black plague—which, if known, might have ruined the exposition.

Woollcott traced this story to Karl Harriman who used it in 1898 in a column in the Detroit *Free Press*. Because Harriman did not remember whether he made it up or obtained it from an earlier source, Woollcott believes it originated earlier. In 1911 the plot was the basis of a news story in the London *Daily Mail*; in 1913 it was the motif of Mrs. Belloc-Lowndes' novel, *The End of Her Honeymoon*; and it also was made into the novel *She Who Was Helena Cass*, by Lawrence Rising.

The Spider Farm story which Ralph Delahage Paine invented in the 1890s for the Philadelphia *Press*, on which he was then a young reporter, is another which refuses to die and which, because of its comparative youth, may be just gathering momentum. The story, as told originally by Paine, was that one Pierre Grantaire, somewhere on the Lancaster Pike, was raising elegant spiders to sell to wine merchants to be used to "cob-web" their wine bottles to give them the appearance of age.

According to Paine's son and namesake, business editor of *Time*, the story was a huge success, a quantity of letters being received. In 1902, when he was on the copy desk of the New York *Herald*, the elder Paine spiked a plagiarized version of it. In the July, 1936, issue of *Mechanics and Handicraft* it was retold seriously under the title, "Webs for Sale," the setting, however, being shifted to France. In the Contributors' Club of the *Atlantic Monthly* for June, 1937, it appeared again as the true experience of the anonymous contributor's grandfather.

Fifty years after its first appearance as a space filler in the Victoria (Texas) *Advocate,* the story of a ranchman's having imported monkeys which he trained to pick cotton still was alive. In 1934 the executive editor of a publishing house wrote to the secretary of the Chamber of Commerce of Victoria that he had been assigned to trace the origin of the story, and that the trail had led to that community. The inference of the letter was that in the interim the story had had other resurrections.

Familiar campfire story with which to frighten tenderfeet is that of a timid person who goes to a cemetery at midnight and dies of terror because some part of his clothing becomes caught on a tree or fence or from his kneeling on it. After Ed Sullivan, columnist, used this in 1937 in his "Broadway" column in the New York *Daily News* and it circulated as news under a Wranowitz, Czechoslovakia, date line in the same year, a correspondent of *Letters* revealed that his father first heard the story in the 1890s in Russia.

Similarly resurrected in new settings and passed off as of recent origin, the next two examples differ from the six just given in the important respect of being grounded in fact.

In the May 6, 1915, issue of the *American Machinist* appeared an advertisement of the Cleveland Automatic Machine Company which, because of its fiendish frankness, caused a great popular outcry and led Secretary of Commerce Redfield to issue a severe rebuke to the magazine. Dubbed by its horrified critics "the advertisement of death," it read in part:

The material is high in tensile strength and *very special* and has a tendency to fracture into small pieces upon the explosion of the shell. Two explosive acids are used to explode the shell in the large cavity. . . . The combination of these two acids causes a terrific explosion, having more power than anything of its kind yet used. Fragments become coated with the acids in exploding and wounds caused by them mean death in terrible agony within four hours . . .

From what we are able to learn of conditions in the trenches it is not possible to get medical assistance to anyone in time to prevent fatal results. It is necessary to cauterize the wounds immediately, if in the body or head,

or to amputate if in the limbs, as there seems to be no antidote that will
counteract the poison.

Forgotten during the decade and a half of comparative peace which
followed World War I, this bloodcurdling testament to the rapacity of
munitions makers was restored as an object of public attention by Hel-
muth Carol Engelbrecht and F. C. Hanighen, who included it in their
Merchants of Death, published in 1934. They gave it its proper historic
setting, but pacifists and other opponents of an American rearmament
program quoted it widely as of contemporary origin.

Senator Gerald P. Nye of North Dakota, leading congressional investigator of the munitions industry and strong isolationist, quoted it in the
Senate without indicating its date. The *New Republic* picked it up from
the *Congressional Record* and commented in its usual pungent editorial
manner. In a letter to the editor of the Baltimore *Sun,* a reader quoted
from it as of recent origin. On a lecture trip in California, Norman
Thomas, the Socialist leader, received a copy of the advertisement from a
Berkeley comrade; and he used it in his "Timely Topics" column in the
April, 1934, issue of the *New Leader.* Seeing it there, Wallace Watson
copied it in his editorial column in the *Kern County Union Labor Journal,*
published at Bakersfield, California. Karl Lore, columnist for *Labor
Action,* organ of the American Workers' Party, lifted it from that publication. After *Time,* in its issue of June 11, 1934, traced the genealogy of
the advertisement, an English reader of that magazine wrote that it had
appeared in a newspaper in London some time previous, suggesting that
it probably made the European as well as the American journalistic
rounds.

Also of World War I origin was a collection of hilarious quotations supposedly from letters received by the War Risk Insurance Bureau. Typical
"howlers" were:

1. I cannot get sick pay. I have six children, can you tell me why it is?
2. This is my eighth child. What are you going to do about it?
4. I am glad to say that my husband, who was reported missing, is
now deceased.
8. Unless I can get my husband's money soon I shall be forced to lead
an immortal life.
12. In answer to your letter I have given birth to a boy weighing ten lb.
I hope this is satisfactory.
15. I have no children yet. My husband is a bus driver and works day
and night.

A few years later, with slight alterations and additions, the list reappeared as from the files of the Veterans Bureau. In 1934 it cropped up in different places all over the United States. *People's Opinion* of Valley City, North Dakota, received it from the Bismarck, North Dakota, relief headquarters as originating there; after several North Dakota newspapers copied it from that publication, it was picked up by *Captain Billy's Whiz Bang* in January, 1935. *Publishers' Auxiliary* for January 26, 1935, used the list as originating in Washington. A correspondent of *Letters* sent it in as coming from the Home Owners Loan Corporation at Jefferson City, Missouri. *Letters,* November 12, 1934, accused the H.O.L.C. office in Washington of having resurrected it, but Theodore Tiller, director of public information for the H.O.L.C., writes:

I have received other references to this list but it was not issued by this office, nor do I know where it originated. My impression is, however, that this humorous correspondence is not entirely authentic, and has been bruited around several government departments with the text changed to suit. It is "just one of those things."

Strikingly similar was another list of "boners" which, early in January, 1936, the New York *Times* said was collected by social service workers in New York, and which Robert S. Allen and Drew Pearson, in their syndicated "Washington Merry-Go-Round," simultaneously credited to correspondence received by President Franklin D. Roosevelt. Headliners in the compilation were the following:

Applicant and wife are not at home. Grandfather was at home, but illiterate.

The only food in the house was a loaf of bread and a pot of caviar.

The woman is troubled with obsessed ears.

The applicant is a typical real American and is the father of eight children.

The mother is very intellectual, speaks three languages and has even written a poem that nobody will buy.

Woman still owes $25 for funeral she had recently.

They endeavor to live nicely, having a little flower pot in the kitchen.

Apparently this list also is "just one of those things."

That "folklore in the making" circulates by word of mouth before being dignified by presentation as authentic news is suggested by the following "coincidence."

An Associated Press story of 1937:

RICHMOND, VA., Aug. 13.—Frank Moran, secretary-treasurer to the state police superintendent, told this one today: A rookie state patrolman, feeling his authority, stopped a tourist car which was several inches out of the right highway lane.

"Where are you from?" he demanded.

"Cincinnati," replied the tourist.

The new officer smiled triumphantly. "Well, buddy, suppose you explain why you've got Ohio tags on your car."

From the *New Yorker* of August 21, 1937:

There is nothing a cop likes better than to catch someone in a lie. Our favorite instance of this sort is the time a traffic policeman in the town of North Woodstock, New Hampshire, stopped a car for speeding. The driver was a woman.

"Where you from?" the cop demanded.

"Philadelphia," replied the lady.

The cop put on a wise look and nodded his head.

"Oh, so you're from Philadelphia, eh?" he said sarcastically. "Well, if you're from Philadelphia, whatcha doin' with them Pennsylvania license plates?"

When a hoax achieves the longevity to qualify for classification as either myth or legend, hope of stopping it almost may be abandoned. One sociological distinction between a myth and a legend is that the former includes fictitious personages as well as facts, whereas the latter involves real persons but fallacious facts. It often is a matter of scholarly dispute whether a particular example is myth or legend, as, for example, the stories of William Tell, Robin Hood, Helen of Troy, King Arthur and Roland. To illustrate with less shopworn examples: Hi-Brazil was a myth, and Johnny Appleseed is a legend.

Hi-Brazil, for about five centuries up to one hundred years ago, was supposed to be a small island west-southwest of Ireland. It appeared on all maps of the North Atlantic and was sought by many mariners. When Christopher Columbus discovered the mainland of South America, many believed he had landed on Hi-Brazil.

Other explorers, including Madoc ap Gwayned, reported that they had sighted Hi-Brazil, and in 1636 a Captain Rich gave bearings which appeared in marine catalogues up to and including that of John Purdy, printed in 1825: *Memoir, Descriptive and Explanatory, to Accompany the New Chart of the Atlantic Ocean.* Purdy wrote:

It has been variously represented on different charts, although its existence has been doubted. Messrs. Verdun and Borda have added to their remarks upon this rock that they do not believe it to exist. It was, however, seen in the year 1791, by the company and master of an English merchant ship, the commander of which favored the editor with a description of it, stating that it is really a high rock, or islet, apparently bold-to, and to which he passed so near that he could have cast a biscuit on shore.

Guillaume de Lisme, famous cartographer during the reign of Queen Anne, Genderville in his *Le Nouveau Théâtre du Monde* (1713) and Bellin (1742), all gave bearings for Hi-Brazil, calling it however, a rock rather than an island.

The only reported case of anyone's capitalizing upon the myth by claiming to have set foot on Hi-Brazil dates from September, 1674, when Captain John Nisbet of Fermanagh returned to Killibeg with a fantastic account and some carefully coached Scotch "castaways" he had "rescued." Hi-Brazil, he said, was inhabited mostly by large black rabbits but was ruled by a diabolical necromancer who lived in a strong castle in which he held the refugees prisoners for years. By building a fire on the shore he and his men had broken the black magic and enabled the Scotsmen to escape.

There is, of course, no Hi-Brazil, island or rock; and there never was, according to modern cartographers.

There once was, however, a Johnny Appleseed. Jonathan Chapman, to use his real name, was born during the Revolutionary War in or near Springfield, Massachusetts. Grown to manhood, he moved, first to Pittsburgh and then to Marietta, Ohio, where he became an orchardist and a Swedenborgian convert. Disappointed in love, he took to wandering with a Bible and a sack of appleseeds. Wherever he went for fifty years, he preached and gave away seeds which the pioneers planted to start the apple orchards which now dot the Middle West.

There are monuments to Johnny Appleseed in Indiana and Ohio; two leading brands of apples are the Jonathan and the Chapman, and the Johnny Appleseed Memorial Commission of Fort Wayne, Indiana, where Johnny is supposed to have died, insists that his story is history and not legend. Nevertheless, in 1936 Harry A. Wright resigned as historical adviser to the committee planning the celebration of the three hundredth anniversary of the founding of Springfield, Massachusetts, because it insisted upon dedicating a monument to the city's famous son. Wright declared the Johnny Appleseed story had been fostered by "some nice old

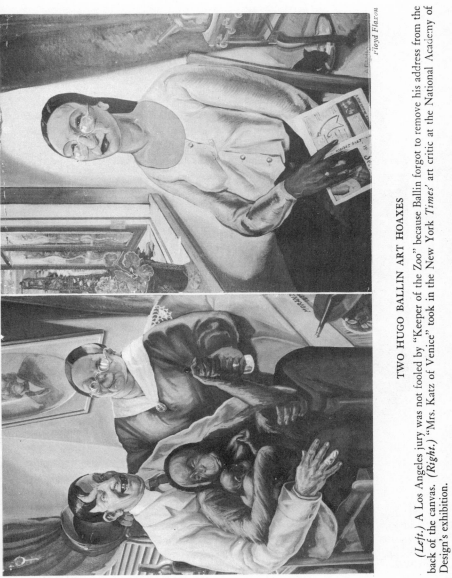

Lloyd Flaxon

TWO HUGO BALLIN ART HOAXES

(*Left.*) A Los Angeles jury was not fooled by "Keeper of the Zoo" because Ballin forgot to remove his address from the back of the canvas. (*Right.*) "Mrs. Katz of Venice" took in the New York *Times'* art critic at the National Academy of Design's exhibition.

FAMOUS ART IN HOAXDOM

(Above.) Paul Chabas, minor French artist, is shown in his Paris studio with a copy of "September Morn," the mediocre painting which became famous after Harry Reichenbach persuaded Anthony Comstock to have it suppressed.

(Below.) "Parson Weems' Fable" was the first of a series of paintings by Grant Wood to "debunk" leading American legends. It shows Parson Mason Locke Weems lifting a cherry-tasseled curtain on a portrayal of the George Washington cherry tree and hatchet story which he invented. The face of the boy is that of the mature Washington as painted by Gilbert Stuart and Weems' facial expression suggests "tongue in cheek."

ladies whose knowledge centered around the knitting bag and kitchen pantry." A horticulturist himself, Wright insisted that, in 999 out of 1,000 cases, trees grown from seeds yield knurly little apples unfit for human consumption, and that the Midwest's apple orchards were planted, not by Johnny's gifts but by cows who ate apples and evacuated the seeds richly fertilized.

To be assured of long survival a hoax must be made a part of a written record. In book form it is admitted to libraries, where it remains unaltered to trap the unsophisticated regardless of how many other books are written to debunk it. Writes K. D. Metcalf, chief of the reference department of the New York Public Library:

The problem which you bring up regarding unreliable books is a difficult one for librarians. The first duty of a library is to make available information of all kinds, not to decide for others whether the books which are available are absolutely correct in all ways. I think that most libraries do make an effort to bring out any definite information that is available in regard to the authenticity of books. When it comes to expressing an opinion as to the correctness of the information contained in a volume, a library cataloguer hesitates to make any statement that might well be contradicted by specialists.

The writer's experience in bringing to the attention of librarians the presence of thoroughly discredited works, such as George Psalmanazar's *Travels* (Chapter IX) and William Francis Mannix's *Memoirs of Li Hung Chang* (Chapter XII), however, contradicts Mr. Metcalf's statement that most librarians are interested in the subject. In at least twenty-five public and college libraries, he has met with virtually complete indifference.

The Library of Congress, which issues catalogue cards for subscribing libraries, has contributed to the correcting of false impressions in a number of cases. Jessica L. Farnum, secretary to the librarian, writes:

Dr. Childs, the chief of the catalogue division, to whom your letter was referred, reports that in cataloguing every reasonable effort is made to represent books accurately as regards title, imprint, physical makeup and content. Entries and cards are corrected and reprinted whenever any important additional information becomes available, particularly when the discovery is made that a work is a forgery or hoax.

One outstanding clever hoax still to be found on library shelves and listed in the *Encyclopædia Britannica* without any indication that, from beginning to end, its contents are fictitious, is William Beckford's *Biographical Memoirs of Extraordinary Painters.* This book by the author of *Vathek* was written as a practical joke in 1780, when Beckford was twenty years old. The eccentric youth was inspired by the "howlers" of the housekeeper at Fonthill Abbey, who displayed great ingenuity in inventing names and details when put to it by visitors to whom she showed paintings by Murillo, Rubens and other masters.

Ostensibly to assist her, and at the same time to indicate his low opinion of certain Dutch and Flemish schools of art, Beckford wrote his volume to serve as her guide. In it works of many masters are credited to such painters as Og of Bason, Herr Sucrewasser of Vienna, Blunderbussian of Venice, Watersouchy of Amsterdam and others equally nonexistent. Beckford created biographies for these ghost painters, and the housekeeper was not the only reader to be taken in. Lockhart saw in the book "the results of already extensive observation and the judgment of a refined taste."

In libraries, public and private, in governmental archives and other places where scholars do their research, there exist innumerable pitfalls, to avoid which the careful historian, as Allan Nevins emphasizes in *The Gateway to History,* must go to original sources. It is from their resting places in libraries that hoaxes often are rescued by well intentioned but naïve or careless scholars who are joyful to announce the rejuvenation of some bit of forgotten lore.

When, for instance, James de Voraginus, Peter Nodal and Peter Ribadeneira set about gathering material for their *Lives of the Saints,* they went to the monastic libraries, according to Isaac D'Israeli in *Curiosities of Literature,*

awakening from the dust these manuscripts of amplification, imagined they made an invaluable present to the world, by laying before them these voluminous absurdities. The people received these pious fictions with all imaginable simplicity, and as the book is adorned with a number of cuts, these miracles were perfectly intelligible to their eyes.

The specious material to which D'Israeli refers consisted of compositions which students, during the early days of the Christian era, wrote for their monastic professors in rhetoric. It was the custom, D'Israeli declared on the authority of Jortin, for the young men to ransack the writings of Livy, Ovid and other pagan poets and historians for miracles and portents which they ascribed to their own spiritual leaders and saints.

The monks, delighted, collected these miraculous compositions, "not imagining that, at some distant period, they would become matters of fact."

Capital example of the scholarly grief which may result if researchers fail to take adequate pains to verify material is that of the discovery in the British Museum in the last decade of the nationalistic eighteenth century of what for fifty years was believed to be a copy of the world's first newspaper, the *English Mercurie,* containing an account of the defeat by the British in 1588 of the Spanish Armada and published by British authorities under Queen Elizabeth "for the prevention of false reports."

Actually the *English Mercurie* was issued by the practical joker, Philip Yorke, the intended victim being his friend, Dr. Thomas Birch. At the height of an international controversy over where the first newspaper was published, Yorke caused to be published a few copies of what seemed to be an old paper in small quarto with news from the principal cities of Europe in the manner of eighteenth century gazettes. The account of the Spanish Armada was plagiarized from Thomas Lediard's account.

When Birch died three copies of the fake passed into the possession of the British Museum. They were mentioned in 1782, with no indication of spuriousness, in Ayscough's *Catalogue of the Sloane and Additional MSS.;* but the world first become aware of them with the publication in 1794 of George Chalmers' *Life of Thomas Ruddiman.* Proudly Chalmers wrote:

After inquiring in various countries for the origin of newspapers, I had the satisfaction to find what I sought for in England. It may gratify our national pride to be told that mankind are indebted to the wisdom of Elizabeth and the prudence of Burleigh for the first newspaper. . . . Yet we are told that posts gave rise to weekly newspapers which are, likewise, a French invention. . . . The dates demonstrate that the pleasures and benefits of newspapers were enjoyed in England more than forty years before the establishment of the Paris *Gazette* by Renaudot in France. And the *English Mercurie* will remain an incontestable proof of the existence of a printed newspaper in England at an epoch when no other nation can boast a vehicle of news of a similar kind.

Once started, according to D. T. B. Wood, the statement passed uncritically into every department of literature. It was copied by Nichols in the *Gentleman's Magazine* and appeared in Volume IV of his *Literary Anecdotes.* It was adopted by Isaac D'Israeli in *Curiosities of Literature,* a source containing iconoclastic material regarding several other cases. Thomas Wright, a serious historian, used it in *Queen Elizabeth and Her Times* as late as 1838. "It appeared," says Wood, "unquestioned in dictionaries and encyclopedias, and for forty years it, in fact, was a standard article of curious information, familiar to almost every desultory reader." The story is in *The Art of Needlework* edited by the Countess of Wilton but written by Mrs. Stone, and in *Lives of the Queens of England,* by Agnes Strickland, who, however, admitted it had "incurred the suspicion of being a forgery of modern times but on what grounds I know not."

It was not until 1839, when Thomas Watts, superintendent of the reading room of the British Museum, had occasion to refer to the originals, that suspicion first was aroused regarding the *Mercuries.* In "Letter to Antonia Panizzi" in the *Gentleman's Magazine,* November 16, 1839, he disclosed that the typography of the alleged first newspapers was distinctly of the eighteenth century.

Then began a search of manuscripts in the Museum for the identity of the real author. In a letter to the *Gentleman's Magazine* in 1850, Watts told of the discovery by Sir Henry Ellis, chief librarian, of the handwriting of Lord Hardwicke, otherwise Philip Yorke, which corresponded with that of a manuscript edition of the *Mercuries* which also was discovered in the papers of Dr. Birch.

A Mr. Holmes of the Museum found an entry, *"English Mercuries,* published by authority in Queen Elizabeth, King James and Charles I times," in *Catalogue of the MSS. in the Possession of the Earl of Hardwicke* (1794) and also the preface to *Athenian Letters* (1741 and 1743) in Yorke's handwriting.

Finally the correspondence was found which passed between Birch and Yorke from 1740 to 1745, and this clearly proved the hoax. A study of Thomas Lediard's *Naval History* (London, 1735) revealed where Yorke had obtained his material. All the evidence seems to show that there was no intention to defraud the literary world, the *Mercuries* being merely an idiosyncrasy of the eccentric Yorke to amuse himself and Birch.

Wood commented in the February, 1914, *Nineteenth Century:*

Never was there a better example of innocent fraud, of the credulity of an uncritical antiquary and of the difficulty of catching up a lie which has a good start, than is afforded by the history of these reputed newspapers.

In the British Museum also are to be found two numbers of the *Commonwealth Mercury,* a newspaper of the sixteenth century dated

"From Thursday, Sept. 2, to Thursday, Sept. 9, 1568," and "From Thursday, Novemb. 18, to Thursday, Novemb. 25, 1568." The account of the death and funeral of Oliver Cromwell in *Historical Memorials of Westminster Abbey* by Dean Stanley is based mainly on these two papers, whose spuriousness has been proved.

In the United States it is not necessary to go to a library to find facsimile copies of a number of faked editions of newspapers, notably: the *Boston News Letter* for April 24, 1704; Benjamin Franklin's *New England Courant* for February 11, 1723; the *Boston Gazette and County Journal* for March 12, 1770, containing an account of the Boston Massacre; *Gazette of the United States* for May 2, 1789; the *Ulster County Gazette* for January 4, 1800, with an account of the death and funeral of George Washington; the Vicksburg (Miss.) *Citizen* for July 2, 1863, printed on wallpaper, and the New York *Herald* for April 15, 1865, with an account of the assassination of Abraham Lincoln.

These relics survive today in the long neglected trunks and boxes containing grandmother's souvenirs of the Philadelphia Centennial Exposition of 1876 or the Chicago World's Fair of 1893, and are not originals or, in most cases, even facsimiles of the originals. Despite the efforts of the Library of Congress, of *Editor and Publisher,* of *Publishers' Auxiliary,* and of other newspapermen's trade journals, hardly a month passes without a newspaper somewhere being fooled into printing a feature article about the discovery of a copy of one of these interesting publications. As B. W. Talcott of Aberdeen, Washington, wrote in *Publishers' Auxiliary,* January 29, 1929:

The papers were packed away with the curl from Johnny's head and the piece of Mary's shroud. The possessors died. Their children or their children's children, finding the papers, musty and old, very naturally believed they were the originals instead of facsimiles.

The finders, without the slightest doubt, turned the papers over, probably to a local editor, an enterprising young fellow always seeking the unusual, and he "played them up" very effectively as well as very innocently.

Most frequently reproduced have been the *Ulster County Gazette* and the Vicksburg *Citizen*. R. W. G. Vail of the New York State Library has collected sixty-seven reprints of the former, and it is estimated that more than a million copies of them were distributed. First reprint was made in 1825 in the shop of the *People's Advocate* at Kingsport, New York, as a quarter-century memorial to Washington. In 1848 there was another reprint edition in honor of the fiftieth anniversary of the founding of the paper, successor to the original, and again, in the same shop, in 1850, a half-century after the first president's death.

It was not until 1930 that a genuine original copy of the *Ulster County Gazette* for January 4, 1800, was found. It differs somewhat from the many reprints and is now in the Library of Congress, which has issued pamphlets to help editors, historical societies and others to distinguish authentic from spurious copies of all of the papers mentioned.

The Vicksburg *Citizen* is of interest because it was printed on wallpaper as were many southern newspapers during the last months of the Civil War when their newsprint ran out, and because, after General Grant's soldiers entered the city, they changed Editor J. M. Swords' "On Dit" column to announce their arrival and published the edition two days late.

The actual copies of the *Citizen* were printed on only three styles of wallpaper, whereas the imitators have used many different kinds. The type used by Swords was badly worn; that on which the reprints were produced was in good condition. In addition to these clues, there are many others by which an expert can prove that almost all of the copies now in circulation are fakes.

That old books as well as old trunks may contain traps for the unwary was learned by the editor of the *Golden Book*, who, in July, 1925, used three stanzas which purported to be additions to "The Diverting History of John Gilpin" and a picture of a maiden astride a fence. He got them from Hone's *The Table Book*, Volume III, page 79, where they appear under the title "Mrs. Gilpin Riding to Edmonton" with a notation that they were sent in July 16, 1827, by "A Sojourner at Enfield" who said he found them among the papers of the late Mrs. Unwin in the handwriting of Samuel Cowper. The sketch was believed to be by Romney.

Almost a year later he purchased a set of Charles Lamb's letters published in 1905 by the Bibliophile Society, and discovered among them one confessing that the additional "Gilpin" stanzas had been written by Lamb as a joke. Lamb's house was in the vicinity of Edmonton, from which he sent the verses to a friend to be submitted to Hone. The sketch was of Mary Lamb by Thomas Hood.

"It's a distinction," commented the editor in the May, 1926, *Golden Book*, "to feel one's self hoaxed by Charles Lamb, even almost a century after his death. But surely, surely anybody (except myself) ought to have known the facts and immediately and superiorly corrected the editorial ignorance."

In November, 1939, the *Reader's Digest* innocently used as a "filler" an alleged letter by Cotton Mather, Puritan pastor, stating that a boatload of "100 or more of the heretics and malignants called Quakers, with W. Penn who is the chief scamp at the head" was to be waylaid before it reached Massachusetts Bay colony, "so that the Lord may be glorified and not mocked on the soil of this new country with the heathen worship of these people." According to William F. Poole, founder of *Poole's Index to Periodicals*, this hoary hoax first appeared in the Easton (Pa.) *Argus* in 1870. The *Reader's Digest* got it from *American Government and Its Problems*, by Robert Phillips.

Today the motion pictures are rapidly outdoing gossips, public speakers, newspapers, magazines and book authors in creating and perpetuating historical untruths. Despite the meticulous care with which costumes and furniture are made to seem true to the period of the plot, most films with historical settings are a nightmare for scholars. It is not the introduction of a love theme, recognized by everyone to be an interpolation, but the irreverence shown to easily learned historic facts which causes controversy. For example, Ferdinand de Lesseps was forty-five, not twenty-five, years old when he began supervising the digging of the Suez Canal, and he was not assisted by Napoleon III, who did not mount the French throne until afterward. Nevertheless, Hollywood thought its "Suez" was improved by making De Lesseps younger and Napoleon older.

Historically minded critics have gone into paroxysms over *The Great Waltz* (based on the life of Johann Strauss), *Jesse James, Marie Antoinette, The Buccaneer* (story of the War of 1812 and the pirate Lafitte), *If I Were King* (the chief character of which is François Villon), *Parnell, Zola, Alexander Hamilton, Abraham Lincoln, Rembrandt* and many another so-called historical movie. With the advent of the motion picture, the biographers, poets and historical fictionists have strenuous competition to be first as disseminators of incorrect impressions regarding the past.

Whenever Hollywood starts a new cycle of pictures, all dealing with the same profession or business, those actually engaged in it emit howls of protest. Newspapermen, for instance, complain regretfully that their lives are not so romantic as the movies would lead one to believe: They do not always get their story and their girl, they do remove their hats in the presence of ladies, and they seldom tell an unreasonable, unscrupulous managing editor where to get off. On vacations, Hollywood notwithstanding, they do not always find it impossible to escape revolution, rum and romance, and it is not vouchsafed to every tough cub with a heart of gold to break up at least one criminal gang or prevent one war during his career.

On the 1939 wave of pictures dealing with medical subjects, *Hygeia,* in June, 1939, commented as follows:

Unfortunately in many motion pictures we see too great a departure from reality. No doubt, for purposes of drama, the writer and producer are warranted to take some license with pure fact. . . . In *Dark Victory,* however, the girl suffers with some sort of brain tumor, not to be found in any of the records of brain tumors known to medical science. . . . This was perhaps necessary for timing and emphasis in the drama but may give many a patient with a brain tumor and the families of many such patients hours of unnecessary anguish. . . . The motion picture might be a great force for dramatic education of the public in regard to disease and health and in the campaign for good medical service. What a pity that producers have not seen the possibilities and utilized the public's interest for this purpose!

For the "grand finale" of this entire book nothing can be better than Henry L. Mencken's famous bathtub hoax, which, to a connoisseur of hoaxes, "has everything."

As originally published in the New York *Evening Mail,* December 28, 1917, under the title, "A Neglected Anniversary," it contained information regarding the first American bathtub which, in the years since then, has found its way into innumerable newspaper and magazine articles, into speeches by leading persons in public life, into advertisements for plumbing concerns, into official federal government publications and into serious books on American social history.

Innumerable attempts have been made to check its spread, but it refuses to be downed and is well on its way toward immortality. If someone were able to kill it in this generation, part of the oversized written record unquestionably would be uncovered by some future historian.

The familiar "facts" are as follows:

The first American bathtub was displayed December 10, 1842, by Adam Thompson of Cincinnati, inspired on a European trip by the example of Lord John Russell who, ten years earlier, had introduced the convenience in England. Thompson's tub was constructed of mahogany and lined with sheet lead; he inaugurated it with a stag party at which the entertainment consisted of trying it out.

Although Thompson, a wealthy cotton and grain dealer, looked upon himself as a public benefactor, he was surprised and chagrined to find that others thought otherwise. Physicians denounced the bathtub as a menace to public health. In Boston a city ordinance prohibited its use except upon medical advice. Virginia imposed a thirty-dollar tax on each installation of a bathtub. Hartford, Connecticut, Wilmington, Delaware, and Providence, Rhode Island, all charged extra rates for water used in bathtubs. The Philadelphia city council considered an ordinance forbidding its use from November to May, but the measure was defeated by two votes.

Despite this opposition, it was impossible to legislate the bathtub out of existence. President Millard Fillmore had one put into the White House in the fifties and took the first presidential bath.

"My motive," writes Mencken of his most celebrated brainchild, "was simply to have some harmless fun in war days. It never occurred to me that it would be taken seriously."

How seriously it was taken, the author himself indicated in a syndicated article, "Melancholy Reflections," which appeared May 23, 1926, in thirty widely separated big-city newspapers. It contained the following paragraph to explain the alarm which caused its author to confess:

Pretty soon I began to encounter my preposterous "facts" in the writings of other men. They began to be used by chiropractors and other such quacks as evidence of the stupidity of medical men. They began to be cited by medical men as proof of the progress of public hygiene. They got into learned journals. They were alluded to on the floor of Congress. They crossed the ocean, and were discussed solemnly in England and on the continent. Finally, I began to find them in standard works of reference.

This article, Mencken revealed in his sixth volume of *Prejudices,* appeared, among other places, in the Boston *Herald* with a four-column head and a two-column cartoon labeled satirically, "The American Public Will Swallow Anything." "And then, three weeks later, on June 13, in the same editorial section, but promoted to page one, the same *Herald* reprinted my ten-year-old fake—soberly and as a piece of news," the disillusioned Mencken declared.

The *Herald's* faux pas elicited a second Mencken confession which received wide publicity July 25, 1926. To make a compilation of the later vicissitudes of the bathtub hoax which the compiler would have confidence is anywhere near complete, is impossible. Nevertheless, the following chronology will give some idea of what the situation has been and continues to be:

October, 1926: *Scribner's* includes an article, "Bathtubs, Early Americans," by Fairfax Downey, based almost entirely on Mencken's story.

December 7, 1926: Feature article, "Bathtub Once Forbidden by Law in America," Chicago *Evening American.*

March 21, 1927: Colonel W. G. Archer, representing the National Trade Extension Bureau of the Plumbing and Heating Industry, tells the complete story in an address, "Sanitation and Civilization," before the Commercial Club of Clearfield, Pennsylvania, as reported by the Clearfield *Progress* the next day.

July 15, 1927: *Survey* includes the report of a meeting of social and health workers of New York City. Among the speakers was John H. Finley, chief editorial writer of the New York *Times,* who told Mencken's story as fact. (Within a week, Paul Kellogg, editor of *Survey,* received a letter from Nolan R. Best, of the Baltimore Federation of Churches, pointing out Mencken's confession of the year before. Correspondence between Kellogg and Dr. Finley revealed that the latter had obtained his information through the Cleanliness Institute of New York. Ames and Norr, publicity agents for that organization, subsequently wrote Dr. Finley that the Institute was making "a desperate effort" to find some pre-Mencken authority on the case and in the meantime was making no further use of his data.)

November 7, 1927: The *Chiropractor* for this date contains an article, "S-P-L-A-S-H," by A. J. Pufahl, D.C., beginning: "Did you ever hear the story of the bathtub and its trials before it became popular in America? Did you know that the medical fraternity fought it and condemned baths as dangerous to health?"

November 15, 1927: Mr. Pufahl's article, word for word, appears in the correspondence column of the Cleveland *Press,* over the signature of E. Herschey, D.C., Ph.C. (Evidently it became part of the duty of members of the profession to keep it in circulation.)

February 13, 1929: The *American Baptist* of Lexington, Kentucky, tells the story in an article, "The Bathtub Innovation."

March 16, 1929: In "Baltimore Day by Day," by Carroll Dulaney, in Mencken's own newspaper, the Baltimore *Evening Sun,* the story is told under the heading, "Painting the Lily."

September 26, 1929: The Paris, France, edition of the New York *Herald* rewrites an article by Ruth Wakeman in the New York *Sun* entitled, "Americans Once Frowned on Bathtubs, Condemning Them for Fancied Hazards."

1929: *Saga of the Bathtub,* a pamphlet by Walt Dennison, is published by the Le Roy Carman Printing Company of Los Angeles.

May, 1930: In the "Over the Editor's Desk" column in *House Beautiful* for this month, the story is retold as true.

September, 1930: The *Golden Book* this month prints "Bathing Through the Ages," by Leonora R. Baxter.

October 11 or 12, 1930: In a release which newspapers used on one of these dates, W. Orton Tewson, private syndicate manager, includes in a column of curiosities the origin of the bathtub in Cincinnati and its introduction into the White House.

November 20, 1930: An encouraging sign that the hoax may be beginning to lose its power to convince, is a letter from Edward C. Aswell, assistant editor of *Forum,* to Mencken, asking him to comment on an article by George T. Nieberg which has been submitted to that magazine. (As a result of Mencken's critical examination, this article appeared without inaccuracies as "Endless Saturday Nights" in the February, 1931, *Forum.*)

November 28, 1930: A Western Newspaper Union release of this date is an article by Elmo Scott Watson, "James, Draw My Bawth," in which Mencken's part in the story is frankly revealed. Much of the article is taken from Mencken's 1926 confession.

January, 1931: Charles Scribner's Sons publish *Puritan's Progress,* by Arthur Train. Readers may turn to page 51 for "facts" about the bathtub in early days.

February 17, 1931: Although a minor feature of Train's book, the "facts" about the bathtub are considered significant enough to figure in the review given it by the New York *Sun.*

March 4, 1931: The New York *Herald Tribune* rewrites Mrs. Baxter's *Golden Book* article, heading it "Baths in Disfavor for Long Periods, History Recalls."

May 22, 1931: In a letter which the editor heads, "Isn't It Marvelous How Much One Head Can Hold?" consisting of a series of paragraphs of useless facts, the bathtub is said to have been originated in Cincinnati. This is in the Baltimore *Evening Sun,* in whose office Mencken has a desk.

December 1, 1931: The Tucson, Arizona, *Daily Star* interviews C. R. King, manager of the Standard Sanitary Manufacturing Company branch in Tucson, on the imminent birthday of the bathtub. Mr. King, who according to the *Star* "had apparently studied the matter considerably," hands out the same old facts, which are printed under a two-column head, "Bathtub Will Have Birthday in America During December."

December 22, 1931: The New York *Sun* again tells the story, "When Bathtubs Were Luxuries and Soap Seemed Lost to Civilization." This is a reprint from the *Military Engineer*.

August 21, 1932: An editorial in the Macon, Georgia, *Telegraph* tells of Mencken's confession and of the distribution in that city of a pamphlet, *The Story of the Bath,* by the Domestic Engineering Company of Chicago, reviewed seriously some time before by the *Telegraph*.

1933: Joseph Nathan Kane writes his 757-page *Famous First Facts,* which the H. W. Wilson Company publishes. On page 81 the "first facts" concerning the bathtub are entirely Mencken's.

April 27, 1933: A United Features Syndicate feature, "How It Began," by Russ Murphy and Ray Nenuskay includes an illustration of Adam Thompson in his first bathtub.

October 12, 1933: In an advertisement for "Blue Coal" in the New York *Sun,* a policeman of about the year 1842 is shown threatening to arrest a man in a bathtub.

1935: Dr. Hans Zinsser, professor in the Medical School of Harvard University, says on page 285 of his best-selling *Rats, Lice and History*: "The first bathtub didn't reach America, we believe, until about 1840."

January, 1935: In the Federal Housing Administration Clip Sheet, Vol. II, No. 9, is an article, "Bathtub History in U. S. Traced to Days of Benjamin Franklin," which contains all the spurious facts. (Many newspapers undoubtedly used it.)

February 24, 1935: Alexander Woollcott in his "Town Crier" radio broadcast says of the year 1841, "The first bathtub had not yet been installed in the White House."

August 4, 1935: In an article, "The Bathtub Wins Wider Patronage," based on a petition of East Side tenants for installation of bathtubs, the New York *Times* says in part: "It was with fear and travail that bathtubs were introduced in these United States. One of the first bathrooms appeared in Cincinnati, Ohio, about 1850, and certain clergymen hearing of it preached that such luxury meant nothing less than degeneracy."

September 26, 1935: The United Press includes in its *Red Letter* the following under an Allentown, Pennsylvania, date line: "In the middle of the nineteenth century the bathtub was classed as a 'curse' to humanity and measures were taken to discourage its use, according to James Weiss, manufacturer of bathtubs." (The St. Louis *Star-Times* used this as late as June 23, 1936, evidently having kept it in its tray of "fillers" all that time.)

October 5, 1935: In a letter to the *New Statesman* J. Vijaya-Tunga repeats the story.

October, 1935: A bulletin of the Department of Health of Kentucky includes the "facts."

November 15, 1935: R. J. Scott's "Scott's Scrapbook," syndicated by the Central Press Association, includes a sketch of a policeman chasing a bather away from his bath, together with the caption: "As late as 1842 some American cities prohibited the use of bathtubs."

December, 1935: The *Digest and Review* prints the "facts."

December 31, 1935: The Melbourne *Australia Age* reprints J. Vijaya-Tunga's letter.

January 23, 1936: The Chicago *Times* quotes a speaker at a meeting of the American Institute of Banking in Chicago as saying: "Why, do you know that when the first bathtubs were introduced in America, intellectual Boston passed an ordinance making it unlawful to bathe in a bathtub except on medical advice?"

March 31, 1936: One of the "Twenty Questions" in *Liberty* is: "In which city of the United States was it against the law to take a bath in 1845?" To which the answer is: "In Boston, Mass. It was then deemed unlawful to take a bath except when prescribed by a physician."

May 27, 1936: Dr. Shirley W. Wynne, former commissioner of health for New York City, uses the "facts" in a radio address, "What Is Public Health?" over WEAF.

July 11, 1936: Under the heading "Bathtub Suffered Same Fate in U. S. As Most Pioneers," the Chicago *Daily News* tells the story with credit to a recent issue of *Architecture.*

October 19, 1936: The author of an article, "Some Historic Lore of the White House," in the *United States News* declares that Dolly Madison established the first bathroom but that "so great was the hue and cry against this innovation from a nation which saw no literal connection between cleanliness and godliness that it caused a minor scandal. Bathing of that nature was considered not merely unhygienic and undemocratic but very close to immorality." Andrew Jackson, the article says, eliminated the bathroom, but Millard Fillmore restored it: "Even then there were memories, at least, of a Philadelphia ordinance which prohibited intemperate bathing without a physician's sanction except in summer."

January 25, 1937: At the time of the devastating Ohio Valley flood, the Associated Press sends out the following under a Cincinnati date line: "A wry smile from the flood zone: Cincinnati, where there is plenty

of water but little to drink and none in which to bathe, is generally credited with the origin of the bathtub. The first tub, built by Adam Thompson of mahogany and sheet lead, was installed in his house in 1842. It
is recorded that the first day Thompson took two baths in it, and on
Christmas Day invited 40 guests, all of whom tried a plunge."

February, 1937: The United Press *Red Letter* includes a story from
Cambridge, Massachusetts, that Dr. Cecil K. Drinker, dean and professor of physiology at the Harvard School of Public Health, has discovered
that his great-great-grandmother, Elizabeth Drinker of Philadelphia, had
a bathtub in her home as early as 1803, thus disputing Cincinnati's claim to
fame for having the first American bathtub. (The Chicago *Daily News*
used the story March 27, 1937.)

February 20, 1937: As an advertisement of a syndicated feature, Western Newspaper Union, in *Publishers' Auxiliary*, which it publishes, runs
a sample of a column, " 'Twas This Way," by Lyle Spencer including the
entire story under the subhead, "The First Bathtub."

April 11, 1937: An article, "The Bathtub as a Symbol of Equality,"
by Donald B. Willard, syndicated by the North American Newspaper
Alliance, appears in the Detroit *News,* with all the "facts."

May 25, 1937: On its editorial page the Kansas City *Star* reprints the
following by Representative Frank Carlson in Quinter *Advocate*: "President Fillmore installed the first bathtub in the White House, while Boston still had a law against taking a bath without medical advice."

June 19, 1937: The Akron *Beacon-Journal* published the Adam Thompson myth as a research discovery of A. W. Dickson, executive secretary to
the Builders Exchange.

1937: "the slow acceptance of the bathtub" was used by Lyndon Brown,
then associate professor of marketing and advertising at Northwestern
University and later president of Knox College, as an illustration of how
slowly market changes occur, on page 41 of *Marketing Research and
Analysis* (Ronald Press, 1937).

1941: A more elaborate use of the "facts," including mention of specific
laws, was given in Paragraph 2 of Chapter 1, "Why Study Advertising?"
of *Effective Advertising* (McGraw-Hill, 1941) by Harry Walker Hepner
of the College of Business Administration of Syracuse University. In the
1956 edition, renamed *Modern Advertising,* the author still insists that advertising popularized bathtubs but omits the spurious Mencken information. In a footnote in the earlier book authority is cited as *Advertising—the
Accelerator of Civilization* by Alfred T. Falk, published by the Bureau of
Research and Education of the Advertising Federation of America, as No.
3 of its 1931 series:

August 17, 1938: Flora MacFarland in her "Look for Your Answer Here" column in the Cleveland *Plain-Dealer* informs a correspondent that the first user of a bathtub in this country was Eli Whitney, inventor of the cotton gin, who imported one in 1820 from England, and that the second user was Adam Thompson of Cincinnati in 1842. She then proceeds to tell the rest of Mencken's story, explaining that President Fillmore's action was intended to prevent malaria, then prevalent in the nation's capital.

September 28, 1938: Hearst's *American Weekly* includes an article, "There's a Lot of History Behind Your Bathtub," by Virginia S. Eiffert, research expert and contributor to *Natural History*, official magazine of the American Museum of Natural History, New York City, and other publications. Miss Eiffert's research has uncovered the old stand-by.

Jan. 10, 1942: Included in an editorial, "Imagineering," in the Chicago *Sunday Times* was the following: "The anti-imagineer was against bathtubs when they were invented. He insisted that bathing was unhealthy."

Sept. 20, 1942: Julia Spiegelman retold the entire Adam Thompson tale as fact in an article, "Bathtub's United States Centennial" in the Baltimore *Sun*, Mencken's own newspaper.

April 28, 1951: In this day's issue of *The New Yorker* John Hersey revealed, in a profile on Harry S. Truman, that "the president seemed reluctant to let go of his belief" in the fact that Millard Fillmore introduced the first bathtub into the White House in 1850. President Truman was known to include the spurious facts in the "lecture" he gave visitors to the renovated executive mansion.

Sept. 16, 1952: In a speech in Philadelphia, President Truman told the story to illustrate what great progress has occurred in public health.

April 13, 1954: Paul Gibson, radio commentator, used the story in its entirety in a broadcast from Miami Beach, Fla.

If the publishers will include a blank page or two after this one, dear reader, you can continue this chronology yourself. Your alertness soon will be rewarded if you keep on the outlook for the "facts" regarding the introduction of the bathtub in America. In fact, if you are so minded, within a comparatively brief space of time, you can produce a fair-sized scrapbook containing, not only this classic of classics but others of the five-hundred-odd anecdotes with which the writer hopes he has both entertained and instructed you.

Index

Abbeville, France, 114
Abbot, Willis J., 166, 250
Aberdeen, Scotland, 92
Aberdeen, Wash., 299
Ackley, Iowa, 101
Acme Newspictures, 192
Acquanetta, Burnu, 59
Adalbert, Max, 54
Adams, James Truslow, 88, 90, 169
Adams, John Quincy, 90, 286
Adams Manuscript Trust, 10
Adams, Samuel Hopkins, 170, 177
Adrian I, Pope, 198
Adrianus of Troy, 171
Adventure. *See* Travel
"Advertisement of death," 290–291
Africa, South, 143–144, 229–231
Agar, Herbert, 163
Agricultural Adjustment Administration, 94
Aiken, S.C., 132
Ainsworth, F. C., 115
Ajax, 264
Akron, Ohio, 57; *Beacon Journal*, 308
Alabama, 15, 284; University of, 165
Alaska, 9, 16–17
Albany, N.Y., 259
Alberti, Leandro, 220
Albion, Nebr., 285
Alcibades, 219
Alden, John, 159
Alexander, John M., 111
Alexander II, Czar, 202
Alexander the Great, 117, 148
Alexandria, Egypt, 149, 194
Alexandria, Va., 131
Alfred the Great, 86
Allegheny City, Pa., 37
Allen, Robert S., 292
Allen, Sally Sue, 226
Allentown, Pa., 306
Alleyn, Ned, 215
Alligators, 12, 31–32
Almanacs, 30, 223, 235, 269
Alvord, F. Reed, 108
Ambigat, 117
American Baptist, 304
American Board of Commissioners for Foreign Missions, 168
American Civil Liberties Union, 280
American Historical Association, 167
American Historical Review, 107, 111
American Journal of Sociology, 41
American Legion, 277
American Machinist, 290

American Magazine, 26, 29
American Mercury, 168
American Museum of Natural History, 208, 309
American Patriotic League, 258
American Press, vi
American Weekly, 96, 309
American Writing Company, 85
Amphion, 149
Amsterdam, 127
Amtorg Trading Corporation, 191
Anacreon, 219
Anastasia Romanoff, 58
Ancestry, 86
Ancient Mariner, 26
Anderson, Andrew, 111
Anderson, Prof. Rasmus, 110
Andover, Mass., 82
Andrea del Sarto, 152
Angle, Paul M., 164
d'Angoulême, Duc, 108
Animals, 3–5, 11–12, 15, 17–18, 24–27, 63, 232, 243, 282
Anne, Queen, 172, 294
Annius of Viterbo, 220
Annual Register, 167
Anthropology, 114, 126–128, 206–208
Antiques, 81–82
Antoninus Pius, 220
Ants, 11
Anu-Heliopolis, 97
Apes, 207–208
Apocrypha, 195–197
Apostles' Creed, 199
Appleseed, Johnny, 293, 294–295
Appleton (Wis.) *Crescent*, 283
Appleton's Cyclopedia of American Biography, 227
April Fool, 9, 40, 224, 247
Aquinas, St. Thomas, 197
Arbiter, Petronius, 221
Arbuthnot, John, 224
Arcadia, 123
Arcadia, Mo., 93
Arch Street Museum, 32, 136
Archaeology, 125–128, 206–207
Archer, Robert, 60
Archer, Col. W. G., 304
Architecture, 307
Archko Volume, 95–96
Arctic, 22, 119–121
Aristotle, 117, 148, 149, 199
Arizona, 16, 248
Arkansas, 16, 264

311

A CATALOGUE OF SELECTED DOVER BOOKS
IN ALL FIELDS OF INTEREST

A CATALOGUE OF SELECTED DOVER BOOKS
IN ALL FIELDS OF INTEREST

THE NOTEBOOKS OF LEONARDO DA VINCI, edited by J.P. Richter. Extracts from manuscripts reveal great genius; on painting, sculpture, anatomy, sciences, geography, etc. Both Italian and English. 186 ms. pages reproduced, plus 500 additional drawings, including studies for Last Supper, Sforza monument, etc. 860pp. 7⅞ x 10¾. USO 22572-0, 22573-9 Pa., Two vol. set $15.90

ART NOUVEAU DESIGNS IN COLOR, Alphonse Mucha, Maurice Verneuil, Georges Auriol. Full-color reproduction of Combinaisons ornamentales (c. 1900) by Art Nouveau masters. Floral, animal, geometric, interlacings, swashes — borders, frames, spots — all incredibly beautiful. 60 plates, hundreds of designs. 9⅜ x 8 1/16 . 22885-1 Pa. $4.00

GRAPHIC WORKS OF ODILON REDON. All great fantastic lithographs, etchings, engravings, drawings, 209 in all. Monsters, Huysmans, still life work, etc. Introduction by Alfred Werner. 209pp. 9⅛ x 12¼. 21996-8 Pa. $6.00

EXOTIC FLORAL PATTERNS IN COLOR, E.-A. Seguy. Incredibly beautiful full-color pochoir work by great French designer of 20's. Complete Bouquets et frondaisons, Suggestions pour étoffes. Richness must be seen to be believed. 40 plates containing 120 patterns. 80pp. 9⅜ x 12¼. 23041-4 Pa. $6.00

SELECTED ETCHINGS OF JAMES A. McN. WHISTLER, James A. McN. Whistler. 149 outstanding etchings by the great American artist, including selections from the Thames set and two Venice sets, the complete French set, and many individual prints. Introduction and explanatory note on each print by Maria Naylor. 157pp. 9⅜ x 12¼. 23194-1 Pa. $5.00

VISUAL ILLUSIONS: THEIR CAUSES, CHARACTERISTICS, AND APPLICATIONS, Matthew Luckiesh. Thorough description, discussion; shape and size, color, motion; natural illusion. Uses in art and industry. 100 illustrations. 252pp. 21530-X Pa. $2.50

TEN BOOKS ON ARCHITECTURE, Vitruvius. The most important book ever written on architecture. Early Roman aesthetics, technology, classical orders, site selection, all other aspects. Stands behind everything since. Morgan translation. 331pp. 20645-9 Pa. $3.50

THE CODEX NUTTALL, A PICTURE MANUSCRIPT FROM ANCIENT MEXICO, as first edited by Zelia Nuttall. Only inexpensive edition, in full color, of a pre-Columbian Mexican (Mixtec) book. 88 color plates show kings, gods, heroes, temples, sacrifices. New explanatory, historical introduction by Arthur G. Miller. 96pp. 11⅜ x 8½. 23168-2 Pa. $7.50

How to Solve Chess Problems, Kenneth S. Howard. Practical suggestions on problem solving for very beginners. 58 two-move problems, 46 3-movers, 8 4-movers for practice, plus hints. 171pp. 20748-X Pa. $2.00

A Guide to Fairy Chess, Anthony Dickins. 3-D chess, 4-D chess, chess on a cylindrical board, reflecting pieces that bounce off edges, cooperative chess, retrograde chess, maximummers, much more. Most based on work of great Dawson. Full handbook, 100 problems. 66pp. 7⅞ x 10¾. 22687-5 Pa. $2.00

Win at Backgammon, Millard Hopper. Best opening moves, running game, blocking game, back game, tables of odds, etc. Hopper makes the game clear enough for anyone to play, and win. 43 diagrams. 111pp. 22894-0 Pa. $1.50

Bidding a Bridge Hand, Terence Reese. Master player "thinks out loud" the binding of 75 hands that defy point count systems. Organized by bidding problem—no-fit situations, overbidding, underbidding, cueing your defense, etc. 254pp. EBE 22830-4 Pa. $3.00

The Precision Bidding System in Bridge, C.C. Wei, edited by Alan Truscott. Inventor of precision bidding presents average hands and hands from actual play, including games from 1969 Bermuda Bowl where system emerged. 114 exercises. 116pp. 21171-1 Pa. $1.75

Learn Magic, Henry Hay. 20 simple, easy-to-follow lessons on magic for the new magician: illusions, card tricks, silks, sleights of hand, coin manipulations, escapes, and more —all with a minimum amount of equipment. Final chapter explains the great stage illusions. 92 illustrations. 285pp. 21238-6 Pa. $2.95

The New Magician's Manual, Walter B. Gibson. Step-by-step instructions and clear illustrations guide the novice in mastering 36 tricks; much equipment supplied on 16 pages of cut-out materials. 36 additional tricks. 64 illustrations. 159pp. 6⅝ x 10. 23113-5 Pa. $3.00

Professional Magic for Amateurs, Walter B. Gibson. 50 easy, effective tricks used by professionals —cards, string, tumblers, handkerchiefs, mental magic, etc. 63 illustrations. 223pp. 23012-0 Pa. $2.50

Card Manipulations, Jean Hugard. Very rich collection of manipulations; has taught thousands of fine magicians tricks that are really workable, eye-catching. Easily followed, serious work. Over 200 illustrations. 163pp. 20539-8 Pa. $2.00

Abbott's Encyclopedia of Rope Tricks for Magicians, Stewart James. Complete reference book for amateur and professional magicians containing more than 150 tricks involving knots, penetrations, cut and restored rope, etc. 510 illustrations. Reprint of 3rd edition. 400pp. 23206-9 Pa. $3.50

The Secrets of Houdini, J.C. Cannell. Classic study of Houdini's incredible magic, exposing closely-kept professional secrets and revealing, in general terms, the whole art of stage magic. 67 illustrations. 279pp. 22913-0 Pa. $2.50

HOUDINI ON MAGIC, Harold Houdini. Edited by Walter Gibson, Morris N. Young. How he escaped; exposés of fake spiritualists; instructions for eye-catching tricks; other fascinating material by and about greatest magician. 155 illustrations. 280pp. 20384-0 Pa. $2.75

HANDBOOK OF THE NUTRITIONAL CONTENTS OF FOOD, U.S. Dept. of Agriculture. Largest, most detailed source of food nutrition information ever prepared. Two mammoth tables: one measuring nutrients in 100 grams of edible portion; the other, in edible portion of 1 pound as purchased. Originally titled Composition of Foods. 190pp. 9 x 12. 21342-0 Pa. $4.00

COMPLETE GUIDE TO HOME CANNING, PRESERVING AND FREEZING, U.S. Dept. of Agriculture. Seven basic manuals with full instructions for jams and jellies; pickles and relishes; canning fruits, vegetables, meat; freezing anything. Really good recipes, exact instructions for optimal results. Save a fortune in food. 156 illustrations. 214pp. 6⅛ x 9¼. 22911-4 Pa. $2.50

THE BREAD TRAY, Louis P. De Gouy. Nearly every bread the cook could buy or make: bread sticks of Italy, fruit breads of Greece, glazed rolls of Vienna, everything from corn pone to croissants. Over 500 recipes altogether. including buns, rolls, muffins, scones, and more. 463pp. 23000-7 Pa. $3.50

CREATIVE HAMBURGER COOKERY, Louis P. De Gouy. 182 unusual recipes for casseroles, meat loaves and hamburgers that turn inexpensive ground meat into memorable main dishes: Arizona chili burgers, burger tamale pie, burger stew, burger corn loaf, burger wine loaf, and more. 120pp. 23001-5 Pa. $1.75

LONG ISLAND SEAFOOD COOKBOOK, J. George Frederick and Jean Joyce. Probably the best American seafood cookbook. Hundreds of recipes. 40 gourmet sauces, 123 recipes using oysters alone! All varieties of fish and seafood amply represented. 324pp. 22677-8 Pa. $3.50

THE EPICUREAN: A COMPLETE TREATISE OF ANALYTICAL AND PRACTICAL STUDIES IN THE CULINARY ART, Charles Ranhofer. Great modern classic. 3,500 recipes from master chef of Delmonico's, turn-of-the-century America's best restaurant. Also explained, many techniques known only to professional chefs. 775 illustrations. 1183pp. 6⅝ x 10. 22680-8 Clothbd. $22.50

THE AMERICAN WINE COOK BOOK, Ted Hatch. Over 700 recipes: old favorites livened up with wine plus many more: Czech fish soup, quince soup, sauce Perigueux, shrimp shortcake, filets Stroganoff, cordon bleu goulash, jambonneau, wine fruit cake, more. 314pp. 22796-0 Pa. $2.50

DELICIOUS VEGETARIAN COOKING, Ivan Baker. Close to 500 delicious and varied recipes: soups, main course dishes (pea, bean, lentil, cheese, vegetable, pasta, and egg dishes), savories, stews, whole-wheat breads and cakes, more. 168pp.
USO 22834-7 Pa. $1.75

EAST O' THE SUN AND WEST O' THE MOON, George W. Dasent. Considered the best of all translations of these Norwegian folk tales, this collection has been enjoyed by generations of children (and folklorists too). Includes True and Untrue, Why the Sea is Salt, East O' the Sun and West O' the Moon, Why the Bear is Stumpy-Tailed, Boots and the Troll, The Cock and the Hen, Rich Peter the Pedlar, and 52 more. The only edition with all 59 tales. 77 illustrations by Erik Werenskiold and Theodor Kittelsen. xv + 418pp. 22521-6 Paperbound **$4.00**

GOOPS AND HOW TO BE THEM, Gelett Burgess. Classic of tongue-in-cheek humor, masquerading as etiquette book. 87 verses, twice as many cartoons, show mischievous Goops as they demonstrate to children virtues of table manners, neatness, courtesy, etc. Favorite for generations. viii + 88pp. 6½ x 9¼. 22233-0 Paperbound **$2.00**

ALICE'S ADVENTURES UNDER GROUND, Lewis Carroll. The first version, quite different from the final *Alice in Wonderland,* printed out by Carroll himself with his own illustrations. Complete facsimile of the "million dollar" manuscript Carroll gave to Alice Liddell in 1864. Introduction by Martin Gardner. viii + 96pp. Title and dedication pages in color. 21482-6 Paperbound **$1.50**

THE BROWNIES, THEIR BOOK, Palmer Cox. Small as mice, cunning as foxes, exuberant and full of mischief, the Brownies go to the zoo, toy shop, seashore, circus, etc., in 24 verse adventures and 266 illustrations. Long a favorite, since their first appearance in St. Nicholas Magazine. xi + 144pp. 6⅝ x 9¼. 21265-3 Paperbound **$2.50**

SONGS OF CHILDHOOD, Walter De La Mare. Published (under the pseudonym Walter Ramal) when De La Mare was only 29, this charming collection has long been a favorite children's book. A facsimile of the first edition in paper, the 47 poems capture the simplicity of the nursery rhyme and the ballad, including such lyrics as I Met Eve, Tartary, The Silver Penny. vii + 106pp. (USO) 21972-0 Paperbound **$2.00**

THE COMPLETE NONSENSE OF EDWARD LEAR, Edward Lear. The finest 19th-century humorist-cartoonist in full: all nonsense limericks, zany alphabets, Owl and Pussycat, songs, nonsense botany, and more than 500 illustrations by Lear himself. Edited by Holbrook Jackson. xxix + 287pp. (USO) 20167-8 Paperbound **$3.00**

BILLY WHISKERS: THE AUTOBIOGRAPHY OF A GOAT, Frances Trego Montgomery. A favorite of children since the early 20th century, here are the escapades of that rambunctious, irresistible and mischievous goat—Billy Whiskers. Much in the spirit of *Peck's Bad Boy,* this is a book that children never tire of reading or hearing. All the original familiar illustrations by W. H. Fry are included: 6 color plates, 18 black and white drawings. 159pp. 22345-0 Paperbound **$2.75**

MOTHER GOOSE MELODIES. Faithful republication of the fabulously rare Munroe and Francis "copyright 1833" Boston edition—the most important Mother Goose collection, usually referred to as the "original." Familiar rhymes plus many rare ones, with wonderful old woodcut illustrations. Edited by E. F. Bleiler. 128pp. 4½ x 6⅜. 22577-1 Paperbound **$1.50**

DECORATIVE ALPHABETS AND INITIALS, edited by Alexander Nesbitt. 91 complete alphabets (medieval to modern), 3924 decorative initials, including Victorian novelty and Art Nouveau. 192pp. 7¾ x 10¾. 20544-4 Pa. $4.00

CALLIGRAPHY, Arthur Baker. Over 100 original alphabets from the hand of our greatest living calligrapher: simple, bold, fine-line, richly ornamented, etc. — all strikingly original and different, a fusion of many influences and styles. 155pp. 11⅜ x 8¼. 22895-9 Pa. $4.50

MONOGRAMS AND ALPHABETIC DEVICES, edited by Hayward and Blanche Cirker. Over 2500 combinations, names, crests in very varied styles: script engraving, ornate Victorian, simple Roman, and many others. 226pp. 8⅛ x 11. 22330-2 Pa. $5.00

THE BOOK OF SIGNS, Rudolf Koch. Famed German type designer renders 493 symbols: religious, alchemical, imperial, runes, property marks, etc. Timeless. 104pp. 6⅛ x 9¼. 20162-7 Pa. $1.75

200 DECORATIVE TITLE PAGES, edited by Alexander Nesbitt. 1478 to late 1920's. Baskerville, Dürer, Beardsley, W. Morris, Pyle, many others in most varied techniques. For posters, programs, other uses. 222pp. 8⅜ x 11¼. 21264-5 Pa. **$5.00**

DICTIONARY OF AMERICAN PORTRAITS, edited by Hayward and Blanche Cirker. 4000 important Americans, earliest times to 1905, mostly in clear line. Politicians, writers, soldiers, scientists, inventors, industrialists, Indians, Blacks, women, outlaws, etc. Identificatory information. 756pp. 9¼ x 12¾. 21823-6 Clothbd. $30.00

ART FORMS IN NATURE, Ernst Haeckel. Multitude of strangely beautiful natural forms: Radiolaria, Foraminifera, jellyfishes, fungi, turtles, bats, etc. All 100 plates of the 19th century evolutionist's Kunstformen der Natur (1904). 100pp. 9⅜ x 12¼. 22987-4 Pa. $4.00

DECOUPAGE: THE BIG PICTURE SOURCEBOOK, Eleanor Rawlings. Make hundreds of beautiful objects, over 550 florals, animals, letters, shells, period costumes, frames, etc. selected by foremost practitioner. Printed on one side of page. 8 color plates. Instructions. 176pp. 9³/₁₆ x 12¼. 23182-8 Pa. $5.00

AMERICAN FOLK DECORATION, Jean Lipman, Eve Meulendyke. Thorough coverage of all aspects of wood, tin, leather, paper, cloth decoration — scapes, humans, trees, flowers, geometrics — and how to make them. Full instructions. 233 illustrations, 5 in color. 163pp. 8⅜ x 11¼. 22217-9 Pa. $3.95

WHITTLING AND WOODCARVING, E.J. Tangerman. Best book on market; clear, full. If you can cut a potato, you can carve toys, puzzles, chains, caricatures, masks, patterns, frames, decorate surfaces, etc. Also covers serious wood sculpture. Over 200 photos. 293pp. 20965-2 Pa. $3.00

VISUAL ILLUSIONS: THEIR CAUSES, CHARACTERISTICS, AND APPLICATIONS, Matthew Luckiesh. Thorough description and discussion of optical illusion, geometric and perspective, particularly; size and shape distortions, illusions of color, of motion; natural illusions; use of illusion in art and magic, industry, etc. Most useful today with op art, also for classical art. Scores of effects illustrated. Introduction by William H. Ittleson. 100 illustrations. xxi + 252pp.

21530-X Paperbound $2.50

A HANDBOOK OF ANATOMY FOR ART STUDENTS, Arthur Thomson. Thorough, virtually exhaustive coverage of skeletal structure, musculature, etc. Full text, supplemented by anatomical diagrams and drawings and by photographs of undraped figures. Unique in its comparison of male and female forms, pointing out differences of contour, texture, form. 211 figures, 40 drawings, 86 photographs. xx + 459pp. 5⅜ x 8⅜.

21163-0 Paperbound $5.00

150 MASTERPIECES OF DRAWING, Selected by Anthony Toney. Full page reproductions of drawings from the early 16th to the end of the 18th century, all beautifully reproduced: Rembrandt, Michelangelo, Dürer, Fragonard, Urs, Graf, Wouwerman, many others. First-rate browsing book, model book for artists. xviii + 150pp. 8⅜ x 11¼.

21032-4 Paperbound $4.00

THE LATER WORK OF AUBREY BEARDSLEY, Aubrey Beardsley. Exotic, erotic, ironic masterpieces in full maturity: Comedy Ballet, Venus and Tannhauser, Pierrot, Lysistrata, Rape of the Lock, Savoy material, Ali Baba, Volpone, etc. This material revolutionized the art world, and is still powerful, fresh, brilliant. With *The Early Work*, all Beardsley's finest work. 174 plates, 2 in color. xiv + 176pp. 8⅛ x 11.

21817-1 Paperbound $4.00

DRAWINGS OF REMBRANDT, Rembrandt van Rijn. Complete reproduction of fabulously rare edition by Lippmann and Hofstede de Groot, completely reedited, updated, improved by Prof. Seymour Slive, Fogg Museum. Portraits, Biblical sketches, landscapes, Oriental types, nudes, episodes from classical mythology—All Rembrandt's fertile genius. Also selection of drawings by his pupils and followers. "Stunning volumes," *Saturday Review*. 550 illustrations. lxxviii + 552pp. 9⅛ x 12¼.

21485-0, 21486-9 Two volumes, Paperbound $12.00

THE DISASTERS OF WAR, Francisco Goya. One of the masterpieces of Western civilization—83 etchings that record Goya's shattering, bitter reaction to the Napoleonic war that swept through Spain after the insurrection of 1808 and to war in general. Reprint of the first edition, with three additional plates from Boston's Museum of Fine Arts. All plates facsimile size. Introduction by Philip Hofer, Fogg Museum. v + 97pp. 9⅜ x 8¼.

21872-4 Paperbound $3.00

GRAPHIC WORKS OF ODILON REDON. Largest collection of Redon's graphic works ever assembled: 172 lithographs, 28 etchings and engravings, 9 drawings. These include some of his most famous works. All the plates from *Odilon Redon: oeuvre graphique complet*, plus additional plates. New introduction and caption translations by Alfred Werner. 209 illustrations. xxvii + 209pp. 9⅛ x 12¼.

21966-8 Paperbound $6.00

AGAINST THE GRAIN (A REBOURS), Joris K. Huysmans. Filled with weird images evidences of a bizarre imagination, exotic experiments with hallucinatory drugs, rich tastes and smells and the diversions of its sybarite hero Duc Jean des Esseintes, this classic novel pushed 19th-century literary decadence to its limits. Full unabridged edition. Do not confuse this with abridged editions generally sold. Introduction by Havelock Ellis. xlix + 206pp. 22190-3 Paperbound **$2.50**

VARIORUM SHAKESPEARE: HAMLET. Edited by Horace H. Furness; a landmark of American scholarship. Exhaustive footnotes and appendices treat all doubtful words and phrases, as well as suggested critical emendations throughout the play's history. First volume contains editor's own text, collated with all Quartos and Folios. Second volume contains full first Quarto, translations of Shakespeare's sources (Belleforest, and Saxo Grammaticus), Der Bestrafte Brudermord, and many essays on critical and historical points of interest by major authorities of past and present. Includes details of staging and costuming over the years. By far the best edition available for serious students of Shakespeare. Total of xx + 905pp. 21004-9, 21005-7, 2 volumes, Paperbound **$11.00**

A LIFE OF WILLIAM SHAKESPEARE, Sir Sidney Lee. This is the standard life of Shakespeare, summarizing everything known about Shakespeare and his plays. Incredibly rich in material, broad in coverage, clear and judicious, it has served thousands as the best introduction to Shakespeare. 1931 edition. 9 plates. xxix + 792pp. 21967-4 Paperbound **$4.50**

MASTERS OF THE DRAMA, John Gassner. Most comprehensive history of the drama in print, covering every tradition from Greeks to modern Europe and America, including India, Far East, etc. Covers more than 800 dramatists, 2000 plays, with biographical material, plot summaries, theatre history, criticism, etc. "Best of its kind in English," *New Republic*. 77 illustrations. xxii + 890pp. 20100-7 Clothbound **$10.00**

THE EVOLUTION OF THE ENGLISH LANGUAGE, George McKnight. The growth of English, from the 14th century to the present. Unusual, non-technical account presents basic information in very interesting form: sound shifts, change in grammar and syntax, vocabulary growth, similar topics. Abundantly illustrated with quotations. Formerly *Modern English in the Making*. xii + 590pp. 21932-1 Paperbound **$4.00**

AN ETYMOLOGICAL DICTIONARY OF MODERN ENGLISH, Ernest Weekley. Fullest, richest work of its sort, by foremost British lexicographer. Detailed word histories, including many colloquial and archaic words; extensive quotations. Do not confuse this with the Concise Etymological Dictionary, which is much abridged. Total xxvii + 830pp. 6½ x 9¼. 21873-2, 21874-0 Two volumes, Paperbound **$10.00**

FLATLAND: A ROMANCE OF MANY DIMENSIONS, E. A. Abbott. Classic of science-fiction explores ramifications of life in a two-dimensional world, and what happens when a three-dimensional being intrudes. Amusing reading, but also useful as introduction to thought about hyperspace. Introduction by Banesh Hoffmann. 16 illustrations. xx + 103pp. 20001-9 Paperbound **$1.50**

EGYPTIAN MAGIC, E.A. Wallis Budge. Foremost Egyptologist, curator at British Museum, on charms, curses, amulets, doll magic, transformations, control of demons, deific appearances, feats of great magicians. Many texts cited. 19 illustrations. 234pp. USO 22681-6 Pa. $2.50

THE LEYDEN PAPYRUS: AN EGYPTIAN MAGICAL BOOK, edited by F. Ll. Griffith, Herbert Thompson. Egyptian sorcerer's manual contains scores of spells: sex magic of various sorts, occult information, evoking visions, removing evil magic, etc. Transliteration faces translation. 207pp. 22994-7 Pa. $2.50

THE MALLEUS MALEFICARUM OF KRAMER AND SPRENGER, translated, edited by Montague Summers. Full text of most important witchhunter's "Bible," used by both Catholics and Protestants. Theory of witches, manifestations, remedies, etc. Indispensable to serious student. 278pp. 6⅝ x 10. USO 22802-9 Pa. $3.95

LOST CONTINENTS, L. Sprague de Camp. Great science-fiction author, finest, fullest study: Atlantis, Lemuria, Mu, Hyperborea, etc. Lost Tribes, Irish in pre-Columbian America, root races; in history, literature, art, occultism. Necessary to everyone concerned with theme. 17 illustrations. 348pp. 22668-9 Pa. $3.50

THE COMPLETE BOOKS OF CHARLES FORT, Charles Fort. Book of the Damned, Lo!, Wild Talents, New Lands. Greatest compilation of data: celestial appearances, flying saucers, falls of frogs, strange disappearances, inexplicable data not recognized by science. Inexhaustible, painstakingly documented. Do not confuse with modern charlatanry. Introduction by Damon Knight. Total of 1126pp. 23094-5 Clothbd. $15.00

FADS AND FALLACIES IN THE NAME OF SCIENCE, Martin Gardner. Fair, witty appraisal of cranks and quacks of science: Atlantis, Lemuria, flat earth, Velikovsky, orgone energy, Bridey Murphy, medical fads, etc. 373pp. 20394-8 Pa. $3.50

HOAXES, Curtis D. MacDougall. Unbelievably rich account of great hoaxes: Locke's moon hoax, Shakespearean forgeries, Loch Ness monster, Disumbrationist school of art, dozens more; also psychology of hoaxing. 54 illustrations. 338pp. 20465-0 Pa. $3.50

THE GENTLE ART OF MAKING ENEMIES, James A.M. Whistler. Greatest wit of his day deflates Wilde, Ruskin, Swinburne; strikes back at inane critics, exhibitions. Highly readable classic of impressionist revolution by great painter. Introduction by Alfred Werner. 334pp. 21875-9 Pa. $4.00

THE BOOK OF TEA, Kakuzo Okakura. Minor classic of the Orient: entertaining, charming explanation, interpretation of traditional Japanese culture in terms of tea ceremony. Edited by E.F. Bleiler. Total of 94pp. 20070-1 Pa. $1.25

Prices subject to change without notice.
Available at your book dealer or write for free catalogue to Dept. GI, Dover Publications, Inc., 180 Varick St., N.Y., N.Y. 10014. Dover publishes more than 150 books each year on science, elementary and advanced mathematics, biology, music, art, literary history, social sciences and other areas.